BLOOD IS THICKER THAN WATER

Sidestone Press

every man is a piece of the continent, a part of the main.

John Donne, Meditation 17,
Devotions Upon Emergent Occasions (1624)

And neither cloud conceal, nor misty air
Bedim, the grand terraqueous spectacle,
From centre to circumference, unveiled!

William Wordsworth, Inscriptions, VI (1813)

Alistair J. Bright

BLOOD IS THICKER THAN WATER

Amerindian intra- and inter-insular relationships and social organization in the pre-Colonial Windward Islands

Published by Sidestone Press, Leiden
www.sidestone.com

ISBN 978-90-8890-071-6

Illustration cover: 'Feet in sand on the beach of Aruba, Dutch Caribbean' by Adriano Castelli (www.dreamstime.com)
Cover design: K. Wentink, Sidestone Press
Lay-out: A.J. Bright / P.C. van Woerdekom, Sidestone Press

Contents

Chapter 1

INTRODUCTION AND RESEARCH OBJECTIVES

> *"In both cases of 'geographical circumscriptive inversion' the historical 'losers' are forced to the margins of the system and bypassed. In the Amazonian-Orinocan systems this 'marginality' meant the upper tributaries and interfluves (Raymond 1988:289), while in the Antilles it became the windward islands in the Lesser Antilles (Watters et al. 1984:390) [...]"*
> (Roe 1989:271)

1.1. Introduction

From the inception of the professional study of Caribbean prehistory, a marked dichotomy has been perceived between the prehistoric inhabitants of the Greater Antilles and the Lesser Antilles, formalised and exemplified by their division into respectively the Arawak and the Carib by Rouse (1948a, b) and into Circum-Caribbean and Tropical Forest tribes by Steward (1949). The Greater Antillean Taíno Indians were believed to exhibit traces of 'high culture' and incipient centralised organization and the Lesser Antillean Caribs were regarded as primitive and loosely organised in marauding bands or tribes. (Ethno)Historical[1] accounts from the contact period as well as rich, monumental sites seemed to offer incontrovertible proof of the existence of so-called *cacicazgos*[2] or chiefdoms in the Greater Antilles (Oberg 1955; Steward 1949:720-721; Steward and Faron 1959:248-249; see also Redmond and Spencer 1994; Wilson 1990). The lengthier and more descriptive (ethno)historical accounts bearing on the Lesser Antilles are generally much later in date and merely make mention of temporary overarching leadership structures in times of war. The apparent lack of monumentality in this area seemed to represent further proof of the lower level of social complexity in these parts. Only in recent years has research involving a reconsideration of early sources (acknowledging primary bias and dispelling secondary bias), new interpretations of material culture and more refined theoretical frameworks, brought about a changing mentality towards this alleged dichotomy (*cf.* Hofman, Bright, Hoogland and Keegan 2008). This changing perspective has led to a reconsid-

1 The terms (ethno)history and (ethno)historical will be adopted throughout this dissertation. The 'ethno' part is bracketed to indicate that while this study's approach to historical sources on the Caribbean can generally be termed ethnohistory, not all sources are ethnohistorical in nature, *i.e.* written with the intention of providing insights into indigenous culture per sé. Some are simply historical in nature, but provide snippets of information on Amerindian customs and lifeways.

2 But see Curet and Stringer (2010:4) for a cautionary note on the use of the term cacicazgo and the suitability of the cacicazgo model for the analysis of social organization in the Greater Antilles in particular.

eration of the nature and characteristics of social structure and material culture throughout the Leeward Islands, as well as interactions with the Greater Antilles. It is only logical therefore to subject the Windward Islands to similar scrutiny.

There is a curious parallel between the levels of social complexity ascribed to the Lesser and Greater Antilles in the Caribbean, and those ascribed to two archipelagos on the other side of the globe, namely Melanesia and Polynesia in Oceania. Years ago, Pacific scholars noted apparently divergent societal trajectories in these two areas in late-prehistoric times; Polynesian society being characterized by ranking and great paramount chiefdoms, and Melanesia by "underdeveloped" autonomous kinship-residential groups, typically of the big or great man type (Sahlins 1963). Naturally, the contrast was in reality never as stark as portrayed, and more aptly considered a grading continuum from west to east rather than step-like or oppositional in nature (Sahlins 1963:286; see also Spriggs 2008a), but nevertheless, a divergence was detectable, or at least, detected.

This dichotomy finds its parallel equally in continental arenas.[3] Archaeologists working in the northeastern United States for instance have long held that the coastal Algonquian Indians were less developed than their Iroquois neighbours further inland. Differences in archaeological remains, divergent Colonial period political strategies and relative interest taken in the two areas by archaeologists all appeared to proffer evidence that Iroquois society was complex and advanced and New England Algonquian society little more than a cultural backwater (Chilton 2005:138-140). Chilton (2005:155) rejects conventional dichotomizing approaches, rigid complexity models and traditional cultural classifications in favour of a more flexible perspective on the nature of transegalitarian societies and the inter-related factors of "*power relations, social organization, cultural traditions, environment, and history*".

Closer to home, Betty Meggers, author of Amazonia: man and culture in a counterfeit paradise (1971), posited human behaviour in the Amazon region as being very much a matter of conditioning by and adaptation to the Amazonian environment. As such, she believed in the circumscribing, at times limiting ecotype terra firme, and the richer várzea or floodplain ecotype. Meggers alleged that subsistence limitations prevented the rise of civilization in the Mesoamerican sense, despite finding evidence for "*the incipient expression of occupational division of labor, social stratification, and other characteristics of urban society among several of the Amazonian terra firme groups*" (Meggers 1971:162). Over the past quarter of a century however, an increasing amount of evidence has come to light that Amazonian and Orinocan populations were much more numerous and societies more complex than hitherto imagined or expected on the basis of existing population numbers and historically known societies (Denevan ed. 1976; Heckenberger *et al.* 2008; Roosevelt 1994; Spencer and Redmond 1998). This only underscores once again that we can never unproblematically project the present or recent past back into pre-Colonial times.

---

3 For discussion of the prevalence of the simple-complex dichotomy in contemporary Western ideology, see Chapman (2003:7).

1.2. Social complexity in the Caribbean: current state of affairs

The Taíno of the Greater Antilles have long been characterised unanimously and conclusively as made up of chiefdom societies (Curet 2002; Keegan 2007; Redmond and Spencer 1994; Rouse 1948a; Siegel 1992; Steward 1949; Veloz Maggiolo 1991; Wilson 1990). These chiefdoms or cacicazgos ranged from simple two-level hierarchies to paramount chiefdom structures (Curet 2002), and there was a clear social hierarchy present, with the top tier occupied by the nitaínos (elite), the middle tier represented by the naborías (commoners) as well as an underclass of slaves (Wilson 2007:110). Social status was hereditary, although opinions differ as to how chiefly power was transferred from one generation to the next (*cf.* Curet 2002).

It has proved rather more problematic to reach a consensus regarding the level of social organization characterising Lesser Antillean societies however. Hypotheses advanced have ranged from multi-island chiefdoms (Crock 2000; Crock and Petersen 2004) and complex tribes (Hoogland 1996; Siegel 1989; Versteeg and Schinkel eds 1992:229) in the Late Ceramic Age Leeward Islands to tribal societies dominated by Big Man collectivities in the Early Ceramic Age southernmost Lesser Antilles (Boomert 2000:392-403). These multi-island chiefdoms are supposedly somewhat analogous to paramount chiefdoms, in that they comprise a network of settlements of varying size, the largest of which would represent the top tier in a settlement hierarchy extending over a number of allegedly interconnected islands. Besides population size, high status goods, prominent ceremonial trappings, advantageous geographical location and rich maritime resources underpin the hypothesis for the existence of such a regional seat of power (Crock 2000:325-329). Complex tribes are regarded by Versteeg and Schinkel (1992:229) as societies that display few status indicators and as a result suggest no significant status differentiation. Accordingly, these archaeologically documented societies are therefore comparable to many Amazonian societies recorded ethnographically. The concept of complex tribe was originally proposed by Hoopes, in a paper that remains unpublished to this day (*cf.* Boomert 2000:392). However, according to Curet (1996:124), the term *"describes those archaeological cases where material evidence of 'communal architecture, long-distance trade, specialized crafts, and a degree of social differentiation' appears in the absence of evidence for centralized authority or individual chiefs"*. Boomert (2000:393-394) hypothesizes that some members of Saladoid society may have been organised into Big Man collectivities, characterised by community-level craft specialization, public displays of materials as part of competitive demonstrations of wealth, gift-giving and destruction of property. He later qualifies the statement somewhat, by claiming of the ritual associated with the disposal of the dead that it is *"not suggestive of status differences in Saladoid/Barrancoid society compatible with a socio-political organization beyond that of the 'big man collectivity' type of tribal society"* (Boomert 2000:403). A number of other researchers have chosen to be more cautious in their ascription of type of social organization, preferring to note a growing or increasing social complexity (De Waal 2006; Hofman and Hoogland 2004; Knippenberg 2006).

One of the problematic factors in coming to an agreement has been disagreement between archaeologists as to how to interpret the archaeological record of the late phase of the Late Ceramic Age. For a start, it has been stated by several researchers that the northern Lesser Antilles were more or less abandoned or at least heavily depopulated towards the end of the Late Ceramic Age (De Waal 2006; Hofman and Hoogland eds 1999, 2004; Wilson 2006). Researchers base themselves on the absence of late phase Late Ceramic Age radiocarbon dates for the Leewards, absence of diagnostic late phase Late Ceramic Age material culture and information drawn from (ethno)historical sources. The depopulation or abandonment argument, a questionable hypothesis that is running the risk of becoming uncritically accepted and engrained within the discipline, should be provided with some counter-weight. Firstly, as Fitzpatrick (2006) argued, radiocarbon dating in the Lesser Antilles is still in its infancy, with many existing dates either proving unreliable or unsupported by additional dates. Furthermore, the absence of radiocarbon dates for the late phase of the Late Ceramic Age at present has more to do with a collecting bias rather than an actual void. Not enough samples have been sought for the period, particularly in the northern Lesser Antilles. When they have been sought and taken (*i.e.* on Saba, Anguilla, Guadeloupe, La Désirade and St. Martin), they have yielded dates well into the Late Ceramic Age, several even stretching into the latest pre-Colonial period. However, if one examines the radiocarbon evidence for the Windward Islands, one remarks that the majority of the Late Ceramic Age radiocarbon dates terminates before 1300 as well (see also Appendix 2), and yet no one questions the late phase Late Ceramic Age occupation of this region (*cf.* Boomert 1987a; Bullen and Bullen 1972).

What then of the other argument, that of lacking archaeological evidence for late occupations? While this position appears to hold true for St. Kitts, the islands of Nevis, Saba, Anguilla, Guadeloupe and St. Martin were all settled deep into Late Ceramic Age times, and possibly into Colonial times. Problematically, despite intensity of research on many islands in the area being as high as that on the southern Lesser Antillean islands, material culture developments in the area during this late period are still poorly understood. Allaire (1974b:161), while noting the general absence of Suazan Troumassoid material on St. Kitts, was quick to point out that this statement should not be taken to mean there were no post-Saladoid developments on the island. Rather, he believed that these later developments must have assumed a course different from the Windward Islands, one not yet properly understood. Furthermore, Allaire (1974b:158) remarked upon the difficulty of distinguishing between Amerindian pottery and Colonial period Creole coarse-ware on St. Kitts, a problem common to other islands as well (Bullen and Bullen 1972:148; Hofman and Bright 2004; Vérin 1961:75-76). In any case, the latest pre-Colonial assemblages on many Leeward Islands are characterized not by Suazan Troumassoid influences, but rather by Greater Antillean Ostionoid influences (Bonnissent *et al.* 2007; Crock 2000; Hofman 1993; Hoogland and Hofman 1999; Hofman, Bright, Hoogland and Keegan 2008). If anything, this suggests population of the region from the Greater Antilles or at least a cultural reorientation of the inhabitants of the Leeward Islands towards their north-western neighbours. Naturally, post-depositional processes may also account to a degree for missing late pre-Colonial remains, given that these would be closest to the surface and hence first to be destroyed by natural or human activity.

The last argument concerns the conditioning influence of the earliest European accounts of the region (Cardona 1974; Columbus 1997; Coppier 1645). Montserrat, Redonda and Nevis were reportedly uninhabited at the time of Columbus' second voyage, but other islands were either not visited or explored adequately to gain an impression of their occupancy. There is strong (ethno)historical evidence for an Amerindian presence on St. Croix and Guadeloupe and activity on some of the Virgin Islands during the 1490s (Chanca 1993:19; Columbus 1997:205), for presence on St. Croix and Guadeloupe in the late sixteenth century (Champlain 1964; Quinn 1991:518-519), and on St. Kitts (Boucher 1992:33; De Laet 1931:48; Goodwin 1979:53-56; Wilson 2006:212), Nevis, Guadeloupe (Gage 1758) and Montserrat (Hilton in Harlow 1967) in the 1620s, although these later occupations cannot be unproblematically projected back into pre-Colonial times.

The same does not hold true for the Windward Islands however, which have seen continual occupation from earliest prehistory up to Colonial times, as has been attested both archaeologically (Allaire 1977; Bullen and Bullen 1972; Drewett ed. 1991) and (ethno)historically (Anonyme de Carpentras 2002; Breton 1978, 1999; Canner 1907; De Laet 1931; Nicholl 1607; Stoneman 1905-1907).[4] However, here the question is not whether there was an indigenous survival, but rather which (indigenous) peoples survived and hence were reported on in the early Colonial period. Unlike the Greater Antillean islands, which seem to have experienced a relatively undisturbed local development from the Early Ceramic Age onwards, some of the Lesser Antilles (and the southern in particular), apparently saw the continual arrival of mainland South American newcomers, most intensively during the final centuries of the pre-Colonial period. Compounding the hazy view of ethnicity in the area during the early Colonial period, an unknown number of African slaves allegedly survived several shipwreck incidents off the coast of St. Vincent in the course of the 17th century, and were absorbed within the Amerindian communities (Foster 1987; Gonzalez 1990:25; Gullick 1995). In time, this led to the rise of a new people, referred to by the English (Young 1971) as Black Caribs (as opposed to the Yellow Caribs, who had not inter-married with the Africans). These Black Caribs adopted aspects of Island Carib culture, even going so far as to practice cranial modification to set themselves apart from Africans, and called themselves Kalinago (Shepard 1971[1831]:24). Foster (1987) points to the intermixing of Africans with Amerindians borne out by three terms in Breton's Carib-French dictionary: *"Chibárali, cachíonna, yaboúloupou, sont les enfants engendrés des Sauvages et des Négresses, qui sont nommés ainsi"* (Breton 1999:7). Their numbers grew as escaped slaves from other Windward Islands joined up with them in defiance of Colonial authorities (Boomert 2002:150; Gaspar 1979; Gonzalez

4 There are some contradictory accounts concerning Barbados, described by many early visitors as uninhabited (Ligon 2003[1657], but see Hughes 1750 for early scepticism regarding these observations), Grenada and Martinique (Keymis writing in the late 1590s encountered no inhabitants, see Hulme and Whitehead 1992:57-58) and Tobago, confidently recorded as uninhabited *"because the Charibes of Dominica are evill neighbours unto it"* (Hulme and Whitehead 1992:57, but see plentiful evidence to the contrary in Boomert 2002).

1990; Kirby and Martin 1972:9-10). African impact on Amerindian society actually commenced even earlier, in the form of prisoners taken from the Spanish during Island Carib raids on Puerto Rico (Foster 1987:75; Moreau 1992:69).

1.3. Proxies for social complexity in the Caribbean

There is an absence of clear-cut archaeological evidence of social stratification or complexity in the Caribbean, in the form of for instance chiefly residences and burials or great differentiation in grave goods across graves or domestic structures. For this reason, a number of proxies have been adhered to in past research, evidence for which is at times as tenuous archaeologically as the supposed proxy itself. The examples that follow are drawn mainly from Leeward Island and Greater Antillean archaeology, and provide a general baseline for research into social organization in the Caribbean. We will revisit these data in Chapter 7, when we attempt to determine whether this research has any bearing on the archaeology of the Windward Islands.

Settlement structure

In the Greater Antilles, according to Curet and Oliver (1998), clusters of burials in the central clearing of several sites in Early Ceramic Age Puerto Rico are a reflection of linear descent groups operating as economic corporate groups. There is some differentiation in the burial gifts (Hofman and Hoogland 2004:53). Siegel (1996a) considered the phenomenon of central plaza burials as indicative of ancestor worship, and expressing a form of community identity. In later times, burials at a number of sites in the Greater Antilles apparently shifted from a central plaza to beneath domestic structures, suggesting a shift in the socio-political ideology of the settlement and perhaps society at large, from a communal orientation to one that emphasized the individual and his familial affiliations (Curet and Oliver 1998; Righter ed. 2002; Siegel 1996a; see also Kingsley 1985). Furthermore, it has been suggested that over time, house size decreased during these periods in what amounted to a reorientation of society from a communal base to nuclear families to the extended households known from the European chronicles (Curet 1992a:162, 169; Curet *et al.* 2004). Whereas houses of oblong or elliptical shape may have been the initial habitation type in Late Saladoid/Early Ostionoid Puerto Rico, houses remained similar in shape but became smaller in size during the subsequent Early/Late Elenan Ostionoid times and finally settled on a similarly small but circular shape in Chicoid times (Curet 1992a:169). However, by assembling data from three different locations and numerous time periods, the possibility of regional variation is somewhat overlooked (see also Bright 2003:55).

In the Lesser Antilles, there is no evidence for centralised communal burial grounds in the Early Ceramic Age (Hofman *et al.* 2003; Versteeg and Schinkel eds 1992). However, in a later phase, there is a clear correlation between the location of burials and residential areas, and in many cases even habitation plans most notably at the sites of Anse à la Gourde on Guadeloupe and Kelbey's Ridge on Saba (see also Bright 2003; Hofman *et al.* 2003; Hofman and Hoogland 2004; Hoogland and Hofman 1993). The Anse à la Gourde site does not provide evidence for a diachronic decrease in dwelling structure size, as larger and smaller structures appear to occur interchangeably through time (Bright 2003; see also Morsink 2006). According to Siegel (1996a), many of the plans of Early Ceramic Age settlements in the Caribbean conform to a model of a central plaza or habitation area, skirted by a ring of (mounded) middens (see also Petersen 1996). Regardless of how sceptical one may be of the alleged skirting nature of these mounds/middens, there is the time factor to consider. The configurations presented by Siegel represent an accumulation of settlement features dating to a time period of several centuries at least. As such, while the features may well have been contemporaneous and either short- or long-lived, they were just as likely sequential, detracting considerably from the hypothesis of central plazas and skirting middens (see also Boomert 2000:293). Upon closer inspection, such reservations hold true for the sites of Anse à la Gourde, Punta Candelero, Maisabel and Monserrate (see also Bright 2003:45-46).

Site patterns, carrying capacity and settlement hierarchies

In the Greater Antilles, numerous studies have been carried out into pre-Colonial site patterns (Curet 2005; Curet *et al.* 2004; Torres 2005). Data compiled from the Loíza River Basin in Puerto Rico and Vieques show that settlement and site tallies increased considerably from the early to the late phase of the Early Ceramic Age. The Salinas and Yauco River Basin data could not be separated into early and late phases, and thus merely provided an initial baseline for occupation of these regions (Curet 2005:97-128). During the subsequent early phase of the Late Ceramic Age, the site tally in all surveyed regions of Puerto Rico increases, but if one takes site type into account, the picture becomes more complex. In the Loíza and Yauco River basins, there is a drop in number of settlements (villages) but an increase in small/medium sites and hamlets. On Vieques and in the Salinas River Basin, there is a rise in settlements and villages (Curet 2005:100-128). During the late phase of the Late Ceramic Age, only the Loíza River Basin sees an increase in number of villages from two to four and a rise in small sites as well; all other areas exhibit a dramatic decline in number of sites of all types (Curet 2005:100-128). On the basis of this research and that carried out in the Maunabo Valley (Curet 1992b), Curet (2005:180) concludes that these parts of Puerto Rico never reached carrying capacity, and as such, the carrying capacity argument cannot be invoked as a reason for the emergence of social complexity in this regions. Keegan (1995a:407) has calculated however that populations would have felt the constraints of density-dependent growth by the time one half of carrying capacity was reached, and would have acted to alleviate such stress. Siegel (2004:91) furthermore suggests that social and political dynamics may have exceeded the scale of single valleys during the latest pre-Colonial period, and that population was not so much decreasing absolutely, but rather waning locally under influence of restructuring and consolidation in other areas.

In the Lesser Antilles, in the course of research on Anguilla, Crock (2000:47-48) and Crock and Petersen (2004) allegedly uncovered evidence of a settlement hierarchy on the basis of differential occurrence at post-Saladoid sites of what they termed “wealth” goods and the absence of such a differentiation during the late Saladoid period (see also Knippenberg 2006:272). To be meaningful, this differentiation then had to be corroborated by differences in other domains, such as site size and location (Crock 2000:47). This approach suffers from a number of problems. In reverse order: site location has been found to be a relatively irrelevant characteristic, with surveys throughout the Caribbean showing that large settlements can be expected in coastal as well as inland settings (albeit not in the mountains), depending on local environmental conditions more than any a priori rules such as proximity to the sea or level ground. Next, site size is extremely difficult to determine in the absence of a multi-tiered excavation programme entailing intensive surface survey, testpitting/augering and excavation. All too often, assumptions about site size are drawn on the basis of surface distribution alone, an approach that runs the risk of: (1) conflating a number of sites into one site, (2) underestimating the true extent or misinterpreting the nature of a site due to taphonomical effects, and (3) missing sites altogether. Furthermore, differences in site size can be related as much to a functional difference as to population size or internal political hierarchy. Finally, as De Waal (2006:121) correctly points out in relation to the Anguilla chiefdom hypothesis: *"However, organisation of and maintenance of long-distance contacts, involving exchange of high status objects, does not necessarily require or produce situations of hereditary status variation or institutionalised social stratification, which are essential aspects of chiefdom societies"*. Ultimately then, it is difficult enough to argue for the existence of a settlement hierarchy, let alone a multi-island chiefdom.

Exchange of prestige goods or non-local goods and crafting

In studying the procurement and working of lithic raw materials in the Leeward Islands, Knippenberg demonstrated that the manufacture of flake tools, axes and threepointed stones occurred on a household level of production throughout the entire Ceramic Age. He suggested that though specialised, these craftsmen would not have been full-time specialists able to standardize the production process and its outcome (Knippenberg 2006:267). As such, it is not in the crafting but rather in the changing patterns in the distribution of lithic raw materials through time that Knippenberg sees indications for changes in socio-political complexity. According to Knippenberg (2006:267-270), the Early Ceramic Age long distance exchanges and wide distributions of raw materials (see also Watters 1997) are replaced by more localised procurement, distribution and control of resources within a constellation of micro-regions (*cf.* Hofman *et al.* 2007; Hofman, Bright, Keegan and Hoogland 2008). He sees these restrictions as evidence of the formation of independent sub-regions that are increasingly competing over resources and forming localised networks (Knippenberg 2006:270). The limited production and distribution of calci-rudite threepointers and their increase in size may be evidence of imposed restriction of access to the resource and a role in public display related to the sanctioning or legitimation of would-be elites (Knippenberg 2006:262-263).

Final remarks on archaeological proxies for social complexity in the Caribbean

In sum then, despite the best efforts of certain Caribbean archaeologists, evidence for a form of social organization in the Lesser Antilles beyond that of complex tribes is still extremely thin. It is worth emphasising however that complex tribes should not be placed on an evolutionary ladder that places them a few rungs lower than the cacicazgos (chiefdoms) of Cuba, Hispaniola and Puerto Rico. Paraphrasing Binford, increasing social complexity can be regarded as nothing more or less than a new solution to a problem that has arisen in a given society (*cf.* Binford 2002:221), and takes its particular form on the basis of numerous conditions such as population size, environmental conditions, available resources, organization of labour, social relationships and cosmology. To quote Nelson (in Yoffee 1993), it is better to ask not how complex societies were, but how were they complex? Or even better, as it avoids evolutionist tendencies, how were societies organised socially? It is the latter question that will be answered for the Windward Islands by the end of this dissertation. Finally, Caribbeanists would do well to heed the warning issued recently by Spriggs (2008b), who has pointed to the increasing "Pacific"-ation of parts of Europe, as a result of the tendency of archaeologists to draw freely on ethnographic models from the Pacific and apply them to (archaeological) cultures elsewhere. Spriggs is not against the use of ethnographic analogy, but argues that the historical or even archaeological trajectories of different areas must be closely examined to ensure that they are similar or at least compatible (*cf.* Peregrine 2004). In that respect, it is safer to stick to the direct historical analogies that have always been such a staple of Caribbean archaeology, although even these analogies require the utmost caution and justification.

1.4. Research problem

This PhD research centres on Amerindian occupation and intra- and inter-insular relationships in the Windward Islands (Figure 1.1) with a view to better understanding social interaction and organization within the region and integration with the wider macro-region. It is embedded within the overarching project *"Socio-political complexity in the pre-Columbian Caribbean (500 BC-AD 1492), an integral approach to inter-insular and inter-regional relationships"*, directed by Professor C.L. Hofman and funded by the Netherlands Organisation for Scientific Research (NWO ASPASIA Grant # 015-001-101, promoting women in academic careers). It is a logical extension of the research carried out at an earlier stage by Hofman (1993) and Hoogland (1996), and by Knippenberg (2006) and De Waal (2006) within the framework of the NWO-programmatic funded research project *"Social organisation and inter-insular relationships in the northern Lesser Antilles"*. The results of these projects will be placed alongside those of this project, to enable comparisons to be made between the two regions and conclusions to be drawn on a wider geographical scale than the data-set at hand had previously allowed.

The main problem that informs this PhD research is both how the inhabitants of the Windward Islands related to one another and others on a local, micro-regional and regional level, and how these societies organised themselves socially

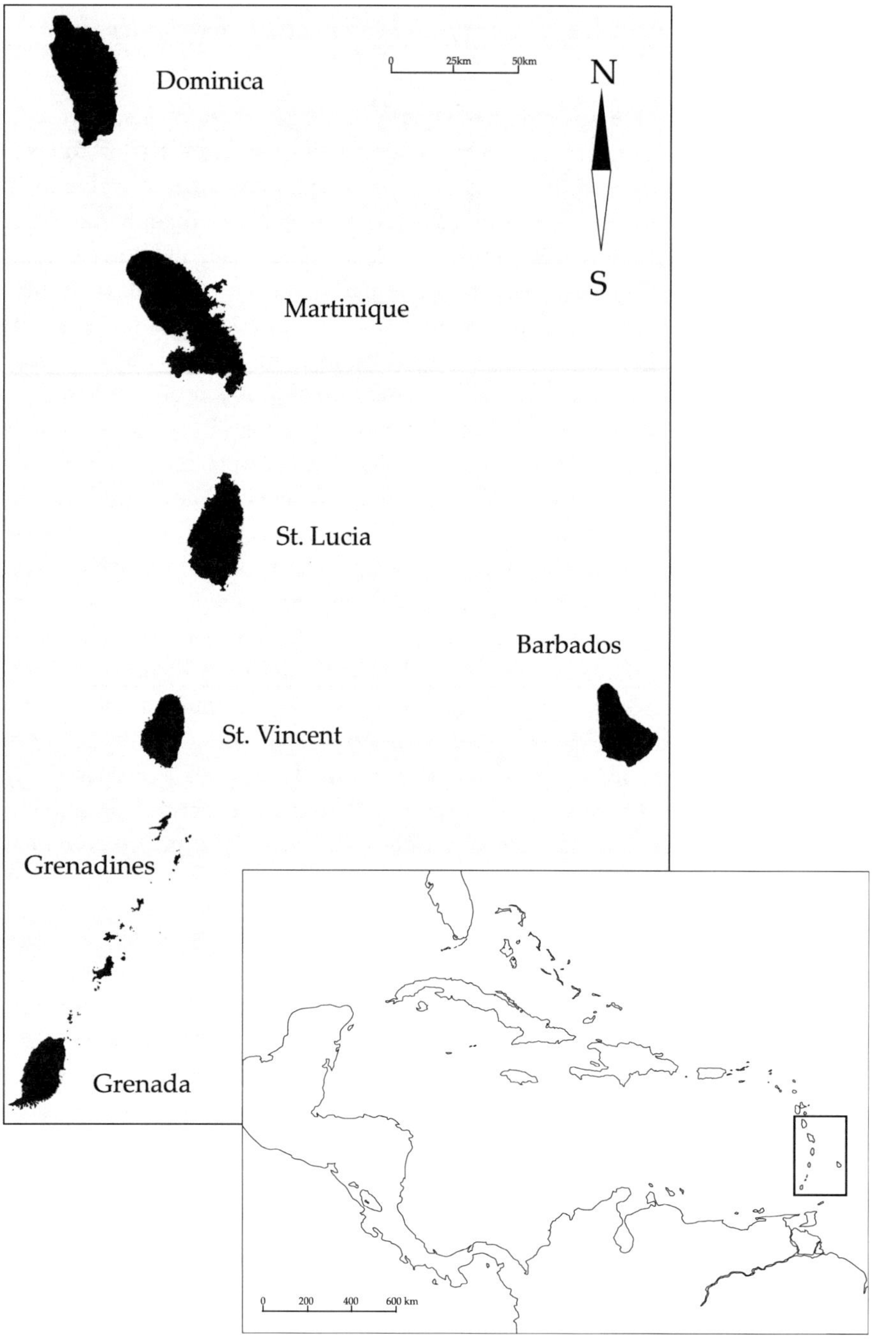

Figure 1.1. Map of the Circum-Caribbean, inset of Windward Islands.

compared to their neighbours to the north and south. Due to the single island perspective adopted by archaeologists in the past (see also Chapter 2) and other reasons such as lack of research uniformity, the multitude of local ceramic typologies in use or the overall lack of research (see below and Chapter 3 for further elaboration), we have a somewhat hazy view of Windward Island archaeology and precisely the inter-island and interregional interrelationships have remained enigmatic until the present. Without a critical re-evaluation of previous research and the forging of some uniformity in the Windward Island archaeological data-set, these data cannot be utilised to address the primary issues of social relationships and organization.

This hazy situation that has come to light reflects a larger issue, namely the political-historical developments of the respective islands. The French islands, known affectionately as DOMs (Départements d'Outre-Mer) have retained strong political and economical ties to France.[5] As these islands hold the political status of departments of France, French and, by extension, E.U. laws apply to them, including and most significantly laws that bear on cultural heritage. This has had significant consequences for funding, political infrastructure and legislation, and an institutionalised concern for cultural heritage manifests itself in excellent fieldwork, well-curated remains, outstanding museums, and frequent publications (Delpuech 2001). The "British" islands have distanced themselves from their colonial past, and many are now independent governments within the British Commonwealth, a far looser overarching structure, but retaining the Queen of England as nominal head of state.[6] Archaeology on these islands is directed by NGOs such as archaeological/historical societies, museums and national trusts that are technically quango's (Watters 2001:85-6) as well as by the University of the West Indies (Barbados, Trinidad and Tobago). Unfortunately, it cannot be denied that archaeological and historical heritage are less protected (if at all) by national legislation and that archaeological enterprise on these former British islands is less well coordinated and receives substantially lower funding (if at all) than in the French départements. Thankfully, these shortcomings have been mitigated to a considerable degree, thanks to numerous examples of fruitful and mutually rewarding cooperation between westerners and the island inhabitants, for instance between University College London and the Barbados Museum & Historical Society, between Leiden University and the Saint Lucia Archaeological and Historical Society, the University of the West Indies (Trinidad) and the Dominica Museum, between the University of Calgary and The National Trust of St. Vincent and the Grenadines (Callaghan 2007) and between the University of Vienna, St. Lucia's National Trust and St. Lucia's Folk Research Centre (Kremser and Wernhart eds 1986), and between Carriacou's Museum, University College London and North Carolina State University (Fitzpatrick *et al.* 2004; Kaye *et al.* 2004).

A concomitant problem in Windward Island archaeology is that of the "divide and conquer" approach wielded by archaeologists. Whether due to nationalist concerns, protectionist fancies, historical accident or lack of funding for archaeology (or a combination of all of the preceding), certain islands have seen investigation by just one researcher, research school or institute over the course of time. The same applies to an even greater degree when one is speaking of individual sites, not islands. It is obvious that every researcher has his/her own interests and biases; without empirical checks, his/her conclusions cannot be falsified. The re-

5 http://www.outremer.com.
6 http://www.thecommonwealth.org.

verse situation, yet obviously equally problematic, is the application of idiosyncratic methods and interpretational frameworks to the archaeology of one and the same site, island or culture by various independent (or more likely cooperating) researchers. Therefore, there is a need to return to the findings of past archaeological fieldwork, in order to examine critically old assumptions and conclusions and re-evaluate them in terms of the current state of the discipline.

Another fundamental problem is the lack of archaeological investigations in general. Some islands have simply seen too little investigation to support any interpretation of their archaeology. Dominica is such a case, with only a handful of publications on what must be an incredibly rich archaeological heritage. Much of the cultural chronology of various islands is also still shrouded in mystery, with radiocarbon dates scant and at times unreliable, not having been calibrated or corrected for the marine reservoir effect (see Appendix 2). Generally speaking, quite a number of statements that have been made in the past concerning settlement, lifeways and social organization are either too vague to have any explanatory worth, or have been drawn from a selective or limited data-set, making their reliability questionable.

Although it may seem that more archaeological fieldwork is the solution, this statement requires immediate qualification; from an epistemological perspective, more data will not necessarily lead to a better, fuller understanding of the archaeological problems at hand, as problems may also be caused by the approaches or frameworks of the archaeologists and the publications they produce. These latter issues need to be resolved first, to avoid an increase of problematic data. Thus, revisiting original data can be just as vital to the advancement of the discipline as new research. Highly significant in this regard is the culture-historical paradigm that has held sway over much Latin American archaeology (Politis 2003), as well as Caribbean archaeology until relatively recently (Rouse 1992). By and large, much research in the Caribbean has taken place without overt reference to theoretical fields such as processualism and post-processualism (although many researchers would perhaps identify themselves with one or the other, and influences are certainly detectable[7]). One exception is perhaps Marxism, which has had a large impact on Greater Antillean (Davis 1996; Vargas and Sanoja 1999) and mainland South American (Politis 2003) archaeological practice. All of this is not to say that Caribbean archaeology operates in a theoretical and methodological wasteland (Fitzpatrick 2004a; see *e.g.* Curet 2005; Newsom and Wing 2004; Oliver 2008), merely that it has developed into a methodologically sound and innovative discipline (see also Keegan 2008) that has for some reason failed to make its presence felt in general theoretical debates in archaeology.

7 Much research that has taken place from the 1960s onwards, for instance on subsistence, site catchment and site patterns, could certainly be classed as processual, and by the same token some research into Amerindian cosmology and societal complexity could be classed as post-processual or cognitive.

1.5. Ceramic (decorative) traits and site patterns: an archaeological approach to social networks and complexity

> *"These changes in style form a useful way of making fine distinctions between the cultural groups who made the pottery; where absolute dating is not possible they may be the only way of dating occupations. In an area like the Caribbean, where islands are separated by sea passages but close enough so that such passages do not prevent communication, stylistic similarities in pottery may also show the pattern of such intercommunication"* (Hill Harris in Drewett ed. 1991:37).

Caribbean archaeology has seen tremendous developments over the course of the last two decades, with a flood of new studies on the Greater and Lesser Antilles. While work carried out over the past 20 years has shed much light on the northern Lesser Antilles, the southern Lesser Antilles have been relatively understudied or, perhaps more accurately, characterised by a lack of reflexive research. While much work was done in the 1960s and 1970s, this work has tended to be uncritically subsumed into later research, and has rarely been re-evaluated, especially in light of recent theoretical developments. Furthermore, there has been little inter-regional comparison of archaeological assemblages, resulting in a proliferation of island-specific approaches and descriptions and hence lack of clarity of the regional situation.

A new study focusing precisely on the Windward Islands is deemed vital for a proper understanding of the micro-region as well as the Caribbean region as a whole. This is not to suggest that this area ever claimed centre stage in any time period, only that the role it played was always less marginal and more internally varied than has been expounded occasionally in the past. The main themes that will run through this thesis are those of variability, dynamism and complexity. As will become clear, the recognition or perception of dynamism and variability requires a perspective that focuses not merely on a grand, generalising scale with low resolution, but also on a small, particularising scale with high resolution. Archaeology as a discipline is notoriously weak at yielding high resolution, individualistic data, which is why the support of (ethno)history and ethnography will be enlisted at various junctures (see also Bright and Hofman in press). While there are certainly methodological complications involved, the careful marriage of these disciplines can offer a balanced, judicious take on the past in all its complexity. As such, this study will reconsider past work - necessary in order to bring cultural taxonomy and frameworks up to date – as well as incorporate new data from fieldwork and investigations of a more recent nature. Only then can the archaeological record from these southern isles be wielded meaningfully in the light of current research advances, with a view to contributing to archaeological problems in the wider fields of Caribbean archaeology and island archaeology at large.

This dissertation aims to study inter-island interrelationships and socio-political developments in the Windward Islands over the entire pre-Colonial Ceramic Age (400 BC – AD 1492) through a dualistic approach: an island-by-island study of both site patterns and ceramic assemblages (Chapters 3, 4 and 5). These two data-sets are intrinsically bound to one another, as we are often reliant upon ceramic typology to provide us with an estimated site chronology given the dearth of radiocarbon dates (see also Chapter 3). An overview of sites and their ceramics through time will not only reveal relative frequency of settlement and activities over time (Chapter 4), but will also point out various configurations of sites, united by shared ceramic styles (Chapter 5). These configurations will be examined in the light of graph-theory (see Chapter 6). Crucial for this study is the abandonment of the island as analytical unit, to be replaced by the site as analytical unit, but within the wider context of the Windward Island archipelago (see also Chapter 2). This has implications for the analysis of the ceramics, because there is a wider framework of reference when looking for possible similarities between assemblages or origins. An assemblage that is unique on one island may be commonplace on another. The challenge is to find a methodologically sound, descriptively comprehensive approach that could facilitate inter-island comparisons without negating inter-island or even inter-site variability. Finally, the findings from the research into the archaeology of the Windward Islands will be placed within the larger framework of contemporaneous developments in the Caribbean, and a number of inferences related to the domains of social interaction and organization will be made (Chapter 7).

Practically speaking, once the basic chronology of sites in the region and the characteristics of their ceramic assemblages have been established, this data-set can be further analysed. It is believed that pottery can inform on many aspects of society such as subsistence, population numbers, resource utilization, manufacturing traditions, prevalent symbols and belief systems among other things. For this research, pottery is employed as a means of determining contact and interaction between pottery-manufacturing communities living on the islands and even between insular and mainland communities.[8] The following section will briefly summarise a number of archaeological approaches to style and then centre on the assumptions underlying the interaction theory of stylistic communication, deemed particularly germane to this study.

Ceramic style and communication

Material culture is inherently manipulable, from the choice for and procurement of particular raw materials through an intricate, poly-facetted manufacturing sequence to the distribution and use of the finished product. The various steps inherent in the manufacture of products from a wide range of materials, such as general forming, carving or modelling, baking and casting and surface decorating or finishing, were methodically and admittedly rather drily detailed by Hodges (1995). However, Hodges drew the line at detailing the manufacturing procedure, and paid little attention to the differential outcome of the manufacturing process, and its possible social significance. For the likes of Sackett (1977, 1982), Wiessner (1983, 1985) and Hodder (1982), this manufacturing process (or the doing) and its result (the expression or manifestation) are not the end of the story at all, but

8 For adoption of this approach in a continental setting, see Parkinson (2006) among others.

rather a departure point from which to seek greater understanding of the reasons behind the choices made by the manufacturer and their societal grounding or impact (Hegmon 1992).

If the archaeological literature of the past decades has proven anything, it is that the notion of style is far from the undiscussed self-evident concept that Gadamer held it to be (Hegmon 1992:517). Indeed, once one moves beyond the extremely general and hence universally accepted tenets that style is a way of doing and that it involves a choice among various alternatives (Hegmon 1992:517-518), one encounters a plethora of varying perspectives on and interpretations of the concept of style and formal variation.

At an earlier stage, stylistic variability in material culture was analysed to determine the time-space systematics of the prehistoric groups held responsible for creating the material culture and its variability (Hegmon 1992:518). However, as material culture variation cannot by definition be regarded synonymous for human activity or even stylistic communication, archaeologists have increasingly sought bridging arguments to tie these phenomena together.

One of the most influential of these arguments has been the information-exchange theory of style (Wobst 1970). Wobst's fundamental tenet was that style functions in cultural systems as an avenue of communication and that artefacts participate in processes of information exchange (Hegmon 1992:519). While many criticisms have been leveled at his theory, Wobst's ideas helped shape future debate on style and material culture variability, and he pioneered the crucial insight that not all material variation is style (Hegmon 1992:521). While the theory recognized style as playing an active part in a cultural system, the motives and actions of the people creating and using style remained understudied. Numerous ethnographic and ethnoarchaeological studies since the 1980s have taken up this tack, emphasizing the role of individuals in stylistic expression and manipulation of (inter-)group relations (Bowser 2000; DeBoer 1990; Hodder 1982; Longacre ed. 1991; Wiessner 1983), but it is particularly the correlation between material culture style and the group or sub-group which Hegmon (1992:527) calls social distinctions that is of prime concern to the present research. In fact, this study will be concerned less with the concept of style than that of the aforementioned formal variation (or conversely homogeneity) in ceramic assemblages, and what such variation may say about inter-community interaction.

The first Americanist studies to suggest some relationship between the extent to which potters, wards or communities at large interacted and the degree of ceramic similarity between intra- and inter-site assemblages date to some four decades ago (Deetz 1965; Hill 1970; Longacre 1970). The discussion was furthered by the publication of Flannery's Early Mesoamerican Village (Flannery ed. 1976), particularly in contributions by Plog (1976) and Pyne (1976), who applied statistical analysis to the occurrence of stylistic/decorative attributes within and across assemblages. For this research, variation and homogeneity in ceramic decoration and morphology between assemblages are regarded as expressions of stylistic diversity or variability, attributable to the variable intensity of social interaction between the groups responsible for their production. Generally speaking, *"if two as-*

semblages are very similar they will be assigned to the same phase and culture; if more different, to separate phases of the same culture or to different cultures" (David and Kramer 2001:168). This study will take a higher resolution perspective though, regarding similarities and differences between assemblages of the same culture and phase as reflecting the relative degree of inter-community interaction. In essence, this perspective harks back to the work of Wobst, who claimed earlier that *"[s]tyle helps to mark, maintain, and further the differences between [socially differentiated] groups at little cost"* (Wobst in David and Kramer 2001:178). Though not mentioned explicitly, one assumes that the inverse of this statement, namely that style would help mark, maintain and further the commonalities between socially related groups at little cost, is equally valid (*cf.* Terrell 2010:3). Later research has emphasized that style is *"used for communication over a wide range of social distances"* and that *"much style is passive rather than active"* (David and Kramer 2001:183).

Of course, decoration and morphology are just one of many potential avenues that can be followed to arrive at an analysis of stylistic behaviour, and not necessarily universally suitable. Technological choices (Lemonnier 1993; Stark *et al.* 2000), or more subtle variations that were not picked up as a result of this study's resolution and approach are equally valid and informative strains of evidence (see *e.g.* De Waal 2006, Hofman 1993 and Hofman and Jacobs 2003 for approaches to ceramics that take a higher resolution perspective and include technological analysis). Furthermore, other material culture categories may be equally or more informative, or even informative in a different way, concerning stylistic and social behaviour, but time constraints meant a choice had to be made (see *e.g.* Knippenberg 2006 for variability in lithic use, Lammers-Keijsers 2007 for variability in shell tools and paraphernalia, and Isendoorn *et al.* (2008) for variability in clay source exploitation and technological choices, all within the Lesser Antillean region). Finally, it goes without saying that the literature on style is much more dense and far-reaching than the single tack pursued here, but given the purposes and limits of this research, this tack alone will suffice.

From theory to approach

Before analysing the Windward Island ceramics, the approach must be detailed. Realizing that a complete characterization of the ceramic inventory under study would be impossible to achieve (*cf.* Sinopoli 1991), a choice had to be made of relevant variables to record. Pottery decoration, one of the characteristics indicative of shared practice, was chosen as the primary focal point for this study, not based on the a priori assumption that it would deliver better results than study of (an)other characteristic(s), but rather because it facilitated a particularly efficient analysis of a vast amount of pottery from the region. As such, this study can also be considered a test of the success of employing mainly pottery decoration traits for studies of interaction. The nature of the materials at hand favoured an approach that centred on decoration, as in many cases, the (decorated) ceramics are quite fragmented, making vessel shape and function difficult to determine, although for the same reason the approach utilized understandably had to be qualitative rather than quantitative. It is hoped that the correlation between decoration and vessel shapes (the grammar of pottery decoration according to Roe [1989]) may be drawn in the future, when hopefully a larger inventory of (more) complete vessels will have been unearthed and documented, both in depots and in future excavations. Having said that, a number of well-documented vessel types have also been taken into account, and in one case, even a whole ware (*i.e.* a group of ceramics that share characteristics of composition, manufacturing technology or surface treatment [Rice 2005:287]).

The results of the stylistic analysis will then be used in tandem with the site pattern data to model the degree of social integration and community interaction within the Windward Islands during the Late Ceramic Age. In practice, this approach will take shape as follows. First, sites contemporaneous with one another during a given period will be established; these sites will represent the baseline for ceramic assemblage comparison. Next, the distribution of individual ceramic traits across the Windward Islands will be examined, to provide an idea of how widely or restrictedly these traits are shared throughout the research area. Analysis of multiple decorative/morphological trait similarities in unison and/or differences between assemblages will then determine which sites interacted with each other either more or less intensively. The more traits that are shared between sites, the more intensive the interaction or the closer the inter-community relations can be expected to have been, following the basic tenets of interaction theory and graph-theory analysis (Hage and Harary 1996; Scott 2005). However, to compensate for potential research intensity bias (*i.e.* sites only known through survey as opposed to excavated settlements with representative assemblages), only the settlement data will be quantified. Other settlements' assemblages can then be more or less safely assumed to really not possess a certain trait, allowing for a measure of certainty in the recognition of community ties or social networks and absences thereof.

A multi-scalar approach

As Wilson explained in his synthesis on the archaeology of Nevis:

> *"In attempting to understand the settlement history and prehistoric population dynamics of the Caribbean, we must incorporate successively larger regions into our synthetic framework; for Nevis, we must look at the island, the Leeward Islands group, the Lesser Antilles, and the Caribbean archipelago generally. Larger and more comprehensive syntheses rely directly on the quality and comprehensiveness of data collected from island to island. This paper has been an attempt to provide reliable settlement data from Nevis for future regional syntheses"* (Wilson 1989:445).

In similar vein, the distribution of ceramic decorative traits will be determined within the study area, but whereas Wilson stopped at the level of the island concerned, this study will attempt to further contextualize its data within the wider region, by approaching the archaeological record on two additional levels besides the local, namely the micro-regional and regional.[9] To that end, site patterns are discussed at both the particularising island scale as well as the generalizing archipelagic scale and ceramic (decorative) traits are conceptualised as occurring at various geographical scales: (1) local, which refers to developments that affect a limited number of sites, either on the same island or on neighbouring islands, (2) micro-regional, which refers to traits or developments that take place at a number of sites across several, geographically bounded islands, and (3) regional, which refers to those stylistic phenomena and/or developments that affect a number of sites in a given region and that are clearly related to phenomena and/or developments outside the region under study, or originate outside the region. This approach will ensure that correct research questions are posed of the dataset. It will also allow recording of all relevant decorative characteristics of the ceramics, not just at a fine-grained site resolution, but at island level as well as coarser region-wide resolution. This approach is incidentally not unique to the Caribbean: slightly different but analogous scalar approaches have recently been taken to assemblages of Neolithic Hungary (Parkinson 2006) and the Bronze Age Cyclades (Hilditch 2008). Ultimately, this approach will result in an overview of archaeological developments in the Windward Islands over a period of some 2000 years, contribute to a diachronic picture of social interaction and organization within the study area and, by placing the Windward Islands within a comparative wider Caribbean framework, will elucidate the relationships maintained between Windward Islanders and their neighbours to the north and south.

However, the multi-scalar nature of this research resides not only in the geographical. In considering the position of Windward Island communities within pre-Colonial Caribbean society as a whole, one runs into a last form of multi-scalarity in the sense of mode or manner of societal social organization. At one end of the spectrum is egalitarian society, at the other cacicazgo society. In between lies a vague no-man's land often defined as complex tribal, for lack of a better term (see above). The types of social organization ascribed to various archaeological cultures throughout the wider Caribbean area will be examined in detail in Chapter 7. Comparison between societies that have been ascribed various types of social organization can be instructive not only in order to re-evaluate argumentation for complexity and archaeological proxies utilised (see above), but also to anticipate the various emergent actors and societal structures that accompany different stages/phases of social complexity and particularly the role of specialists in mediating contact and exchanges between groups with different social, economic, and political organizations (Oka and Kusimba 2008:347-348).

1.6. Data collection and fieldwork methodology

Finally, all that remains is to outline the data collection method employed for this dissertation research, which breaks down into study of ceramic collections, literature study, archaeological surveys and site-visiting.

---

9 A similar tripartite division has been adopted in the Caribbean previously by Hofman (1993), who considered phenomena at assemblage, insular and inter-insular level, and by Curet (2005).

Study of ceramic collections (photography/inventory)

In order to take on a ceramic stylistic study at such extensive geographic and temporal scales as was envisioned, it was necessary to make an inventory of what ceramic materials were extant in collections throughout the Windward Islands (and beyond). Given that only a fraction of these materials had been published and even then often only as low-quality reproductions, it was vital to gain access to collections and photograph as much as possible or at least obtain a representative sample. To that end, visits were made to all major museums and storage depots in the region and three outside the region (see also Appendix 1). The time available to document materials varied in each instance, ranging from ten days at St. Lucia's Depot Vigie to just an afternoon at Martinique's SRA storage facility. The photographing and inventorying itself focused predominantly on decorated pottery, given its highly diagnostic character. Where possible, ceramics were photographed against a black background with a scale and from two sides, and relevant information was recorded on the spot. Sometimes time constraints meant that the description process had to be completed at a later stage. In some cases, no permission could be obtained to photograph collections, in other cases photographing had to been done from behind glass, to understandably detrimental effect. The photographs taken of ceramic assemblages in the course of this research naturally emphasize the decorated, the unique, the diagnostic, in short the most favourable to establish the cultural period at hand. The risk of this focus is that special finds are overrepresented in the database, for little or no plain ware was catalogued or photographed. In an ideal situation, equal attention would be given to plain ware and a representative ratio of decorated vs. undecorated pottery would be established (*cf.* Keegan 2004). However, as was already noted by the Bullens (1972:35), it proved almost impossible to distinguish between the plain ware of various series, both contemporaneous and successive. Thus, for the purpose of establishing a cultural chronology and comparing the sharing of stylistic traits between island or site assemblages, the present emphasis on decorative traits should prove the most effective.

Literature study

Physical examination of archaeological assemblages was complemented by an intensive study of all major publications on Windward Island and Caribbean archaeology, from 19th-century reports to recent PhD dissertations, and anything in between (see bibliography). With the quality of reproduced illustrations of artefacts and sites differing enormously, ranging from excellent (Bullen and Bullen 1972; Petitjean Roget 2002) to awful (plates in McKusick 1960a, Allaire 1977)[10], written description is all-important. Unfortunately, as has been detailed above, descriptions of sites and collections are of equally variable quality, making standardization of information one of the prime concerns and challenges of this re-

10 It should be remarked that this is not the fault of the authors, but rather wholly attributable to UMI dissertation services.

search. Furthermore, the individual islands making up the Windward Islands have been given unequal attention by archaeologists, either avocational or professional, in the past, which needless to say has had an impact on the relative coverage some of these islands' archaeology has received.

Survey campaigns

In addition to study of collections and revisiting of the archaeological literature, the author was fortunate to participate in numerous survey campaigns on St. Lucia and Martinique, which not only uncovered a great number of previously unknown sites, but also yielded new insights into the archaeology of the Windward Islands. Particularly two surveys carried out by Hofman, Hoogland and Keegan on St. Lucia (Hofman *et al.* 2004; Keegan *et al.* 2003) provided an extremely rich data-set, adding dozens of sites to the existing tally. The opportunistic character of the surveys (relatively random fieldwalking in areas considered to have high potential or surface visibility, such as agricultural fields, riverbanks and roadcuts) did however preclude the results from holding any statistically testable or quantifiable value (see above). Also, while surveys proved to be highly effective in coastal settings, where they were aided by favourable circumstances, they appeared to lose some potential in inland settings, where less favourable conditions predominate. Settings devoid of agriculture or other ground disturbances were clearly less conducive to rapid ground surveys than for example highly rural southern St. Lucia (see also Bright 2007). Areas of dense vegetation would perhaps benefit from auguring and surface cleaning in combination with surface surveying. Alternatively, one could compensate for poor visibility with a visibility factor (estimating the percentage of bare soil visible, and multiplying up the number of recorded sherds accordingly), which is a standard practice in the Mediterranean (*cf.* Bintliff *et al.* 1999). Nonetheless, rapid ground surveys remain the most efficient means of gathering a significant amount of preliminary information within a short space of time with a small team. Furthermore, they are an excellent means of verifying or updating information in the archaeological literature.

Site visits

Finally, both in the course of as well as subsequently to fieldwork in the region, countless archaeological sites were visited on Trinidad and Tobago, Barbados, Grenada, the Grenadines, St. Vincent, St. Lucia, Martinique, Dominica and Guadeloupe. This site-seeing process afforded valuable insights into local and (micro-)regional differences and similarities in environment and general site setting. For example, it underscored the environmental heterogeneity of the region, from lush, undisturbed tropical rainforest and traditionally cultivated agricultural plots to grazing pastures, barren coastlines and highly manicured and landscaped residential areas. It also helped prime one's understanding of the sites' immediate surroundings, resources and aspects such as accessibility or defensibility of a site location. Of course, these insights cannot be accorded too much value, in light of for instance centuries of vegetation modification and our undoubtedly inferior motor skills when it comes to ascending or descending a steep incline or making our way through dense undergrowth. However, basic observations such as (perennial or seasonal) streams, offshore coral reefs and beaches or low lying bays (potential canoe landing spots) are insightful with respect to understanding a settlement system, as opposed to simply determining a site pattern, as emphasised above.

Having outlined the research problem, objectives, and methodological and theoretical underpinnings of the chosen approach to tackling the research problem, the following chapter will proffer a conceptual framework for envisaging the Windward Islands archipelago as an archaeological and cultural unit of analysis, incorporating geological, environmental, archaeological and (ethno)historical lines of evidence.

Chapter 2

THE WINDWARD ISLANDS STUDY AREA: TOWARDS A WINDWARD ISLANDSCAPE

2.1. Island archaeology and islandscapes

The last decade has seen a tremendous increase in the amount of archaeological research being carried out in island settings. Slowly but surely, 'island archaeology' is starting to conquer a niche for itself as an alleged subdiscipline of archaeology (*"the subfield of island archaeology* [...] *as a unique entity"*, Fitzpatrick 2004b:xiii), nestling alongside other subdisciplines such as wetlands archaeology, montane archaeology and coastal archaeology (*cf.* Fitzpatrick ed. 2004 and the birth of the Journal of Island and Coastal Archaeology). Initially issuing from predominantly Oceanic and Mediterranean quarters and comprising archaeological case studies largely inspired by island biogeography (Cherry 1984; Evans 1973; Goodenough 1957; Keegan and Diamond 1987; Mead 1957; Terrell 1977)[11], island archaeology is now practised in or at least preached about in most insular environments throughout the world (Broodbank 2002; Gosden and Pavlides 1994; Irwin 1992; Kirch 1997, 2000; Patton 1996; Spriggs 1997; Rainbird 2004; also see Fitzpatrick ed. 2004, Boomert and Bright 2007, Rainbird 2007 and Spriggs 2008b for an overview).

The fact that a distinction is being made would seem to suggest that island archaeologists consider the form of archaeology they are practising as inherently different to that practised by others, in other settings. However, thus far, few researchers have succeeded in formulating what makes islands archaeologically distinctive from other settings (Fitzpatrick 2004b/c), so that one cannot help concluding that there is no theoretical or methodological basis underlying the nomer island archaeology. Rather, it is a purely descriptive nomer, that stands for archaeology conducted on islands (Boomert and Bright 2007; however, see Fitzpatrick *et al.* 2007 for a considered riposte).

One indubitably useful concept that has arisen from research in island settings is that of the islandscape. No doubt inspired by developments in the field of landscape archaeology and its cautious application to Oceania (Gosden and Head 1994) leading to the birth of the concept 'seascape' (Gosden and Pavlides 1994), Broodbank (2002) launched the concept 'islandscape' in his treatment of the Greek Cyclades. It has since been cautiously applied in both northwest European (Cooney 2004) and Caribbean (Hofman *et al.* 2007) settings. Torres and Rodriguez-Ramos (2008) have gone so far as to style the Caribbean archipelago a "continent of islands". For Broodbank, the term islandscape is nothing more and nothing less than the unison of island landscape and seascape, the two do-

11 That is not to discount an early, sound Caribbean contribution provided by Goodwin (1979).

mains straddled by islanders worldwide. The islandscape concept therefore comes to represent the state of the islands and the surrounding or intermediate waters in terms of geology, geography, climate and natural environment, but not only that. Contemporary approaches to the natural surroundings urge us to consider the interaction between the landscape and humans. The landscape is not just a plane traversed by the human species, a silent static witness to the actions of mankind. Rather, it is lived in and through, mediated, worked on and altered, replete with cultural meaning and symbolism. Through this symbolic content, landscape also has the capability to profoundly affect and influence people (Tilley 1994). To put it another way: *"space and society are mutually constitutive"* (Gosden and Pavlides 1994:163). Following from this, it is evident that the mindset of and the experience of land and sea by the original island inhabitants should also fall under the concept islandscape. A fundamental part of that mindset is the maritime orientation of islanders.

While this may strike many as a tautology, for years the study of island life was dominated by an academic canon that stressed islands as isolates (Terrell *et al.* 1997) and perfect "laboratories of change" (*e.g.* Mead 1957 and Evans 1973, but see Rouse 1951 for an early, much-neglected contra-position). Implicit in this line of thinking were two notions: (1) the notion of the sea as a barrier between islands, circumscribing them on all sides and precluding or at least discouraging travel over it, and (2) the notion that humans were basically governed by the same laws as those that governed plants and animals, an early precursor of some archaeologists' forays into island biogeography.[12]

It is now commonly accepted that human islanders were never isolated to the degree that flora and fauna could be, except in very extreme cases that form the exceptions that prove the rule (see also Boomert and Bright 2007). On the contrary, the sea most likely functioned as a waterway, an oft-traversed 'liquid plain' (Braudel cited in Cooney 2003) with which islanders would have been extremely comfortable, despite its occasional unpredictability (Wilson 1993; Terrell *et al.* 1997; Watters 1997; Rainbird 2004). This perspective requires a certain leap of faith on the part of continentally minded individuals and a certain trivialisation of the act of seafaring (*cf.* Di Piazza and Pearthree 2001), although Gell (1985:272) has previously cautioned against underestimation of the degree of skill and knowledge implicit in the art of seafaring:

> *"Can one really assert that navigating a boat, without a chart or a magnetic compass, is really an 'everyday' task? Is it not rather a very special task, requiring long training, memorization of a mass of detailed information, and considerable mental agility in applying this fund of information to the ever-changing circumstances of an actual sea voyage?".*

Applying these ideas to the Caribbean, mobility within and outside this region would have been encouraged by the geographical distribution of the islands, which is such that many of the islands are relatively close to one another and intervisible (Hofman *et al.* 2007; Keegan and Diamond 1987; Sleight 1965:227; see also

12 "The peopling of islands by man in early colonization follows much the same laws as that of plants and animals" (Fewkes 1914:664).

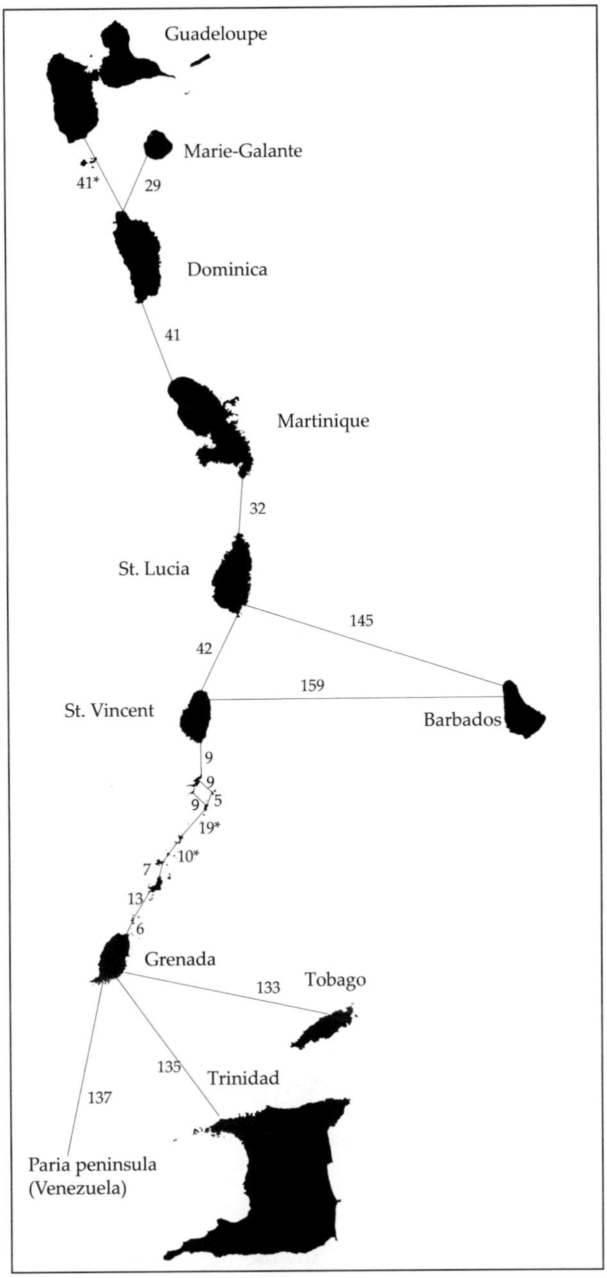

Figure 2.1. The shortest distances in kilometres (rounded up to the nearest whole kilometre) between neighbouring islands. An asterisk denotes the presence of small stepping stone islands / islets along a trajectory, which would have facilitated navigation and reduced the actual distance to be travelled on open sea. Note that Trinidad, Tobago and the Paria Peninsula are not accurately positioned.

figure 2.1). It should also be noted that even when the next island could not be seen from land, there were areas of intervisibility in the sea between neighbouring islands - also termed spaces of intersecting visibility (Torres and Rodriguez Ramos 2008) - reached at variable distances from the shore (*cf.* Callaghan 2008:57-58).

The only broader straits of sea in the Lesser Antilles are those between Grenada and the Paria Peninsula (137 km), Trinidad (135 km) and Tobago (133 km) respectively, and between Barbados and St. Vincent (159 km) and St. Lucia (145 km) respectively. That is assuming that direct crossings between Barbados and Tobago (216 km) or Grenada (234 km) would not have been hazarded. Further north, broad stretches of open sea are encountered at the Anegada Passage, between the outermost Leeward Islands and the Virgin Islands. It is some 138 km from Saba to St. Croix, 116 km from Dog Island to Anegada and 94 km from Sombrero to Virgin Gorda. The last great expanses to be crossed were those in the Greater Antilles, between western Dominican Republic and the Turks and Caicos Islands (141 km), between Haiti and Jamaica (190 km), between Haiti and Great Inagua Island (103 km), between Jamaica and Cuba (164 km) and between central Cuba and the Bahamas (113 km), assuming that such direct crossings were made.[13]

The dominant ocean currents together with the annual debouching of floodwaters of the Amazon and Orinoco rivers during the South American rainy season facilitate sea travel from south to north, though the winds predominantly blow from a north-easterly to easterly direction throughout most of the year (St. Vincent and the Grenadines Country Environmental Profile 1991; Watts 1994, 1999). Furthermore, what makes the islands in the Caribbean somewhat exceptional in the world is their high degree of intermediacy. Their linear rather than clustered distribution (as in the Aegean or Polynesia) has catalysing consequences for travel and interaction between island communities, lending the archipelago the character of an avenue, or as Roe (1989: 270) put it, an inverted main-river. Pre-Colonial communities facing each other across a channel of sea would be closer to one another as the crow flies than communities at opposite ends of the same island (Rouse 1951, 1982; Watters and Rouse 1989; see also Bright 2007).[14] This implies that communities did not necessarily have a solely inward, terrestrial outlook, relying on and relating to other communities on the island, but had an outward outlook too, oriented towards communities on other islands (*cf.* Hofman 1993; Hofman *et al.* 2004). But just because islanders could be mobile, does not need entail that they were. It is worthwhile outlining just one of the reasons why Amerindians may have chosen to be mobile and interactive.

The geological and environmental diversity of the region, referred to in more detail below (see section 2.2), has ramifications for the natural environment of islands, especially for their respective biodiversity (Newsom and Wing 2004). The heterogeneous nature of individual islands and the island group as a whole has led

13 The 114 km separating Puerto Rico and the Dominican Republic could be substantially shortened by navigating via Mayaguez and Isla Mona.

14 By positing the simple dichotomy of travel over land between communities on one island versus seafaring between facing communities on different islands past researchers seem to have ignored the possibility that other communities on a single island could equally have reached one another through seafaring, provided the communities were fairly coastal in setting. Boomert (2000) mentions one instance of territoriality and lack of contact between ethnic groups on proto-historic Trinidad, but the same situation need not have pertained to every island. Size and environmental characteristics of islands undoubtedly played a role in intensity of inter-community contacts, besides social concerns.

to a differential distribution of natural resources, both biotic and abiotic (Newsom and Wing 2004). While these island-specific resource configurations may indeed have led to certain island-specific adaptations by prehistoric human groups (*cf.* Newsom and Wing 2004:10), it is believed that this differential or discontinuous distribution (Watters 1997; Crock 2000) would also have led to Amerindians being resourceful, mobile and flexible, as well as maintaining trading and/or kinship contacts with Amerindians inhabiting other settlements either on the same island or on other islands. Non-local resources and manufactures, ranging from the mundane to the extraordinary, from perishable foodstuffs and clays to people and highly valued trade items, were exchanged between these island communities (*cf.* Hofman *et al.* 2007). It must be remembered that although geological and environmental vicissitudes lead to differential raw material availability and hence account to a certain degree for localised craft specialization and interaction (Butt Colson 1973:58), specialization and exchange arise out of "a combination of genuine and pretended lack either of raw materials or the requisite manufacturing skills" (Boomert 2000:423), something Thomas (1972:15) calls the cultural division of labour. Furthermore, stylistic or technological variation applied by others to objects already in common use or manufacture amongst a given group will tend to be appreciated, and may lead to such objects becoming sought after goods in spite of their functional superfluity (Butt Colson 1973:59). In any case, environmental determinism fails to account for the deeper motivations for social interaction and how this interaction took form, *e.g.* marriage links (Thomas 1972) and political alliances.

It now becomes evident that one may have to refrain from assembling cultural typologies and chronologies at an island level, when island community interaction transcended the geographical boundaries of the island (*cf.* Curet 2004; Hofman 1993; Wilson 1993). Put simply, the islandscape concept urges us to broaden our horizons, cast our nets ever more distant and adopt an archipelagic perspective (*cf.* Carlson and Keegan 2004; Hofman, Bright and Hoogland 2006), taking into account the roles played by neighbouring islands and (distant) mainlands (Hofman *et al.* 2007).

While the "primitive isolate" discussion is in danger of becoming an anachronistic, self perpetuating niche for researchers, many of the main points of criticism levelled at the isolation myth have yet to fully permeate archaeological research designs. The overwhelming majority of archaeological fieldwork in the Caribbean for instance is still unit-focused in design, rather than inter-unit, whether these units are sites, regions, islands or archipelagos. Geographical and political boundaries often still determine the archaeological comparative framework (see also Chapter 1). The outcome of much early work therefore still has a rather island-centric ring to it, something this research aims to avoid. That having been said, the danger underlying the present hype of regarding islands as connected and entangled entities must also be acknowledged. As Anderson (2004a) so eloquently points out, archaeologists are running the risk of over-compensating for years of thinking in terms of boundedness and isolation. Examples of true geographical isolation do exist and there are even more examples of true social isolation (see also Boomert and Bright 2007).

It is important that we do not forget, in our enthusiasm to construct interaction networks and island-transcending frameworks, to consider the island as an entity as well. Indeed, while in some cases, similarities in material culture assemblages divided by water passages may be striking (Bright 2007; Rouse 1951), they may be equally or even more striking among assemblages along the coastline of a single island. Furthermore, it is all too easy to minimize the importance of the interior of islands, biased as much research is by the unsurveyable nature of many island interiors and the rich pickings of coastal archaeology. Now that we have opened our eyes to the seascapes that are a fundamental component of our islandscapes, we must not downplay the importance of the lands, which are equally fundamental.

Similarly to how Tartaron (2008) recently presented an overview of Aegean prehistory as world archaeology, it is hoped that this contribution to Windward Island archaeology may be of interest to island archaeologists the world over, not just Caribbeanists. Certainly, other recent publications in Caribbean archaeology could be said to have repercussions outside their direct study field, providing theories and case studies in mobility and exchange (Hofman *et al.* 2007, 2008) maritime voyaging and inter-island visibility (Callaghan 2008; Torres and Rodríguez Ramos 2008), adaptation to insular life and human ecology (Fitzpatrick and Keegan 2007; Keegan *et al.* 2008), and (over)exploitation of terrestrial flora/fauna and marine resources (Newsom and Wing 2004; Steadman and Stokes 2005; Steadman *et al.* 2005), to name but a few.

2.2. Defining the Windward Islands

When defining the geographical scope of the PhD research, one encounters two terms for the general area under study: Windward Islands and southern Lesser Antilles. The term Windward Islands is a construct rooted in maritime history rather than a cultural unit per sé. Columbus had already introduced the term "barlovento" as early as 1492 (Verdera 1994:298-300), and the first English mention of the term Windward Islands dates to at least as early as the seventeenth century[15], when it was applied to the islands from Grenada to Dominica, as they were deemed more windward to the predominant north-north-easterly to easterly trade winds than the islands further north. However, in French, Dutch and Spanish, the term Windward was more logically applied to the entire Lesser Antillean chain, and the term Leeward was reserved for the islands off the coast of Venezuela. The term is adopted as an analytical unit in this research, with full recognition that fluid cultural boundaries do not accord perfectly with rigid geographical boundaries. In this dissertation, the Windward Islands comprise Grenada, the Grenadines, St. Vincent, St. Lucia, Martinique, Dominica and Barbados (*cf.* Allaire 1977). Although opinions vary, the general consensus nowadays is that the islands of Trinidad and Tobago, though a part of the (southern) Lesser Antilles, cannot be considered to belong to the Windward Islands either geologically or cultur-

15 *I.e.* "1657 R. LIGON Barbadoes (1673) 23 The most "windwardly Island of all the Caribbies". http://www.oed.com. See also De Laet (1931:36) for early usage of the Dutch equivalent of Windward Islands, 'Eilanden boven den Wind'.

ally (see also Chapter 7). Culturally, the ceramic assemblages of Trinidad vary substantially from those of the Windwards, particularly during the Late Ceramic Age, exhibiting largely mainland South American characteristics. Assemblages of Tobago exhibit both similarities and differences with those of the Windwards and the South American mainland. The islands off the Venezuelan coast (also known as the Leeward Antilles) fall under the cultural influence sphere of the western and central Venezuelan Dabajuroid culture. The Leeward Islands comprise the northern Lesser Antilles and the British and U.S. Virgin Islands, although in this dissertation, a cultural definition of the Leeward Islands will be adhered to, which excludes the islands to the west of the Anegada Passage. During the Late Ceramic Age, the Leewards were increasingly influenced by developments in the Greater Antilles. The island of Guadeloupe straddles the Windward/Leeward divide both geographically and culturally, and is therefore somewhat difficult to assign to either region.[16] Given that the archaeology of Guadeloupe has been well documented, it was deemed unnecessary to include it in the Windward Islands overview. However, its position as gateway into the Leeward Islands does make it extremely interesting for studies into the precise nature of the Windward/Leeward divide somewhat artificially imposed by the British Colonial authorities, or rather, an evaluation of whether such a divide holds any merit archaeologically or culturally speaking (see also Chapter 7).[17]

Be that as it may, the archaeological record of the islands from Grenada to Dominica (and including the geographical outlier Barbados) does exhibit similarities in material culture through time, homogeneity indicative of some anterior cultural unity. This material homogeneity, though far from perfect, has determined the geographical limits of this study. In this dissertation, the term Windward Islands will be employed to refer to the islands from Grenada up to and including Dominica, whereas the more general and inclusive term southern Lesser Antilles will be employed to refer to all islands from Trinidad up to and including Guadeloupe, which straddles the southern and northern Lesser Antillean divide geographically and culturally.

2.3. Towards a Windward Islandscape: the natural setting

2.3.1. Geography and geology of the southern Lesser Antilles

The Lesser Antilles stretch some 1200 km from north (the westernmost Virgin Islands St. Thomas and St. Croix) to south (the southern end of Trinidad), of which the southern Lesser Antilles - from Trinidad to Guadeloupe – take up about

16 This issue is underscored by the confusing description of the Windward Islands (south of Dominica) and the Leeward Islands (north of Guadeloupe) proffered by Newsom and Wing (2004:77), which leaves Dominica and Guadeloupe unaccounted for, and would appear to view Trinidad and Tobago as belonging to the Windward Islands.

17 It is safe to say that the geographical division between Windward and Leeward islands, imposed and employed by colonial Europeans on the basis of meteorological characteristics affecting sailing in the region, held no meaning for the Amerindian inhabitants. Given their seafaring capabilities, they were affected by currents rather than winds. While the Amerindians were undoubtedly aware of regional geophysical and environmental differences, there is no evidence to suggest that they thought in terms of Windward and Leeward islands.

700 km. The Windward Islands stretch some 400 km, with a total surface area of some 3629 km^2 (see table 2.1). It is important to realize that in comparative archipelagic terms, this is a relatively diminutive arena, dwarfed by the Mediterranean, South-East Asia and Oceania, and more in the order of the various sub-archipelagoes within these regions.[18]

The arc of islands of the Lesser Antilles separates the Caribbean Sea from the Atlantic Ocean. Although general processes underlie the formation of the Caribbean islands, individual islands have extremely varied geological histories. Not even islands individually are of a uniform geological age or make-up; for instance an island such as St. Lucia has a complex geological history, ranging from young deposits in the south of the island and older deposits in the north. Local island geology will be discussed in more detail in the subsections of Chapter 4.

Generally speaking, the Lesser Antillean arc began to take shape after eastward movement of the Caribbean Plate some 38 million years ago led gradually to subduction of the Atlantic oceanic crust, which in turn caused andesitic volcanism (Blair Hedges 2001; Van Soest 2000: 28/9). At present, the island chain splits into two geologically distinct arcs from Martinique onwards, the limestone islands to the east and the volcanic islands veering off to the west. The islands from Trinidad up to and including Dominica are volcanic in geological make-up. North of Dominica, the arc splits into an inner and an outer arc. The islands of the inner arc are geologically younger and consist of active and/or recently extinct volcanoes. This younger arc extends 750 km from Grenada in the south to Saba in the north and further comprises the islands of St. Vincent, St. Lucia, Martinique, Dominica, the western half of Guadeloupe known as Basse-Terre, Montserrat, Nevis, St. Kitts and St. Eustatius. The outer arc islands are of composite nature, predominantly consisting of marine sediments on an old volcanic foundation. This geologically older arc stretches some 375 km and comprises Marie-Galante,

Island	*Area (km^2)*
Dominica	750
Martinique	1100
St. Lucia	616
St. Vincent and Grenadines	389
Grenada	344
Barbados	430
(Trinidad and Tobago)	(5128)
Total (Including Trinidad and Tobago)	3629 (8757)

Table 2.1. Area of Windward Islands in km^2 (Microsoft Encarta Interactive World Atlas 2001).

18 The Kula exchange of Melanesia (which could be considered an attractive analogy for certain exchanges in the Caribbean) takes place over an area roughly the same as that making up the Windward Islands. The matter of scale is obviously important to bear in mind when considering cultural comparisons with other insular areas (*cf.* Broodbank 2002: figures 3 and 5).

Les Iles de la Petite Terre, Grande-Terre (eastern Guadeloupe), Antigua, Barbuda, St. Barthélemy, St. Martin, Anguilla and Sombrero (Knippenberg 2006; Van Soest 2000).

The remaining islands of La Désirade, Barbados, Trinidad and Tobago cannot be assigned to either of the arcs (Knippenberg 2006). Barbados appears to consist of elements of both, but may in fact have a different geological origin from all other islands (Drewett ed. 1991). Trinidad and Tobago are considered to be more related to mainland South America than to the Lesser Antilles in terms of geology, due to their being situated atop the continental South American Plate and once having been connected to the mainland (making them land-bridge islands, *cf.* Keegan and Diamond 1987). As such, they are considerably older than the other islands and their terrestrial flora and fauna reflect their mainland allegiance (Boomert 2000:17).

2.3.2. Palaeo-environment and palaeo-climate

In order to make sense of Amerindian settlement and lifeways throughout the Windward Island archipelago, it is vital to reconstruct its environmental and climatic aspect in pre-Colonial times, for it is this, together with the geological and geographical setting outlined above, that determined the arena within which Amerindians led their lives. This is not to paint an environmentally deterministic view of the island inhabitants, just to detail the surroundings in which they found themselves upon arriving on the islands and to indicate certain conditions they would have faced. While the environment had an undeniable impact on human life, humans were so resourceful as to preclude their placement in environmentally determinist models.

Broodbank, in his discussion of the archaeology of the Cyclades, is able to state with confidence that essentially, the overall outline and appearance of the Cycladic islands has changed little over the last 5000 years (Broodbank 2002:70). The contrast with the Caribbean islands could not be greater. As Watts (1994) details, the Caribbean has suffered one of the most drastic environmental degradations in the world over the last five hundred years alone. In some rare cases, little may have changed, but in many other cases there may be drastic differences between the present setting and the palaeo-setting. Attempting to reset the environmental clock to pre-Colonial times is therefore a hazardous enterprise, entailing various methodological problems; a certain degree of projecting back from early, fallible Colonial-period sources is inevitable and much will rest on assumption rather than assertion. However, it is believed there is more to be gained than lost through this exercise. Various approaches will be employed in unison to paint a picture of pre-Colonial environments.

Delpuech (2004) characterizes the Caribbean archipelago as an astounding mosaic of environments with a great diversity in resources. The same was undoubtedly the case in pre-Colonial times. In characterizing the initial conditions encountered by the first islanders, the most apparent features of islands would have been their relatively depauperate terrestrial faunal assemblages and extremely rich potential for harvesting marine resources. Following the general laws of island biogeography, a drop-off is to be expected in terms of abundance of mainland taxa throughout the archipelago the further one is removed from their mainland origin (MacArthur and Wilson 1967:23; see also Newsom and Wing 2004:205-206). With no predatory species on the islands before the arrival of man, many of the mammals and birds living in the archipelago may have represented easy, rich pickings, as did the unspoiled estuaries, mangroves and reef systems along the coast (Wilson 2007:26). Which species of animals were present on the islands at the time of first colonization? Early visitors to the Greater Antilles probably encountered land mammals like the giant ground sloth and certainly its later, smaller descendants, possibly the Puerto Rican giant cavy, certainly the Greater Antillean spiny rat, the capybara, the hutía, three species of Antillean monkey and shrew-like insectivores (Steadman *et al.* 2005; Watlington 2003:33-47). As far as marine mammals are concerned, the waters were populated by the Caribbean Monk Seal, the West Indian Manatee and numerous whale and dolphin species. Rivers, estuaries and the shoreline were inhabited or frequented by freshwater and sea turtles, iguanas, crocodiles, various freshwater, bank, reef and pelagic fishes including shark, crabs and crayfish, and a large array of shell molluscs (Watlington 2003:48-62). Rounding off the inventory are waterfowl, migrant and native bird species such as ducks, parrots, pigeons, shearwaters and frigate birds and many more (Watlington 2003:63-71). In some cases, occurrence of species is limited to the Greater Antilles or even to one particular island, restricting the degree of their exploitation by Amerindians throughout the region. Also, not all animals and resources listed were necessarily exploited at all, and even those that were may not have been exploited constantly or even intensively through time, some becoming extinct swiftly after humans arrived on the scene.[19]

It had been suggested in the past that the first Amerindians arriving in this island arena would have been at a loss regarding exploitation of marine resources, considering their mainland origin and terrestrial bent. For a while, there even appeared to be evidence for this supposition in the so-called crab-shell dichotomy visible at certain sites, which was attributed to successive migrations of groups practising different economies, one terrestrially-oriented and the other marine-oriented (Rainey 1936). However, this alleged dichotomy was qualified significantly as an adaptive process over time (Goodwin 1980), and has in recent times been explained as an optimistic, flexible attitude towards resource exploitation, in which terrestrial and marine are not easily separated (Boomert 2000:309-310; DeFrance *et al.* 1996; Siegel 1993; Stokes 1995). It is hypothesised that Amerindians from the mainland would at the very least have had experience of riverine fishing, considering their Orinocan origins (*cf.* Allaire 1991:716). They probably acquired further knowledge of and expertise in exploiting truly marine resources thanks to contacts they maintained with the Manicuaroid people during their sojourn along the Venezuelan coast, before moving out into the islands (Boomert 2000:83, 88; McKusick 1960:131-2; Sleight 1965:226).

19 This has prompted endless debate about the cause of their demise. Whether species like the giant sloth were hunted to extinction, or died out as a result of changing climate and concomitant habitat changes is still a matter of great debate.

Generally speaking, the flora and vegetation of the Caribbean islands are highly similar to those of Central and South America, suggesting that the mainland environment came to be replicated on the islands as a result of flotation or aerial transmission of organisms and seeds over time. Therefore, Amerindians would have encountered a fairly familiar natural environment, characterized on the whole by lower species diversity rather than totally exotic biota. The environment ran the gamut from tropical and subtropical rainforest, wet and moist forest and montane and lower-montane forests to coastal mangroves, dry forest, thorn woodland and desert scrublands, occasionally on a single island (Newsom and Wing 2004:21). Amerindians would have likely cultivated or at least targeted for exploitation tree species bearing edible fruits such as soursop, papaya and guava, cockspur, sapodilla, sea grape and hog-plum (Newsom and Wing 2004:108, 143). The calabash tree (gourds), lignum vitae (wood and bark), the silk cotton tree (fibre) and the stinking toe pod (resin) were likely utilised for the resources they offered too (Newsom and Wing 2004:108). Food staples such as manioc and other tubers as well as maize were introduced and cultivated, and panicoid grass and a range of other plants were drawn on for medicinal purposes as well as for basketry and the like.

Inexorably connected to palaeo-environment are the twin factors of palaeoclimate and palaeo-geology. Geology, weather and climate maintained a tenuous balance, affecting life in the short-term as well as in the long-term. In general, Caribbean islands and islanders have been subjected to various geophysical processes such as plate tectonics, subduction, coastal and riverine erosion as well as sedimentation, earthquakes, volcanic activity and hurricanes (Delpuech 2004).

Climatically, the yearly cycle in the Caribbean is characterized by the succession of dry and rainy season, the dry season running from November to April, and the rainy season from May to October. The Caribbean is nowadays renowned for its tropical climate, combining favourable elements such as sun and cooling trade winds with less favourable elements as tropical showers and hurricanes. The trade winds harbour a great amount of moisture, which only results in precipitation if atmospheric cooling takes place. In the Lesser Antilles, this commonly occurs by means of the orographic effect that island relief has in creating instability waves in the trade wind. This phenomenon leads to considerably greater precipitation in the windward parts of an island (north and east) rather than the leeward parts (south and west) (Watts 1994).

While the general climate does not seem to have been radically different in pre-Colonial times than at present, there are indications of climatological fluctuations that may have influenced Amerindian life considerably. The notorious rainy season hurricanes, which plague the Caribbean yearly to this day, would have been a regular feature of pre-Colonial life on the islands, requiring a certain resilience and flexibility (*cf.* Cooper and Peros 2010). Not only would the force of the wind have wreaked havoc upon settlements, but also the storm surges: high waves pummelling and inundating settlements in coastal areas (Davis and Oldfield 2003; Scudder 2001, 2003; Watters and Petersen 1993). Cooper and Peros (in press) suggest that nearby cave systems in their research area in Cuba may have served as temporary shelters during hurricane events (*cf.* De Waal 2006:92, 117 for similar behaviour on La Désirade)[20], but that islanders mitigated the threat of flooding and storm surges by constructing stilted dwellings that partially lay behind protective mangrove islands. There are indications that settlements shifted locally over time, moving back from the beach to a setting further inland behind dunes, perhaps connected to rising sea levels (Delpuech 2004; Hofman *et al.* 2001; Keegan 1995b; Petersen *et al.* 1995; Scudder 2001, 2003). Climate change could have either reduced or greatly enhanced the threat of these destructive forces of nature. Palynological (Bonnissent 2003; Bonnissent *et al.* 2007; Curtis *et al.* 2001; Siegel *et al.* 2001), biological (Curtis and Hodell 1993; Hodell *et al.* 1991), geochemical (Beets *et al.* 2006; Haug *et al.* 2003; Hodell *et al.* 2001), photographic and archaeological evidence amassed over the past decade throughout the wider Caribbean area has started to point to major drought episodes hitting the islands over the last ten thousand years. The implications of these droughts could have been substantial, and while certain researchers have focused on this aspect, the full extent of the effects of drought on Caribbean Amerindian populations is far from known.

According to deposits from Lake Miragoane, from 3200 BP onwards, and especially after 2400 BP a dry episode set in that lasted until 1500 BP. A brief period of wetter conditions prevailed between 1500 and 900 BP after which conditions gradually became those of the present (Hodell *et al.* 1991:792). Considering the implications for island settlement, this means that around 450 BC the Early Ceramic Age island settlers would have encountered a dryish environment until about AD 450, when things became wetter for a period of 600 years, becoming dryer again after AD 1050. However, more recent data from Lake Chichancanab in Mexico's Yucatan peninsula (Hodell *et al.* 2001) and the Cariaco Basin off northern Venezuela (Haug *et al.* 2003) provide a slightly different picture. Hodell *et al.* (2001) establishes numerous dry periods at 475 BC, 275–250 BC, AD 125-210, AD 750-875 and AD 1000 to 1075, whereas Haug *et al.* (2003:1734) provide evidence of multi-year droughts centred at approximately AD 760, 810, 860 and 910. Finally, Beets *et al.* (2006) underscore that dry, stormy conditions prevailed between cal AD 800 and 1000, after which the climate became wetter again. Petitjean Roget (2005) and more recently Blancaneaux (2009) have advanced the hypothesis that the drought or numerous drought episodes that prevailed between AD 800 and 1000 in Middle America and the Caribbean inflicted considerable stress on Amerindian populations throughout the region and were responsible for societal realignment and significant changes in material cultural and cultural practices (see also Chapter 5, section on female statuettes). Possible explanations for changing site patterns will be evaluated later on in this thesis (see Chapter 4).

Intimately related to climate, but also to regional and local tectonics, is the phenomenon of sea level change, both relative and absolute. Debate still rages over when and to what extent sea levels rose and fell, but it is certain that there were considerable changes over time (Delpuech 2004). Not only did climate changes make the sea rise and fall absolutely, local and regional tectonics caused islands to subside or uplift, compounding the overall rising or falling sea level (*cf.*

20 Locals and many archaeologists have have long been aware of the use of the caves as temporary shelters, but little has been published on the topic so far (pers. comm. L.A. Curet, 2010).

Baker Littman 2003). Estimates put the sea level at the time of man's first arrival in the Caribbean (around 7000 BP) at around 40 metres below that of the present, rising to a few metres above present sea level by around 5000 BP (Watts 1994). Trinidad became separated from the South American mainland as a result of the Flandrian eustatic transgression that commenced around 17,000 BP (Fairbridge 1976:531), and by around 6200 BP the Gulf of Paria was completely submerged (Boomert 2000:44). Trinidad and Tobago were separated by a channel as early as the beginning of the Holocene (Boomert 2000:44). Though levels oscillated somewhat, they have slowly fallen since then. Lower sea levels would have had a massive impact on human migration to or presence in the Caribbean (Scudder 2001). Previously submerged land would have been exposed, narrowing channels between islands and altering the form and characteristics of the islandscape entirely. When sea levels began to rise, Amerindians would have lost land to the encroaching water and may have needed to relocate.[21] Increased distances between islands and the disappearance of islets altogether would have rendered navigation more time-consuming and risky and Amerindians would have had to familiarize themselves with altered seascapes. Changing sea levels would also have impacted the availability of a number of resources, as new biotopes (mangroves, tidal shallows, coral reefs and beaches) replaced old ones.

Life on the islands could imply living untroubled and bountifully provisioned one moment and being afflicted by droughts or hurricanes the next (Delpuech 2004). From a long-term perspective, climate and sea level change may have gone largely unnoticed by the Amerindians, prompting gradual, almost natural adjustments through time rather than affecting daily lives. Whereas long-term processes are detectable in various ways as highlighted above, events are more difficult to pick up in the archaeological record, but there are some examples. The site Mount Irvine 1 on Tobago seems to have been covered in boulders as a result of an earthquake or landslide (Cambridge 1967). The Shoal Bay East site on Anguilla revealed storm-deposited bands of sterile sand in profile and the Barnes Bay site shows evidence of erosion and scouring by ground seas (Crock 2000; Crock and Petersen 2001). Volcanism, still plaguing the Caribbean to this day, also played a part in Amerindian lives, as is evident on Martinique, where a volcanic layer is sandwiched between two occupation layers at the sites of Vivé, Fond-Brûlé, St. Pierre, Grande Anse de Lorrain, Anse Belleville and Le Prêcheur (Allaire 1989; Bérard 2004; Mattioni 1984; Roobol *et al.* 1976). Similarly, the Saladoid occupation layer at the Soufrière site on Dominica is sealed by a thick layer of volcanic deposits (Bérard *et al.* 2005). The Trants site on Montserrat (Petersen *et al.* 1995) has likewise yielded evidence of pyroclastic flows that certainly predate, but are possibly coterminous with, Saladoid settlement, as indicated by huge boulders covering and in turn covered by human deposition. On Saba, a number of shell tools lying atop a pyroclastic deposit were uncovered during construction activities, and at the Sugar Factory site on St. Kitts, a layer of volcanic tephra sepa-

21 There is a distinct possibility that Lithic or Archaic age sites have been lost to the encroaching sea (*i.e.* Baker Littman 2003:63), and increasingly, Ceramic Age sites are in danger of being washed away (*i.e.* Morel and Anse à la Gourde on Guadeloupe among many others, see Hofman *et al.* 2001, De Waal 2006).

rates Saladoid and Archaic deposits (Roobol and Smith 1980:169-170). The sites of Fitz-Hughs, Hermitage, Queensbury, Owia Bay 2 and 3, Buccament West, Cumberland Ravine, Camden Park, Kingstown Post Office, Stubbs and Lot 14 on St. Vincent all exhibit layers of volcanic tuff or ash in their profiles or deposits attributed to slope wash or run-off as a direct result of volcanic activity (Bullen and Bullen 1972; Callaghan 2007).

The danger of living under the constant threat of an active volcano seems to have played no deterring role in the settlement choice of the Amerindians, or, more probably, the benefits of the extremely fertile soil were considered to outweigh the risks of rare eruptions that arrived with advance warning. While Allaire (1989:154) suggests that natural disasters may have had severe mental repercussions on the Amerindian mindset, little direct evidence exists that they severely impacted Amerindian life in the long run.[22] Delpuech (2004:12) points out that natural catastrophes and where they struck may have been accorded geosymbols in the mental cartography of the Amerindians and been replete with mythical meaning (*cf.* Harris 1999, 2001). Presumably though, then as now, islanders took various environmental and climatological vicissitudes in their stride.

Increasingly over the past decades, evidence has come to light that the Amerindians of the Caribbean did not merely haplessly, passively adjust to the natural environment, but rather actively tinkered with and altered their surroundings from the moment they arrived (Watlington 2003:73). Recent studies (Berman and Pearsall 2000; Bonnissent *et al.* 2007; DeFrance *et al.* 1996; Fitzpatrick and Keegan 2007; Newsom 1993; Newsom and Wing 2004; Pagán Jiménez *et al.* 2005) have indicated that Amerindians on the islands altered their natural environment by introducing plants and animals from the mainland as well as other Caribbean islands both intentionally (so-called 'transported landscapes'; *cf.* Kirch 2000:109) and accidentally (so-called 'portmanteau biota'; see Kirch 1997:218-220) as well as by carrying out a range of (subsistence) activities, in effect domesticating the landscape (Terrell *et al.* 2003). Manioc, and perhaps papaya, sweet potato, pepper, peanut and tobacco are all introduced species from mainland South America, and therefore not an original part of the natural environment of the Windward Islands (Newsom and Wing 2004:200). On the Leeward Antilles, the remains of animals not indigenous to those islands such as monkeys, deer and peccary have been recovered from archaeological sites, although it is impossible to determine whether they were transported alive or dead (Newsom and Wing 2004:72-73). Dogs (Schwartz 1997) as well as guinea pigs and agouti were certainly introduced to the Caribbean islands and transported in live form from the South American mainland, whereas hutía were most abundant on Puerto Rico, and thus presumably transported from there to other islands. According to Curet (personal communication 2010), hutía were introduced to Puerto Rico early on

22 The island of Montserrat in the Leeward Islands forms an interesting contemporary parallel, with communities having lived on the island in the shadow of the Soufrière Hills Volcano from pre-Colonial times right up to the disastrous eruptions that commenced in 1995. Furthermore, Martinique's Mount Pelée, whose eruption in 1902 claimed over 30,000 victims, is also an active volcano, a fact that has not deterred people from settling in its direct vicinity.

from Hispaniola. The decline of these species in relative abundance with increased distance from their source suggests that Amerindians may have found it difficult to maintain population levels (Newsom and Wing 2004:204-206).

Activities such as slash-and-burn agriculture, slope agriculture, predation of faunal species leading to their extinction and whole-scale forest clearing all took their toll on the surroundings. In many cases, primary vegetation was replaced by secondary vegetation (*cf.* Drewett ed. 1991:178), slopes saw erosion as the soil was no longer held together by root systems and the increase in sediment flowing into the sea as a result of deforestation likely caused the destruction of coral reefs along the coast of several islands (Crock 2000:9).

2.4. Towards a Windward Islandscape: an archaeological perspective

Let us now paint a picture of the current state of affairs or general consensus in Caribbean archaeology, from first occupation until the present, centring on the themes of settlement, lifeways and social organization. A more detailed, island-by-island review of Windward Island archaeology will follow in Chapter 3. An attempt has been made to avoid equating ceramic styles with ethnic groups or 'peoples' (though not explicitly, the spirit of V.G. Childe still drifts through some works implicitly), and to stop thinking in terms of periods whose parameters are determined by the dated occurrence of ceramic styles. This practice has already been adopted by numerous researchers in recent times (Curet 2003; Hofman and Hoogland 2004; Petersen *et al.* 2004), though Allaire (1999) was presciently one step ahead, presenting Caribbean prehistory in arbitrary 500-year time blocks, namely 500 BC–0, 0–AD 500, AD 500–1000 and AD 1000–1500.[23] This study will adopt a chronological framework encompassing Early and Late Ceramic Ages, themselves subdivided into an early and late phase, more or less analogous to the chronological framework of recently published research in the Leeward Islands (*cf.* De Waal 2006; Knippenberg 2006; Petersen *et al.* 2004). However, slightly different dates pertain to the various phases in the Windward Islands. The early phase of the Early Ceramic Age dates 400 BC–AD 300/400, the late phase of the Early Ceramic Age AD 300/400-700, the early phase of the Late Ceramic Age dates AD 700–1000 and the late phase of the Late Ceramic Age AD 1000–1500.[24]

23 It will be argued by some that this is pure semantics, as the dates of these 'arbitrary' time blocks are suspiciously similar to the generally accepted dates of the occurrence of Saladoid, Troumassan and Suazan Troumassoid pottery. However, with developments on various islands hardly running in perfect synchrony, one island's "Saladoid period" can be another's "Troumassan Troumassoid period". For this reason, it is much more sensible to use a typo-chronological system that does not conflate ceramic styles with periods. Also, chronological parameters without an explicit ceramic or cultural basis allow for various simultaneously occurring developments and are therefore far better suited to dealing with transitional periods, when various wares (or by extension even technologies or lifestyles) could be in use simultaneously, the one waxing and the other waning.

24 As the dates remain roughly inspired by the dated occurrences of major changes in material culture, the Leeward Island phases do not perfectly match those of the Windward Islands.

First inhabitants

While the debate concerning the initial peopling of the Americas continues to rage between 'early' or pre-Clovis and 'late' or Clovis camps (Adovasio and Pedler 2005:44-49; Haynes 2005:4)[25], it is acknowledged among Caribbeanists that the first Amerindians were roaming the Antilles by 5000/4000 BC (Kozłowski 1974; Rouse 1992; Wilson 2007; Wilson *et al.* 1998). They have been called either Paleo-Indians (Kozłowski 1974) or Lithic/Archaic Age Amerindians, which is a more preferable nomer given the conditions set by the term Paleo-Indian worldwide, and not replicated in the Caribbean (Lundberg 1980:134). Sea levels at that time were between 9 and 20 meters lower than at present (Wilson 2007:26), which would have facilitated navigation, though not low enough to restore the land bridges that existed earlier between the mainland of South America and Trinidad (Boomert 2000; Guarch-Delmonte 2003). These first migrants would have been well adapted to varied environments (terrestrial, riverine and marine) and have been capable of picking up on faunal movements (Watlington 2003). Few sites datable to this period are currently known, but it is remarkable that the earliest are all located far up the Antillean island chain, in Cuba, Haiti and the Dominican Republic (Wilson 2007:27).

Various hypotheses have been advanced regarding the mainland provenience of the early Amerindians. South America and Central America, particularly the Yucatán Peninsula) are considered likely places of origin on the basis of assemblage similarities (Boomert 2000; Wilson 2007), North America is not. Predominantly lithic assemblages are all that remain of these first inhabitants. The discovery of one Joboid spearhead near Biche, Trinidad (Harris 1993) provides tantalising evidence of true Palaeo-Indian presence (ca. 10,000 BP or earlier) in the southern Lesser Antilles, although technically speaking, Trinidad was still attached to mainland South America at the time (Boomert 2000). Trinidad also has the oldest remains of human occupation, the site Banwari Trace yielding a date of ca. 6000 BC. The material culture of these Archaic Age groups has been termed Ortoiroid, which comprises the Banwarian (6000-2500 BC) and Ortoiran (1500 BC-500 BC) subseries (Boomert 2000).

Thus far, only Trinidad, Tobago, Martinique and Barbados have yielded sites or finds attributable to these cultures in the southern Lesser Antilles. Sea level rise, local isostatic uplift and subsidence, sedimentation and erosion are likely to blame for the low number of Archaic Age sites discovered so far. Recent finds on Saba (Hofman and Hoogland 2003; Hofman *et al.* 2006) suggest that the hitherto largely unsurveyed interiors of other volcanic islands may have preserved Archaic Age remains as well, similar to Martinique's Boutbois and Le Godinot (Allaire and Mattioni 1983; but see Bérard 2006c/d for question marks surrounding their periodisation).

25 For early dates in South America, see for instance the Monte Verde site in Chile (Meltzer *et al.* 1997) and Taima-Taima in Venezuela (Oliver *n.d.*).

Lack of evidence precludes an elaborate discussion of the Archaic Age in the Windwards. Thus far, only two sites have yielded dates that fall before 400 BC, the date that arguably pinpoints the earliest Saladoid assemblages in the islands, Fond-Brûlé on Martinique (2480±40 BP: Bérard 2004:26, 60) and Heywoods on Barbados (3980±100 BP: Drewett ed. 2007) (see also Appendix 2). Interestingly, the researchers recently involved with the Fond-Brûlé site have dismissed these early dates gathered by their predecessors as being unreliable (*cf.* Bérard 2004:62), leaving Heywoods as the only site in the Windward Islands ascribed to the Archaic Age with a trusted date to match. All other supposed Archaic Age sites remain circumspect without bolstering radiocarbon dates. However, if we can consider the Archaic Age in the Windward Islands as analogous to that in other parts of the Caribbean, then we must have been dealing with small bands or groups of versatile, hunter-fisher-collectors, who traversed the islandscape frequently, perhaps even seasonally (Hofman *et al.* 2006). Temporary camps and activity areas were primarily located along the coast (Lundberg 1980) but also incidentally high up in the interior (Hofman and Hoogland 2003), perhaps reflecting the range of resources targeted and procurement strategies adopted. Material culture was relatively simple and portable, comprising millstones, pounders, cobbles, flint cores and flakes as well as shell axes and undoubtedly many artefacts made of perishable, organic material. Though highly mobile and self-sufficient, these groups would have probably interacted with each other now and then, to socialize and ensure reproductive health, as well as to exchange raw materials (Hofman *et al.* 2006). Archaeological evidence indicates that the diet of these first islanders in the main consisted of (shell)fish, crustaceans, and sea mammals, as well as land mammals and birds, in frequencies that varied per site (Davis 2000; Hofman and Hoogland 2003:16-17, 20; Lundberg 1980).

Early Ceramic Age society (400 BC – AD 700)

There are two main hypotheses regarding the origins of lower Orinocan and, by extension, Antillean Saladoid culture (Boomert 2000). The first argues that around 4000 years ago, a culture arose somewhere in the Central Amazon, near the confluence of the Upper Amazon, the Negro and the Madeira, that was to form the Middle Orinocan Ronquín culture, the basis for the Saladero culture which developed in the lower Orinoco basin some 1000 years later (Boomert 2000:101-105; see also Cruxent and Rouse 1982; Lathrap 1970:112; Vargas Arenas 1979, 1981). Around 800 BC, this culture spread increasingly downriver, then along parts of the Venezuelan coast, before ultimately crossing to the islands. The alternative hypothesis postulates that the origins of the Saladoid are actually Andean rather than Amazonian, from the highlands of Colombia, Ecuador and Peru (Meggers and Evans 1978; Sanoja and Vargas 1978, 1983). According to Boomert (2000:114-15), both theories are based on superficial stylistic comparisons that highlight a number of resemblances between the respective material assemblages, but fail to account for numerous discrepancies. Whatever the case, Saladoid influence or carriers of the culture showed up in the lowlands and coastal areas of Venezuela by around 1000 BC (Boomert 2000).

In recent years, new life has been breathed into the theory discussed by Rouse and Cruxent (1969:58), namely that once there, the Saladoid horticulturalists interacted intensively with the resident arboriculturalist Manicuaroid hunter-gatherers, who introduced them to the new environment's resources and, crucially, aided them in their transformation from proficient riverine travelers into the fully-fledged maritime voyagers the hunter-gatherers themselves evidently already were (*cf.* Boomert 2000; Curet 2005; Hofman *et al.* in press; Keegan and Rodriguez Ramos 2005; Newsom and Wing 2004; Rodriguez Ramos 2007). In return, the Archaic groups may have benefited from horticultural knowledge and other traits afforded by a more sedentary lifestyle.

This scenario still upholds, in a more moderate fashion, the idea of groups carrying culture forth from one point to another. The potential for cultural learning, diffusion and cross-group symbiotic relationships offers a number of alternative scenarios: (1) the "Saladoid" groups moving into the archipelago were in fact Archaic Age groups influenced by Saladoid culture, or, more likely, the outcome of a merger of the two cultures, a new Archaic-Saladoid culture (*cf.* Curet 2005:67-68) and, (2) the islands were not vacant gardens of Eden, but settled semi-permanently by Archaic groups, who took on board aspects of Saladoid culture through diffusion by way of the Lesser Antillean islands or directly across the Caribbean Sea from coastal north-east South America or through independent innovation. Either way, there was less movement into the archipelago by agriculturalists than previously hypothesized (Curet 2005; Hofman *et al.* in press).

While the latter hypothesis is probably overstating matters slightly, evidence is increasingly showing that the idea has some validity at least for the Greater Antilles. Indeed, mounting evidence for Archaic Age pottery (Rodriguez Ramos 2007; Rodriguez Ramos *et al.* 2008; Ulloa Hung and Valcárcel Rojas 2002) in Cuba, Puerto Rico and the Dominican Republic, the long-standing debates surrounding the relationship of Huecan/La Hueca pottery to Saladoid pottery (see Oliver 1999), studies of the lithic assemblages of the respective cultures (Bérard 2008; Rodríguez Ramos 2007) and research into the alleged arboricultural practices of Archaic Age groups (Newsom and Wing 2004; Pagán Jiménez *et al.* 2005; Petersen 1997) all point to the conclusion that the mainland and potentially resident insular Archaic groups were highly sophisticated, and that the Saladoid groups (if they can be called such) were not the great bringers of culture they have so long been considered (*cf.* Rouse 1992).

The discovery of a spatially segregated, aberrant ceramic assemblage - alternately termed Huecoid, Huecan Saladoid, La Hueca style or La Hueca complex (Chanlatte-Baik 1984; Curet 2005; Oliver 1999; Rouse 1992) – on Puerto Rico, Vieques, St. Martin and Guadeloupe has led some scholars to question the dominant Saladoid migration paradigm. The intriguing possibility that Archaic Age groups were already manufacturing ceramics well before the arrival of Saladero horticulturalists has only added fuel to the fire (Ulloa and Valcárcel 2002; Keegan and Rodríguez Ramos 2005).[26] The La Hueca phenomenon has so far failed to manifest itself in the Windwards though, bar one or two trade items, and Archaic Age remains are scarce enough, let alone evidence of co-mingling.

Returning to the Saladoid phenomenon, no researcher of the Caribbean has failed to note the remarkable linear, arching distribution of the islands across the Caribbean Sea (Barbados forming the only exception), which would appear to lend the archipelago a stepping-stone, avenue-like quality when it comes to movement through the area (*i.e.* Keegan 2004; Hofman *et al.* 2007; Roe 1989). The earliest archaeologists assumed that an initial Ceramic Age entry was made into the archipelago at either the Venezuelan or Floridian end of the chain (or both), and that the Amerindians would have ventured forth from one island to the next consecutively (island-hopping). Once the material cultural link between the first ceramic assemblages on the islands and the Venezuelan Saladero and Ronquín culture was discovered, Florida was dismissed as a possible cultural donor area. The advent of radiocarbon dating offered the first opportunity to test the migration pattern of the Saladero Amerindians. Initial results were somewhat unexpected, as there were very early dates for Puerto Rico and a number of Leeward Islands, and dates of similar or slightly younger age for the Windward Islands and Trinidad. However, give or take a century, the dates more or less fitted the accepted scenario of sequential settlement from south to north, although the migration must have been a fast event. By 400 BC then, Saladoid groups had manifested themselves on many of the Caribbean islands up to Puerto Rico, fleetingly in some cases and permanently in others.

The penecontemporaneity of settlement at both northern and southern ends of the Lesser Antilles and the generally homogeneous style of the ceramics found across almost the entire archipelago seem to suggest that the islands were occupied (either briefly or more lengthily) by a number of highly mobile, inter-related settler groups (*cf.* Rouse 1992). The traditional view of the early phase Early Ceramic Age settlement is one where the first settlements were established predominantly in the north and east of volcanic islands (*cf.* Haviser 1997), a little back from the shore, in the vicinity of a perennial river and amid forest, which Rouse (1992:79) regarded as a predilection for environments reminiscent of ancestral homelands with suitable agricultural land in the near vicinity. Haviser (1988:33) suggests that Saladoid people would have been unsure of their surroundings and more defensive in their selection of site location. Fertile soils and abundant freshwater supplies would have been essential, and food acquisition centred on terrestrial resources. However, other locations were also settled, that appear to be dependent on the presence of reefs, attesting to the mixed economy that these colonists had started to practise. Villages were apparently relatively large and long-lived (Bérard 2004; Keegan 2000:141; Petersen 1996; Watters 1994), although settlement dimensions may have been overestimated, by interpreting sheet deposition caused by diachronically shifting settlement locations as contemporaneous occupation.

26 While the introduction of pottery is most readily associated with sedentary, agricultural groups, it would be fallacious to assume those traits from the presence of pottery or to dismiss the possibility that hunter-gatherers manufactured pottery (Arnold 1989; Hoopes and Barnett 1995:2).

Furthermore, the duration of single phase occupations can easily be overestimated by the general absence of radiocarbon dates for many sites and the large margin of uncertainty pertaining to those dates that are available. Possible site abandonment and re-occupation either within one phase or between successive phases is also effectively impossible to gauge. Be that as it may, these earliest settlements consisted of one or a number of large roundhouses or oval structures with rubbish middens located directly behind them, a (central) clearing or plaza and gardens outside but in the vicinity of the settlement (Boomert 2000:292-297; Hofman and Hoogland 2004). Subsistence practices comprised the cultivating of root crops (horticulture), fishing, hunting and collecting, amounting to a broad-spectrum diet.

Archaeologists adduce that these tribal societies (*cf.* Boomert 2000:392; Curet 1996; Keegan 1996:144; Roosevelt 1994:6; Siegel 1992; Steward and Faron 1959:17) were egalitarian in nature, perhaps allowing temporary leadership in times of environmental stress or warfare. Levelling mechanisms would presumably have been in place to prevent the rise of institutionalised or ascribed leadership. Amerindian worldview was highly animistic, characterized by the belief that everything in the world was animated or imbued with spirits. Safely negotiating the human world required frequent mediation with the spirit world, a role that was performed by the shamans. By entering into drug-induced trances, they bridged the human and spirit world, asking the spirits for guidance, manipulating them for good or evil purposes and to heal sickness. Although egalitarian, these early societies would have relied greatly on their shamans, who as a result of the faith vested in them, were prestigious and highly powerful individuals (Boomert 2003; Hofman and Hoogland 2004). Amerindian Windward Islanders manufactured Saladoid ceramics during this period. This ware is thin yet durable, highly decorated by painting, incising, engraving and modelling. Equally impressive is not so much the quality of the ceramic assemblage, but also its enormous variety in terms of vessel shapes and decorative motifs (Roe 1989). Delicate, intricately carved items of personal adornment were fashioned from lithic, shell and bone material (Chanlatte-Baik 1984).

The later phase of the Early Ceramic Age is characterized by a continuation of proceedings of the prior centuries, though markedly intensified, with more dense settlement of the already inhabited islands and initial settlement of islands that had been uninhabited until that period, like Barbados. Social organization and lifeways appear to be unchanged compared to the early phase Early Ceramic Age. Later Saladoid (also called Modified Saladoid) ceramic assemblages in the southern Windwards have been determined to exhibit Barrancoid influences, prompting the hypotheses that the Barrancoid influence sphere was expanding at this time, up to the East Venezuelan coast and Trinidad (Boomert 2000:246), or that there was actually a migration of Barrancoid-culture people to the islands (Rouse 1992; Sanoja 1979). Towards the end of the later phase of the Early Ceramic Age, there is a slight yet detectable decrease in the quality and appearance of the ceramics, which are now also referred to as Terminal Saladoid.

Early phase Late Ceramic Age society (AD 700-1000)

The traditional view of early phase Late Ceramic Age settlement is one of continuation and consolidation of the Early Ceramic Age, although the early phase of the Late Ceramic Age is often glossed over in favour of the later period. Allaire (1977) postulated that the Amerindians of Martinique moved into more arid areas at this time, perhaps because they had become less dependent on terrestrial (rainforest) resources or had over-exploited them. Alternatively or coevally, Amerindians may have gained a better understanding of the marine environment and the resources it harboured (Serrand 2007:425). Petitjean Roget advances yet another hypothesis: the dryer climate forced populations to give up on agriculture and rely more on the marine resources offered by the mangrove and reef systems of south-east Martinique. Settlements remain similar in appearance to the earlier period, still comprising a number of round or oval structures, loosely grouped around a central plaza or clearing, with rubbish middens behind the houses and gardens nearby (Hofman and Hoogland 2004).

Subsistence practices similarly held over from the Early Ceramic Age, entailing the cultivating of root crops (horticulture), fishing, hunting and collecting, although Serrand (2007) notes an increasing exploitation of marine resources, especially bivalves, starting in this period, which she relates to the relocation of Troumassoid settlements to mangrove-rich areas. Allaire (1991) has suggested that cotton cultivation and salt exploitation picked up during this period, perhaps under influence of drier climatic conditions.

Little has been written about social organization during this period, which is seen as transitional and difficult to get to grips with. Haviser (1988:33) has suggested that populations were increasing and that competition over resources may have started to arise. He relates the orientation towards marine resources, and the increasing distance of settlements from freshwater supplies to a growing familiarity with the surroundings. He further posits that defensive strategies decreased, as there was less uncertainty about neighbours, allowing local interaction spheres to arise (Haviser 1988:33).

Initially seen as the material manifestation of a second wave of migrants into the Lesser Antilles, the Troumassoid series of the early phase of the Late Ceramic Age is nowadays considered a local development that evolved from the Saladoid series some time after AD 600 (Hofman *et al.* 2007; Rouse 1992:127-128). Both positions are still evident in the taxonomical nomenclature however: the former in the fact that Troumassoid pottery was deemed to represent a new series, the latter in that the early Troumassan ware for instance on St. Lucia (Troumassée A style) is now classified as a local style belonging to the Saladoid series, and its successor Troumassée B as a local style of the Troumassoid series. A number of Saladoid decorative traditions persist, such as painting in red, black or white, curvilinear incision and wedge-shaped lugs. As the period wears on, the pottery gradually becomes cruder, painting occurs less and less frequently and loop handles and a number of vessel shapes in general disappear. On the other hand, a number of new phenomena such as elaborate rim lugs and clay spindle whorls (associated with the rise of cotton production during this period) are introduced and vessels (including griddles) are increasingly furnished with legs or pedestal/annular bases (Rouse 1992:127-129). Also, a highly elaborate polychrome ware (called Caliviny Polychrome) appears at select sites throughout the Windwards (see Chapter 6).

It is perhaps worth noting that the Saladoid-Troumassoid break, however weak or strong it is perceived to be, is not an isolated phenomenon within the greater Caribbean area. Similar breaks in material culture apparently occurred at around the same time on the South American mainland (Saladoid/Barrancoid–Arauquinoid), in the Leewards (Saladoid–Mamoran Troumassoid) and in the Greater Antilles (Saladoid–Ostionoid). These more or less coeval societal realignments taking place in different areas throughout the region suggest that the Saladoid cultural template was definitely on the wane (see also Chapter 7).

Late phase Late Ceramic Age society (AD 1000-1500)

As mentioned above, it has been suggested that settlement during the Late Ceramic Age moved from allegedly wetter parts of the island to more arid regions, exemplified on Martinique by a shift from the north-east to the south-east (Allaire 1991). In general, settlements are postulated to have been situated along the coast, and close to mollusc-rich mangrove habitats and offshore coral reefs, rather than to the moist, forested areas and freshwater rivers that were so important in earlier times (Bérard and Vidal 2003:26; Keegan 2000:146). Evidence points to an increase in the number of sites during this period, although the number of settlements remained relatively unchanged (see Chapter 5). Settlement layout likewise appears to hold over from earlier times, with no apparent single structuring principle, and dwellings of varying shapes and sizes (Bright 2003). Burial practices are more complex though, with a noticeable shift from communal to private interment and all kinds of post-mortem manipulation of the grave and the interred taking place (Hofman and Hoogland 2004).

Allaire (1991:716-717) characterized Late Ceramic Age Windward society as Amazonian in the broadest sense of the word, with its tropical forest ecosystem setting, subsistence based on slash-and-burn cultivation of manioc, supplemented by hunting and fishing, relatively low populations and simple, village-based social organization. Allaire (1991:717, 722) also advanced the possibility of an incipient, more integrated level of social development, in deference to Roosevelt's work (*e.g.* Roosevelt 1991) (underscored by later developments in Amazonian archaeology, see also Chapter 1) and cross-comparative research on coastal societies worldwide. Already a mosaic in earlier times, Windward Island society takes on a polyfacetted appearance in final pre-Colonial times. Regional unity appears to give way to more localized contact networks and increasing influx of people from the mainland of South America and perhaps the Greater Antilles and Leeward Islands (Hofman *et al.* 2007).

Regarding material culture, ceramics become more sober, as painting and incision are very rare (although the manufacture of Caliviny Polychrome seems to continue for a while into this period), replaced by scratching and a renewed interest in modelling, particularly of human-like faces and figurines. The quality of these Suazan Troumassoid ceramics cannot however be compared to those of earlier periods. Perhaps the craft of ceramic manufacture was on the wane at this point, though whether artisanship was being simply redirected to other (friable) materials is a moot point. Whatever the case may be, it is clear that pottery had lost some of the roles it used to play in Amerindian society if not its overall importance, obviating the need for highly elaborate decoration and processing of ceramics. Another possibility is that old contact and exchange networks had broken down, disrupting not only the spread of important trade and craft materials, such as pigments, clays and temper materials, but perhaps even the ancient manufacturing know-how (see also Hofman *et al.* 2007). Furthermore, vessel legs become more elaborated, and a number of new decoration modes, vessel shapes and artefacts appear such as finger indentation, female figurines, (body) stamps and support rings.

A number of late pre-Colonial/early Colonial-period ceramic assemblages evince a marked Guianan influence, and have been termed Cayo ware (Boomert 1987a). These ceramics are tentatively linked to the historically recorded Island Carib, who recount stories of their migration from the South American mainland to the islands (see below).

2.5. Towards a Windward Islandscape: an (ethno)historical perspective

From the late 1400s onwards, we move into the realm of written records for the Caribbean region, although the accounts discussing the Lesser Antilles remain sparse and unrepresentative until the advent of the 17th century. The (ethno)historical record will now be considered, first for the Caribbean in general, and then for the Windward Islands in particular.

First European impressions of the "New World"

From the moment that Columbus inadvertently stumbled upon the Caribbean islands – thus discovering the New World to the Old – the area sparked the imagination of the Western world, and it has continued to do so unfailingly over the course of the last 500 years. The interests of outside parties in the Caribbean may have changed in character over time, from pure wonder at the unknown, through economic and political interests right up to the eco-tourism, rich cultural heritage and relaxation that the area offers to the modern-day traveller, the fascination has remained. The first reports to reach Europe outdid one another in superlatives and enthusiasm for the newly encountered lands across the ocean. De Las Casas records the words of an over-awed Columbus: *"The Admiral says that he never saw a more beautiful place* [...] ". Columbus clearly considered the Indies to be an "earthly paradise" (Jane ed. 1988; Moffitt and Sebastián 1998). In his own words, Columbus later reports of the surroundings:

> *"There are six or eight kinds of palm, which are a wonder to behold on account of their beautiful variety, but so are the other trees and fruits and*

> *plants. In it are marvellous pine groves, and there are very large tracts of cultivatable land, and there is honey, and there are birds of many kinds and fruits in great diversity. In the interior are mines of metal, and the population is without number. Española is a marvel"* (Jane ed. 1988:6).

Not just the natural environment, but also the population of the Caribbean was greatly admired; the Indians were regarded as handsome, well built and friendly. Initial favourable tidings soon came to be replaced by more negative accounts, as the wonder and delight of first contact gave way to disillusionment and malice and, in its wake, calculated and coloured reports that cast the Amerindians in a bad light to justify Colonial design (Whitehead 1984). Be that as it may, every early account emphasizes the overwhelming effect of this encounter on the European voyagers. A cornucopia of unknown faunal and floral species, an unfamiliar climate and humans unlike any encountered before amounted to a total culture shock. Lush vegetation seemed to indicate that Caribbean soils were incredibly fertile, and the temperature appeared particularly conducive to agriculture. In short, the Caribbean seemed a sort of Arcadian place, holding unlimited promise. It took a while before the Caribbean climate was characterized more accurately in the wake of the advent of hurricanes and the marked succession of wet and dry season (Watts 1999). Discomforts such as gnats and mosquitoes as well as various diseases would all serve to change the positive tone of the first reports.

First reports of the Windward Islands and European settlement

The Windward Islands first became known to Europeans through Columbus's conversations with the Taíno. The Taíno spoke to him of their fear of the man-eating Carib who allegedly inhabited an island called Quaris to the south-east (see also Keegan 1996), and of the island of women, Matinino, likewise supposedly located to the south-east.[27] Columbus believed he had found evidence of these reported islands on his second voyage in 1493[28], although controversy surrounds the precise identification of the island, particularly as the term Quaris has since been linked to the generic Arawak term caeri or 'island' (Laurence 1967). After stopping off at several islands and taking note of certain habits (observations that were to lay the basis for five hundred years of debate on issues of ethnicity and behaviour[29]), Columbus swiftly travelled along the rest of the archipelago on his way to the men he had stationed at La Navidad. He returned to the area on his third voyage, skirting the southern end of the archipelago (Trinidad) before exploring the Venezuelan coast. The islands further north went unexplored. The lack of interest in the *islas inútiles* evinced by Columbus cleared the way for other European nations to involve themselves in the Lesser Antilles during the ensuing centu-

---

27 Recorded in the Santangel letter and the letter of Columbus, which were printed in 1493. Lengthier descriptions of the neighbouring Caribs are to be found in the journals of Columbus, transcribed by De Las Casas and not published until 1825 by Navarette, in a number of letters written by Columbus as well as the accounts of Dr. Chanca and Michele da Cuneo (Taviani *et al.* 1994:41-45).

28 Recorded in the letter of Dr. Chanca (1993).

29 See *e.g.* Davis and Goodwin 1990 and Whitehead (ed.) 1995.

ry. However, the islands were only sporadically visited or described at any great length and rather than successful ventures, plans for colonization and aborted attempts abounded throughout the 16th century (Moreau 1988). Occasional trading encounters, skirmishes or other incidents set the tone for the profile of the islands in the European mindset. Spain had designs mainly on the Greater Antilles (bar a number of colonization attempts on Guadeloupe), considering the Lesser Antilles initially as a nuisance and later as little more than a potential source of slaves as outlined in the Cedula Réal of 1511 (Jesse 1963; Whitehead 1984).

By the late 1500s and early 1600s, other colonial powers, somewhat slow on the uptake, started to manifest themselves in earnest on the Caribbean stage. Initially, the islands were seen as handy stop-offs en route to the South and North American mainland, where fresh food, water and other provisions could be taken on board after the Atlantic crossing (Myers 1978). Over time, the Europeans also became interested in trade goods that could yield a profit at home or elsewhere in the Americas (Moreau 1988). Finally, European nations succeeded in gaining a permanent foothold on many of the Lesser Antilles, despite fierce indigenous resistance from the Island Carib, inheritors of many cultural traditions of the native Caribbean people and the mainland Kalina who asserted themselves vigorously on the vacuous stage of the early colonial period (Allaire 1977; Boomert 1986, 1995; Sued-Badillo 1978; Whitehead 1995:105). Relations between European nations were anything but peaceful either, as shared interests and shrinking territories led to frayed tempers; emblematic of this was England and France warring over the Lesser Antilles for the greater part of 200 years, while the indigenous Amerindians, tenacious and wily, switched alliances from one side to the other side depending on the situation at hand. The islands were finally split up between the two nations in 1763 with the signing of the Treaty of Paris, an agreement that has had lasting implications for the political, economical and cultural development of the islands.

Accounts of this period, particularly those related to the Windward Islands are overwhelmingly positive in tone, both towards the natural surroundings as well as the island inhabitants. There is a wealth of (ethno)historical information on the Amerindians occupying the Windwards at this time, ranging from brief accounts of a trading encounter (*e.g.* Canner 1905-1907; Myers 1978; Percy 1969; Perkin 1969) to entire (parts of) monographs (Anonyme de Carpentras 2002; Breton 1978; Castres 2002; Nicholl 1607). These are tremendously insightful sources dealing with lifeways, customs and beliefs of the indigenous inhabitants, although one has to take into account the inevitable biases pervading some of the works. Furthermore one must remember that there is a gap in the reporting on these islands between Columbus in the late 15th century and the first English and French accounts, many of which date to the 17th century. There are also doubts as to how representative of past cultures the Carib of historical times are, as they may have been relative newcomers to the scene (the 'Island Carib' debate, *cf.* Allaire 1997; Boomert 1995; Davis and Goodwin 1990; Sued-Badillo 1995). Indeed, although it is difficult to date the alleged arrival of the Island Caribs in the Windward Islands, most sources agree that they were indeed newcomers from the mainland (Gullick 1980). Breton (1978) refers to an unspecified mainland origin, and Du Puis (1652) and Du Tertre add that they were descended from the mainland Kalibis (*i.e.* Galibi).[30] All three agree that the newcomers first settled on Dominica (Verrand 2001:103-104). Rochefort records that the Island Caribs themselves claimed descent from the Galibis of Guiana, and first settled on Tobago, one of the islands closest to the mainland (Rochefort 1658:324-330). Rochefort also refers to the mainland origin of the earlier inhabitants of the islands, highlighting the similarity in language between that spoken by Arawaks of the mainland and Island Carib women (Hulme and Whitehead 1992:120). Castres (2002:70) does not make mention of a mainland origin, but writes that the Amerindians believe in a great flood, which only a man named Loveco survived, from whom they are all descended.

The 17th century Island Carib represented an egalitarian society with considerable local autonomy; each village was more or less its own entity. The sources contradict each other somewhat on the issue of leadership. Breton and Du Tertre are generally dismissive of the Caribs' capacity for what they call 'polity' (Hulme and Whitehead 1992:117), but Breton refers to some form of leadership in his dictionary (Breton 1999:208). Most other sources speak of between two and five levels of political authority, ranging from the leader of the household and the chief of the carbet/village or the canoe, to two great captains of the island, a council of nine elders and a supreme chief or leader, deferred to only in times of war (Anonyme de Carpentras 2002; Castres 2002; Rochefort 1992). A number of sources stress however that in the absence of a strict form of government or laws, on the whole, people were free to do as they pleased, and could not be forced to comply with orders. Earlier sources refer to Amerindian villages as comprising a number of houses, typically a men's house (táboüi or carbet) and a number of family dwellings, one or two later sources appear to be testimony to European encroachment and Amerindian demise, in offering up a view of hamlets or single households dispersed across the landscape. The majority of the sources paint an overlapping picture of Amerindian lifeways: subsistence practices entailed hunting, fishing and growing produce in gardens, social life revolved around a great number of drinking parties (termed caouynages) and visiting the parties of relatives, and when not occupied with subsistence needs, men and women undertook various segregated activities such as weaving, basketry, crafting weapons, tools and utensils and manufacturing pottery. It is immediately apparent that perishables make up a substantial part of Amerindian material world. More insights into

30 See also a highly significant, detailed passage written by James Ley a little after 1608: "*The Carybes have tenn Rivers, owya Kayani, Macullia, Cawrur, Surinamma. Towpannoma and one other little River. And one other little Iland called Dominica; And one Iland called santa bissin, And one Iland called santa Luea, and an Iland called Camawya, their Captaine is Mayerawon.*" (Ley in Lorimer 2006:326-327). The rivers that have been identified (Macouria, Kourou, Suriname and Coppename) are all located in Surinam and French Guyana, the island referred to are Dominica, Saint Vincent, Saint Lucia and Grenada (see also Lorimer 2006:318-320, 326-327). In addition, Keymis reported that Amerindians of the Malmanoury River, French Guiana spoke the same language as those of the island of Dominica (Boomert 1986:12).

Amerindian subsistence practices, lifeways and settlement will be furnished in Chapter 4.

Colonial period in the Windward Islands

When the European Colonial powers began to exploit the Windward Islands in earnest, they in no way encountered a pristine natural environment, as detailed above. However, Amerindian activity was made to look relatively conservative compared to the far-reaching impact of European industry. By the 1700s, plantation industry was in full swing, and forests were stripped bare to provide lumber and firewood and transform them into land where profitable crops could be grown (Chew 2001). Even on islands unsuited to large-scale plantation agriculture, the planting of subsistence crops, acquiring of charcoal and the grazing and trampling of cattle modified the environment substantially (Watters and Miller 2000; Watts 1999). French missionary Jean-Baptiste Labat deplored the actions of the islands' colonists, who "had overcut mahogany and other valuable woods and had hunted manatees, sea turtles, water and land fowl, and feral pigs to near extinction" (Boucher 2002:207). Besides overexploitation, Europeans introduced many exotic species that fared so well that one readily associates them with the Caribbean, and cannot imagine them ever not having occurred there naturally. However, bananas, breadfruit and sugar cane all originate from southeast Asia, and were introduced during Colonial times (*cf.* Fitzpatrick and Keegan 2007). The origins of other "typically Caribbean" species like pineapple and coconut are still being debated. Closer to home, numerous species of wood and timber products were introduced in the region either from other islands in the Caribbean or from North America, to keep up with the demands of the sugar plantations and rum industries (Carrington in Watters and Miller 2000:26). This wholesale transformation of the natural environment resulted in the replacement of primary by secondary vegetation and a great increase in soil erosion and slope-wash, as well as ultimately the impoverishment of the soil (Watts 1994).

Not only the natural environment but also the original human population was replaced over time, through a combination of disease, over-exploitation, absorption into the growing African populations on the islands and even forced migration (*e.g.* Conzemius 1928; Gonzalez 1988; see also Chapter 1). By the 19th century, the only Amerindians that remained in the Windward Islands had been confined to the north-east coast of St. Vincent and the Carib Territory on Dominica. Renowned anthropologist Douglas Taylor devoted much of his life to studying the mid-20th-century Carib of Dominica, producing several ethnographic monologues and a steady stream of shorter contributions from the 1930s until 1980, the year of his death.

The Windward Islands today

Traveling through the Caribbean nowadays, one is confronted by a wonderful array of ethnicities and identities. Interestingly enough, whereas ethnicities bridge islands and water passages separating them, identities appeared to be very much island-based. Thus, the entire archipelago is currently inhabited by a mixture of people of Amerindian, African, Indian, Asian and European descent, but identity is expressed in national, island-centric terms, such as Looshan (St. Lucian), Bajan (Barbadian), Grenadian, Vincentian, Trinidadian, Tobagonian and so on. Crucially, the descendents of the Carib survive to this day on Dominica and St. Vincent, resilient and defiant, increasingly identifying themselves as either Kallinago or Garifuna (Honychurch 1997a; Smith 2006; Twinn 2006).

At this point in time, two opposing forces are at work in terms of the conservation of the natural resources of the islands. On the one hand, there is the work of heritage groups, who have done a good job of monitoring archaeological sites and securing tracts of land for the purpose of turning them into nature reserves. On the other hand, in an ironic repetition of history, the islands of the Caribbean are once again being visited, settled and in-filled intensively, although this time the settlers are in the main wealthy retired or second-home-desiring Westerners.[31] Crown Land is being sold off to opportunistic property developers, and while it is not necessarily a bad thing that land is being emancipated from Crown ownership, the motives behind its sale are less idealistic. In Bequia's case for instance, the revenue generated from the sale is needed to continue work on the construction of the new international airport, which will be able to accommodate more tourists from more destinations, which will mean more Western interest in Bequia, which will entail… and so on. Other goings on include the buying up of large tracts of islands or entire islands being privatized, for the construction of luxury resorts, golf courses or villas for the rich and famous jet-set (The Mustique Company's ownership of Mustique is a case in point). It is a sad development for archaeologists and conservationists, as many archaeological and environmental contexts are being destroyed or irreparably damaged.[32] It is equally sad for the local islanders, who find themselves being bought out of their own islands and restricted in their freedom of travel, all in the interest of creating manicured 'paradise islands'.

2.6. Concluding remarks

During the Colonial period, Windward Island Amerindians certainly knew of the South American mainland, recalling it as the landmass from whence they had departed and made their way to the islands, settling there under varied circumstances, depending on which (ethno)historical source is consulted (Boomert 1995:31; see also above).[33] Hoff (1995) hypothesizes that the Carib influence (Kaliña/Kariña words with an Arawak syntax) on the Island Carib linguistic rep-

31 Not all development can be condemned of course, as no one could begrudge local expansion or the return of 'expats' who, having worked outside the Caribbean, want to enjoy retirement on their home island.

32 There have been a number of positive developments in this regard though, entailing developers working together with Leiden University archaeologists to mitigate the destruction and loss of archaeological heritage by means of partially funded rescue excavations (most notably on Curaçao and St. Vincent).

33 Breton (1998) noted different terms for mainland (baloué) and island (oúbao) in use among the 17th-century Caribs of Dominica. It is reasonable to assume that similar concepts were in use among pre-Colonial Amerindians.

ertoire derives from the Kariña-speaking men who invaded the society of Igneri[34]-speaking islanders. They continued to use their native language for all affairs in the male realm, and reverted to a pidgin Kariña to communicate with the women and children who had been permitted to retain their own native Igneri language (Hoff 1995:46). The pidgin Kariña was probably also used during trading encounters with coastal mainland groups (Dreyfus 1983/1984; Gonzalez 1990:36; Hoff 1995:39). Island Carib conception of the Greater Antilles, far off to the northwest, was presumably somewhat vaguer, although the Virgin Islands and Puerto Rico in particular were the destination of many an Island Carib raid (Dreyfus 1976; Figueredo 1978; Moreau 1992:64-72). Additionally, a Windward-Leeward distinction may have held some significance for Amerindians at the island-level, although this may have more to do with a mountain range running across certain islands physically dividing one group from another. The marked difference in precipitation between the two sides of an island could also have been a determining factor in Amerindian settlement strategy, especially during the numerous dry periods that have affected the region in the past. (Ethno)Historical sources reveal that Amerindians had distinct names for islands (Breton 1999:204-207; De Waal 2006:80; Hofman 1987; L'Etang 2004; see also figure 2.2), settlements (Taylor 1956, 1958a) and rivers (Breton 1978, 1999:235-237; Taylor 1958a), and there is linguistic evidence that they identified themselves and each other with reference to a particular island using a locative suffix –ri or –na, meaning inhabitant of (Breton 1999:207; see also Taylor 1958b:156). At the very general level, the Amerindians of the Windward Islands called themselves callínago or kallinago in the male language, and callíponam or kalliponam[35] in the female language (Breton 1999:55; see also Hoff 1995:39, Taylor 1958b and Wilson 2007:147) and made a distinction between islanders and mainlanders.[36]

Early Europeans referred to the Amerindians in vaguely ethnic, extremely generalizing terms that (one suspects) transcended geographical and possibly ethnic boundaries. Even the general ethnic terms employed by archaeologists to describe the different indigenous peoples of the Caribbean are of questionable veracity. The (mis)nomer Taíno for instance, first employed as an ethnic term by Rafinesque-Schmaltz (1836) in describing the Amerindians of Haiti and their language[37], is nowadays regarded a handy yet faulty umbrella-term that effectively effaces considerable regional variation (Petersen *et al.* 2004:18-21). The term (Island) Carib is equally problematic, as has been well documented over the last few decades (Hofman 1993; Keegan 1996; Petersen *et al.* 2004:19-21; Whitehead 1995).

---

34 Igneri was an Arawakan language (Hoff 1995:46).

35 By taking recourse to mainland Lokono, Taylor (1958b:57) interprets the name Calipona as consisting of the elements kaoi: bitter manioc, -fo: plant suffix and -na: clan of, resulting in clan of the bitter manioc plant. Kallina refers to the mainland Kalina Carib group to which the male invaders of the islands belonged, -go probably represents an honorific suffix (Taylor in Hoff 1995).

36 Breton records the geographical ascription of mainlander, balouöouri (Wilson 2007:147).

37 The term was adopted by archaeologists (De Hostos 1923; Fewkes 1904, 1907; Harrington 1921) in the early 1900s, see also Hulme (1986:60-61).

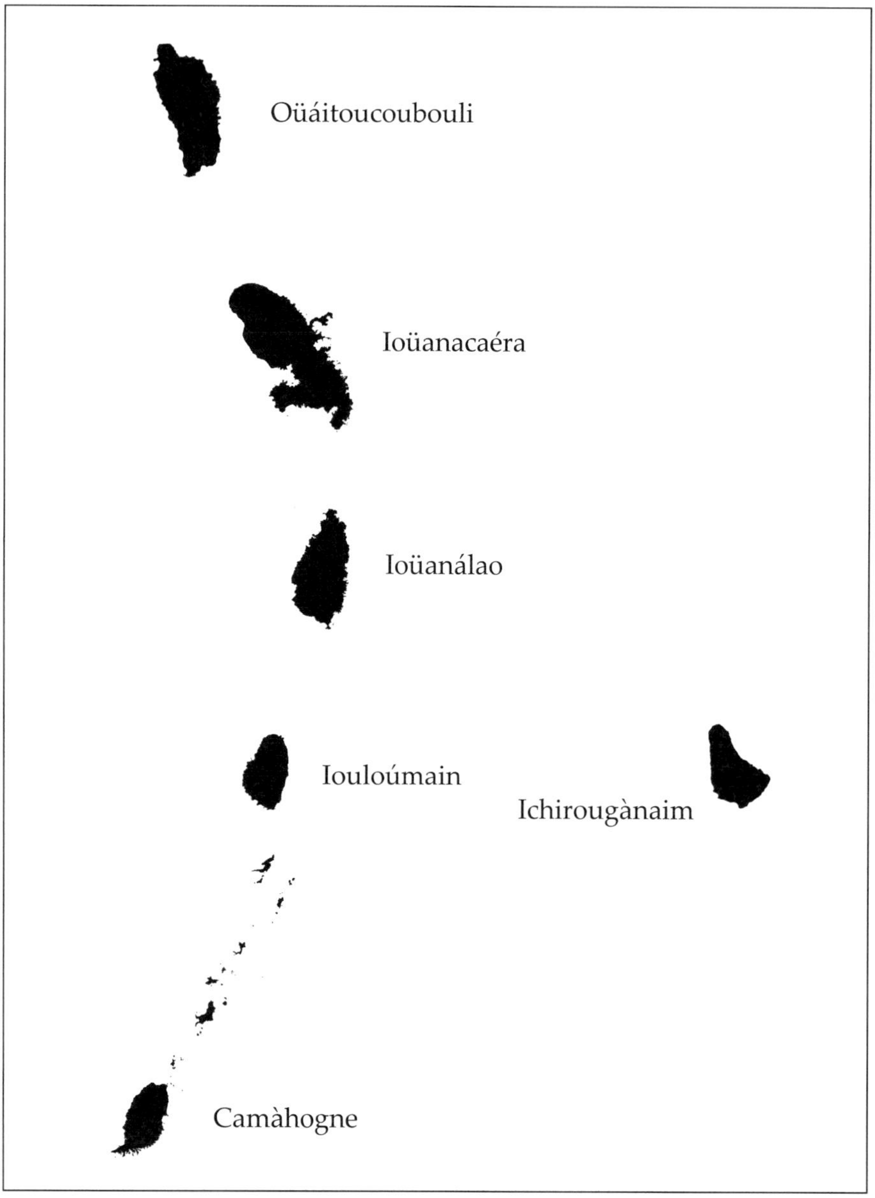

Figure 2.2. Island Carib toponyms for Windward Islands and Guadeloupean micro-region (included for its wealth of toponyms as well as its attested Colonial period ties with Windward Islands), as recorded by Breton (1999) in the mid-17th century.

The islands in the Windward chain may have functioned as stepping-stones for colonizing groups from the South American mainland, leading them all the way to the Greater Antilles, but recently objections have been raised to the rather naïve stepping stone model by those favouring a more stochastic view of movement (*i.e.* Callaghan 2001; Keegan 2004; see also Chapter 4). It cannot be denied however that the Lesser Antillean arc as a whole is favourably situated between the Greater

Antilles and the South American mainland, facilitating communication between these two other areas of cultural development (Hofman *et al.* 2007). In turn, both regions appear to have been of great importance for the cultural developments of groups inhabiting the smaller islands of the Lesser Antilles. Traditionally, communities inhabiting the whole island chain up to the Dominican Republic have been regarded as under influence from South American mainland cultures during the Early Ceramic Age, those on Trinidad and Tobago particularly profoundly. During the Late Ceramic Age, influences become more diversified, with Trinidad continuing to fall under South American influence, Tobago and the Windward Islands forming a somewhat homogeneous and independent unit and the northern Lesser Antilles becoming increasingly caught up in developments taking place on the Greater Antilles (Hofman and Hoogland 2004). Despite these varied affiliations, inter-regional influences continued to operate, coeval to local developments and particular interaction spheres that characterized the regions or various islands within them individually. This current perspective will be examined and evaluated in the chapters to come.

Chapter 3

SITE DISTRIBUTION AND CERAMIC ASSEMBLAGES IN THE WINDWARD ISLANDS: CURRENT STATE OF AFFAIRS

Having outlined the cultural, geographical and geological setting of the Windward Islands in the preceding chapter, this chapter will introduce the two main datasets (archaeological sites and their ceramic assemblages) that have been analysed for the present study. First an historical overview will be provided of past approaches to these data (archaeological surveying and ceramic classifications) within the (wider) study area, as this past research has to a large degree determined the availability, type and quality of data at hand and occasionally introduced an unmistakable research bias. Then the current state of affairs[38] regarding site pattern and distribution of ceramic styles in the Windward Islands will be presented in the form of an island-by-island overview of the distribution of sites and the characteristics of ceramic assemblages in the Windward Islands, except for the Grenadines, which are taken as an entity.[39] Each island is dealt with under four subheadings: geographical and geological setting, history of archaeological research, habitation history and an overview of the ceramic traditions on the island.[40]

3.1. Site pattern archaeology and the Windward Islands

> *"'You can't fool him on settlement patterns,' said the Skeptical Graduate Student, looking over his shoulder. 'There's nothing he likes better than a lot of black dots on a map.'"* (Flannery ed. 1976:161)

In examining the archaeological record of a number of islands, one is led initially to study the "*spatial relationships among human entities and between them and the nonhuman physical world*", also termed regional archaeology (Kantner 2008:42-43). Such a regional, wide-ranging approach *"contrasts with the smaller spatial scale of site-focused approaches, although of course the results of the latter provide critical data for the former"* (Kantner 2008:43). The fundamental backbone of such research is the elucidating of regional settlement patterns, recently characterized as *"significant research and exciting, intellectually challenging work"* (Kowalewski 2008:225). Regional settlement patterns are defined as *"the arrays formed by sets of interacting, interdependent local groups of people"* and regional systems as *"the processes behind the patterns"* (Kowalewski 2008:226). While the approach has been implemented in the study of a wide range of societies, from hunter-gatherer

38 This current state of affairs has been assembled through literature study, study of collections and personal observations in the field; see also Chapter 1.

39 Although this goes against the current political division of the islands, it is deemed the most neutral starting point for research.

40 Appendix 1 provides detailed information on every individual Windward Island site under consideration in this research.

and 'tribal' societies to chiefdoms and states, it is particularly in studies of quasi-egalitarian village and community societies that it shows its value to the current research. Some of the questions the approach raises (without necessarily answering them) are: what are communities, what are the reciprocal relations between sets of villages and regional society (to which one could add the prefacing question: what are the relations between villages), how and why do local and regional groups form, what kinds of exchanges crosscut these communities (Kowalewski 2008:234). Although such questions cannot be answered at this point in time, an attempt will be made in this dissertation to at least establish likely connections between communities both locally and (inter-)regionally (see Chapters 5-7).

This research adopts the conceptual framework of regional settlement archaeology, albeit with the slight modification of the term settlement into site, for two reasons. The first is that the current state of research throughout the Windward Islands is often insufficient to determine a site's functional character, *i.e.* to distinguish between an activity area, a pottery scatter or a settlement. It is therefore deemed more sensible to adopt the more inclusive term 'site' until we have more clarity on site characteristics. The second reason is that within the context of the archaeological reflection of the actions of interacting peoples, activity areas and other non-settlement sites are just as important, if not quite equally informative, as settlement sites, and therefore should be accorded some if not equal consideration (see also Chapter 4).

Next, one has to define one's region as embedded in the term 'regional'. Kowalewski (2008:226) uses the term region in a geographical sense; that is as a geophysical region (drainage basin, coastal plain, mountain plain) or more often as a behavioural region. The latter is defined as *"an interacting set of settlements or central places forming an integrated social whole* [...] [containing] [...] *multiple communities and one or more politically autonomous societies* [...] *more or less economically self-sufficient in most things, or* [...] *more or less demographically autonomous"* (Kowalewski 2008:226). Kantner (2008) recognizes that regions can be conceptualized at many different scales, varying from the large continental expanses to highly localized drainage systems. Also, he states that regions tend to be demarcated by the archaeologist themselves, independent of any existing physical or cultural boundaries (Kantner 2008:41-42). In the case of the Windward Islands, the region is defined geophysically as a group of islands that make up an (artificially circumscribed) archipelago (see Chapter 2). However the supposed behavioural interrelations between the communities inhabiting these islands are merely hypothetical conjecture awaiting archaeological testing.[41] Furthermore, a focus on a particular region should not blind us to potential connections with other regions (see also Chapter 5).

Finally, Kowalewski points out a number of caveats. First is that regional settlement pattern study and archaeological surface survey should not be regarded as synonymous or indeed equivalent (Kowalewski 2008:227). This is particularly

41 That is to say that communities on a number of the Windward Islands appeared to be closely tied together during the 17th and 18th centuries (see also Chapters 2 and 4), but it is unknown to what extent – if at all - these relationships can be projected back past the Columbian divide (but see Chapter 5).

true in the case of the current research, which, for reasons enumerated above and elaborated below, relies on data drawn from numerous types of archaeological fieldwork, ranging from survey and excavation to literature and collections study. Second, that different techniques of archaeological data collection naturally vary in their objectives, coverage and intensity, and that the *"more fragmented or discontinuous the coverage, the greater the difficulty in representing relational features of settlement patterns (vertical complexity, horizontal complexity, boundaries, interaction etc.)"* (Kowalewski 2008:227). Obviously, this is a germane concern for the current research, which not only takes on board data gathered through application of a variety of archaeological techniques, but also has to deal with the widely divergent personal approaches and practices of the dozens of archaeologists and researchers whose work is synthesised here. It is in this aspect then that my definition of the concept of regional (settlement pattern) archaeology differs most from that as defined by Kowalewski, namely that his is a view proffered by one, and mine an amalgamated view pieced together from the observations of many.

Determining settlement patterns or, more correctly, site patterns for the Caribbean is an essential undertaking if we desire to track and make sense of Amerindian movement through and settlement and enterprise within the Caribbean, from the time of initial colonisation right up to and beyond the Columbian divide. Establishing the extent of the distribution of Amerindians across the landscape and the dating of their vestiges can help piece together the order in which and the extent to which islands were successively or simultaneously inhabited, visited or avoided (see also Chapter 4). It should be noted though that even the archaeological site patterns established are *"inferences derived from the numbers, associations, and spatial distributions of the surviving residues of the range of activities carried out over the course of time at different places in landscape"* (David and Kramer 2001:227). This quote will be revisited below, when the many caveats in the realm of taphonomy and survey biases are discussed.

Determining site patterns should not be considered a satisfactory end in itself, however. Instead, it is argued that the real challenge facing archaeologists is regarding the determining of site patterns as a means towards the end of understanding site patterns, which involves scrutinising the pattern in order to draw up settlement determinants, reconstructing landscape use, formulating a subsistence-settlement system out of a site pattern (sensu Binford [1980], an enterprise which the same Binford [1982] would be first to admit is fraught with difficulties), and determining more precisely the coevality of sites to better approach the erstwhile contact networks between pre-Colonial islanders. Sites are more than just dots on the map; they represent specific locales of specific enterprise within a total social landscape. Only by trying to explain the presence of sites rather than just add to the site inventory can we advance in our understanding of Amerindian settlement and lifeways. This will ultimately do justice to the Caribbean region as a very socialised islandscape, an arena made up of inter-connected, interactive island communities now sparsely dotted across, then jostling for space in the Caribbean archipelago (see also Chapters 5 and 6).

Before continuing, a definition of the term 'site' should be provided. Willey, in his monumental work on the prehistory of the Virú valley, Peru, famously declined to discuss the question of what a site is (1956:8). However, he is not referring to a matter of typological distinction, but rather to geographic boundedness. All he means is that in his analysis he may have lumped separate sites together, or actually falsely split up one site into multiple sites. He provides a general site classification, which was an easier task in his particular area due to the excellent visibility on the ground and the nature of the archaeological remains. One could take as a starting point the definition provided by Renfrew and Bahn: *"a distinct spatial clustering of artifacts, features, structures, and organic and environmental remains, as the residue of human activity"* (Renfrew and Bahn 1998:46). This extremely broad characterisation forms an umbrella over many a site subcategory. Various site typologies (*i.e.* Flannery ed. 1976) have sprung up in different regions, in an attempt to cover the full spectrum of archaeological remains present. In some cases, this has led to a multi-tiered typology, comprising over a dozen site-types, differentiated from one another on the basis of size, function and length or time of occupation. These various site definitions, necessarily more precisely determined than that of the all-encompassing site, and drawn from ethnography, can be problematic. Of course, the definitions are guidelines more than strict rules, but archaeological reality can confound even the most general guidelines. Precisely the three aforementioned distinguishing features of size, function and length/time of occupation, can be very difficult to determine in the field, as a result of numerous factors that adversely affect the archaeological remains, our view and understanding of them, or even prohibit our discovery of remains in the first place (see also Bérard 2004; De Waal 2006).

To begin with, there are geological factors such as sedimentation (particularly problematic in riverine environments), volcanic eruptions, sea level rise and tectonic subduction that all conspire to conceal remains from view. There are environmental factors such as wind, wave and hurricane erosion that actively conspire to remove the archaeological record from underneath our feet (see also section 2.3). Wilson (1989:435) alluded to this problem, stating that the *"taphonomic problems of differential site survival in diverse Caribbean environments could potentially introduce a systematic bias into our understanding of settlement systems throughout the Lesser Antilles"*.

Then there are factors related more to the material remains themselves and the discipline of archaeology, such as friable remains (*i.e.* organic materials, low-fired ceramics), the low density of remains (an activity area, a hunting camp), diagnostic versus non-diagnostic materials and the poor dating resolution as a consequence thereof as well as bias inherent to survey design. For instance, it is common knowledge that surveys are difficult to carry out in the tropics, as a result of dense vegetation and bioturbation that obscure even substantial architectural remains in some cases (Johnston 2002; Zeidler 1995). Archaeologists out to discover sites are usually forced by time and budgetary constraints to limit their survey to areas with high promise. This could be called an opportunistic yet flawed survey design, as it may recover a greater number of sites, but one will not be able to quantify or extrapolate the results, significantly limiting its research potential.

The other method is to carry out a full coverage or at least a representative survey, at the risk of expending valuable time and resources to little gain other than statistical validity of the findings or non-findings. Finally, there are other human factors that are beyond the control of the archaeologist such as construction activities (houses, hotels, airports, industry) and related activities such as logging, sand mining and landscaping.

The above points to the difficulty archaeologists can encounter when attempting to discover sites initially, and subsequently determine the site type that corresponds with a given find scatter/deposit. The problem gets worse when one takes into account that any one site may have had various functions, either during the annual round or successively over time (Binford 1982). This phenomenon is particularly prevalent in hunter-gatherer as well as (semi-)sedentary societies that experience periodic shifting settlement. Faced with such seemingly insurmountable obstacles, one could almost be forgiven for asking whether it is even worth attempting an archaeology of sites at all. Flannery, already recognising the pitfalls of determining function on the basis of surface remains alone, chose to forge ahead in the best manner possible: "[...] *preferring to light one small candle rather than curse the darkness* [...]" (Flannery ed. 1976:165).

In similar fashion, Caribbeanists continue to undertake surveys as the preferred method to elucidate site patterns in the Caribbean and draw preliminary conclusions about issues of settlement, landscape use and increasing socio-political complexity. Such surveys have been carried out at all geographical scales, from micro-regional and regional to island and inter-insular level, with various aims in mind. A number of these surveys will be reviewed below. However the earliest significant observations of archaeological sites and materials in the Caribbean date to the late 19th and early 20th century, when a spate of travellers began to explore the Caribbean. Many noted the presence of archaeological artifacts, structures or sites in accounts of their journeys (Ober 1899; Sapper 1903). Indeed, several visitors amassed collections of artefacts that later made their way into established museum collections such as the Latimer collection (Puerto Rico, now at the Smithsonian, Washington D.C.), the Guesde collection (Guadeloupe), and the Heye collection (now at the Museum of the American Indian). Over the course of a century or so, the British Museum acquired a number of artefacts from individuals or at auction, ranging from Greater Antillean Taíno wooden sculptures to Lesser Antillean stone threepointers and axes (Joyce 1907, 1916). Jesse Walter Fewkes was one of the first to document archaeological remains in the Lesser Antilles (including the Windward Islands), through rudimentary archaeological reconaissance, the use of local informants (personal communication Curet, 2010) and study of collections (Fewkes 1907, 1915, 1922). His studies are still of importance to Caribbean archaeologists, not only due to the impeccable illustrations and detailed observations with which they are furnished, but also given the disappearance over time of a considerable number of the archaeological objects and sites Fewkes described. However, his observations on sites were few and understandably limited, so that little insight into site patterns can be gained from the work bar general location and presence of remains.

Mason (1941), De Booy (1919), Harrington (1921) and Hatt (1924) excavated at a number of sites throughout the Caribbean in the 1910s and 1920s, though many of these earliest site inventories consisted almost exclusively of highly recognizable sites such as large shell middens and petroglyph sites (*cf.* Huckerby 1914; Lovén 1935). Many therefore see Rouse's survey work on Haiti and Cuba (Rouse 1939, 1942) as the start of a professional, systematic approach to site archaeology proper in the Caribbean. As the 20th century progressed, many local island archaeologists picked up where others had left off or carried out their own pioneering work. One of them, Pinchon (1952), may have been the first Windward Island archaeologist to draw tentative conclusions from the distribution and dating of sites, noting as he did the remarkable shift in settlement location on Martinique from early Saladoid to post-Saladoid times. Whereas the earliest Saladoid sites are located along the north-east coast (with fertile soils due to volcanic eruptions), many post-Saladoid sites are located along the south-eastern coast, which though arid offers access to plentiful marine resources (Allaire 1977; Bérard 2004). Allaire (1977:347) suggested that competition over land, the threat of a volcanic eruption or climatic change may have led Amerindians to broaden their horizons and make further adaptations to (small) island environments. Bérard's research on Martinique has underscored the early Saladoid settlement pattern, from which he attempted to draw a number of general settlement rules or determinants, such as proximity to shore, mangroves, potable water and jasper sources, the geomorphological environment, the vegetation and the fertility of soils (Bérard 2004:76). For the early phase of the Early Ceramic Age, the majority of these determinants holds true, except proximity to mangroves and jasper. The Late Ceramic Age sees sites adhering less to fertile soils and a decreased proximity to potable water, in favour of locations in the more barren south, near mangroves and coral reefs (Bérard 2004:80; Bérard and Vidal 2003). Unfortunately, such a distinctive (shift in) site pattern has as yet not been found on other Windward Islands, but that need not compromise the validity of the Martiniquean case.

Opportunistic surveys, testpitting and small-scale excavations were the norm in the Windward Islands throughout the 1960s and much of the 1970s. The Bullens for instance intensively surveyed and excavated on Grenada, the Grenadines, St. Vincent, St. Lucia and Barbados, uncovering information on many new and known sites throughout the region (Bullen 1964; Bullen and Bullen 1972). They concluded that the main settlement determinant is access to water (either fresh or brackish), in the form of streams and ponds. Sites were mainly found along the coast, except on St. Vincent, where many sites were found inland, always close to a stream. The Bullens considered these inland sites ("kitchen gardens") places to which Amerindians would have resorted in case of population pressure or as temporary refuges in times of floods, volcanism or invasion (Bullen and Bullen 1972:150). They further noted the remarkable settlement mode on Grenada, St. Vincent, St. Lucia and Barbados of late pre-Colonial sites atop high headlands or bluffs along the windward coast, without attaching any interpretation to the phenomenon. They go on to suggest that the lack of inland sites in general on the islands except St. Vincent is probably a survey/visibility bias, and that increasing human activity in the non-coastal areas will no doubt turn up traces of

Amerindian activity (Bullen and Bullen 1972:150). Be that as it may, it is still no explanation for the inhospitable location on top of ridges, away from fresh water and access to the sea. Researchers studying similar patterns on other islands have suggested that beach sites may have become too vulnerable to attacks in late pre-Colonial times, forcing Amerindians to relocate to more inaccessible, easily defensible points offering wider views of the sea in all directions (*cf.* Hofman 1995). One last interesting point raised by the Bullens is that of water shortage. Despite finding numerous quite substantial sites on many of the Grenadines, they claimed that:

> *"The Grenadines are satisfactory for a short stay but their small size and scarcity of water make them undesirable for permanent occupation. This is reflected in their archaeology as large sites were only found on Carriacou, the largest and best endowed of the Grenadines. Bequia has many more sites but those on Carriacou cover much larger areas"* (Bullen and Bullen 1972: 9).

The sheer number of sites and density of remains uncovered by themselves, let alone by many others both prior and subsequently, would seem to debunk this statement. While water was undoubtedly of great importance, its only source was not (perennial) streams or ponds. The Amerindians may well have collected rainwater, which falls profusely during the rainy season and even at times outside it. In addition, over the past decades a number of large, bottomless stacked ceramic vessels have been excavated from beach contexts on Carriacou, Mustique and Barbados, suggesting that Amerindians frequently extracted brackish to sweet water along the coastal zone from the top of the fresh water lens, striking a balance between accessibility of the water table and salinity of the water (Drewett ed. 2000; Hinds and Harris 1995; Schultz 1995).

Surveys were also carried out on Dominica during the late 1960s and 1970s. First was Evans (1968), who bemoaned the 'lack of archaeology on Dominica' but discovered ten pre-Colonial or early Colonial period Amerindian sites. These sites were all coastal in setting and showed little patterning. However, Evans' survey design and its execution were no doubt influenced detrimentally by the team of biologists he was accompanying. He was followed by Petitjean Roget (1978b/d) and Myers (1978) who sought archaeologically (the former) and (ethno)historically (the latter) to prove that Dominica had been occupied more intensively than asserted by Evans. Petitjean Roget did indeed find many new sites that Evans had missed, indicating that the west coast had mainly been occupied during the late phase of the Early Ceramic Age (AD 400-700), whereas late phase Late Ceramic Age material was encountered at just three sites: Kachacru, Soufrière and Salisbury. Honychurch (1997a/b, 2006) carried research on Dominica into the 1990s and beyond, and his site inventory finally revealed an island-round occupation on the island, though diachronic aspects of the site pattern have yet to be explored. In 2005, an international team undertook test excavations at various sites on Dominica (Bérard *et al.* 2005), but the research project was tragically cut short by the death of James Petersen in that same year.

By the late 1970s and early 1980s, the first truly systematic surveys started being carried out on St. Kitts, Barbuda and Montserrat (Goodwin 1979; Watters and Scaglion 1980). These were to be followed by surveys on many of the other Leeward Islands such as Anguilla (Crock 2000), Anegada (Davis and Oldfield 2003), Nevis (Wilson 1989) and parts of Guadeloupe (De Waal 2006) and the Windward Island of Grenada (Cody 1991). Drewett's work on Barbados in the 1980s and 1990s provided a comprehensive overview of Amerindian sites on the island, painting a picture of predominantly coastal sites and settlements along with a number of cave sites. Drewett suggests that average site size decreased after Early Ceramic Age times, although site number increased, particularly during the late phase of the Late Ceramic Age, resulting in a gradual infilling of much of the coast. Regarding settlement location, Drewett concluded that the coastal fringe was the preferred settlement location, with its easy access to a range of marine resources and potential for manioc cultivation behind the beach, with inland locations possibly being frequented seasonally or temporarily for the procurement of specific resources such as clays, plants or animals (Drewett ed. 2000:178).

In 2000 and 2001, a team led by Callaghan (University of Calgary) carried out a site survey programme on St. Vincent, which involved archaeological prospection and a coring programme at a number of sites. Building on earlier work (Allaire and Duval 1995), some 30 new sites were discovered, predominantly on the eastern side of the island, during the course of the month-long survey. As the survey was focussed specifically on river valleys and terraces, sites were discovered both in coastal and inland locations. Given the repeated occurrence of pottery scatters stretching from settlements near the coast further inland, albeit with breaks in between, Callaghan and Moravetz suggest that rather than "new" sites, these scatters may represent one settlement's shifting location along a watercourse over time (Callaghan 2007; Moravetz 2005).

Bradford (2001a/b, 2003) carried out a survey of Windward Island archaeological literature to compile a database of its archaeological sites from which inferences could be drawn. She provided a useful overview of a great many sites (408, two thirds of the number covered in this thesis), analysed a number of site-location correlations and generated a number of interesting statistics, although many aspects of archaeological and anthropological interest were only dealt with cursorily.

Starting in 2002 with preliminary survey and testpitting of a number of sites and areas across St. Lucia (Keegan *et al.* 2002), a team headed by Leiden University and the Florida Museum of Natural History carried out a three-year multi-disciplinary project in cooperation with the Saint Lucia Archaeological and Historical Society, comprising archaeological survey, testpitting and excavation as well as ethnographic observation and recording of traditional craft activities and use-wear experiments (Hofman *et al.* 2004; Keegan *et al.* 2003). Intent on assembling an accurate picture of Amerindian settlement and utilization of the entire island, the team designed a research strategy that involved surveying any promising (*i.e.* flat, inhabited, disturbed or eroded) land along St. Lucia's dense infrastructure. The method was highly successful and uncovered sites in coastal settings as well as deep inland in the foothills. The survey strategy was aided by the fact that St.

Lucians still inhabit more or less the same spots as the Amerindians did many generations earlier. Furthermore, many still work the land to grow agricultural produce, bringing Amerindian artefacts to the surface. It became clear that while most Saladoid sites were large and concentrated at more or less regular intervals along the coast, post-Saladoid sites were generally smaller and dispersed across the entire island, from coastal and islet settings to spots some 5 km inland. The small size of many of these inland sites may indicate that these were not permanent settlements but rather temporary dwellings, activity areas or garden plots. Proximity to water once again seems to be the major determinant, paramount over specific locations or proximity to other resources. The Leiden/Florida surveys confirmed the pattern of windward coast occupation signalled by the Bullens (1972), but with much of the leeward coast still awaiting survey, this pattern may yet turn out to be an outcome of research bias. Furthermore, the settling of seemingly inhospitable, elevated areas is by no means the standard in Late Ceramic Age St. Lucia, with numerous large Suazan Troumassoid sites being established on low-lying promontories or just behind beaches in both the north and south of the island (*i.e.* Giraudy, Saltibus Point, Lavoutte, Comerette Point). It may be more accurate to claim that the high, defensible spots were settled in spite of their inaccessible nature rather than representing a prime settlement choice, reflecting the high degree of Amerindian adaptability to the characteristics of specific microenvironments.

Carriacou, one of the largest of the Grenadines Islands, was the next island to be surveyed systematically, through a multinational cooperative effort. Campaigns in 2003, 2004 and 2005 led to the mapping of twelve sites of varying dimensions, spanning the entire Ceramic Age. Eleven of the twelve sites were located in a coastal setting, and a number of them are suffering from severe erosion (Fitzpatrick *et al.* 2004; Kappers *et al.* 2007; Kaye 2003; Kaye *et al.* 2004).

In 2004, to support an on-going reconsideration of the Late Ceramic Age in Martinique and the site of Macabou (Allaire *et al.* 2002; Bérard and Vidal 2003; Vidal *et al.* 2004), Benoît Bérard undertook a survey of southernmost Martinique, focusing on the coastal strip and offshore islets. His findings echoed those of Leiden's St. Lucia coastal results, namely dense occupation of the shoreline encompassing both larger and more ephemeral sites as well as utilization of offshore islets. This seemed to tie in with earlier hypotheses of the likes of Allaire (1977) and Petitjean Roget (1978b) that the late pre-Colonial populations were overwhelmingly outward-looking, maritime resources-oriented peoples, living on the cusp of the land. To counter the coastal bias inherent in the research design, Bérard enlisted a team from Leiden to replicate their inland St. Lucia survey in southernmost Martinique. Over the course of ten days, a meagre ten sites were discovered (of which only three can be considered 'inland'), most ephemeral, late pre-Colonial and non-diagnostic. It would appear that this is down to the xerophytic, resource-bare, almost a-riverine environment of southernmost Martinique compared to the lush, tropical surroundings of inland southern St. Lucia, although different visibility factors cannot be ruled out as yet either (Bright 2007). Bérard has since suggested a theory that makes sense of the more dispersed, extensive site pattern of late pre-Colonial times. He hypothesizes that during the Early Ceramic Age, populations had a dense, clustered nature, gathering in large numbers at large sites, and carrying out many activities at the site. By contrast, in later periods, there was a more dispersed mode of settlement by smaller groups across the landscape, that carried out many activities away from the site at processing stations or other activity areas, before finishing off the processing at the settlement. This theory is supported not only by the increase in number of (ephemeral or activity) sites, but also by the type of remains encountered at settlement sites dating to the late pre-Colonial period, *i.e.* less lithic debitage and semi-finished items (Bérard, personal communication 2005; see also De Waal 2006:117 for similar reasoning regarding Late Ceramic Age settlement patterns in a Guadeloupean micro-region).

In conclusion, Caribbean archaeologists have been steadfastly recording archaeological sites on maps of all scales for nearly a century. The resolution of site studies has been gradually increased to include and distinguish between all manner of archaeological manifestations from settlement sites to activity areas and singular finds. The results of these and other surveys are discussed in more detail in Appendix 1 and the data issuing from them are utilised in Chapters 4 and 5. The foregoing overview of site patterns in the Windwards suggests that ultimately there may be no one settlement/subsistence pattern that can be applied to all Amerindians throughout the Windward Islands (and beyond). Rather, each microenvironment may have imposed its own limitations and demands on those who would settle there, and no one strategy could be implemented successfully regardless of the surroundings. This preliminary conclusion will be revisited in Chapter 4 on the basis of the new additional data compiled during the course of this dissertation research.

3.2. Ceramic classification and the Windward Islands

Caribbean archaeology has in the past been dominated and shaped to a large degree by ceramic studies (Keegan 2000:135). This is a logical result not only of the relatively and absolutely vast number of ceramics unearthed during most archaeological fieldwork, but also of the seemingly endless study potential of these omnipresent, durable and diagnostic ceramics as a material category. Not only do ceramics inform on aspects of local quotidian life (Espenshade 2000; Heidke and Stark 2001) and manufacturing choices (*cf.* Arnold 1989; Gosselain 1992; Hofman and Jacobs 2003; Lemonnier 1986; Rice 2005), they can also reflect such diverse phenomena as intergroup communication, group identity and ritual knowledge, to name but a few (Bowser 2000; Hodder 1982; Rice 2005). While the emphasis in this study will later shift to ceramic decoration modes or traits as markers of intergroup communication, the most basic use of ceramics in Caribbean archaeology must first be expounded, namely as temporal markers for assembling cultural chronologies. It is this line of research that informs much of the existing work on diachronic site patterning and cultural chronology in general, largely due to the continuing absence of radiocarbon dates for all but the most prominent archaeological sites in the region.

In an area where radiocarbon dates are still far from common (and recognizing that radiocarbon dating is by no means unproblematic and the answer to all questions), archaeologists are out of necessity forced to seek other means of determining a cultural chronology. In the 1940s and 1950s, when the first truly academic archaeological research began to take place in the Caribbean, the culture-historical approach was still very much en vogue. Stratigraphically separated ceramics were ordered into a successional scheme, which came to define the cultural sequence of the region. Rouse (1992; Rouse and Faber Morse 1999) was instrumental in defining this general, unifying scheme for much of the Caribbean area. However, a far from straightforward situation presently obtains in the archaeology of the Windward Islands, where various distinct manners of classifying ceramics have developed side-by-side yet independently of each other. These distinctive approaches have had a fundamental influence on the way with which the archaeology of the Windward Islands has been dealt, both in the field and in the literature. There are advantages and disadvantages to all approaches utilized and the main challenge is to find a way of characterizing ceramics that does not detract from their heterogeneity, but equally does not efface all homogeneity to the extent that one cannot make any inter-assemblage comparisons that transcend the level of the island or site-specific complex.

The first systematic approach to the study of Windward Islands ceramics was developed by McKusick (1960), a student of Rouse, who carried out excavations on St. Lucia and Dominica. McKusick *"used a modal approach to the analysis of the artefacts in order to define ceramic styles, study their distribution and establish a local sequence for the island"* (Allaire 1977: 126). Unfortunately, McKusick soon moved on to other research areas, which meant that his approach and many of his suggestions were never followed up. After McKusick, the three main classifications to be applied to Windward Island ceramic assemblages were: (1) Irving Rouse's modal approach, (2) Ripley and Adelaide Bullen's type-variety method, and (3) Jacques and Henri Petitjean Roget's type-variety method (see also Hofman, Hoogland and Van Gijn 2008). The origins, developments and consequences of these classifications will be outlined below.

3.2.1. Irving Rouse and the modal approach

The most influential and widely applied ceramic classification in Caribbean archaeology has been and still is that of Irving Rouse (1951, 1966, 1992), whose "lust for taxonomy" (Siegel 1996b) led him in due course to assemble a typological chronology for the entire Caribbean on the basis of a modal approach. This modal approach was first introduced to the Caribbean by Rainey (1941) and Rouse (1941) and later extended to Rouse's dissertation work dealing with Haiti (Rouse 1939).[42] Rouse based himself on earlier work on pottery such as McKern's Midwestern Taxonomic system, Shepard's work on Pecos pottery, and the studies by both Clellan and James Ford (Rouse 1939:9, 13; see also Willey and Sabloff 1980). Rouse devised a phylogenetic, hierarchical system structured in such a way that complexes or styles are classified within subseries and subseries within series (Lundberg 2002). A complex or style represents *"the entire pottery repertoire of a people made during a single cultural period in a particular geographical location"*

42 Due to publishing delays, Rouse's later work Prehistory in Haiti was actually published before the earlier work by Rainey and Rouse on the Fort Liberté region in Haiti (Rouse 1939:7).

Description	*Date*
Cedrosan Saladoid	250 BC–AD 250
Cedrosan Saladoid with Barrancoid influence	AD 250–500/550
Troumassan Troumassoid	AD 500/550-1000
Suazan Troumassoid	AD 1000-1450

Table 3.1. Cultural chronology of Rouse (Rouse et al. 1995).

(Petersen *et al.* 2004:21). How particular varies from case to case, but tends to be local or island-bound. A style is defined by assemblages containing a similar set of attributes or modes (such a set also being designated a type) in the realm of material, shape and/or decoration (Petersen *et al.* 2004:21; Rouse 1939:11). A series is a group of styles related throughout space and time that are known to have descended from a common ancestor (Petersen *et al.* 2004:21). Vescelius (1980) proposed the addition of the intermediate subseries (a (sub)division of a series consisting of smaller geographical, chronological and cultural units that share a common ancestor), a suggestion that was duly implemented by Rouse in later publications (Petersen *et al.* 2004:22).

As one moves down from series to complex/style, one is reducing the geographical range of a ceramic phenomenon, as well as the duration of its manifestation, thereby gradually working towards an ever-higher archaeological resolution. It goes without saying that the higher the resolution for which one strives, the less comparable the archipelago's ceramic assemblages become. This typology has been modified from time to time and place to place and has seen application especially in the Greater Antilles and the northern Lesser Antilles. The approach was never utilised directly in the Windward Islands, but served as an overarching paradigm for research carried out on numerous islands throughout the region.

Rouse initially distinguished three ceramic series in the prehistory of the Windward Islands: Saladoid, Troumassoid and Suazoid (Rouse 1992). The occurrence of Saladoid was dated between approximately 400 BC and AD 600, Troumassoid was dated AD 600-1000 and Suazoid AD 1000-1500. He later revised this scheme to include just two series, Saladoid and Troumassoid, the former of which he subdivided into Cedrosan and Cedrosan with Barrancoid influence subseries, the latter into a Troumassan and Suazan Troumassoid subseries (Rouse *et al.* 1995; see also table 3.1). The dating remained more or less the same, although Rouse recognized that developments were not exactly coeval across the islands. Despite having provided two seminal contributions on Caribbean ethnicity (Rouse 1948a/b) to Steward's Handbook of South American Indians, Rouse was extremely cautious in relating ethnicity to material culture assemblages. Rather, he preferred to adopt the material culture nomer as a sort of shorthand for the people allegedly responsible for the materials' manufacture.

The framework, though slightly outdated and bemoaned for its geographically sweeping, generalizing scale, is extremely useful for discerning broad developments over a large area and represents a good general narrative and solid basis from which to deviate at a more localized level when necessary. In addition, its wide-ranging nature serves as a useful reminder when it comes to seeking out potential stylistic similarities between widely dispersed assemblages or stylistic influences originating outside one's main study area. Rouse's typology can foster a tendency to mask variability and force data into an ill-fitting straitjacket at times (see also Curet 2003, 2005). This tendency, by the way, should not be blamed on Rouse and his approach, but rather on the misuse and abuse of the approach by fellow archaeologists (Curet 2003).

3.2.2. Ripley and Adelaide Bullen and the type-variety approach

The 'type-variety' approach was adapted from the archaeology of the U.S. Southeast and introduced to the Caribbean in 1962 by the Bullens (Bullen 1962, 1964; Bullen and Bullen 1972) as a means to describe the pottery of the Virgin Islands.[43] It had earlier been adopted by Evans and Meggers (1960) in classifying the ceramic assemblages of British Guiana (now Guyana). Within the space of some ten years the system developed into the most widely-applied approach to describing pottery in the Windward Islands, mainly as a result of the Bullens' prolific, wide-ranging fieldwork and impressive publication rate. The Bullens' binominal or at times trinominal typology is made up of a ware defined on the basis of the quality of the clay, surface treatment and tempering materials (its 'paste'), to which they add as a second term a distinctive feature of shape or decoration, and sometimes a third term, that details the position of said decorative or morphological feature on the vessel (Bullen 1964:38). For their 1972 publication on the archaeology of St. Vincent and the Grenadines, the Bullens modified Ripley Bullen's original 1964 ceramic typology. Advances in the study of Caribbean ceramics had allowed their pottery type names for sherds to better represent the vessels that the sherds once constituted. Their system now comprised series (ceramics of similar paste and surface treatment) and refined types and was implemented on Barbados, Grenada, the Grenadines, St. Vincent and St. Lucia in the Windward Islands as well as a number of other islands throughout the region (*cf.* Bullen and Bullen 1973). As Allaire points out: *"Each series is named after a type site and is strongly correlated with a period or phase, for which it is often synonymous in their works"* (Allaire 1977:127). This is of course equally true of Rouse's typology.

Description	*Date*
Insular Saladoid	260 BC–AD 295
Modified Saladoid	AD 295-710
Terminal Saladoid	AD 710-1000
Caliviny-Suazey	AD 1000–1580

Table 3.2. Cultural chronology of the Bullens (1972:152-166).

43 Haag (1965) adopted a similar approach, but like McKusick, failed to make a lasting impression on the Caribbean scene.

Basically the Bullens distinguished between five subsequent ceramic "periods" or "traditions" in prehistoric Windward Island archaeology. The first of these they termed Insular Saladoid, dated roughly 200 BC to AD 300, followed by Modified Saladoid, which lasted from around AD 300 to 650. Then came Terminal Saladoid, a transitional phase that lasted from approximately AD 650 to 950. It was followed by an entirely new pottery "tradition" called "Caliviny" which supposedly lasted until AD 1100 when, according to Bullen, a final pottery "tradition" called "Suazey" became established in the region, which allegedly continued into the Colonial era (Bullen and Bullen 1972:151-167; Boomert 1987a:22; see also table 3.2). Where Rouse was hesitant to link ethnicity to material remains, the Bullens proved eager to do just that, assigning Caliviny Polychrome ceramics to "pre-Carib Arawaks" or "proto-Carib invaders" and later Suazey ceramics to the historically reported Island Carib (Bullen and Bullen 1972:165).

The Bullens recognized that the majority of ceramics recovered could not be allocated to narrowly defined pottery types and therefore persisted in including what they call "generalized or single mode types" (Bullen and Bullen 1972:130). These could be of slight chronological value, but perhaps more importantly, underscored the variability inherent in the ceramics. However, unlike the modal approach, their type-variety method was by definition unable to cope with potentially multiple decorative traits present on a sherd, thereby in fact effacing variability. The Bullens expected that the "more specific separately defined types will be the ones used to: (1) divide the long Saladoid influenced period into chronological subdivisions, (2) determine direction of influences and communications, and (3) demonstrate differences between islands which may have important sociological implications" (Bullen and Bullen 1972:130). While their first point is no longer necessarily valid, as it has since been recognized that various ceramic wares may have been manufactured contemporaneously (*cf.* the La Hueca debate [Oliver 1999]), the latter two points are particularly relevant in the context of this research. Although the type-variety approach has its drawbacks, its basic tenets are, in modified form, still germane to the comparative study that lies at the heart of this research.

3.2.3. Jacques and Henri Petitjean Roget and the horizons approach

Roughly around the same time as the Bullens were establishing their type-variety method, Jacques Petitjean Roget conceived a tripartite subdivision of ceramics on the basis of excavations on Martinique. Three horizons were distinguished, coded I, II and III, the last of which was deemed to represent Island Carib ware (J. Petitjean Roget 1970). Henry Petitjean Roget later added another horizon to the Arawak period, making the Carib period Horizon IV. Finally, the typochronology came to include a Caliviny horizon (Horizon IV), making the Carib period Horizon V (H. Petitjean Roget 1978a; see also table 3.3). Significantly, Petitjean underlined the importance of plain wares, which he termed "cold wares", as well

Horizon	Description	Date
Horizon I	Proto Arawak	AD 0-350
Horizon II	Ancient (IIa)	AD 300-500
Horizon II	Recent (IIb)	AD 500-750
Horizon III		± AD 700
Horizon IV	Caliviny	AD 600-800
Horizon V	Carib	± AD 700- historic times

Table 3.3. Cultural chronology H. Petitjean Roget (1978a:3).

Description	Date
Huécoïde	500 BC-AD 100
Saladoïde insulaire	400 BC-AD 350
Saladoïde modifié	AD 350-600
Troumassoïde	AD 600-900
Suazoïde	AD 900-1200
Caraïbe insulaire préhistorique	AD 1000–1635

Table 3.4. Cultural chronology H. Petitjean Roget (2005:41).

as the "warm" decorated wares (Allaire 1977:127).[44] This approach was utilised to classify ceramic assemblages on Martinique, Dominica and Guadeloupe to great effect, but failed to catch on elsewhere.

Petitjean Roget (1968b/c), Mattioni (1968), and Pinchon (1952) before them, believed that Martinique and Guadeloupe had been settled by two Amerindians groups in the past, the Arawaks and the Caribs. Like the Bullens, they were convinced that the two groups could be distinguished on the basis of material culture as well as settlement location preference[45], hence the direct correlation between their horizons and these two ethnicities.

Recently Petitjean Roget has revised his chronology, apparently abandoning the horizons and most of the descriptive nomers, settling on a Bullens-Rouse hybrid (table 3.4).

44 Petitjean Roget drew inspiration from Lévi-Strauss's (1966) hot and cold societies; see Petitjean Roget (1970:5).

45 The timid, fearful Arawak were deemed to prefer settlements in defensible, elevated locations, whereas the Caribs were confident enough of their ferocity that they could settle low-lying, vulnerable plains as well as plateaus (Pinchon in Petitjean Roget 1970:22, 56). Needless to say, this hypothesis has failed to stand the test of time.

3.2.4. *Resolution*

In the last decade or so, these past approaches have come under increasingly heavy fire from a growing number of archaeologists (Bérard 2004; Harris 1995; Lundberg 2002). They claim that the singling out of decorative traits and fabric composition as primary diagnostic markers (particularly germane to the type-variety approach) has reached its limits, and attention should now be focused on vessel shapes. Such an approach, it is argued, ultimately says more about Amerindian society, as it breaks down the ceramic assemblage into functionally meaningful categories. Harris (1995, 2001b) has suggested an alternative chronological framework, based on vessel shapes and function rather than paste/decorations. Harris' approach (subsequently adopted by Lundberg [2002]) is deemed to be a useful addition to the spectrum of frameworks. Unfortunately, time constraints did not permit the author to reconstruct vessel shapes of the thousands of pottery sherds cursorily studied and photographed during the course of fieldtrips, which is why this approach is not referred to in great detail. Besides, a major problem with the approach, as must be readily conceded by its adherents, is that an overwhelming number of sherds encountered in excavations are relatively non-diagnostic body sherds that offer little indication of overall vessel shape. Another problem must be the determination of the alleged function of a particular vessel, once its shape has been conclusively determined. So while the utility of the vessel shape approach is acknowledged, it is not deemed vital to adopt it to a significant degree within this current research. Although a general overview of vessel shapes occurring within assemblages will be provided in below (section 3.3) greater emphasis will be placed in this research on an examination of decorative and morphological traits (see Chapter 5). These elements are diagnostic, distinguishable and easily recorded, all vital characteristics in light of the goals of this research and the approach taken towards realising those goals (see sections 1.5 and 1.6).

Because of the unique trajectory that research in the Windward Islands has taken, the Bullens are either the first or only people to have done archaeological research on a number of the islands, at least until fairly recently. Therefore, little or no revision of their research has occurred, rendering it outdated and making intra- and interregional comparison between their work and that of others extremely difficult.

As far as justification for the merits of either modal or the type-variety approach is concerned, the matter can be somewhat simplistically reduced to the argument between 'lumpers' and 'splitters', Rouse representing the former and the Bullens the latter. Rouse may be accused of oversimplifying inherent variability in his efforts to identify ceramic (sub)series or styles and construct a broad, general framework, whereas the Bullens may be accused of spawning a proliferation of analytical categories in their search for ceramic types, which are useful at a local or micro-regional level but hamper study on a wider scale. Additionally, not all ceramics cleanly fall into one or the other compartment. Some sherds may exhibit both white-on-red painting (WOR) as well as incision, in which case it is impossible to classify them as one or the other exclusively. Bullen acknowledged the problem with his model, stating:

"After examination of the typology presented below, many may feel I have been too much of a "splitter" of pottery types. It is very difficult at this stage in our research to determine just what are significant differences in various ceramic modes. [...] Pottery types are analytical tools. It seems better to have too many types at first, even if some are eliminated later, than to have to split a type at a later date" (Bullen 1962:5-6).

Furthermore, its emphasis on individual sherds and reliance on decoration as prime diagnostic means that other potential sources of information are ignored, such as vessel shapes, rim and lip profiles and appendages (*cf.* Allaire 1977:128). The non-decorated ceramics are also largely ignored, despite constituting the overwhelming majority of pottery in any assemblage.[46] *"Moreover, their use of clay and tempering material as criteria in the definition of their series is subject to too much ambiguity and their chronological significance can be seriously questioned"* (Allaire 1977:128).

Considering that this study attempts to compare ceramic assemblages both intraregionally and interregionally, both the modal and type-variety approaches have merit and this study will draw on elements of both the Rouse and the Bullen methods. It is a matter of fine-tuning and according the right model to the right research question. For detailed comparisons between sites on one island or several islands, an approach focusing on unicity can be vital. On the other hand, to be able to draw general conclusions on interregional relationships, one requires a more workable, coarse-grained model. As detailed above, the study of the archaeology of the Windward Islands has been unnecessarily and perhaps even falsely complicated by the introduction of a plethora of terms to describe variation in ceramic style.

Rouse's general framework and terminology will be taken as a starting point, to ensure the compatibility of the results from the Windward data-sets to data-sets from other regions. However, in comparing site assemblages, many of the type-varieties first described by the Bullens will be upheld in somewhat modified form, to make optimal use of their fine-grained work. Taking Rouse's approach as a starting point is easier said than done however, as much of the earlier research in the Windwards is steeped in either the terminology of the Petitjean Rogets or the Bullens. In effect, the first step to take before any meaningful comparative work can be done is one of translation or conversion, to arrive at a uniform data-set (see also Chapter 5 and Appendix 1).

3.3. Windward Islands typo-chronology

Before reviewing the ceramic developments on individual islands, it may be useful to examine the broader ceramic developments in the region of which the local developments are to a lesser or greater extent a reflection.

46 "[...] 5 eroded sherds that might have originally been either Suazey or Simon Plain [...]" (Bullen and Bullen 1972:35), a prime example of how ineffective their approach is when dealing with non-decorated pottery.

Saladoid series

The first ceramic series present in the Windward Islands is Saladoid, which appeared in the lower Orinoco Basin around 1200 BC and was named after the type-site Saladero, and predominantly its subseries Cedrosan Saladoid, named after the type-site Cedros on Trinidad (Boomert 2000). Characteristic of Cedrosan Saladoid pottery, distributed from Trinidad up to Puerto Rico, is the combination of plain ware, zoned incised crosshatching (ZIC) and white-on-red painting (Rouse and Alegría 1990). Painting is more common than crosshatching and occurs on a variety of vessel shapes, whereas ZIC decoration only occurs on hemispherical bowls. As a possible explanation for the co-occurrence of both decorated wares, Rouse and Alegría (1990) have suggested that they could have been used in different rituals. The painted motifs are often stylized geometrical figures. Other diagnostic decorative features are curvilinear and linear incised lines (sometimes used to outline painted designs), simple linear incision (occasionally filled with white paint) and modelled-incised hollow-backed anthropomorphic and zoomorphic adornos (rim lugs representing animals or humans), tabular lugs and nubbins. Vessels are characterized by a variety of shapes including bell-, boat- or kidney-shaped bowls, bottles and jars with circular to ovoid shapes as well as hemispherical bowls, to which D-shaped handles are often attached. Griddle rims have a variety of forms, but all have an enlargement of the top of the griddle rim (Bérard 2004; Hofman 1993; Faber Morse 1989; Rouse 1992:81; Petersen *et al.* 2004; Rouse and Alegría 1990).

From about the fifth century AD the Cedrosan pottery is enriched by areal painting, heavy modelling, and deep, broadline incision (Wilson 2007:66). Rims are often thickened, triangular or flanged, sometimes painted red and surfaces are mostly polished and of a pinkish-buff colour (Drewett ed. 1991). The pottery, on the whole, is heavier, thicker and softer (Rouse 1986:136-138). These new elements are thought to represent influences of the Barrancoid series, which occurred along the lower part of the Orinoco from 800 BC onwards. On the Windward Islands this phase is also known as Troumassée A (McKusick 1960) or as Modified Saladoid (Mattioni and Bullen 1970). According to Rouse (1989:387) there is evidence of interaction between the Barrancoid and Cedrosan Saladoid potters in coastal areas of Venezuela. Cedrosan-style pottery has been found at Barrancoid sites on the lower part of the Orinoco Valley and Barrancoid-style pottery has been recovered from Cedrosan sites in Trinidad and Tobago and from the adjacent Venezuelan coast. This intrusive pottery is often called 'trade pottery', although many other mechanisms than trade might have caused this phenomenon, *e.g.* reciprocal exchange and marriage ties. Considering it to be trade pottery Rouse has hypothesized that the islands of Trinidad and Tobago may have served as ports of trade from which Barrancoid influence spread to the people who made the Cedrosan pottery of the Windward Islands between AD 300 and 500 (Rouse 1992:85). Boomert (2000:441) has criticised this notion as ill-befitting Saladoid society under study, considering that by definition, ports-of-trade typically feature in early state level societies. On some of the islands, for example Barbados (*i.e.* Chancery Lane and Hillcrest sites, see Drewett ed. 1991), it is likely that

Barrancoid-influenced Modified Saladoid pottery is the first pottery style that was introduced. Boomert has suggested that this pottery should be grouped into a Palo Secan subseries, named after the Palo Seco type-site on Trinidad (Rouse *et al.* 1985; see also Drewett ed. 1991). Barrancoid influences are further evident at the sites of Chatham Bay on the Grenadines (Rouse 1992), Salt Pond on Grenada (Rouse 1992), Arnos Vale Field on St. Vincent (Rouse 1992), Troumassée A on St. Lucia (McKusick 1960), Diamant II on Martinique (Petitjean Roget 1968a; Allaire 1977), Vieille Case on Dominica and Morel II on Guadeloupe (Rouse and Allaire 1978; Rouse 1992). Barrancoid influences did not spread further north to the rest of the Leeward Islands or the Greater Antilles.

Troumassoid series: Troumassan Troumassoid

On the Windward Islands, the Cedrosan Saladoid slowly developed into a Troumassoid series around AD 500/600, although the nature of the transition is rather overstated by the alleged sudden replacement by a new series, Troumassoid (coined by McKusick (1960) after the type-site of Troumassée on St. Lucia). Numerous researchers have since pointed out that particularly the Troumassan Troumassoid subseries is a somewhat unfortunate classification, exhibiting as it does both hold-over traits from the Saladoid series as well as a number of innovations in morphology and decoration. Indeed, the problem is best illustrated by McKusick's (1960) original subdivision of Troumassée A (with a median date of AD 430) and B (with a median date of AD 730), the former of which is more aptly considered a terminal Saladoid ware (classified by Rouse as Cedrosan Saladoid with Barrancoid influences), and the latter as something that breaks away resolutely from the Saladoid series, or what has since been termed the Troumassan Troumassoid subseries, persisting in the Windward Islands until around AD 1100. Clearly, some of the ongoing confusion with the Troumassan subseries arises from its Saladoid holdovers, making some of its ware indistinguishable from Late Saladoid ware. The lack of sound stratigraphical excavations confounds the issue to this day, and future research may conclude that there is no such thing as Troumassan Troumassoid, or at least not as it is currently defined, and that it is rather a waning, terminal Saladoid style, that could better be referred to as for instance Troumassan Saladoid (*cf.* Boomert 2000:245).

Bullen and Bullen (1972) had called this phase 'Calivinoid' after the Caliviny Polychrome decoration they initially believed typical for it and which they had identified at the Caliviny Island site of Grenada. It has since been recognized however that the suite of traits that the Bullens classed as Caliviny occurs throughout the Late Ceramic Age, and is not particularly useful as a chronological marker (Allaire 1977; Boomert 2000). Indeed, Allaire's excavations on Martinique showed that both Bullen's culture-chronological division of the post-Palo Secan ceramic evolution in the Windward Islands and his ethnic identifications were wholly incorrect (Allaire 1977, 1980, 1984). Early Troumassan Troumassoid pottery, as exemplified by the l'Espérance complex from Martinique, is characterized by a fine, sand-tempered pottery, scratched surfaces, inward thickened rims, legged, pedestal or annular bases, legged griddles[47] and triangular griddle rims (Allaire 1977). Decoration is rich, though less complex than on Saladoid pottery, comprising polychrome painting with white, red and black or red and black combined with curvilinear incisions. Modelled-incised designs are present on some lugs. Vessel shapes include a variety of boat-shaped, kidney-shaped, bottomless, double, simple open, hemispherical and inverted-bell shaped bowls. Cylindrical pot stands, jars and effigy bowls are also common, and of course the Troumassée cylinder, which probably saw its first occurrence in late Saladoid assemblages though (Allaire 1977; Hofman 1993; Rouse 1992).

Later Troumassan Troumassoid, as exemplified by Allaire's Paquemar complex on Martinique, tends to comprise thicker, more coarsely tempered and softer pottery. Typical vessel forms are open bowls, trays and basins with an inward thickened rim. Composite vessels, generally restricted, also occur, as do footed vessels and plain and footed griddles. Circular and pedestal bases occur, though handles generally do not. Surfaces tend to be pitted and irregular despite finishing techniques such as burnishing or scratching. Decoration is still common, though mainly in the form of overall red paint. Some incision is evident, but modeling is generally absent, except in the form of rim modifications, which are typically convex and horn-shaped extensions of the rim. An interesting appearance during this period is the clay spindle whorl (Allaire 1977; Rouse 1992).

Troumassoid series: Suazan Troumassoid

After around AD 1100, Troumassan Troumassoid gradually turned into the Suazan Troumassoid subseries, which is distributed from Guadeloupe and La Désirade in the north to Tobago in the south, although a number of individual decorative traits occur sporadically further north as well. Suazan (named after type site Savanne Suazey on Grenada) was initially deemed significantly different from Troumassan as to warrant its ascription to a separate series, but it has since been recognized as more or less a continuation of many Troumassan traits, albeit with the introduction of a number of novel traits. It is relatively homogenous in terms of style and type of decorative attributes, notwithstanding a certain degree of variation in the eventual execution of shared ideas. This pottery was long considered the least finished and crudest pottery of the Caribbean, *e.g. "the sloppy, easily made, artistically destitute pottery named Suazey"* (Bullen 1964:56). But for quite some time it has been recognized that Suazan also comprises a finer, well-executed ware as well as the plain, crude ware for which it became (in)famous (Allaire 1977;

47 According to Allaire (1977:312-13), who did not find griddle legs in his l'Espérance assemblage, these may be a later Troumassan Troumassoid development, which fits the predominantly post-AD 700 dates for the Mill Reef complex on Antigua (Rouse 1976) and the Troumassée B complex on St. Lucia (McKusick 1960) that both contain griddle legs.

Boomert 1987a; Boomert and Kameneff 2005). Drewett recently suggested that the whole idea of a post-Saladoid slump in material culture and society at large is a misconception. He argued that while Saladoid ceramics may have been technically superior, the Suazan Troumassoid material may represent the pinnacle of a creative society, not bound by stylistic convention: *"Instead of the rather dull and stylised, if technically highly accomplished, pottery of the Saladoid period, the pottery of the Suazoid on Barbados is exciting, free flowing and individualistic"* (Drewett 2004:215).

While that may be overstating the case somewhat, it is true that the range of decorations applied is extensive, even if the execution of these decorations is rather less refined than before. General vessel shapes of Suazan Troumassoid assemblages are restricted and large open bowls, necked jars and legged bowls and griddles, the legs having a number of forms: U-shaped, V-shaped, tubular (both flaring and tapering) and rectangular (Allaire 1977). Utilitarian vessels tend to be thick and badly made, coarsely tempered and undecorated bar scratching or scraping, with diameters reaching 40 cm. Finer ware is slightly better made, has polished surfaces and is decorated with red paint, linear or areal painting, or simple incisions of parallel lines, circles or scrolls on the rims or walls. Other decorative traits are fingertip and fingernail indentation along the vessel rim and a wide variety of lugs, including single and double horns, rounded and tab or trapezium-shaped lugs. Anthropomorphic adornos, figurines and clay pestles or loomweights (often given rudimentary facial features) are typical, as are clay stamps, (perforated) discs (spindle whorls) and pot stands (Allaire 1977; Hofman and Bright 2004; McKusick 1960; Petersen *et al.* 2004).

Cayo

Faint as its presence may be, Cayo is presumably the latest pre-Colonial and earliest indigenous Colonial period pottery style in the Windward Islands (*cf.* Allaire 1994). First recognized by Kirby (1974), Cayo was initially thought to predate the Suazan ceramics on St. Vincent, but it was later recognized that Cayo probably occurred simultaneously with later Suazan Troumassoid ceramics throughout the Windwards and outlasted them (Allaire 1984; Boomert 1986, 1995, 2004). Boomert (1986) associated this pottery with the Island Carib occupation of the Windward Islands and he argued that the Cayo ceramics show some strong similarities in decoration and shape to the Koriabo complex of the Guianas. On the basis of this affiliation, Boomert dates Cayo to some time between AD 1000 and 1500, and more precisely ca. AD 1250 (Boomert 2004; see also Petersen *et al.* 2004:29).[48] Allaire (1994:1-2) found evidence of Cayo remains intermixed with Colonial-period artefacts such as glass beads and metal, suggesting that the Cayo complex extended into Colonial times. Cayo is recognizable as dark-brown, greyish or yellowish-red pottery, comprising such vessel shapes as constricted and open bowls, bowls with composite contours (*e.g.* globular with straight necks), jars with

48 It must be stressed however that this is a relative date, as there are as yet no radiocarbon dates for Cayo material in the Windward Islands.

convex necks, and large straight-walled vessels, more aptly describes as vats. A host of decoration modes are applied to the vessels, including indented and incised rims, strips of filleted and punctated appliqués, plastic modelling and curvilinear incisions (see also Boomert 1986; Cody Holdren 1998). A number of sherds exhibit a distinct black slip or residue on their interior, and the trait of exterior scratching appears to hold over from Suazan Troumassoid ceramics. The temper of some Cayo ceramics consists of caraipé, or the crushed, burnt bark of the kwepi tree (Chrysobalanaceae; Licania spp.), which only occurs on the mainland of South America and Trinidad (Boomert 1986; Hofman *et al.* 2008:11).

3.4. Windward Islands archaeology: current state of affairs

In the following subchapters, we will examine how these sites are distributed geographically and diachronically, and delve into the research history underlying their discovery.

3.4.1. Grenada

3.4.1.1. Geographical and geological setting

Grenada is the southernmost of the Windward Islands, a fact that is emphasized by the considerable (at least for Antillean standards) stretch of sea between Grenada and either Tobago or Trinidad (some 150 km). In that sense, Grenada, rather than Trinidad or Tobago would have represented the first navigating challenge for voyaging mainlanders. Grenada is oval-shaped, measures approximately 16 by 30 km and encompasses a total area of 367 km^2. It is a typical Windward island, in the sense that it is characterized by a landscape that generally grades from sandy beaches through low valleys or river plains to hilly slopes and volcanic peaks. Its indented southern coastline is particularly stunning, and provides the island with a large number of natural inlets and bays. Vegetation and microenvironments are typically varied, ranging from mangroves, xerophytic headlands and lowland dry forests to lush rainforests and elfin woodlands. The southern coast is almost entirely skirted by coral reefs, as are parts of the remaining coastline, providing rich offshore marine habitats. Overall, Grenada is teeming with wildlife, from landcrabs, lizards, bats and monkeys to fishes, turtles, armadillos and nesting seabirds (Grenada Country Environmental Profile 1991; Groome 1970).

3.4.1.2. History of Grenada archaeology

Fewkes was the first archaeologist to visit Grenada (Holmes 1907) and study Grenadian prehistory (see Fewkes 1922 for a discussion of mainly lithic artefacts attributed to Grenada from the Heye collection). Lovén (1935) described the same lithic materials and additionally some ceramic material from Grenada. Huckerby (1921) was the first to survey Grenada and pinpoint the location of petroglyph sites on the island, but it was Bullen who provided the first general overview and numerous follow-up articles on the archaeology of Grenada (Bullen 1964, 1968, 1969; Bullen and Bullen 1968a). Bar some surveying and testpitting by Petitjean Roget (n.d.) in the eighties, little other than avocational work was carried out until Keegan (1991) carried out some excavations at the heavily disturbed Pearls site. Fandrich (1991) dealt shortly with stone tools from Grenada and Cody (1991, 1995; Cody Holdren 1998) chose Grenada as a case study for her study of contact-period Carib social and political networks, carrying out test excavations at various late pre-Colonial sites. Most recently, Harris (2001) also selected Grenada as a test case for his ethno-archaeological approach, but worked from existing data. The most recent work on Grenadian archaeology has been an analysis of Saladoid adornos (Byrne and Keegan 2001) and a study of exotic lithics from the Pearls site (Boomert 2007a). At present, there is little or no pre-Colonial archaeology being undertaken on the island.

3.4.1.3. Habitation history Grenada (fig. 3.1)

Grenada was first settled during the early phase of the Early Ceramic Age, as evidenced by the ten sites belonging to this period. The late phase of the Early Ceramic Age sees 30 sites on the island. Mainly the south-western and north-eastern coasts were inhabited during this period. Average distance between site clusters is around 7 km. The ensuing early phase of the Late Ceramic Age numbers 19 sites, most of which are a continuance of earlier sites. A number of settlements and sites in the south-west were abandoned, leaving the entire western coast of Grenada seemingly unoccupied. The period does see Ile de Ronde being inhabited for the first time however (an island just 7 km north of Grenada, visible from the coast, and discussed here on account of its close proximity). Late phase Late Ceramic Age Suazan Troumassoid sites are 27 in number, 14 of which represent a continuation of early phase Late Ceramic Age sites and another 18 of even earlier late phase Early Ceramic Age sites. A number of sites in the southwest were apparently re-occupied during this period. Two Cayo sites have been discovered thus far, one of which is located along the northern coast, facing Ile de Ronde, which also happens to be the location of the only known Cayo site in the Grenadines. Besides settlements and scatters, Grenada also numbers five petroglyph sites, one non-descript Ceramic Age site and two altogether non-diagnostic sites, although one of them was adjudged a settlement by Bullen (1964).

3.4.1.4. Ceramics Grenada

A share of ceramics from Grenada is on display or stored at the Grenada National Museum, another share is in storage at the Florida Museum of Natural History (Bullen 1964; Keegan 1991). The Yale Peabody Museum also holds numerous ceramics and other artefacts from various sites on Grenada. Furthermore, there are numerous other private collections of Grenadian Amerindian artefacts (notably those of Leon Taylor and Kachelriess; Boomert 2007a) on the island. In addition, there is a small collection of material from Pearls in the Vigie Depot, St. Lucia, and in the National Museum and Art Gallery, Trinidad. The site of Pearls in particular has suffered from incessant looting over the years, resulting even in the online sale of countless Saladoid adornos a few years ago.

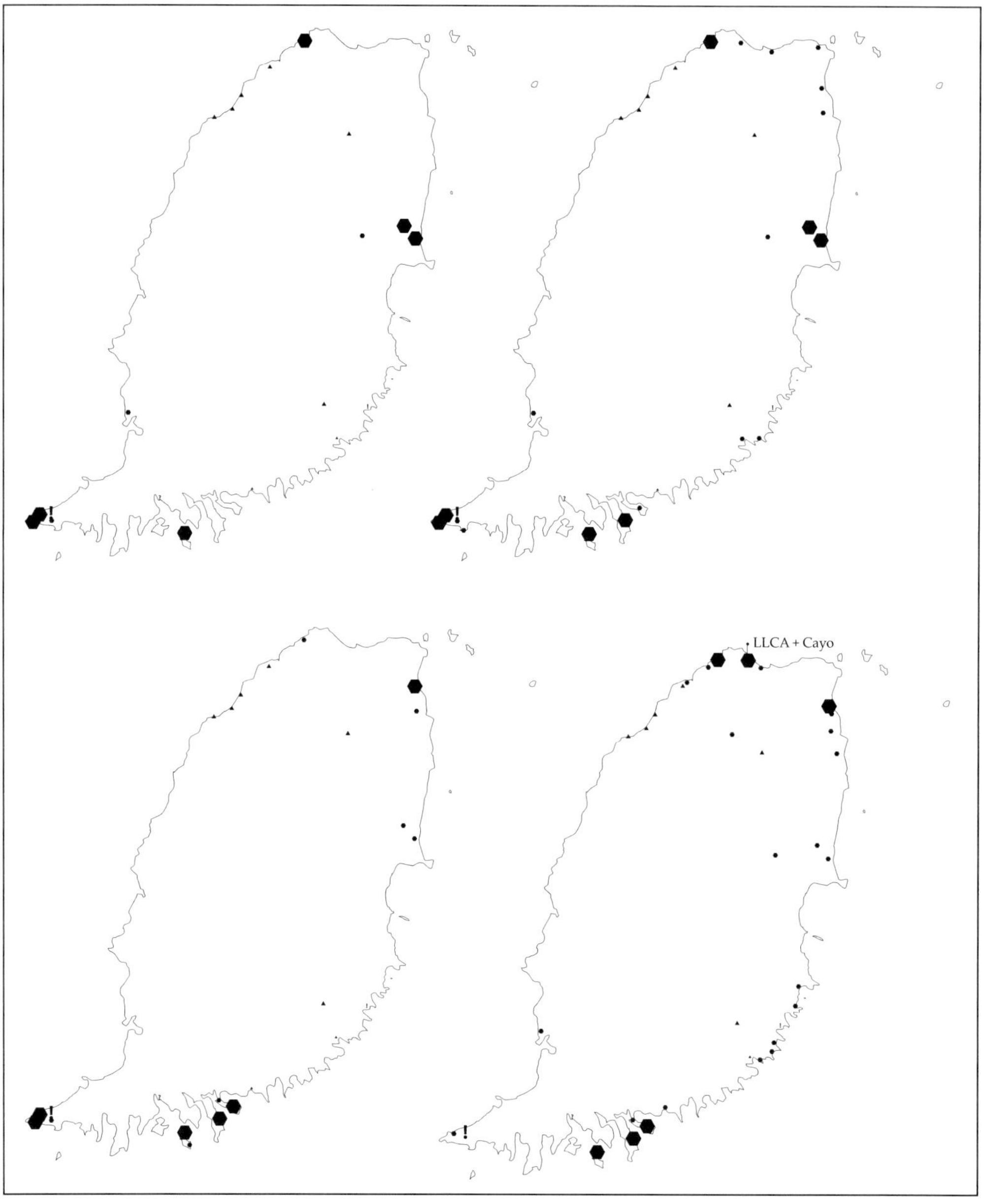

Figure 3.1. Grenada site pattern, (top left to right) early phase of the Early Ceramic Age, late phase of the Early Ceramic Age, (bottom left to right) early phase of the Late Ceramic Age, late phase of the Late Ceramic Age (+ Cayo). Large hexagons represent settlement sites, small hexagons represent pottery scatters, large exclamation marks represent nondiagnostic settlement sites, small exclamation marks represent nondiagnostic pottery scatters, large question marks represent undescribed settlement sites, small question marks represent nondiagnostic sites, triangles represent lithic finds or petroglyph sites. The same conventions apply to all following site distribution maps in Chapter 4.

The Bullens were the first to propose a typology for Grenadian ceramics, arriving at a tripartite division into the Pearls-Simon-Saline series (representing the Saladoid tradition as previously defined by Rouse and Cruxent), the Caliviny series and the Suazey series (Bullen 1964:3). This division generally accords quite well with the currently employed division Saladoid, Troumassan Troumassoid and Suazan Troumassoid, with the exception of the Saline series, which is now deemed Troumassan Troumassoid rather than terminal Saladoid on the basis of its rim modifications. The Bullens also distinguished a further two series, the Airport and Westerhall series, but did not utilize these on St. Vincent and the Grenadines (Bullen and Bullen 1972), suggesting that these are local complexes or that the subdivisions has not stood the test of time. A small number of ware types could not be assigned to any particular series. Other ware types were stratigraphically segregated to such a degree that the Bullens ascribed them to phases; these would be termed complexes nowadays. The Pearls series comprised an Early or Black Point phase, a Middle or Pearls phase and a Late or Salt Pond phase. Suazey pottery comprised a prehistoric and historic component (Bullen 1964). Rouse *et al.* (1995:fig. 7) arranged the various local ceramic complexes into his series as follows: Pearls (Saladoid), Salt Pond (Saladoid), Caliviny (Troumassan Troumassoid) and Suazey (Suazan Troumassoid). Boomert (1986), following up on pioneering work by Kirby (1974), took the Bullens' Savanne Plain types to represent a Cayo component (strongly related to the Koriaban Marajoaroid subseries of the Guianas). While there certainly are Cayo ceramics among these assemblages, it is probably incorrect to assume that all Savanne Plain and Peasant Ware ceramics represent Cayo ceramics. Cody Holdren (1998) was the first to determine the presence of Cayo ceramics on Grenada on the basis of personal observation and excavation.

3.4.2. The Grenadines

3.4.2.1. Geographical and geological setting

The Grenadines form an island group that stretches roughly 90 km, filling the gap between Grenada and St. Vincent. They comprise some 35 islands, islets and cays, ranging in area from 32 km^2 (Carriacou) to a few hundred square meters. They are geologically older than St. Vincent and Grenada, but have had a complex history, having re-emerged above sea level only since late Pleistocene times due to regional uplifting of the seafloor. The islands have varied rock types of both volcanic and sedimentary origin. Union island, Mustique and Mayreau possess mangrove areas as well as one or more salt ponds, and Cannouan numbers as many as four salt ponds. Most of the Grenadines have some offshore coral reefs, but the most extensive are around Mayreau, Union Island and the Tobago Cays (St. Vincent and the Grenadines Country Environmental Profile 1991). Interestingly, all the larger islands have yielded some evidence of Amerindian activity, from settlements to isolated ritual finds.

3.4.2.2. History of Grenadines archaeology

The earliest recorded archaeological forays in the Grenadines are perhaps those of Ober (1899 [1879]), who found not only Amerindian pottery and lithics, but also a wooden carving in a cave on Battowia. Fewkes (1922) visited Bequia and Balliceaux, noting the presence of several midden deposits and excavating at the site of Banana Bay. Decades later, the Bullens (1972) surveyed and excavated on St. Vincent and many of the Grenadines. Research was continued into the 1980s and 1990s (Sutty 1976a/b, 1978, 1983, 1985, 1990, 1991a/b), and in recent years, a collaborative team has carried out surveys and excavations on Carriacou (Fitzpatrick *et al.* 2004; Kaye *et al.* 2003; Kaye *et al.* 2004, Kaye *et al.* 2005).

3.4.2.3. Habitation history Grenadines (fig. 3.2)

It has been suggested (Sutty 1991a) that two sites on Carriacou date to the Archaic Age, however, evidence for this is unconvincing, as it is negative (absence of ceramics) rather than positive (Archaic Age assemblage), and not supported by radiocarbon dates thus far. For the time being, it is safer to consider the Grenadines to have been first settled during the Ceramic Age, with eight sites designated as early Saladoid, and a further 34 as later Saladoid. Particularly Carriacou, Union Island, Mayreau, Cannouan, Mustique, Balliceaux and Bequia show evidence of intensive settlement. The early phase of the Late Ceramic Age numbers nineteen Troumassan Troumassoid sites, seventeen of which overlie earlier sites. Habitation persists on the aforementioned islands, albeit considerably less extensively, and Ile de Ronde sees its first settlement during this period. Settlement intensity increases again during the late phase of the Late Ceramic Age, with 32 sites designated Suazan Troumassoid. Of these, seventeen are a continuance of earlier Troumassan Troumassoid (and in sixteen cases also Saladoid) sites. Particularly Bequia and Carriacou seem to recover from the settlement slump of the previous period. Even tiny Frigate Island off the coast of Union shows traces of late phase Late Ceramic Age activity. One Cayo site has been discovered in the Grenadines so far, on Île de Ronde. A petroglyph site, two polissoir sites and eight undiagnostic ceramic sites (one of which, a cave on Battowia, also yielded remarkable wooden carvings) round off the inventory.

Reviewing the data, it is clear that the Amerindians were more resourceful than the Bullens had expected. Indeed, only the very smallest islets have thus far failed to yield evidence of settlement, although many may have been utilized for various activities or as a stop-offs. Furthermore, Amerindian occupation of the Grenadines was remarkably stable over time, with only minimal changes in location of smaller sites and a great number of settlements seeing permanent occupation from Early Ceramic Age to late phase Late Ceramic Age times. This could be a logical consequence of the limited dimensions of the Grenadines, which would have offered fewer options for relocation. Recent archaeological research on Carriacou (Kaye *et al.* 2003, Fitzpatrick *et al.* 2004) has underlined the rich nature of archaeological heritage on Carriacou and may suggest that the other islands in the Grenadines should not be discounted so easily. If not supportive of autono-

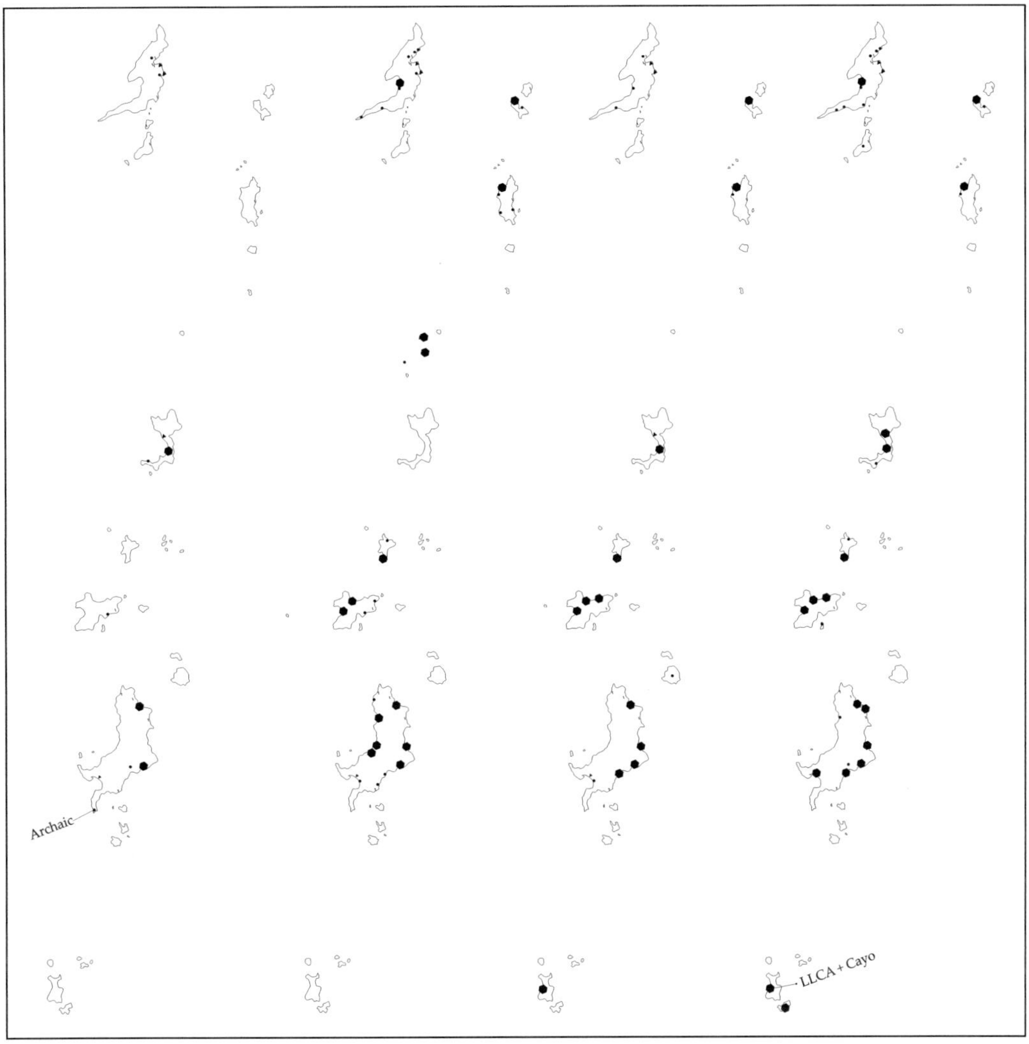

Figure 3.2. Grenadines site pattern, (left to right) early phase of the Early Ceramic Age (+ Archaic), late phase of the Early Ceramic Age, early phase of the Late Ceramic Age, late phase of the Late Ceramic Age (+ Cayo).

mous settlements, these islands may have functioned within an island network or influence sphere of Carriacou. This would imply that while deposits may not be so rich or continuous as those on Carriacou, the islands may have been utilized throughout the entire pre-Colonial time, for longer or shorter periods and with more or less settled uses in mind.

3.4.2.4. Ceramics Grenadines

Ceramics from the Grenadines are understandably scattered. A significant portion of Carriacou's ceramics is housed at the Carriacou National Museum. Other ceramics are stored among the collections of the Saint Vincent & the Grenadines

National Trust / Museum in Kingstown, St. Vincent. More Grenadines artefacts are probably either on display or in storage at the Grenada National Museum, but the Florida Museum of Natural History certainly has ceramics from a number of the Grenadines derived from the Bullens' surveys and excavations (Bullen and Bullen 1972). Martinique's Musée Régional d'Histoire et d'Ethnographie has a number of artefacts from the Grenadines (Petitjean Roget 2002) as does the Yale Peabody Museum. The Tobago Historical Museum has one piece from Petit Martinique, incidentally the only find known from this islet. Furthermore, there are undoubtedly numerous private collections on the islands, one of which, on Bequia, was viewed by the author.

The Bullens were also the first to systematically study the ceramics in the Grenadines, applying their previously constructed tripartite division for Grenada to St. Vincent and the Grenadines, with the addition of a number of new types and the omission of the Saline series (Bullen 1964; Bullen and Bullen 1972). A further innovation was the introduction of the terms Insular Saladoid (Pearls series), Modified Saladoid (Simon series) and Terminal Saladoid (not defined), apparently inspired by Mattioni (Mattioni and Bullen 1970). Allaire justly criticised their so-called Terminal Saladoid phase for not being documented by any empirical data. Indeed, its very vagueness reflects the general lack of clarity within Caribbean archaeology at large regarding the Troumassan Troumassoid manifestation, transitional between the late phases of the Early and Late Ceramic Ages. The Bullens adhered to the belief that their Modified Saladoid or Simon series was followed by a poorly attested deteriorated Saladoid type called Terminal, which was followed no later than AD 1000 first by Caliviny and then by Suazey ceramics (Bullen and Bullen 1972:161). At present, Caliviny is seen not so much as a phase, but rather as a type that bridges and occurs within the Troumassan and Suazan Troumassoid subseries. The first and only reference to Cayo ceramics in the Grenadines was made by Petitjean Roget (2002) for a site on Île de Ronde.

3.4.3. St. Vincent

3.4.3.1. Geographical and geological setting

St. Vincent is roughly oval-shaped, measures some 28.4 km north-south and 17 km west-east, and covers an area of roughly 390 km^2. The island is basically made up of a north-south running chain of hills, skirted by a coastal plain. The northern end of the chain is dominated by the Soufrière volcano, which has erupted many times, even in recent times. Vegetation, though lush, is rarely primary, as a result of both human activities as well as volcanic eruptions. Rather, St. Vincent is mainly characterized by small patches of elfin woodland, palmbrake, secondary rainforest, deciduous seasonal forest, littoral woodland and cactus scrub. Stretches of the west and east coast are skirted by coral reef, and there are only a very few areas of mangrove on the island (St. Vincent Environmental Profile 1991).

3.4.3.2. History of St. Vincent archaeology

While the occasional early mention was made of St. Vincent's Amerindian heritage (*e.g.* Ober 1899 [1879]; Sapper 1903; Fewkes 1907), the first person to have a major impact (in more ways than one) on the archaeology of St. Vincent was Reverend Thomas Huckerby. Huckerby was a Methodist minister who, while living at Chateaubelair, acquired the incredible number of 3000 artefacts, which he later sold to the Heye Museum and also inventoried, described and photographed the majority of the petroglyphs of St. Vincent (Huckerby 1914). A portion of the Heye collection was later described by Joyce (1916), Fewkes (1922) and Lovén (1924, 1935). There was a subsequent lull in activity, until the late 1960s, when Kirby (1970, 1974, 1976) and the Bullens (1972) put St. Vincent back on the map again. Sutty (1983) and Boomert (1986) discussed aspects of St. Vincentian archaeology in the 1980s, and since the 1990s, Hackenberger (1991) and various researchers from the Universities of Manitoba and Calgary have worked on the island (Allaire and Duval 1995; Callaghan 2001, 2007; Moravetz 2005). Since the passing away of Earle Kirby in 2005, things have been somewhat in a state of disarray, but the National Trust is now finding its feet again and funding as well. The extensive collection of artefacts has been moved from the old archaeological museum in the Botanical Gardens to the National Trust's headquarters in Kingstown, where some select materials are now on permanent display. In 2009 and 2010, teams from Leiden University excavated several sites in the south-east of the island that were threatened with destruction by the construction of a new international airport (Hoogland *et al.* in prep; Van den Biggelaar and Boomert 2010).

3.4.3.3. Habitation history St. Vincent (fig. 3.3)

St. Vincent was first settled in the early phase of the Early Ceramic Age, with eighteen sites attributable to the period. The late phase of the Early Ceramic Age numbers 56 sites, almost half of which appear to have been large settlements.[49] There appears to have been no preference for location, although the north-west quadrant is barely settled, and remains almost empty in later periods.[50] St. Vincent (along with St. Lucia) is quite unique to the Windward Islands in having quite a number of truly inland sites, dating from Early Ceramic Age times and enduring until the late phase of the Late Ceramic Age. Some of the settlements and sites are still in view of the coast, at about 500-1500 metres distance, but as many as seven are located at least three and as much as five km inland. Interesting to note is also that the average distance between site clusters is 2-3 km in the south and a little more in the north. A number of settlements appear to be clustered very close together as well, perhaps indicative of a shifting settlement or settlement

49 It should be noted that the site numbers for St. Vincent at my disposal differ significantly from those published (though not specified) by Callaghan (2007). Callaghan tallies 33 sites with a Saladoid component, 63 with a Troumassoid component and 63 with a Suazoid component. The larger site tally is presumably attributable to (unpublished) research such as Allaire's field notes, work on the Kirby collection and the University of Calgary survey (Callaghan 2007: table 1).

50 See also Callaghan (2007) for attribution of the dearth of finds in this sector to the inherent difficulty of surveying this area.

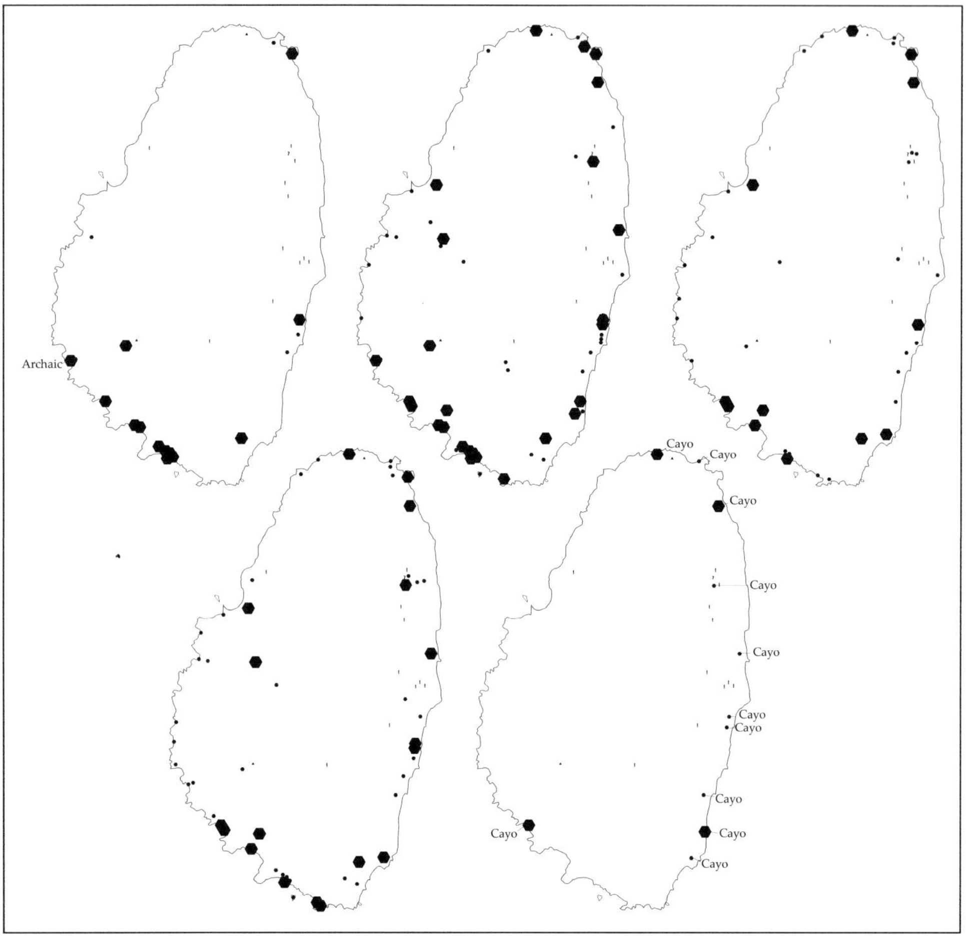

Figure 3.3. St. Vincent site pattern, (top left to right) early phase of the Early Ceramic Age (+ Archaic), late phase of the Early Ceramic Age, early phase of the Late Ceramic Age, (bottom left to right) late phase of the Late Ceramic Age, Cayo.

fissioning during the Early Ceramic Age (see also Chapter 4). The ensuing early phase Late Ceramic Age period numbers 39 sites, 32 of which are a continuance of earlier sites. A number of settlements and some smaller sites disappear, indicating a slight depopulation in certain areas, in particular along the southern coastline, although the population were presumably incorporated by other communities. Suazan Troumassoid sites are 58 in number, 32 of which are a continuance of earlier Troumassan Troumassoid (and in 28 cases also Saladoid) sites. This late phase of the Late Ceramic Age seems to represent a period of consolidation, re-occupation and some minimal occupation of new areas (*i.e.* Young's Island). Eleven Cayo sites have so far been discovered (remarkably the entire west coast is abandoned by this time) as well as 18 petroglyph sites. Some 17 sites yielded only undiagnostic remains, and could not be ascribed to any given period. A number of isolated and clustered stone tool finds have also been reported. Descendants of the historically recorded Island Caribs and Black Caribs live scattered along the north-east coast of the island to this day.

3.4.3.4. Ceramics St. Vincent

The extensive collections formerly housed at Earle Kirby's archaeological museum in the Botanical Gardens are now stored at the National Trust headquarters, where they have been photographed and inventoried by a team from the University of Calgary. Some ceramics are on display at Fort Duvernette, Kingstown. There are undoubtedly numerous private collections on St. Vincent, one of which, Russell's Wallilabou collection, was viewed by the author. Outside St. Vincent, the National Museum of the American Indian in New York holds the Huckerby/Heye collection. The Florida Museum of Natural History has ceramics from a number of St. Vincent sites, derived from the Bullens' surveys and excavations (Bullen and Bullen 1972), as does the Yale Peabody Museum.

As mentioned above, the Bullens were the first to systematically study the ceramics in St. Vincent (Bullen 1964; Bullen and Bullen 1972). They saw the ceramic developments through time as follows: Pearls series (Insular Saladoid), Simon series (Modified Saladoid) and an ill-defined Terminal Saladoid, followed by the Caliviny and Suazey series, to which Kirby (1974) added another ware, Cayo, which he deemed to be chronologically placed between the Saladoid and Caliviny series. While subsequent research has dismissed Kirby's chronological conclusions, the existence of a Cayo ware is widely accepted (Boomert 1986; Cody Holdren 1998). Rouse *et al.* (1995:fig. 7) furthermore arranged the various ceramic assemblages into a series of local complexes named Post Office (Saladoid), Arnos Vale (Saladoid), Indian Bay (Troumassan Troumassoid) and Fitz-Hughs (Suazan Troumassoid). Since the late 1990s, researchers from Calgary University have been carrying out fieldwork on St. Vincent, including the mammoth task undertaken by Joe Moravetz of photographing the entire archaeological collection formerly housed at the Archaeological Museum in the Botanical Gardens. Unfortunately, the provenance of the majority of these artefacts has been lost, so that the artefacts can only be used to make general observations on ceramic style traits.

3.4.4. St. Lucia

3.4.4.1. Geographical and geological setting

St. Lucia is situated roughly in the middle of the Windward Islands. It is leaf-shaped, narrow in the north and fanning out towards the south. A peninsula juts out in the extreme south. It measures 43 km from north to south and 22 km at its widest point from west to east, encompassing a total area of 620 km^2. Belonging to the so-called volcanic Caribbees (Van Soest 2000:33), the island is largely volcanic in geology. The central part of the island consists of a north-south running mountain chain, which grades into montane slopes, river plains and beaches and headlands successively as one moves east and west. Southern St. Lucia is particularly diverse, with features such as a glacial fan at Vieux Fort and the geologically younger caldera at Soufrière (Stark *et al.* 1966).

3.4.4.2. History of St. Lucia archaeology

St. Lucia played a key role in the earliest systematic study of Caribbean prehistory, seeing the establishment of the first Lesser Antillean archaeological society in 1954, The Saint Lucia Archaeological and Historical Society. Despite its early role in stimulating archaeological research in the West Indies, little extensive archaeological work has been conducted on the island in the past 25 years. The first major field investigations were conducted by Marshall B. McKusick as part of his Ph.D. research in 1956 and 1957 (McKusick 1960). When McKusick came to St. Lucia, he limited his excavations to the southeast coast of St. Lucia, bar one excursion to the west coast at Choc Bay. He was basing himself on earlier reports of sites and choosing the destinations that presented few logistical problems, namely Troumassée, Choc, Micoud Beach, Grand Point, Massacre, Point Canelles and Point de Caille (McKusick 1960:59). William G. Haag (1964) and the Bullens (1970, 1973 with Branford) carried out research throughout the 1960s. The last major summary of St. Lucian archaeology was compiled by the Reverend C. Jesse in 1960 and revised in 1967, to which Devaux (1975) added a number of sites, both Colonial period and pre-Colonial. During the 1980s, research was undertaken by the University of Vienna (Friesinger 1986; Friesinger and Devaux 1983) and research into historical sites was initiated by the University of Bristol in 2000. In 2002, an international cooperation programme was established between the St. Lucia Archaeological and Historical Society, the Florida Museum of Natural History and the Faculty of Archaeology at Leiden University (Keegan *et al.* 2002, 2003; Hofman *et al.* 2004). The aims of this project are manifold: to compile an inventory of archaeological sites on the island through extensive archaeological surveys, to develop a better classification of St. Lucian pottery and to place it within a broader, Windward Islands context and finally to conduct ethnographic and ethnoarchaeological investigations on the island (*e.g.* Hofman and Bright 2004). The project was continued in 2003 and 2004, the focus shifting first to the southwest and then to the east. The project awaits completion, with the mid-western and northern parts of St. Lucia remaining unsurveyed. However, a team from Leiden returned to the island in 2009 and 2010 to carry out rescue excavations at the site of Lavoutte, where tropical storms and tourism had exposed numerous skeletal remains that were in danger of being destroyed (Hofman and Branford 2009; Hofman and Hoogland 2009a,b).

3.4.4.3. Habitation history St. Lucia (fig. 3.4)

So far, no convincing Archaic Age sites have been discovered on St. Lucia, although the Coulon River site could be a contender if it withstands closer inspection (Stokes *et al.* 2002). For now, first occupation must be deemed to have taken place in Early (though not earliest) Ceramic Age times: 30 sites have thus far been designated as Saladoid, ten of which can be considered settlements on the basis

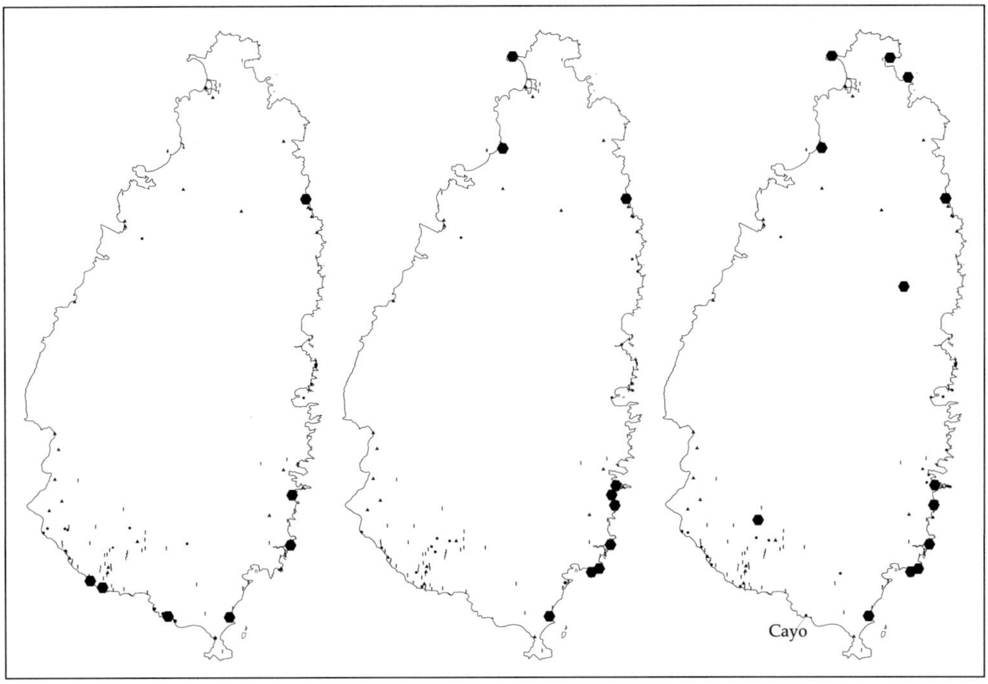

Figure 3.4. St. Lucia site pattern, (left to right) Early Ceramic Age, early phase of the Late Ceramic Age, late phase of the Late Ceramic Age (+ Cayo).

of evidence gathered thus far. Four settlements are located along the southern coast, with the site of Black Bay falling almost exactly in between Giraudy and Balembouche/Anse Touloulou, and Grande Anse, Troumassée and Canelles Point are on the east coast. Another 32 sites fall within the Troumassan Troumassoid category, including twelve overlaps in location from the previous period. Troumassée is the type-site for this period, albeit only as far as the Troumassée B component is concerned. The late phase of the Late Ceramic Age sees the most widespread occupation, with a total of 43 sites. The Windward coast is settled more intensively than before, numerous sites being located on rocky headlands jutting out into the sea or along cliffs high above sea level (see also Keegan *et al.* 2002). It appears that defensibility and better visibility of the surrounding land and sea were indeed important locational strategies in this period (*cf.* De Waal 2006; Hofman 1995). It should be noted that despite their elevated position, the sites are generally still near bays and rivers, just not located directly at or beside them. Some 56 sites yielded entirely undiagnostic ceramic material, and could not be assigned to a given period. Five sites have been reported in the literature, but not explored since. Fifteen petroglyph or rock carving sites round off the total.

3.4.4.4. Ceramics St. Lucia

The overwhelming majority of archaeological artefacts on St. Lucia is stored at the depot of the St. Lucia Archaeological and Historical Society at Vigie, Castries. Material excavated and collected all over the island over the last hundred years or so has been stored there, after surviving the vicissitudes of nature and man (see Jesse, 1960). Most has been furnished with a find number and site provenience, and some even have stratigraphic layer recorded on them, others are completely without context. Furthermore, there are a number of smaller collections, like the one at the Pigeon Point Museum, at the office of the Saint Lucia Archaeological and Historical Society and at the CARDI Agricultural Centre in La Ressource as well as a number of private collections such as the Barnard and Balembouche collections, both viewed and photographed by the author. Outside St. Lucia, the Barbados Museum has a collection of lithics and ceramics (see Jesse 1967), the Florida Museum of Natural History holds a collection of St. Lucian artefacts from a number of sites, as do Louisiana State University (the Haag collection) and the Yale Peabody Museum (the McKusick collection).

The first to publish on ceramics from St. Lucia was Father Jesse in his overview of St. Lucian archaeology (Jesse 1967). Despite not working within a cultural/stylistic framework, his careful descriptions allowed later archaeologists to subsume his findings into their own models. One such later archaeologist was McKusick. On the basis of careful excavations at various sites around the island, McKusick proposed a sequence of local complexes, which he aligned with Cruxent and Rouse's chronological scheme (Cruxent and Rouse 1982: 34, table 1), starting with their period IIb, questionably alleged to commence around 150 AD on the basis of undiscussed linguistic evidence.[51] Leaving the Saladoid or Cedros-like material aside, McKusick recognized a Troumassée A complex, a Troumassée B complex, a Choc complex and a Fannis complex. Recognizing broader stylistic similarities across the Lesser Antilles, McKusick subsequently placed the complexes within overarching series. The little studied Cedros-like ware was housed in the Saladoid series (running from AD 150 to 350), Troumassée A and B were subsumed by a Troumassoid series (running from AD 350 to 750) and Choc and Fannis within a Micoid series, dating AD 1150-1500 (McKusick 1960:152-4). McKusick hardly dealt with the period between AD 750 and 1150 (and left it blank in his typo-chronological chart), although he made one or two references to a late Troumassée ware that he presumably considered to belong to this period. Reconsidering McKusick's typo-chronology, it would appear that his unfamiliarity with Saladoid materials led him to underestimate the duration of the Saladoid cultural tradition, which subsequently made his research on the Troumassoid series problematic. Haag (1964) and the Bullens (Bullen 1968; Bullen and Bullen 1970; Bullen, Bullen and Branford 1973; Bullen, Bullen and Kirby 1973) subsequently excavated on St. Lucia, following the Bullens' established seriation of Pearls, Simon, Caliviny and Suazey types (Bullen 1964; Bullen and Bullen 1972). While doing more justice to the Saladoid component, the Troumassoid component remained enigmatic. A team from the University of Vienna carried out extensive excavations in southern St. Lucia, but have only published a preliminary report which provides a questionable typo-chronology of the ceramics in a micro-region encompassing Canelles, Grand Anse, Troumassée and Point de Caille/Saltibus

51 Probably a reference to Taylor and Rouse (1955), personal communication Arie Boomert, 2007.

Point (Friesinger 1986). Rouse (1992), Boomert (2000) and Harris (2001) finally made some sense of the Troumassoid, by determining that McKusick's Troumassée A was actually a late Saladoid component, and his Troumassée B represented an early Troumassan Troumassoid phase (see also Petersen *et al.* 2004). McKusick's tentative Late Troumassée ware was in fact classic Troumassan Troumassoid and his Choc style probably late Troumassan/Early Suazan Troumassoid. McKusick's Fancy style falls under classic Suazan Troumassoid.

St. Lucia's Troumassan Troumassoid ceramics are thick with relatively soft, grit-tempered paste, which splits rather easily. Vessel shapes are varied with forms including boat-shaped, kidney-shaped, pedestal, bottomless, double, hemispherical, and inverted-bell-shaped bowls. Rims tend to be thickened with a variety of forms including flanges and rim bevels. Painted decoration is common including bichromes and polychromes with red, white, and black. Some modeled-incised motifs are present. Over time the painted decoration disappeared, as did fine-line crosshatching. Tripod griddles were introduced and modeled-incised decorations became more elaborate. The type-site for the Troumassoid series is the site at Troumassée River (McKusick 1960).

Dominant characteristics of the Suazan Troumassan subseries on St. Lucia are the newly-introduced leg bases, clay pestles, and a thickness and crudity of construction. Decoration tends to be garish, with heavy, incised lines and crude model-incised lugs frequently resembling human heads. Overall red paint is common and bichrome is rare. Finger-notched rims become predominant in the later phase of the series (McKusick 1960).

3.4.5. Martinique

3.4.5.1. Geographical and geological setting

Martinique measures 60 by 30 kilometres, encompassing a total area of some 1100 km^2, making it the largest island of the Lesser Antilles bar Trinidad.[52] It is ecologically diverse, harbouring a range of environments from low coastal areas characterised by shrubs and littoral vegetation to mountainous areas covered by dense tropical rainforest. The north of the island is predominantly lush and fertile, while the south is a lot dryer and more barren. This is countered to some degree by the mangrove and coral reef systems along the southern coasts. The most striking feature of the island must be the dormant volcano Mont Pelée, which erupted to devastating effect in 1902 and is known to have had a considerable impact in Amerindian times as well. St. Lucia lies to the south and Dominica to the north, and the resultant island interrelationships have been the subject of discussion (Bérard *et al.* 2005; Bright 2005, 2007).

52 Guadeloupe technically comprises two islands, although the separation between Grande-Terre and Basse-Terre should not be overly stressed as the narrow Rivière Salée is not much of a divider.

3.4.5.2. History of Martinique archaeology

Archaeological work on Martinique commenced in the first half of the twentieth century, with the excavations of Father Delawarde at the sites of Anse Belleville and Marigot. In the late thirties, he participated in excavations by Revert at Paquemar, Lassalle and Vivé.[53] Father Pinchon continued their legacy in the 1940s, excavating at l'Espérance, Vivé and l'Adoration. Pinchon was also instrumental in setting up what is now known as the IACA, and organised the First International Convention for the study of pre-Columbian culture in the Lesser Antilles on Martinique in 1961 together with Jacques Petitjean Roget (Celma ed. 1997; Giraud 2002). Petitjean Roget carried out work at the newly discovered sites of Grande Anse, Fond-Brûlé and Diamant during the 1960s, and established a cultural chronology in the process (Petitjean Roget 1970). During the 1970s and early 1980s, Mario Mattioni became a key figure in Martinique, excavating at Vivé, Fond-Brûlé, Boutbois, Le Godinot, Diamant and Anse Trabaud, lecturing at the Université des Antilles et de la Guyane, and creating the Musée Départemental d'Archéologie Précolombienne et de Préhistoire de la Martinique (Allaire and Mattioni 1983; Mattioni 1980, 1984, 1990). Mattioni was assisted at the latter two excavations by Louis Allaire, whose PhD research had earlier directed him to excavate at Macabou, Séguineau and Diamant. Allaire's contribution to Caribbean archaeology has been immense, as he published widely and extensively on a range of topics (Allaire 1977, 1997, 1999, 2003). Other notable contributions to the archaeology of Martinique have been made over the past decades by Henri Petitjean Roget (1974, 1975, 1978a/c), Benoît Bérard (2002, 2004; Bérard and Vidal 2003) and various researchers employed by the Service Régional de l'Archéologie (SRA, see Bilan Scientifique de la Région Martinique 1994-2007).

3.4.5.3. Habitation history Martinique (fig. 3.5)

Martinique was possibly settled in Archaic times, as hinted at by two sites uncovered somewhat inland in the north of Martinique, Boutbois and Le Godinot (Allaire and Mattioni 1983; Bérard 2002, 2006c/d). The Savanne des Pétrifications site, long considered a possible Archaic Age site, has recently been placed firmly in the Ceramic Age (Bérard 2002). For the ensuing Ceramic Age, a denser and more reliable settlement pattern emerges, although there is still considerable debate over when Martinique's Ceramic Age began. A host of early radiocarbon dates for the site of Fond-Brûlé seemed to point to initial occupation around 400 BC, but subsequent research has cast doubts over the validity of these earlier findings (Bérard 2004). It now seems safer to assume that the Ceramic Age settlement started around AD 1, in accordance with many other dates gathered over the last few decades. There appears to be a preference among the earliest settlers (saladoïde ancienne) for the fertile soils (due to volcanic activity) and proximity to rivers, sea and moist to tropical forest offered by the north-eastern coast of Martinique, exemplified by the sites Vivé and Fond-Brûlé, as well as eleven others (Barrau and

53 The entire Revert collection, previously housed at the Musée de l'Homme, is now stored at the Musée du Quai Branly, and accessible online (http://www.quaibranly.fr/cc/).

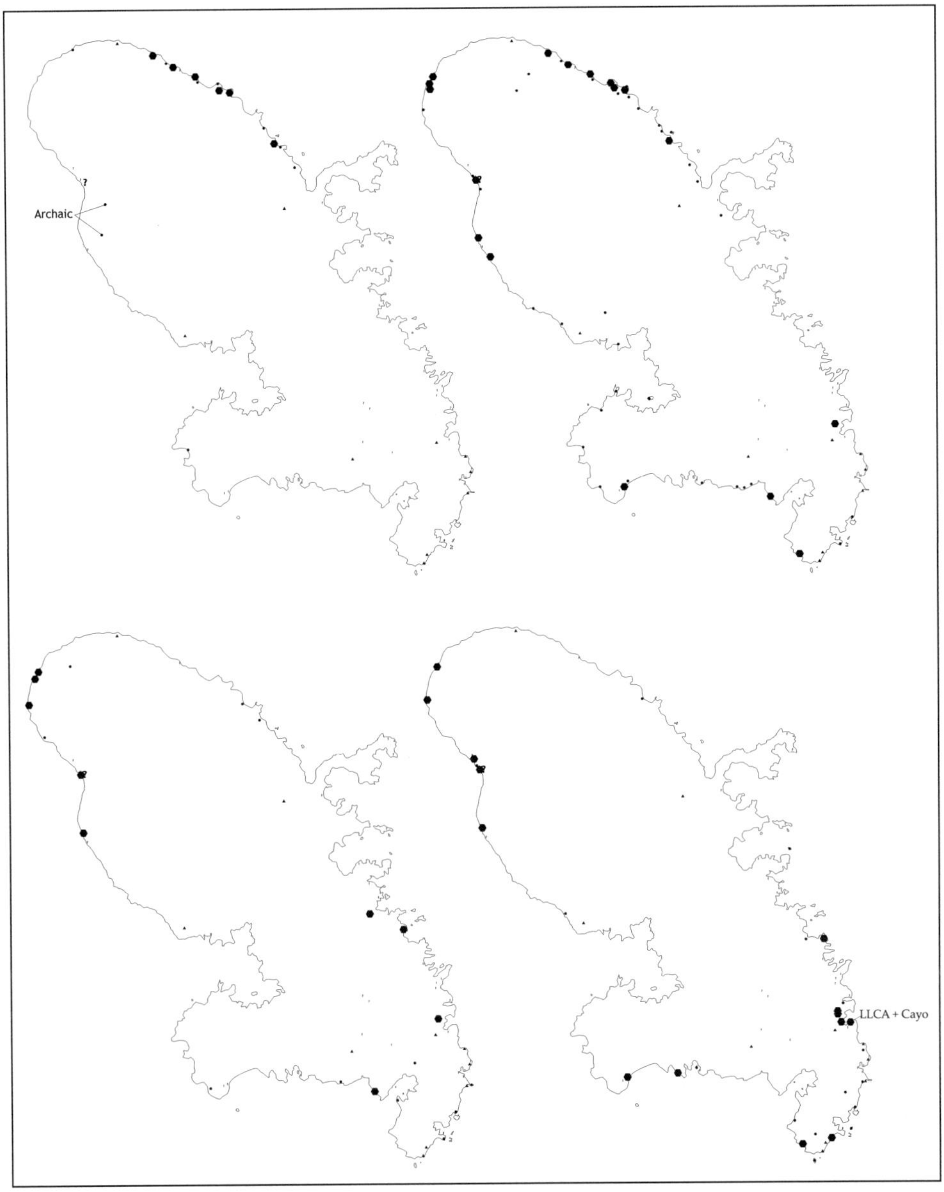

Figure 3.5. Martinique site pattern, (top left to right) early phase of the Early Ceramic Age (+ Archaic), late phase of the Early Ceramic Age, (bottom left to right) early phase of the Late Ceramic Age, late phase of the Late Ceramic Age (+ Cayo).

Montbrun 1978; Bérard 2004). The late phase of the Early Ceramic Age sees 41 new Saladoid sites appear and ten of the early phase sites enduring. The ensuing early phase of the Late Ceramic Age numbers 24 Troumassan Troumassoid sites, thirteen of which represent a continuation of earlier sites. Suazan Troumassoid sites are 30 in number, ten of which are a continuance of earlier Troumassan (and in most cases also Saladoid) sites. One site has yielded Cayo thus far. The site inventory further includes two petroglyph sites, a polissoir site, an area of extensive lithic flaking attributable to the Ceramic Age, a number of isolated finds (shell and lithics), fifteen non-diagnostic Ceramic Age sites and fourteen non-diagnostic sites. This trend of decreasing number of sites over time is most likely a result of the increased attention given to the Early Ceramic Age in recent years, as opposed to the prior emphasis placed on later periods by the likes of Allaire.

3.4.5.4. Ceramics Martinique

Martinique houses one of the most impressive and well-preserved ceramic collections in the Lesser Antilles. The two major collections are housed at the Service Régionale de l'Archéologie and at the Musée Départemental d'Archéologie in Fort-de-France. Smaller collections are scattered around the island, for instance at the Ecomusée de Martinique (Anse Figuier), at the Musée Régional d'Histoire et d'Ethnographie de la Martinique (Fort-de-France), at the Musée Volcanologique (Saint-Pierre) and at Habitation Céron (Anse Céron). Outside Martinique, a various artefacts are stored at the Yale Peabody Museum.

While earlier research by the likes of Pinchon had made a crude distinction between Arawak and Carib ceramics, it was Jacques Petitjean Roget (1970) who first proposed a serious typo-chronology for Martiniquean ceramics. He devised a tripartite division on the basis of stylistic features and stratigraphy of horizons I, II and III, the last of which supposedly represented Island Carib times (Allaire 1977; Petitjean Roget 1970). His son Henri later added two horizons to this scheme, and at the same time re-introduced terminology such as "arawak tardive" and "caraïbe" (Petitjean Roget 1975). Allaire's extensive stratigraphic excavations enabled him to develop a complete sequence of late-prehistoric pottery complexes for the island, which he could correlate to that reconstructed by McKusick (1960) for St. Lucia. He grouped the two complexes he deemed to occur during the period AD 600-1150, Espérance and Paquemar, into a Troumassoid series. He proposed the name Suazoid for the two complexes he determined to occur between AD 1150 and 1450, Macabou I and Macabou II. Including Saladoid, this yielded the following periodisation: Vivé (Early Saladoid), Diamant (Late Saladoid), Espérance (Early Troumassan Troumassoid), Paquemar (Late Troumassan Troumassoid), Macabou I (Early Suazan Troumassoid), Macabou II (Late Suazan Troumassoid) (Allaire 1977; see also Boomert 1987a). Cayo has so far been attested at just one site on Martinique, namely Macabou (Allaire 1984). In recent years, certain functional studies of ceramics have been undertaken, most notably by Bérard (2004), which have further refined our understanding of ceramic assemblages, albeit those of the Early Ceramic Age.

3.4.6. Dominica

3.4.6.1. Geographical and geological setting

Dominica, the most pristine and rugged of the Windward Islands, covers 732 km^2 and measures 46.5 km north to south and 25.5 km from west to east. Many of Dominica's peaks are over 1000 metres a.m.s.l., and the island is dissected by dozens of mountain rivers and streams. It is in essence one of the most challenging islands in terms of physical geography, one of the reasons why Amerindian communities inhabiting it were able to resist Colonial rule longer than many of their neighbours. It does however have a number of river valleys on both leeward and windward sides, and flat or moderately sloped land along or leading to the coast. It is here that habitation and the majority of activities are concentrated, to a greater degree than on any other island. Dominica is heavily forested, with a wide range of vegetation types ranging from elfin woodland and rainforest to littoral and scrub woodland as well as limited fumarole vegetation, swamp and wetlands. Dominica's steep topography limits the presence of seagrass, mangrove and reef habitats; its deep coastal waters are however attractive to various pelagic vertebrates such as whales, dolphins and turtles. Sea birds also frequent and nest on Dominica or its offshore islets (Country Environmental Profile Dominica 1991).

3.4.6.2. History of Dominica archaeology

The archaeology of Dominica unfortunately merits but a small subchapter, through historical contingency and lack of archaeological research. For an island with such a rich Amerindian legacy (*i.e.* Myers 1978), the dearth of archaeological research carried out is astonishing. Collections of Amerindian artefacts were made sporadically in the 19th century by travellers, but the first archaeologist to study Dominica was Jesse Walter Fewkes, whose brief visit in 1912 contributed little to the state of knowledge. Nearly half a century then passed before another archaeologist, McKusick, arrived on the scene, excavating for a short time at Vieille Case. His findings have only been described in manuscript form and extremely concisely in his PhD thesis (1960). In the late sixties, Evans (1968) heralded the lack of archaeology on Dominica, on the basis of questionable (biologist-staffed) fieldwork, but was put straight through archaeological (Petitjean Roget 1978b/d) and (ethno)historical (Myers 1978) research. More recently, Honychurch inventoried the state of archaeological affairs and has kept the Amerindian legacy very much alive since then (Honychurch 1997a/b, 2006).

Most extant ceramic material is exhibited at the Roseau Museum, in Roseau, along with a collection of stone tools and an ethnographic collection of basketry and wooden artefacts. The ceramics recovered during the surveys undertaken by Petitjean Roget in the 1970s appear to have been lost to hurricane Lenny in 1999 (Lennox Honychurch and Henri Petitjean Roget, personal communication 2004). Other artefacts, predominantly lithics, have suffered from insects eating away their paper labels over the years, to such a degree that the provenance of 105 of 159 artefacts, if ever known initially, is now unknown (Petitjean Roget 1978d). Lack of awareness regarding heritage has also led to the loss of artefacts, as an incidence of construction workers discarding skeletal remains and ceramics encountered in association at Soufrière in the past proves (Honychurch 2004, personal communication). However, the recent discovery of Cayo ceramics by archaeology volunteers under supervision of Honychurch indicates a turning point in this regard (Honychurch n.d.).

A new archaeological project was initiated by Bérard (SRA Martinique/ Université Antilles-Guyane), Honychurch (Dominica Museum and Fort Shirley) and Petersen (University of Vermont) in the summer of 2004, focusing on possible parallels between the south coast of Dominica and the northern coast of Martinique. Fieldwork carried out the following year yielded vital new data on the archaeological record of Dominica and its possible connections to northernmost Martinique (Bérard *et al.* 2005), but suffered a tragic setback in Petersen's death in August 2005. Leiden University recently carried out testing at a number of Cayo sites on the island (Boomert 2009). All of this amounts to making Dominica one of the least studied Windward Islands, on equal footing with Grenada (see section 3.4.1.2) in terms of amount of archaeological research carried out.

3.4.6.3. Habitation history Dominica (fig. 3.6)

As evident from the picture painted of archaeological research on Dominica, much of its earliest prehistory remains enveloped in mystery. Not until the ensuing Ceramic Age does a site pattern emerge in the archaeological record. Although the sites Soufrière, Canefield and Cachacrou date to the early phase of the Early Ceramic Age (Boomert 2000:234; Petitjean Roget 1978b), another thirteen Early Ceramic Age sites yielded late Saladoid materials. Petitjean Roget (1978b), drawing on ceramic similarities between some Soufrière and Fond-Brûlé ceramics, hypothesises that the Soufrière site may represent the first inhabitation of Dominica, implying a Martinique origin for the initial Ceramic Age colonizers of Dominica. The ensuing early phase of the Late Ceramic Age numbers eleven sites, three of which are a continuation of earlier sites. Late phase Late Ceramic Age sites are eleven in number, four of which are a continuance of earlier Troumassan sites and four a continuance of an even earlier Saladoid site, either suggesting that the site was reoccupied after some time or that a Troumassan component has been missed or gone unrecognised. Five late phase Late Ceramic Age sites represent new site locations, but may be offshoots of sites in the neighbourhood (*i.e.* Toulaman River of Walkers Rest, Vieille Case of Au Parc, Saint Sauveur 2 of Saint Sauveur 1, Eden 1 of Sophia Bay). Judging from finds reported by Honychurch, Woodford Hill Bay has yielded Cayo remains, and Petitjean Roget (1978b) has suggested further Cayo remains at Melville Hall B. Surveys and test excavations carried out by a team from Leiden in 2008 (Boomert 2009) yielded Cayo ceramics at Woodford Hill Bay, Eden, Sophia Bay, Walker's Rest and Melville Hall. Seven sites have not been described at all, only listed (Honychurch 1997a), making them unknown entities. Another six sites yielded only non-diagnostic ceramics, precluding their ascription to a given time period. Furthermore, one polissoir (Middle Bay) and a large number of isolated (stone) finds from all over the island, both near the coast as well as deep inland, have been reported (Honychurch 1997a; Petitjean Roget 1978d). These are most likely indicative of activity areas or gardens located both close to and at some distance from the habitation sites. The most impressive of these finds must be the large threepointer found in a cave at Soufrière in 1878 (Honychurch 1997a; Soustelle 1934-5), now housed at Musée du Quai Branly, and the wooden duho recently rediscovered among the collections of the Royal

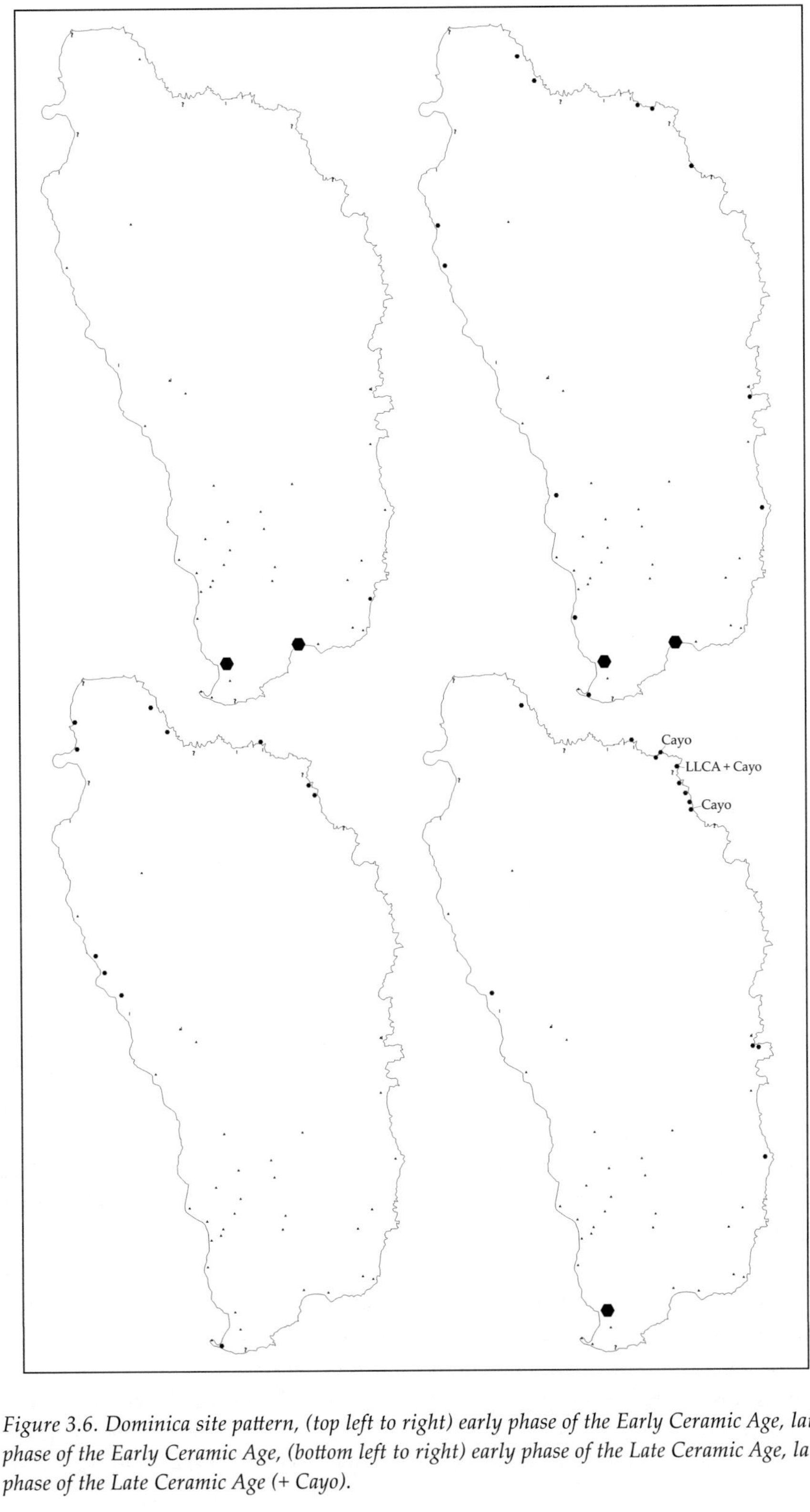

Figure 3.6. Dominica site pattern, (top left to right) early phase of the Early Ceramic Age, late phase of the Early Ceramic Age, (bottom left to right) early phase of the Late Ceramic Age, late phase of the Late Ceramic Age (+ Cayo).

Botanical Gardens at Kew (Honychurch 2001). Descendants of the historically recorded Island Caribs and Black Caribs live in the Carib Territory in the northeastern quadrant of the island to this day.

Reviewing the data, it is clear that while Dominica is still something of an archaeological enigma, it has caught up with other islands in recent years. Its major handicap must be the loss of artefacts recovered during previous fieldwork. Petitjean Roget notes that every bay on the west coast seems to have been inhabited at some point in time, although he is surprised at the lack of early Arawak pottery north of Canefield. He puts this down to riverine activity, both meandering and inundating (Petitjean Roget 1978b:86). This renders all the more credible reports of finds at up to 14 feet (some 5 metres) below the surface (Clarke 1806) and underscores the great lengths to which archaeologists may have to go in order to recover substantial archaeological remains.

3.4.6.4. Dominica ceramics

The ceramics of Dominica unfortunately merit but a tiny chapter, through aforementioned historical contingency and lack of archaeological research. At present, the pottery of only three or four of the forty-odd archaeological sites on Dominica is visible to this day. Much of that material is exhibited at the Roseau Museum, in Roseau. The archaeological depot of Fort Shirley at Cabrits National Park, Portsmouth holds certain materials too. Furthermore, the Yale Peabody Museum has a small collection from Dominica. What has been done with Dominican ceramics while they were still available and what little can be concluded from the remaining ceramics can be briefly summarized as follows:

McKusick (1960) was perhaps the first to classify Dominican ceramics, making brief mention of an excavation at Vieille Case, which turned up some Saladoid-Barrancoid ceramics as well as some Choc-style sherds (*i.e.* Suazan Troumassoid). Evans (1968:99-100) encountered more numerous remains and applied a typo-chronology comprising Caribbean Saladoid-Barrancoid or pre-Arawak, Arawak and Historical Carib. Myers (1978) and Petitjean Roget (1978b) mention some Dominican ceramics, but use rather confusing, undefined terminology such as *arawak terminal*, *arawak tardif*, *saladoide terminal (arawak)*, *caraïbe ancien*, *caliviny*, *horizon I* and *horizon II (ancien)* and so on. Petitjean Roget (1978b: 87, 89) did however introduce Cayo to the typo-chronology, recognizing its presence at the Melville Hall site. Honychurch finally drew all the past work together and applied some uniformity to ceramic descriptions incorporating the Saladoid and Suazoid series, work that was followed up on by Bérard, Honychurch and Petersen (Bérard *et al.* 2005).

Reviewing the literature and taking into account the present author's inventory, Saladoid ceramics on Dominica comprise the usual range of decorative modes (white-on-red, ZIC, red slipped, modelling, burnishing) and vessel shapes such as shallow open bowls with pedestal bases, deeper vessels with numerous keeling points, dishes with elaborate modelled, incised and painted flanges and bowls with handles and lugs (see also Bérard *et al.* 2005; Honychurch 1997a; Roget 1978b). Troumassan Troumassoid is all but absent from existing collections, but what little can be gleaned from existing descriptions seems to attest to similar characteristics as Troumassan on other islands: simpler and more limited range of vessel forms, general decrease in decoration modes (red slip, white paint, incising and modelling remaining, cross-hatching disappearing). Suazan Troumassoid is not clearly represented either, with the lack of typical diagnostic elements such as griddle legs and feet, scratched body sherds (but see Bérard *et al.* 2005: figure 3) and finger indented rims. A number of (fragments of) Cayoid vessels exhibit the characteristics of Form 5 (see Boomert 1986:figure 3.5), *i.e.* small, rather squat vessels with globular bodies, a severe inflection point at the transition to the neck (a structural weak spot) and straight or slightly outward flaring rims. The other complete vessel is less squat, has a more globular body, and a less severe inflection point at the transition to the neck, which is longer and straight, itself giving way to an outward flaring rim, resembling Form 11 of the Koriabo complex (see Boomert 1986:figure 13.3).

3.4.7. Barbados

3.4.7.1. Geographical and geological setting

Barbados, the least volcanic of all the Lesser Antillean islands in terms of geological make-up, covers an area of 431 km^2, measuring 32.5 km from north to south and 22.5 km from west to east at the island's widest point. The most striking Barbados characteristic is that it is the most isolated of Caribbean islands. Its nearest neighbours St. Vincent and St. Lucia lie 150 km to the west. It has been suggested that its relatively remote position led to its later settlement and somewhat divergent cultural development over time. What must be stressed however is that even if Barbados witnessed a different occupation history over time because of its geographical position, its settlement was no less dense than that of other islands, indicating that Amerindians were perfectly capable of finding the island and settling it.

3.4.7.2. History of Barbados archaeology

The first archaeologist to visit Barbados and study Barbadian prehistory was Jesse Walter Fewkes in 1902 (Fewkes 1915) and 1904 (Holmes 1907), but the first archaeological observations were recorded as early as the mid-18th century by Reverend Griffith Hughes, who speaks of the digging up of idols and Indian caves, and includes some illustrations of Amerindian artefacts in his book (Hughes 1750). Lovén (1924, 1935) studied collections from Barbados, Roach (1936, 1938a/b/c, 1939) and Barton (1953) provided an overview of avocational findings throughout the island, and McKusick (1960) collected ceramics from a few sites in 1957, but no controlled excavations took place until those of the Bullens at Chancery Lane and a few other sites (Bullen 1966; Bullen and Bullen 1968b). Incidental work (some of it historical) took place on the island after that (Loftfield 1993; Taylor 1983; Wing 1993), but in the 1980s and 1990s, the archaeology of Barbados became synonymous with the name Drewett and the rest of his team, who uncovered and published a wealth of information on Amerindian life on Barbados (Drewett 1993, 2004; Drewett ed. 1991, 2000, 2007; Drewett and Harris 1991; Hackenberger 1988; Harris 1987, 1989, 1993, 1995; Harris and Hinds 1995). One downside of Drewett's extensive work at a number of sites is his neglect of the dozens of other sites on Barbados. A number of sites have been so cursorily discussed that one is furnished with no information on the nature of the finds recovered or the criteria that determine site type ascription. While Drewett recognizes 54 Amerindian settlements on Barbados, it seems more prudent to only classify excavated sites with relatively abundant remains as settlements. Equally confusing is the lack of attention paid by Drewett to past discoveries on Barbados (particularly of Roach and Barton), resulting (one suspects) in a number of sites bearing two or three different names in the archaeological literature and a number of others disappearing from the map altogether.[54] The situation is compounded by (coastal) construction activities, which have seen large stretches of the Barbadian coastline modified; that is built up, extended or reduced. At present, there is little or no pre-Colonial archaeology being undertaken on the island, although a Caribbean archaeologist was temporarily hired as a university lecturer by UWI Barbados.

3.4.7.3. Habitation history Barbados (fig. 3.7)

Barbados was sparsely settled in the earliest pre-Colonial times. To date, there is only the barest of evidence of aceramic or preceramic activity, at the Heywoods/Port St. Charles site (Drewett 2007). One Strombus gigas shell was radiocarbon dated to the third/second millennium BC (see also Appendix 2), and many associated shell adzes are assumed to date to the same period (Drewett 1993; Drewett ed. 2007:9-13). The Early Ceramic Age fares better in occupancy, with 18 sites falling in this period, one of which, Goddards, has radiocarbon dates that fall deep in the early phase of the Early Ceramic Age. The sites are more or less evenly distributed around the coast, but with a small concentration in the south-west including the site Goddards. The sparse settlement is underscored by the great distances between site clusters, generally some 15 km. The early phase of the Late Ceramic Age sees a marginally denser occupation of Barbados with 23 sites, the majority of which overlie earlier Saladoid sites. Again, site location is more or less even, with a slight concentration in the northern part of the island. This period sees the first "inland" site appear, Greenland, located about 1.5 km from the coast. There is a veritable explosion of Suazan Troumassoid sites, 50 in total, more or less evenly distributed along the coast, with a remarkable cluster of sites in the north-east quadrant. Of the 50 sites, twenty are located atop a Troumassan site, and twelve atop a Saladoid site. Cluffs A and Brandons seem to have been reoccupied after a lull in early phase Late Ceramic Age activity. Three inland sites, between 1.5 and 2.5 km from the coast, are known for this period, two of which are cave

54 Emblematic of this process is the enigma of the Land's End site, a number of whose remarkable post-Saladoid artefacts are on display in the Barbados museum. I have been unable to find out who collected these artefacts and the toponym Land's End has disappeared from Barbadian maps, if it was even ever an official place name (Carrington *et al.* 2004:150). It is highly likely however that Indian River and Land's End are one and the same site.

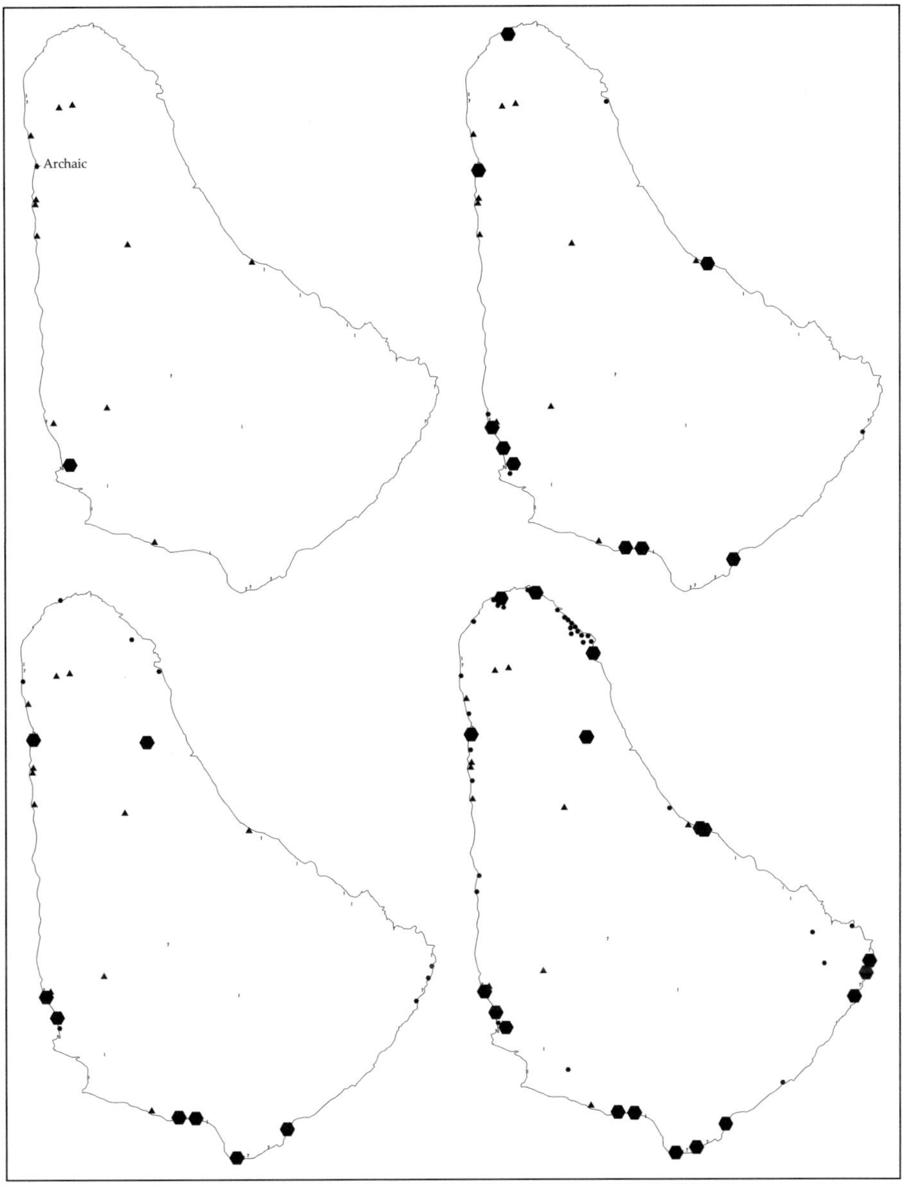

Figure 3.7. Barbados site pattern, (top left to right) early phase of the Early Ceramic Age (+ Archaic), late phase of the Early Ceramic Age, (bottom left to right) early phase of the Late Ceramic Age, late phase of the Late Ceramic Age.

sites. Three sites yielded non-diagnostic ceramics and nine sites cannot be ascribed to any cultural period. There is one petroglyph site at Springhead and a number of caves appear to have been lived in briefly or used for some other purpose.

3.4.7.4. Barbados ceramics

The majority of the Barbados ceramics are housed at the Barbados Museum. The ceramics have been extensively described by Harris (1991, 2000). The Florida Museum of Natural History has ceramics from a number of Barbados sites, derived from the Bullens' surveys and excavations (Bullen and Bullen 1968b). The Museum of the American Indian holds Fewkes' 1912 collection; the Göteborg museum has some Barbadian artefacts, as does the Yale Peabody Museum of Archaeology and Ethnology at Harvard University (Boomert 1987a). Furthermore, the Cambridge University Museum of Archaeology and Anthropology has a 19th century collection from Bathsheba and Maxwell, the H.W. Fielden collection (Harris and Drewett 1995), and the British Museum's Chester collection likewise comprises artefacts from Barbados (Boomert 1987a; Lovén 1935).

Boomert (1987a) was the first to systematically analyse Barbadian ceramics, proposing a sequence of local complexes tied in with Rouse's series. He coined the name Chancery Lane 1 for the modified/Palo Secan/Barrancan-influenced Saladoid, Chancery Lane 2 for the Troumassan Troumassoid ceramics and Peak Bay and Indian Mound for the Suazan Troumassoid assemblages (Boomert 1987a). Cayo ceramics have not been found on Barbados, nor have early Saladoid ceramics. For the last two decades, pottery from Barbados has been studied comprehensively by Mary Hill Harris (Harris 1991, 2000, 2007b), who has further detailed the individual stylistic traits of the assemblages of a number of sites.

Comparing Barbados's ceramic assemblages to those of the other Windward Islands, a number of differences can be noted, particularly within the Suazan Troumassoid assemblages. One major distinction is the absence of U- or V-shaped griddle legs at sites in Barbados. Rather, the main legs are straight and tubular, and many have an inflection point towards the top or a modelled feature resembling a knee joint (see also Chapter 5, section 5.3.7). This trait seems to be unique to Barbados. Also, while finger-indented rims occur throughout the Windwards, many late Barbados vessels have fingernail-indented rims, often in multiple rows, as well as a range of other indentations or punctations, likely created with a tube or stick (see also Chapter 5, section 5.3.6).

3.5. Concluding remarks

In this chapter, the methodologies underlying site pattern archaeology and ceramic classifications in the Windward Islands were discussed, followed by an overview of the history of archaeology on the individual Windward Islands, including site patterns and the characteristics of ceramic assemblages. In the following chapter, these site patterns will be analysed in unison (and in part updated with recalibrated radiocarbon dates) to determine whether any general patterns emerge from the individual island patterns, and to gain a better understanding of the site patterns and ultimately arrive at a (re)construction of a Windward Island settlement system.

Chapter 4

WINDWARD ISLANDS RECALIBRATED SETTLEMENT SEQUENCE AND CERAMIC AGE SETTLEMENT SYSTEM

4.1. Windward Islands (sequence of) settlement, recalibrated

For a long time now, Caribbean archaeologists have been relying on relative, cultural chronologies to establish the date of settlement and site-activities. The problems surrounding cultural chronologies are evident: material can tend to be culturally non-diagnostic and even when it is diagnostic, the question becomes, of what exactly? In the worst case, ceramics cannot be differentiated over a 2000 year-period, *i.e.* from early Saladoid right up to Colonial period Afro-Caribbean ware. In slightly better cases, a distinction can at least be drawn between Saladoid, post-Saladoid and historic period, and if the material is particularly diagnostic it can be classified down to the subseries or to a particular style (*e.g.* Caliviny, Cayo). But even in this best case, we are still dealing with a rather coarse resolution: a subseries can be dated to a time-span of some 300 or 400 years, and in some cases longer still. When this problem is combined with the heterogeneous (temporal and locational) character of material distribution over (an) island(s), dating with any level of precision becomes a hazardous enterprise.

There are various approaches towards getting a better grasp of Caribbean settlement sequence and site chronologies. First of all, to improve cultural classifications of material, ceramics are being subjected to detailed compositional study. Research suggests that provided the sherd is large enough, distinctions can be drawn between periods on the basis of differences in the chaîne opératoire *i.e.* selection of raw materials, addition of temper materials and manufacturing choices in terms of *e.g.* morphology, finishing and firing (Hofman and Jacobs 2003). Ultimately, this research may be equally suited to determining regional variations in contemporary assemblages as it is to detecting diachronic changes. Second, a greater number of controlled settlement excavations should once and for all refine cultural classifications on the basis of stratigraphical levels and accompanying radiocarbon dates. A third approach is to gather more radiocarbon dates, which are noticeably lacking for many Lesser Antillean archaeological sites. In this respect, recent work by Erlandson and Moss (1999) is illuminating: rather than employ radiocarbon dating only at a few large, excavated sites, they wielded it as a surveying tool, dating countless small, ephemeral and exposed sites (often with non-diagnostic remains) along the coast of Oregon. Concurrently, there is a need to perform some chronometric hygiene (Spriggs 1989), as certain radiocarbon dates still circulating in the literature are either uncalibrated, not corrected for marine reservoir effect, are from an unreliable context, or were simply established too long ago to be trusted. Fitzpatrick (2006) undertook just such a task, but discounted many dates.

For the present research, 78 Windward Island radiocarbon dates were taken on board, recalibrated and corrected for the marine reservoir effect (*cf.* Stuiver *et al.* 1986). This resulted in a number of dates becoming considerably younger, rendering some Early and Late Ceramic Age dates late phase rather than early phase, or even Colonial rather than late phase Late Ceramic Age (see also Appendix 2). The following section details this calibrated chronology, providing a sweeping overview of the settlement of the region as a whole through time. Of the 78 dates, one proved Archaic, 24 were purely Early Ceramic Age, seven stretched from the Early to Late Ceramic Age, 31 were purely Late Ceramic Age, eight stretched from the Late Ceramic Age into Colonial times, and one date was purely Colonial.

Early Ceramic Age

Judging from the sparse radiocarbon dates, the Saladoid movement into the Antilles occurred in several stages in a non-linear and seemingly indiscriminate fashion (Callaghan 2001; Haviser 1997; Hofman and Hoogland 2004; Keegan 2004). The oldest radiocarbon dates come from Fond-Brûlé on Martinique and fall roughly between 500 calBC and calAD 300. There is even a pre-500 calBC date, but this may be unreliable, as there have been problems with radiocarbon dates for this site (see Bérard 2004:26 for a discussion hereof). While the early dates for Martinique are exceptional within the Windward Islands, there seems to be no reason to discount them as unreliable outright; the Lesser Antillean archipelago harbours a number of equally old if not older dates: Trants and Radio Antilles on Montserrat, Hope Estate on St. Martin and Morel on Guadeloupe all have dates within the range 500 calBC (or earlier) to AD 1 (Hofman and Hoogland 1999; Petersen 1996). Looking back past the southern periphery of the Windward Islands, one encounters a 381-37 calBC date range at 2-sigma for Trinidad's Cedros site. Trinidad's neighbour Tobago has no radiocarbon dates earlier than about calAD 550, though on the basis of ceramic style, its earliest occupation can be pushed back a few centuries (Boomert 2000). Barbados appears to have been occupied next, with radiocarbon dates for the Goddard site falling within the (admittedly wide) 2-sigma ranges of 402-192 calBC and 236 calBC - calAD 394 (see also Appendix 2). The colonization sequence continues with a 2–sigma calAD 21-661 date for St. Vincent's Buccament West site and first to sixth century calAD date ranges for Martinique's Vivé, Fond Brûlé and Lasalle sites. The Grenadines and St. Lucia are apparently settled later, with a range of fourth to seventh century dates and Grenada's Pearls site now dates calAD 481 to 815 at 2-sigma. No radiocarbon dates are available for Dominica (and there is precious little material to examine), but northern neighbour Guadeloupe was certainly inhabited around the same time as the other islands, if not earlier, leading one to think Dominica would not have seen a much different occupation date. By calAD 500 then, all the Windward Islands had seen Amerindian occupancy (*cf.* Boomert 2000; Fitzpatrick 2006; Hofman *et al.* 2007; see also Appendix 2).

Late Ceramic Age

The majority of the Windward Islands were continually occupied throughout the Late Ceramic Age, as attested by numerous radiocarbon dates for this period. Some forty dates either centre on or stretch into the (early/late phase of the) Late Ceramic Age, until calAD 1300. Furthermore, all islands represented in the sample except Union Island and St. Vincent have dates that fall within the later stages of the late phase of the Late Ceramic Age (*i.e.* post-calAD 1300), seven of these later dates extend into the early Colonial period, and one date falls entirely within that era. One interesting phenomenon on the islands of Martinique and Barbados, and, less convincingly St. Vincent, is that of a dating gap between the late phase of the Early Ceramic Age and the late phase of the Late Ceramic Age. Although there are just five dates for St. Vincent, making it very hard to draw any meaningful conclusions, none of Martinique's 21 dates and only two of Barbados's twelve dates even encroach on the period between roughly calAD 700 and 1000 at 2-sigma, let alone cover the entire range.

Discussion

Concerning the Early Ceramic Age, in the past few years, the radiocarbon-dating plot has thickened, with early dates in the Leeward Islands being upheld and some of the early dates in the Windward Islands (particularly those of Martinique) being dispelled as unreliable (Bérard 2004). The continued absence of fresh early dates for the Windwards or Trinidad and Tobago (despite a considerable research focus on the Early Ceramic Age) has led some researchers to postulate that the migration was anything but a steady uni-directional wave of advance over the stepping-stone islands, but rather a swift migration up the islands with only temporary stop-overs or a direct leap across the sea, followed by back-migration down the chain once Puerto Rico had been reached and settled and/or later infilling from the mainland as groups continued to migrate to the islands (Curet 2005; Keegan 2004; Haag 1965; Wilson 2007). In this scenario, the islands are not being colonized in turn all the way up to the Greater Antilles, in the shape of a patient process driven by population growth, the reaching of carrying capacity, ensuing settlement fissioning and populations advancing onwards in search of new land (Keegan 1985; see also Chapter 2). Rather, it is suggested that the first horticulturalists were driven by an impetuous, exploratory urge that only subsided upon their reaching the large island of Puerto Rico. The homogeneity of widely separated ceramic assemblages of the early phase of the Early Ceramic Age would appear to provide additional backing for this hypothesis (but see Keegan 2001 and section 5.2 for qualification of the connotations of the so-called Saladoid veneer).

Of course, there is a danger in letting ourselves be led to premature conclusions by the handful of radiocarbon dates currently at our disposal. Also, it seems somewhat illogical that fertile islands like Grenada, St. Vincent, Martinique and St. Lucia would be skipped in favour of the smaller islands of the Leeward Islands and the equally promising yet far more distant Virgin Islands and Puerto Rico. One must remember that these were pioneering populations surviving on a very narrow margin, who needed a safety net to fall back on in times of environmental or social stress. In the case of the Antilles, this net would have been provided by one of two things: proximity to neighbouring island communities and proximity to communities in their homeland. So even if the direct leap theory is correct, we need to explain the avoidance of the Windward Islands or, in other words, the attraction of the Leeward Islands and Puerto Rico. The attraction of a relatively large island like Puerto Rico to colonists from the mainland can be readily understood considering its many river valleys with large tracts of fertile land. But why would the small Leeward Islands be selected over the Windwards? Admittedly, the presence of extensive reef and bank systems provide for cornucopian marine resources in the Leeward Islands, but marine resources would have been relatively rich in the Windward Islands too, and larger tracts of land would have been available for agriculture and the hunting and gathering of terrestrial floral and faunal resources.

It would seem that there are two possibilities: (1) the direct leap theory is essentially correct, and explanations for it have to be sought in the realm of replicating familiar surroundings and lifeways, superior Amerindian navigational skills eliminating the problem of distance, and perhaps interaction with or reliance upon the resident Archaic populations (see also Hofman *et al.* in press); (2) there is a paucity of settlement archaeology and available radiocarbon dates, or Windward Island settlement was sufficiently limited during this early phase so as to leave little evidence, yielding an incomplete reflection of the actual situation. The more research is done, the more dates will hopefully become available, pointing either to an incremental colonization of the islands (albeit by successive mainland groups rather than by one expanding group of migrants; see also Hofman *et al.* in press), or supporting once and for all the direct leap hypothesis.

Concerning the Late Ceramic Age, the same danger highlighted above of drawing premature conclusions pertains. Having said that, the large number of late phase Late Ceramic Age and even Colonial period dates is not surprising given the strong presence of Amerindians in the region until late Colonial times as attested by numerous (ethno)historical sources (*cf.* Anonyme de Carpentras 2002; Breton 1999; Labat 1979; Le Breton 1998). It is somewhat ironic that four sites on Barbados can be placed in this very late era though, while Barbados was one of the very few islands not inhabited by Amerindians at the time of the Europeans' permanent arrival on the scene (Dutton, Gordan and Turner in Barton 1953:34; Hughes 1750; Ligon 2003). Apparently there had been a sizeable enough population in the early 16th century however to justify the undertaking of Spanish slaving operations (Figueroa in Barton 1953:25-26). Similarly, St. Vincent is the one island indubitably inhabited by Amerindians up until and even after 1797, yet dates extend no later than calAD 1282. No significance should be attached to this phenomenon however, as it is undoubtedly attributable to restricted sample and sampling bias.[55] The question remains whether the Amerindians encountered by the Europeans in the late 16th and early 17th century were descendants of those that were occupying the islands during the late phase of the Late Ceramic Age, namely carriers of the Suazan Troumassoid culture. Allaire (1991:721) believes

55 Furthermore, the dates for the Banana Bay site on Balliceaux, the island to which the Vincentian Black Caribs were initially deported, accord very well with the established historical time frame.

they were not, and that Suazan Troumassoid culture expired before AD 1450. As yet, this hypothesis cannot be proved on the basis of the limited number and restricted distribution of dates available. The situation is somewhat similar in the Leeward Islands to the north, where occupation seems to decrease dramatically after calAD 1350/1400. In fact, Amerindian presence is so weakly attested that archaeologists believe the area was depopulated to such a degree as to be virtually uninhabited by the early colonial period. Carib raiding, the encroaching Taíno influence sphere or environmental stress are some of the reasons that have been proposed for this large-scale abandonment (Crock 2000; Hofman and Hoogland 1999; Hofman *et al.* 2008; see also section 1.2).

Concerning the dating gap between the late phase of the Early Ceramic Age and the late phase of the Late Ceramic Age evident on Martinique and Barbados, it would be worth revisiting this phenomenon as further radiocarbon dates are gathered to determine whether it is coincidental, a result of a research bias towards either the Early Ceramic Age or the late phase of the Late Ceramic Age on these islands, or whether it represents a localised response to larger events of this period, such as the drier conditions (see section 2.3) and a concomitant slight drop in site number (see below).

Having discussed the absolute, radiometric site data, we now turn to site data derived from (ceramic) material assemblage classification, to examine site type and patterning through time.

4.2. Windward Island site patterns: an analysis

> *"This situation is typical of many locations we have visited on the windward sides of Grenada and St. Lucia where sites producing thick pottery of the Suazey series are in the last stages of erosion by sea and wind"* (Bullen and Bullen 1972:12).

The following section will deal with site patterns in the Windward Islands. This overview should yield a regional perspective on island organization, site function and site hierarchies through time. While offering a broad take on general issues, this overview is of rather low resolution and approximating or conjectural in certain aspects through lack of excavation or surveying. Furthermore, a number of problems in the realm of site pattern archaeology in the Windward Islands hamper the analysis of data. These will be reviewed briefly below.

The first major problem concerns survey methodology and coverage, not just at the island level, but also within islands at the micro-regional level. As alluded to in Chapter 1, and as has become clear from the foregoing overview, certain islands have seen more research and fieldwork than others: Grenada and Dominica are perhaps the most understudied relatively speaking, whereas St. Lucia, Martinique and Barbados may be the best studied.

Furthermore, on those islands where fieldwork has been carried out, this research has not always covered the entire island, and may thus not be fully representative of an island's archaeological record. For instance, as a result of three fieldwork campaigns between 2002 and 2004 as well as much prior research, we have a relatively good picture of the archaeology of southern St. Lucia. However, the northern half of the island remains poorly studied, particularly the leeward coast, giving the (presumably) false impression of a less intense occupation. Similarly, for very understandable reasons, much fieldwork (with notable exceptions) has concentrated on the coastal parts of islands, where visibility and accessibility are generally greater, and archaeological fieldwork often more imperative in light of tourist developments. The unfortunate result is a heavy bias towards coastal areas, and the possible persistence of a hidden landscape further inland.

The third problem concerns the dating of many sites: with 65 non-diagnostic sites and 106 non-diagnostic Ceramic Age sites, a total of 37% of the entire site inventory cannot be assigned to any specific cultural period (see also Figure 4.2). While the non-diagnostic site tally will be hard to reduce, considering it is made up for the most part of petroglyph and rock carving sites, the tally of non-diagnostic Ceramic Age sites is unacceptably high. As long as relative dating methods are employed, sites that do not yield recognizable culturally-specific remains will continue to be earmarked merely dots on the map and therefore be of little value when it comes to determining (shifts in) settlement and site patterns through time.

As highlighted in section 1.3, the representativity of surface scatters for the situation below the surface is extremely questionable. Some of the doubts expressed at the start of this research have only been underscored by the subsequent enumeration and elaboration of the site patterns in the Windward Islands. The archaeological site patterns on most islands are inherently biased and inaccurate reflections of Amerindian settlement. Most islands exhibit the same generic site pattern: a chain of coast-hugging or near-coastal sites and a number of sites located some distance inland from the coast. A markedly different situation pertains to St Lucia. There too is present the all-familiar coast-hugging site pattern, but in addition, a dense pattern of sites has emerged from the areas located further inland (Hofman *et al.* 2004; Keegan *et al.* 2002, 2003). One could dismiss these findings as unique to St. Lucia, however unlikely that may be, but one would be hard pressed to deny the validity of this newly emerging pattern in the light of recent (subsurface) survey fieldwork on Martinique (Bright 2005, 2007) and St. Vincent (Callaghan 2007).

The explanation for the predominance of coastal sites in the archaeological record rests on a number of factors: first and foremost, modern-day habitation and infrastructure are most dense along the coast and construction activities most frequent, resulting in a higher potential for disturbing and uncovering Amerindian remains. An additional problem that was first noted as early as the 1960s is illegal beach sand mining and, increasingly, sea-sand dredging (*i.e.* Kaye *et al.* 2005), usually in aid of aforementioned construction. Secondly, even if no modern-day human activity is taking place at a coastal location, nature tends to step in and lend a hand by means of various taphonomical processes, chief among them being sedimentation, coastal erosion and hurricane and storm surge impacts (Crock and Petersen 2001; Delpuech 2004). Thirdly, archaeologists have tended to favour coastal survey routes, as they are often more easily traversed than interior routes, be it due to local topography, type and degree of vegetation and logistical accessibility. It comes as no surprise therefore that archaeologically empty stretches along the coast on site distribution maps can often be related to the obstructive presence of for instance mangrove vegetation.

In contrast, the Leiden/Florida and Leiden/Martinique surveys were designed to cover not only the coast but also interior areas, inasmuch as they were accessible. By expanding the dimensions of the area under survey, one is potentially increasing the odds of finding archaeological sites, particularly in hitherto largely ignored areas. This is absolutely crucial in escaping self-fulfilling prophecy survey designs that tend to characterize past site archaeology (though De Waal 2006 is a notable exception). A sentence like the following is not uncommon in archaeological literature: "Because previous studies have shown that Lucayan settlements were usually restricted to coastal habitats, these locations have been the focus of most research efforts" (Keegan 1992:68). However, there is always room for improvement, for once survey limits have been tackled and adjusted to make for more representative surveys, the survey methods need to be altered as well, particularly in settings where nature or man is not on hand to facilitate the archaeologist's work. In these cases, surface survey will be of little to no use, and must be replaced by intrusive archaeological methods such as test pit excavation or augering.[56] In extreme cases (such as around the Soufrière volcanoes on Dominica and St. Vincent), deposits may be buried underneath six metres or more of alluvial or volcanic sediment, practically out of reach of the archaeologist's probing tools.

Site classification

A lasting legacy of over a century of surface survey and excavation is that we are dealing with a sizeable site assemblage, although the characteristics of the sites in question are not always readily apparent. Through excavation, sites can fleshed out with more detail on type and dating, but in other cases, one has no idea whether the finds encountered on the surface are representative of the situation beneath the surface. Also, in the absence of diagnostic remains (generally decorated pottery), sites cannot be assigned to any given period. Additional intrusive testing is still required at many sites reported in the literature, to establish even their most basic characteristics. All in all, the site inventory at present numbers 642 pre-Colonial archaeological sites distributed over the seven large Windward Islands and thirteen of the smaller Grenadines.

To provide a realistic view of settlement and lifeways, a distinction was made between sites of different sizes and characters. Because this research draws upon the work of many different researchers, a number of determinations may require further testing in future, but it is believed that more is to be gained from the exercise than from effacing all variability by lumping sites together under a single nomer. Site classifications of previous researchers have been upheld if there is confidence in the determination or have been classified anew if the data permitted on the basis of the following criteria. As such, an individual lithic find represents one isolated find of a lithic artefact, for instance an axe or adze, and a number of lithic finds is a cluster of lithic artefacts, such as lithic debitage, a cache of numer-

56 In recent years, even ground penetrating radar has been tested for its potential for detecting pre-Columbian sub-surface remains, for instance on St. Vincent (Kocks Consult 2008).

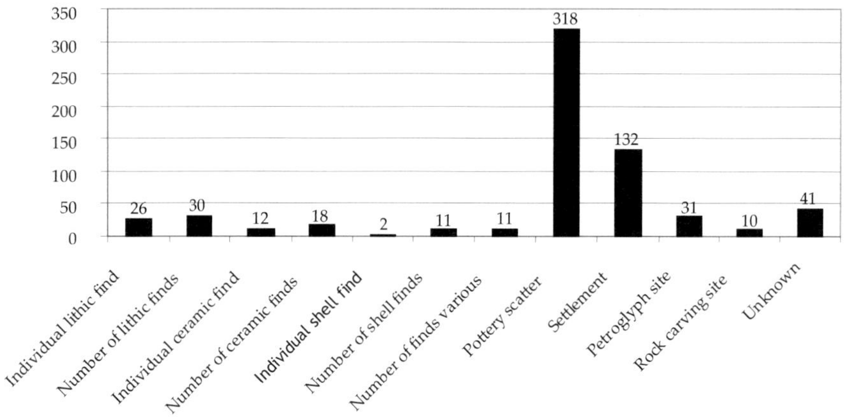

Figure 4.1. Histogram showing the various types of sites in the Windward Islands site inventory.

ous stone tools or a number of stone artefacts found relatively close together. An individual ceramic find represents one isolated find of a sherd or complete vessel, whereas a number of ceramic finds represent between two and five sherds found relatively close together. An individual shell find is one isolated find of a shell artefact or manuport. A number of shell finds represent a cluster of shell artefacts, such as shell debitage, a cache of numerous shell tools or a number of shell artefacts found relatively close together. A number of finds various entail a cluster of artefacts of varying nature, found relatively close together. A pottery scatter means a cluster of five sherds or over, either on the surface or subsurface. A settlement is a high-intensity pottery scatter (over 200 sherds) over a relatively widespread area and/or evidence of habitation such as presence of a shell midden, posthole features or hearths. Finally, there are petroglyph sites, abstract and pictographic man-made rock carvings, and rock carving sites, representing polissoirs or boulders/rocks upon which axes were allegedly ground and sharpened, resulting in cup-like depressions and long, narrow grooves. While hardly fully representative, this division is satisfactory as the groundwork preceding more intensive island-centred research. The 642 sites break down into various subtypes, as illustrated in Figure 4.1.

At over forty, the number of sites classified as unknown is too high, and needs lowering by intensive revisiting of sites themselves or by questioning colleagues if possible.

Site periodisation

Drawing on the results of the various strains of research discussed above, all but a number of non-diagnostic sites have furthermore been ascribed to a cultural period (in the general absence of radiocarbon dates, most sites are relatively dated by assigning material uncovered at them to an archaeological period or (sub)series). In some cases, prior research was of such a high standard that sites could be ascribed to local complexes rather than only subseries or series. Therefore, sites may be identified by Saladoid, Troumassan Troumassoid, Suazan Troumassoid, Cayo and/or Archaic components. That leaves a number of less precisely datable sites. Non-diagnostic ceramic sites are sites that have yielded ceramic material which cannot be assigned to any particular period within the Ceramic Age. Non-diagnostic sites are sites that have been reported or recorded in the literature but not furnished with any details regarding their character or recovered archaeological materials, or whose materials cannot be assigned to any particular period (such as petroglyph and rock carving sites, as well as lithic or undated shell finds). The 642 sites break down into various subcategories, as illustrated in Figure 4.2.

Having acknowledged and taken into account problems and possible biases, it is time to consider the site pattern and characteristics as they now stand diachronically and from a regional perspective. First, some raw data will be presented, which will then be contextualised and made relevant to matters of anthropological and archaeological interest such as human lifeways, shifting settlement strategies and general interaction with the (is)landscape. To help provide a human slant on the bare-bones archaeological data, some recourse will be made to (early) (ethno)historical accounts that make mention of aspects of Amerindian settlement and utilization of the islands. One significant impression that one gets from these accounts is the lack of uniformity inherent in descriptions of Amerindian lifeways across the islands and through time. That is partly a result of the different backgrounds, biases and experiences of the various writers themselves, but also partly attributable to developments over time and intrinsic cultural variability. In an area that – at least during the later Ceramic Age - took on the appearance of a "cultural mosaic" (Wilson 1993), we should expect a plethora of varying customs and behavioural patterns, perhaps overlying the foundations of a vaguely homogeneous mother culture. The chronicles, accounts and brief observations do not disappoint in this regard, as we shall see below. But first the data, which already provide a

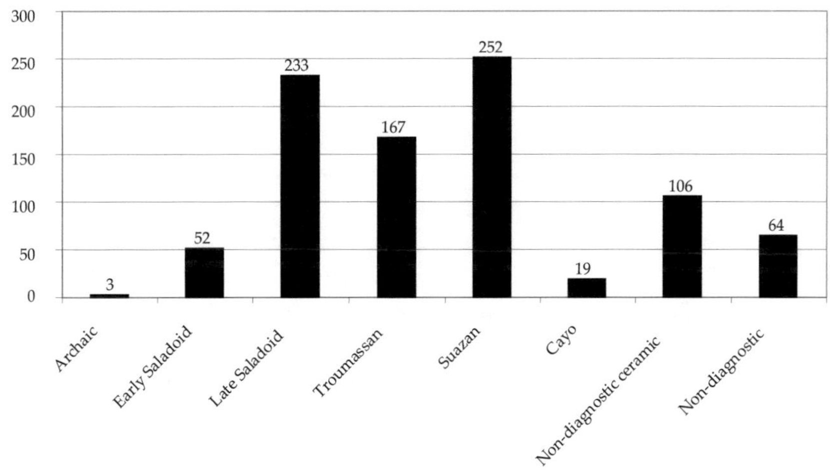

Figure 4.2. Histogram showing the various cultural components present across the Windward Islands site inventory.

number of interesting insights in their own right: Cayo is, as alluded to above, still an extremely rare occurrence in the Windward Islands. Furthermore, Troumassan Troumassoid, though stronger in presence, falls well short of both its predecessor and successor. While this may reflect a population slump between the late phases of the Early and Late Ceramic Age, one suspects that this statistic is more a failure to recognize the full extent of Troumassan remains, both in the past and to this day. By its very transitional nature, Troumassan lacks many of the diagnostic features so characteristic of Saladoid and Suazan pottery (see also section 3.3). Add to that the relatively short time frame within which Troumassan occurred when compared to the other two (sub)series, and it is clear why Troumassan has not been as readily discerned in the archaeological record.

More interesting and valuable statistics are for instance the fact that twenty-one sites are occupied or used apparently continuously until the Colonial period from the early phase of the Early Ceramic Age onwards. Another 88 sites date from the late phase of the Early Ceramic Age onwards, of which six stretch up to and potentially into the early Colonial period, an occupation span or use-life of potentially 1000-1500 years give or take the odd pauses between short-term abandonment and swift re-occupation or re-utilisation, which cannot be detected archaeologically. Another 34 sites may indicate precisely the kind of abandonment that is archaeologically visible, namely when an entire component is absent from a site's occupation history, in this case the Troumassan component between Saladoid and Suazan Troumassoid ones. This phenomenon has interesting ramifications for the drought debate, as has been extensively researched by Blancaneaux (2009). Alternatively, the component may have simply been overlooked or be present at another location in the vicinity, implying shifting settlement (see below for elaboration). Of the 232 sites with a late Saladoid component, 87 see no continuation in later periods and 22 (9.5%) see occupation continued into the early but not the late phase of the Late Ceramic Age. Of the 167 sites with a Troumassan component, 57 represent a new site location not utilized in the foregoing Early Ceramic Age (though one site had an early phase Early Ceramic Age component). 119 of the 167 sites (71.3%) see continued occupation in the late phase of the Late Ceramic Age, suggesting more stable conditions between the early and late phases of the Late Ceramic Age, especially considering that there are fewer sites relatively speaking. Of the 252 sites with a Suazan component, 97 represent new locations, the rest represent re-occupation of Early Ceramic Age sites or continued occupation of early phase Late Ceramic Age sites.

On the face of site numbers and periodisation alone, it would appear that the late phase of the Early Ceramic Age saw the Windward Islands well settled, only for the islands to witness a population slump in the early phase of the Late Ceramic Age before things picked up again during the late phase of the Late Ceramic Age, when islands apparently saw their densest occupation. But what happens to this view when we bring site type into the equation? The early phase of the Early Ceramic Age sees 31 sites categorized as settlements, the late phase of the Early Ceramic Age sees 99 settlements, dropping to 84 during the early phase of the Late Ceramic Age, and rising to 100 in the late phase of the Late Ceramic Age. Nine of these settlements have yielded Cayo ceramics, as have two holdovers from

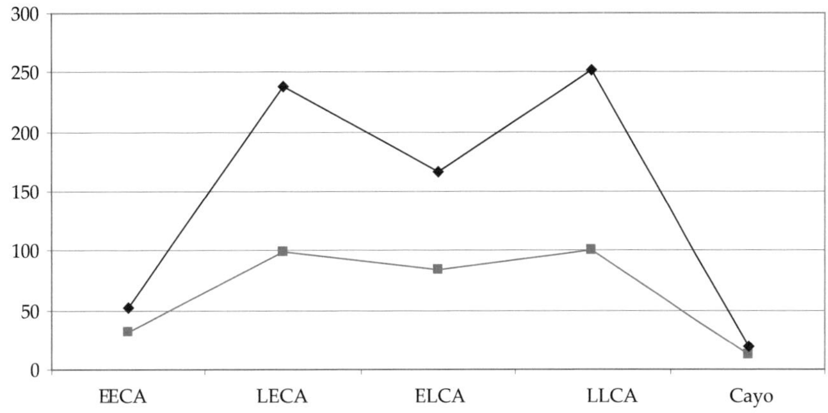

Figure 4.3. Chart showing the absolute frequencies of Windward Island sites (upper line) and settlements (lower line) across different cultural periods. Though exaggerated in this figure, in relative terms, the early phase Late Ceramic Age slump is certainly less marked in settlements than in sites.

the early phase of the Late Ceramic Age, potentially pushing occupation of these settlements into early Colonial times. One site (Argyle, St. Vincent) appears to represent a single component Cayo settlement. While reflecting the general trend of decline during the early phase of the Late Ceramic Age yielded by the general site pattern, the contrast is much less marked (a drop of 15.2% versus 28.1%), suggesting that settlement remained more stable over time and that the difference between the periods mainly concerns activity areas and other non-settlement sites (see also figure 4.3). The 106 non-diagnostic ceramic sites could also have a bearing on this trend, as most pottery that is not easily recognisable as Saladoid or Suazan Troumassoid runs the risk of being classified as non-diagnostic ceramic. Judging from the data at hand, and being mindful of the aforementioned pitfalls and problems, a fair case can be made for occupation in the Windward Islands being remarkably even and stable over a millennium, from the late phase of the Early Ceramic Age until the end of the late phase of the Late Ceramic Age.

Turning to consider not just general site and settlement statistics but rather specific settlement occupation histories, it is possible first of all to rank settlements on the basis of length of occupation, as measured by ceramic series present among settlement assemblages. Of course, this is a somewhat crude gauge, considering the long time periods associated with ceramic series. However, at the very least, multiple-component settlements evidence re-occupation of settlement sites across many centuries, entailing a rudimentary form of social memory (Tilley 1994) and attachment to place. At most, multi-component settlements point to long-lived, stable settlement locations, inhabited in uninterrupted fashion for many centuries.

Surprisingly, there are significantly more multi-component settlements than single-component, and significantly more consecutive than non-consecutive components (see figure 4.4). It is also interesting to see that the more components a settlement has, the more likely these are to be consecutive.

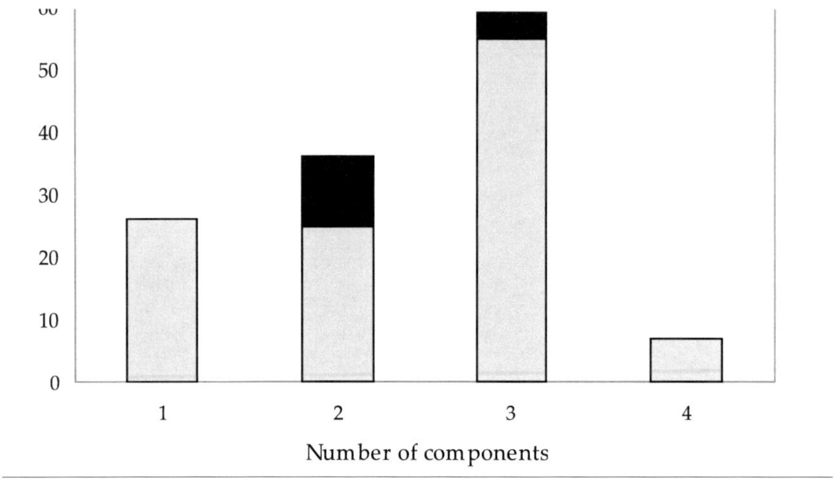

Figure 4.4. Chart showing the number of single- and multi-component settlements in the Windward Islands. Grey represents consecutive components, black represents non-consecutive components.

Breaking down the region-wide data to the level of individual islands, a number of interesting patterns emerge. First of all, Grenada and St. Vincent are the only two islands that harbour settlements with four consecutive components, *i.e.* settlements inhabited during the entire Ceramic Age. In addition, these islands harbour another eight (Grenada) and fourteen (St. Vincent) three-component settlements, the majority of which are consecutive, cementing these islands' top ranking in terms of individual settlement history. Barbados and the Grenadines follow, with just over half of their settlements comprising three consecutive components. St. Lucia is next, as just under half of its settlements comprise three consecutive components, while Martinique (under a quarter three-component settlements) and Dominica (one non-consecutive multi-component settlement) bring up the rear (see also figure 4.5).

Settlement location

Having discussed typology, periodisation and ranking, we now move to a consideration of locational aspects of settlement. Antecedents of this sort of research question have already been discussed (Chapter 3, section 3.1); how do their findings accord with those of this Windward Islands research? To start with the general before moving to the particular, researchers have noted that the earliest Ceramic Age settlement on Martinique and other islands concentrated in the north-east quadrant of the islands (see sections 2.4 and 3.1.1; *cf.* Bérard 2004; Haviser 1997; Rouse 1992). While the situation on Martinique is indubitable, the hypothesis loses much of its strength when extended to the rest of the Windward Islands (*cf.* Callaghan 2007). While it is a worthwhile enterprise to attempt to elucidate settlement mobility at a higher resolution than long-lasting Ceramic periods, previ-

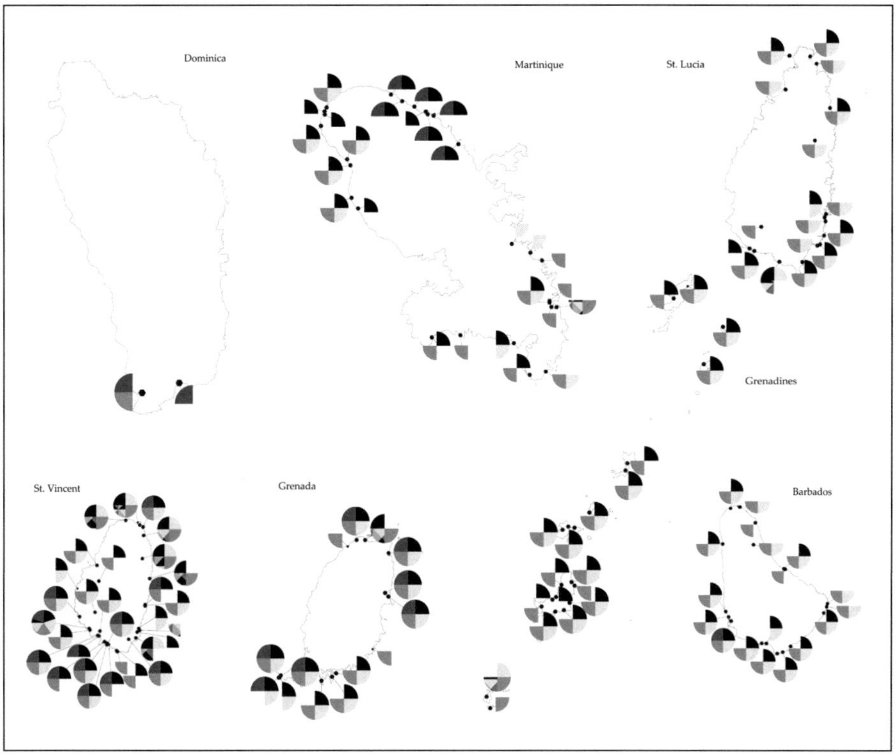

Figure 4.5. Windward Islands settlement histories on the basis of cultural components present (dark grey early phase Early Ceramic Age, black late phase Early Ceramic Age, light grey early phase Late Ceramic Age, medium grey late phase Late Ceramic Age, check Cayo).

ous studies such as that of Haviser (1997) tend to be handicapped by a limited site inventory[57], making various inferences statistically rather meaningless (50% is not as impressive when it refers to five sites as when it refers to 50). There are other problems, including the fact that artefact comparison (Haviser 1997:65) is barely at a level that it can differentiate between earliest and simply early or later Cedrosan Saladoid, particularly given the deceptive homogeneity of the ware over quite a long period of time (see also Chapter 5, section 5.2). Regardless of all that, Haviser's Early Ceramic Age A period Goddards site is located in the south-west of Barbados. The Windward Island sites included in Haviser's Early Ceramic Age B period are located in the south (Chancery Lane [BAR-12], Kingstown Post Office [SVI-48], Arnos Vale [SVI-03/04]), south-west (Black Point [GRE-02/03], Buccament West [SVI-14], Diamant [MAR-33]), west (Chatham Bay [GRS-56], although it hardly makes sense to speak of directionality on tiny Union Island), north (Vieille Case [DOM-63][58]) and north-east (Pearls [GRE-29], Vivé [MAR-121], Lassalle [MAR-66], Grande Anse [SLU-70]), which bespeaks little patterning. Callaghan (2007:19) noted that the south-west quadrant was preferred dur-

57 His site inventory numbers just 35 for the Lesser Antilles and Puerto Rico (Haviser 1997: table 7.1).

58 Vieille Case is in fact not regarded as a settlement in this study, but as a mere pottery scatter (see also Appendix 1).

ing the Early Ceramic Age on St. Vincent, although there are numerous Early Ceramic Age settlement sites along the north and east coasts and inland from the west coast (see subsection 3.4.3.3). The present inventory further indicates a similar preference for the southern part of the island on Barbados, St. Lucia and Dominica, whereas Grenada exhibits an almost even spread between south-west and north-eastern quadrants. Remarkable is the absence of settlements along the (central) leeward coast of all islands bar Barbados and Martinique; on these latter two islands, the opposite, central windward coast is largely empty (see Figures 4.6 and 4.7 as well as various island headings under section 3.4).

Regarding the early phase of the Late Ceramic Age, the present inventory indicates a number of changes in settlement location and intensity. Dominica has no settlement sites attributable to this period at all, nor does Bequia in the Grenadines. However, Ile de Ronde sees initial occupation during this period and occupation on the other Grenadines remains relatively stable. Martinique's north-east coast is apparently abandoned, the north-west and south continue to be settled and a number of new settlements are established along the central windward coast. St. Lucia sees a denser settlement of its northern and south-eastern part, with a slight decline in settlement along the southern coastline. St. Vincent experiences a decline in settlement in most parts, and interestingly, a number of inland settlements disappear or shift towards the coast during this period. Little changes on Grenada, bar the abandonment of a couple of settlements in the south-western quadrant. On Barbados, the only changes are the abandonment of settlement at the northernmost tip and along the windward coast, in favour of a settlement some distance inland in the north (see Figure 4.8 and also various island headings under section 3.4).

Turning to the late phase of the Late Ceramic Age, we see renewed occupation of southernmost Dominica and of the southern coast of Martinique, stable occupation of Martinique's north-western quadrant, intensified settlement in the south-east and the continued shunning of the north-eastern coastline. On St. Lucia, settlement remains dense in the south-east, appears intensified in the north and shifts from coastal to inland in the south. St. Vincent's south and eastern coasts are more intensively settled in the late phase of the Late Ceramic Age, with other areas exhibiting little change. Settlement of the Grenadines picks up as well, particularly on Bequia, Cannouan, Carriacou and Ile de Caille, which sees its first occupation during this period. On Grenada, the north coast is slightly more densely settled, and settlement in the south-western corner shifts further north along the coast. Finally, Barbados sees greatly intensified settlement along the southern, eastern and northern coasts (see figure 4.9 and also various island headings under section 3.4).

Considering the greatly expanded site inventory now at our disposal for the Windward islands (see subsections 3.4.1.3 through 3.4.7.3), one has to conclude that Amerindian settlements in the Windward Islands at least do not conform to any strict locational patterning at a general level. This really should come as no surprise, for there would be no reason for Amerindians to conform to a spatial pattern that has no bearing on the micro-environmental conditions or indeed nec-

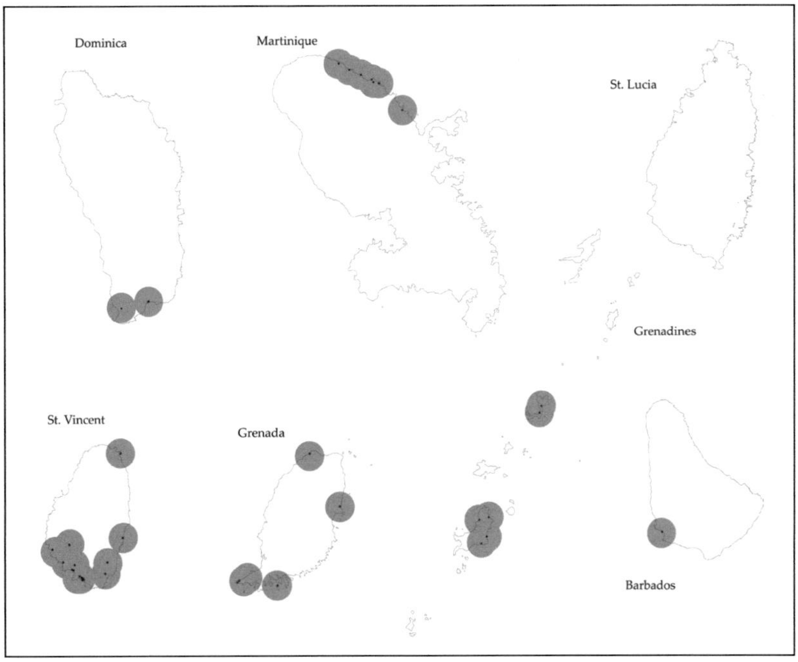

Figure 4.6. Settlement territories (3 km radius) during the early phase of the Early Ceramic Age.

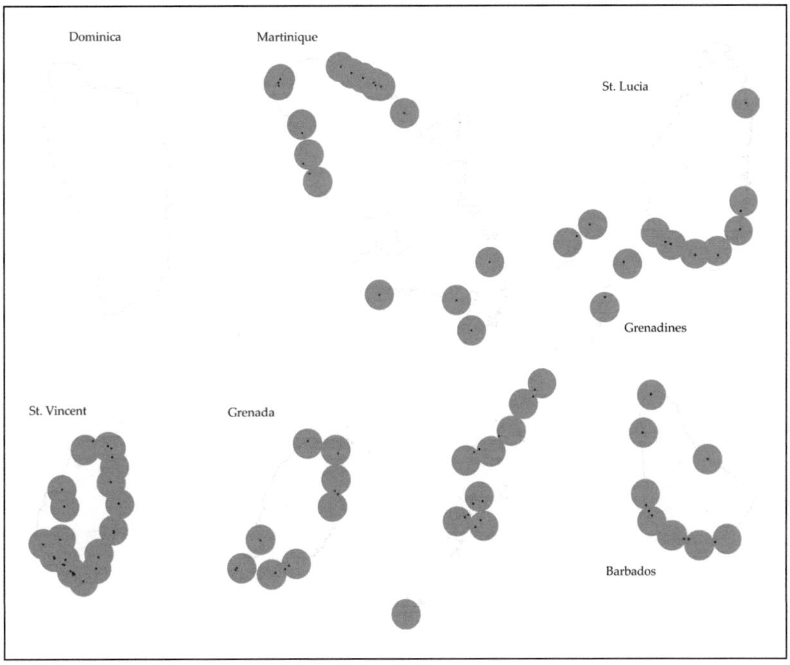

Figure 4.7. Settlement territories (3 km radius) during the late phase of the Early Ceramic Age.

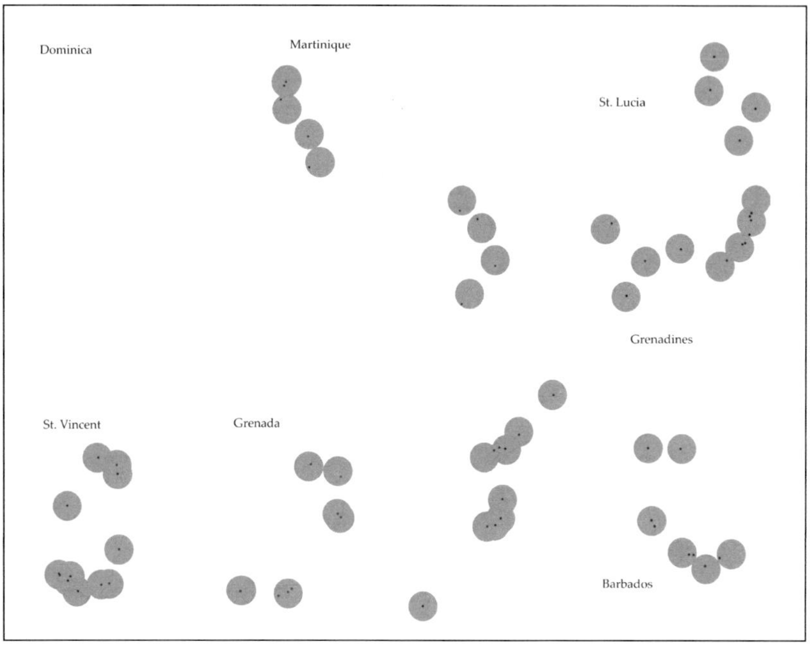

Figure 4.8. Settlement territories (3 km radius) during the early phase of the Late Ceramic Age.

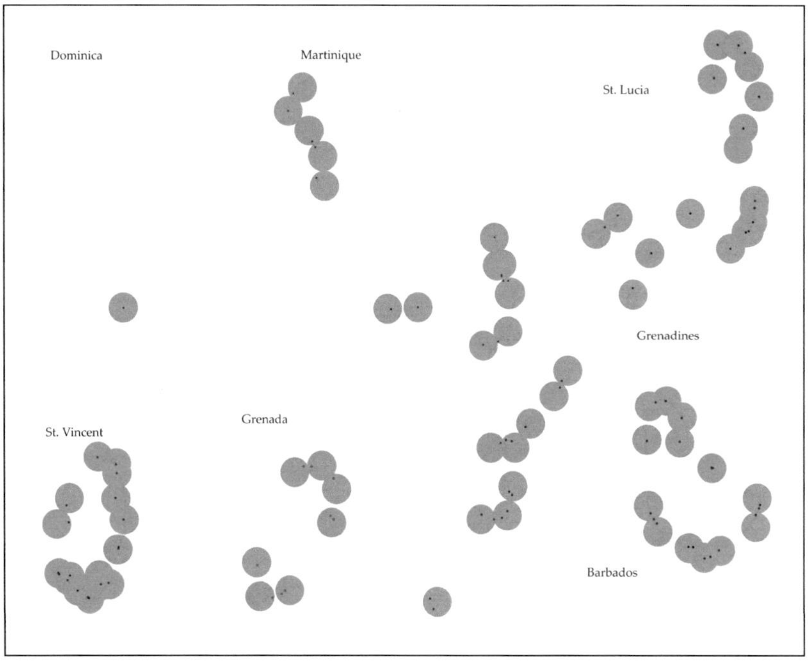

Figure 4.9. Settlement territories (3 km radius) during the late phase of the Late Ceramic Age.

essarily conform to environmental strictures at all. Having said that, a number of islands demonstrate a distinct pattern of settlement of extremities, rendering the central part of the island void of settlement. This is particularly true of Grenada and Martinique, throughout the entire Ceramic Age, and to a lesser degree of St. Lucia and Dominica (only during a certain period).

Another locational aspect that has been discussed in the archaeological literature is site distance from the shore. Haviser has earlier pointed out that the overwhelming majority of Early Ceramic Age sites were located on the coastal strand or the coastal plain (Haviser 1997:67). This Windward Island inventory certainly upholds that statistic and extends it to the entire Ceramic Age, with 497 sites lying within 500 metres of the shore. However, notwithstanding the considerable fieldwork biases toward the coast, numerous sites and settlements have been discovered at inland locations, most notably on St. Vincent and St. Lucia, although (paene-)coastal sites greatly outnumber them. Furthermore, settlement sites are relatively under-represented, with the majority of inland sites being formed by pottery scatters and individual finds. Adapted survey designs and increasing development of the islands will undoubtedly reveal more sites in non-coastal locations in future. Perhaps the most important conclusion to draw from the foregoing is that despite being predominantly oriented towards the coastal ecotope from the start, the Amerindians occupied a number of (well-watered) inland locations as well and certainly made extensive use of this territory (see below).

4.3. Windward Island settlement system: an interpretation

Having acknowledged in Chapter 1 that site patterns are at best inferences, we shall now proceed to pile inference upon inference, in an attempt to render the Windward Island site patterns more than just dots on the map.

4.3.1. Settlement territories

Taking the site pattern of the Windward Islands at face value, a clear distinction can be drawn between large settlement sites and small, rather more ephemeral sites that lie within the daily round or catchment radius (Higgs and Vita-Finzi 1972) of the settlements. Whether these small sites represent the material reflection of various daily activities emanating from central settlements, or indeed whether such sites represent small-scale or temporary habitation away from large, well-established settlements is a moot point until such sites see (further) excavation. One possible approach to interpreting these enigmatic, small-scale finds, and particularly their relationship to the larger, better researched and more informative settlement sites, is to group all sites that fall within a certain radius of a larger settlement to that same settlement on the basis of period and/or proximity (in the absence of chronological information). To assume that all discovered sites were contemporaneous with the nearest settlement is admittedly somewhat unorthodox, but perhaps forgivable when considering that one retrieves only a fraction of what is actually present beneath the soil. While in no way all-encompassing or definitive, the hypothetical activity spheres radiating outwards from main settlements can be considered as a cautious approximation of some Amerindian engagements with the landscape. Needless to say, the catchment areas are circular and regular by default, and must be regarded as preliminary and uncalibrated to geographical and environment particularities (*cf.* Haviser 1993:240). Most notably, the catchment area concept is biased towards land, based as it is on the time spent covering a certain distance on foot. Travelling by water, much greater distances can be traversed, and greater loads carried in the same time. This insight was applied early on, for instance by Boomert (1985:114, 124), who determined that the shellfish catchment area of the Mayo and St. Joseph sites on Trinidad extended some 7.5 to 10 km and 14 km from them respectively.

A number of Caribbean archaeologists have dealt explicitly with the relationship between settlement sites and their surrounding environment, by furnishing these settlements with hypothetical settlement radii or catchment areas, though opinions differ as to how large or inclusive they should be made. Keegan (1992:83) adopted a 1.5–2 km site catchment radius for his study of Bahamanian site patterns. Haviser adopted a 3-km site catchment radius for his studies of settlements on Bonaire, Curaçao and St. Martin (Haviser 1987, 1989, 1993). Drewett (ed. 1991: figure 91) illustrates the range of activities that could have been undertaken both offshore Barbados and deep inland on the island (up to 10 km from the shore), but does not explicitly tie this information in to any one site or mention the concept of site catchment areas. Siegel (1993:317) referred to research carried out among the Kuikuru (by Carneiro), the Waiwai (by Mentore), the Yaruro (by Leeds) and the Siona and Secoya (by Vickers), before deciding to test a range of catchment radii (0.5, 1, 2 and 3 km) for Early Saladoid sites. Murphy and Healy (1995: figure 2) examined a similar range for the Muddy Bay site on Antigua, though starting at 1 km and extending it to 5 km. Boomert likewise invoked radii of 1, 2, 3 and 5 km for his analysis of the catchment area of the Early Ceramic Age Golden Grove site (Boomert 2000:370-373).

Under the same heading as small or ephemeral sites fall the many individual finds - generally stone axes or tools - dotted across the islands. Though frustratingly non-datable, these objects can afford some interesting insights within the context of site patterns and site systems. In a number of cases, such objects are found relatively near to or on the very spot of an identified Amerindian settlement or site, in which case it is reasonable to assume a functional relationship to that site. For example, the Balembouche area in southern St. Lucia harbours two very distinct sites. South of the main road lies Balembouche Estate (SLU-13), a large Amerindian settlement occupied from the late phase of the Early Ceramic Age onwards that has yielded copious amounts of pottery (see also Appendix 1). Across the road to the north lies the Morne Lezard (Balembouche Barnard) site (SLU-102), which has yielded numerous jasper flakes and dozens of stone axes of all shapes and sizes. On St. Vincent, there is the case of the site of Fancy Fields (SVI-35), which represents a number of stone axes, celts and a chisel, found in agricultural fields close to the site of Fancy (SVI-34) (see also Appendix 1). It does not require a great stretch of the imagination to regard these lithic finds as representing activities linked to the neighbouring settlement, perhaps related to agricultural activities, woodworking and procurement of natural resources within the wider periphery of the site (Bullen and Bullen 1972:62-63; see also Siegel 1993:284 for Amazonian ethnographic examples of agricultural field camps). Drewett (ed. 1991: figure 91) has referred to this landscape zone or resource area behind the settlement as the locus for tree felling, hunting, gathering, collecting and cultivating on Barbados (see also section 5.3 for (ethno)historical evidence). Recently, ethnoarchaeological research has been carried out among the Yanomamö to determine the spatial relationship between villages and garden plots (Craig and Chagnon 2006).

For this analysis, I am not interested directly in gaining a view of the availability of resources within a catchment area, but rather with the availability of land in general, which may be called a site's territory or territorial unit (*cf.* Torres 2005). I take site catchment areas as a rough proxy for site territories because in ideal circumstances, a settlement would have to be able to provision itself adequately without encroaching upon another's terrain. Torres (2005:215) similarly establishes cost boundaries at 2.5 and 5 km distance from settlements, the former representing an area within which face-to-face interaction was potentially consistent, the latter representing the upper limit of the intensively used area around the settlement. As such, for my purposes, these hypothetical domains need not be centred upon the settlement in question, but may be shifted, so as not to overlap with a neighbouring settlement's territory. My hypothesis is that in ideal circumstances, communities would prefer not to share territories to keep social tension at a minimum and alleviate the impact of exploitation on the environment, but as time passed and populations grew on the islands, they may have been forced to suffer overlaps. Alternately, overlapping territories could point to networks of socially or economically related communities (Torres 2005:215). My site territories will assume the size of the average site catchment areas as detailed above, namely a circle with a 3 km radius. What does the application of these territories to the archaeological map reveal about settlement spacing through time in the Windward Islands?

Little can be said about settlement spacing on Dominica in the general absence of settlement sites, but it is interesting to see that during the Early Ceramic Age, the only two settlements are found in the southernmost part of the island, about 6 km apart. This suggests a high degree of interaction, for while settlement territories were respected, these communities chose to settle as close to one another as possible without mutual territorial or resource encroachment. There is no evidence for settlements during the early phase of the Late Ceramic Age, and apparently just one settlement for the late phase of the Late Ceramic Age.

Martinique saw dense settlement of particularly its north-western and north-eastern parts during the Early Ceramic Age, with various settlements exhibiting overlapping territories, regardless of how one positions them. The settlements further down the north-west coast and in the south are all far enough apart so as not to have overlapping territories. The early phase of the Late Ceramic Age sees most settlements well-spaced, bar two in the upper north-west. During the late phase of the Late Ceramic Age, settlement was quite dense along the north-west and south-east coasts, but would only have resulted in territorial overlap between Paquemar (MAR-81) and Paquemar Nord (MAR-82), and A-Tout-Risque (MAR-13) and Macabou (MAR-73), although this may be a case of shifting settlement or settlement pairing (see below).

During the Early Ceramic Age, the settlements along St. Lucia's south coast would all have had overlapping territories to a greater or lesser degree, whereas the settlements along the Windward coast are dispersed. The early phase of the Late Ceramic Age sees settlements in the north and south well spread out, and the six settlements in the south-east clustered, unavoidably encroaching upon each other's territories. The encroaching increases in the late phase of the Late Ceramic Age, with settlements in the extreme north jostling for space along with those in the south-east.

On St. Vincent, most of the Early Ceramic Age settlements along the eastern and southern coasts are located within each other's territories, to say nothing of the many paired settlements. There is a visible drop in settlements during the early phase of the Late Ceramic Age, but what settlements there are have territories that overlap with those of other settlements. The late phase of the Late Ceramic Age sees infilling of the landscape once again, with settlements in the north and south once more crowding one another. Potentially, the settlements in the centre of the island had territories that did not encroach upon others, but only if the territories are adjusted extremely off-centre.

During the Early Ceramic Age on the Grenadines, most islands harbour either one or two settlements, effectively subsuming within their territory either the entire island (and even offshore islets in some cases) or half of the island. The great exception is Carriacou, whose six settlements are visibly short of space, even if they are grouped in three pairs. During the early phase of the Late Ceramic Age, the number of settlements drops slightly, leaving certain islands like Bequia, Cannouan and Carriacou less crowded, though Union Island is actually settled more intensively. The situation during the late phase of the Late Ceramic Age mirrors that of the Early Ceramic Age, with most islands fully occupied and some seemingly overcrowded.

On Grenada, settlements are relatively well-spaced, except in the south where territories overlap, and possibly once on the east coast as well. Settlement is slightly less intensive during the early phase of the Late Ceramic Age, yet some crowding persists in the south and on the eastern coast. Settlement picks up during the late phase of the Late Ceramic Age, although little changes in terms of spacing, except that the south becomes a little less crowded and the north a little more so.

Settlements in southern Barbados exhibit a degree of territorial overlap during the Early Ceramic Age; settlement in the north is light and well-spaced. Small changes in settlement occur during the early phase of the Late Ceramic Age, but they have little effect on the overall level of crowding, which basically carries over from the previous period. The situation changes drastically during the late phase of the Late Ceramic Age, when there is a veritable settlement explosion, and there is territorial overlap between settlements along the northern and southern coastlines.

4.3.2. Settlement pairs

The above exercise assumed that all settlements assigned to a certain period were completely contemporaneous. This need not necessarily have been the case however. An intriguing phenomenon one encounters when studying inter-settlement spacing, and one that holds true for Martinique, St. Lucia, Grenada and St. Vincent[59], is that of site clusters, *i.e.* possibly related sites located in relative proximity to one another. First noted in the Caribbean by Keegan (1985:227-239) for the Bahamas and named settlement pairs[60], Keegan and Maclachlan (1989) subsequently posited that these settlement pairs came about through population growth, when a new settlement would be established close to the old one. It has been alleged that spouses were exchanged within paired communities as well as between opposite moieties on different islands (Bradford 2001a:80; see also Keegan 1992:106-107). There are several possible explanations for this clustered appearance in the archaeological record: (1) these findspots represent one extensive site whose actual dimensions and contiguity have been obscured by post-depositional processes, (2) the findspots represent related and contemporaneous settlements or (3) the findspots represent successive occupations by an expanding or shifting population. Site abandonment by the entire population of a village or a segment thereof (*i.e.* house abandonment) is a common enough occurrence, and the ethnographic literature centring on lowland South America abounds with examples of such behaviour. The many reasons advanced for the phenomenon range from resource depletion and deteriorating hygienic and sanitary conditions to death of a household member, fear of spirits and the centrifugal behaviour of an expanding or fissioning population (Århem 1996:45; Carneiro in Heckenberger *et al.* 1999:364; Chagnon 1997:71-81; Clastres in Hornborg 2004:319; Fock 1963:204-205; Gillin 1975:31-32, 165; Rivière 1984). In some cases, settlements or residences are moved many kilometres away, in others, a few dozen metres.

Returning to the archaeology of the Windward Islands, and adopting a conservative 1.5 km settlement radius, which settlements do indeed cluster into pairs? On Grenada, the settlement sites of Black Point 1/2 (GRE-02/03) and Salt Pond 1 (GRE-34) cluster together during the Early Ceramic Age only, whereas the settlements of Westerhall Point 2/3 (GRE-45/46) and Chemin Bay (GRE-10) on the one hand and Pearls (GRE-29) and Simon Beach (GRE-39) on the other remain twinned throughout the entire Ceramic Age. The Big David Bay (GRE-01) and Sauteurs (GRE-37) settlements fall just outside each other's radius during Early Ceramic and late phase Late Ceramic Age times.

On St. Vincent, the settlement sites of Owia Bay 2 (SVI-71) and Espagnol Point South (SVI-32) cluster together during the Early Ceramic Age (New Sandy Bay [SVI-62] falls just outside the 1.5 km radius extending from the latter site), as do Kingstown Post Office (SVI-48), Red Cross Hut (SVI-83) and

59 Settlement pairs in the Grenadines are excluded from the analysis due to the limited dimensions of the islands that make most contemporaneous settlements on these islands pairs by default.

60 A settlement pair as defined by Keegan (1985:236, 1992b:83) refers to settlement sites situated within each other's catchment areas, defined as a 1.5-2 km radius around the settlement.

Government House (SVI-40). The Carib Piece, North Union (SVI-19) and South Union (SVI-88) sites form a pair during the Early Ceramic Age and late phase of the Late Ceramic Age and Flour Mill (SVI-37) and Camden Park (SVI-16) are paired throughout the entire Ceramic Age. During the Late Ceramic Age, the Government House (SVI-40) and Red Cross Hut (SVI-83) settlements cluster together, whereas Stubbs (SVI-90) and Mount Pleasant/Rawacou (SVI-57) fall just outside each other's radius. The Careenage (SVI-18) and Sharp's Bay (SVI-86) settlements are paired only during the late phase of the Late Ceramic Age.

On St. Lucia, only the Early Ceramic Age sites of Anse Touloulou (SLU-09) and Balembouche Estate (LU-13) are paired. The early phase of the Late Ceramic Age reveals a settlement cluster comprising Massacare (SLU-96), Troumassee (SLU-143) and Micoud Beach (SLU-97). The settlements of Saltibus Point (SLU-120) and Point de Caille (SLU-119) are paired throughout the entire Late Ceramic Age (Canelles Point [SLU-32] falls just outside the 1.5 km radius). The late phase of the Late Ceramic Age sees Massacare (SLU-96) and Micoud Beach (SLU-97) still paired, with Lavoutte [SLU-91] and Comerette Point (SLU-42) lying just outside each other's radius.

The Early Ceramic Age on Martinique sees two settlement clusters: La Pointe (MAR-63), Séguineau (MAR-112) and L'Adoration (MAR-65) on the one hand, and Anse Céron (MAR-05), Anse Couleuvre (MAR-07) and Habitation Céron (MAR-53) on the other. In the early phase of the Late Ceramic Age, Anse Céron (MAR-05) and Anse Couleuvre (MAR-07) are paired, and in the Late Ceramic Age late phase Macabou (MAR-73), A-Tout-Risque (MAR-13), Paquemar (MAR-81) and Paquemar Nord (MAR-82) and Saint Pierre Centre (MAR-17) and Périnnelle (MAR-84) form a cluster and a pair respectively.

In conclusion then, the phenomenon of settlement pairs is indeed present on most of the Windward Islands. Interestingly enough, in a number of cases, not two but three or even four settlements are found in close proximity to one another during the same period. This could be interpreted in a synchronic way, *i.e.* a number of contemporaneous settlements were established near to each other, or perhaps we are dealing with one large settlement, whose true dimensions have been obscured by post-depositional processes or misreading of the archaeological record. A diachronic interpretation on the other hand would regard the pattern as a number of successive residential moves within one and the same period, highly feasible considering the dynamic settlement patterns exhibited by many mainland South American groups past and present (see above).[61] Such micro-scale mobility may also be responsible for the shifts in settlement location from one period to the next, visible in the abandonment of a settlement or its diminution into a site and the simultaneous appearance nearby of a new settlement or – more arguably – the expansion of what was earlier just a site into a settlement (see following section). A number of potential settlement pairs were discounted as they fell just outside the 1.5 km radius. Extending the radius to the initial upper limit of 2 kms imposed

61 *Cf.* the micro- and macro-village movements documented by Chagnon (1997:71-81) among the Yanomamö. Rivière (1970:245-246) remarks that Trio village sites were moved frequently, sometimes as often as every five years.

by Keegan (1985) would have made them eligible for inclusion. Conversely, an upper limit of 1 km would have resulted in the loss of just one or two existing settlement pairs and the realigning of some existing clusters of multiple sites into pairs, suggesting that a 1 km radius may well provide the most accurate reflection of settlement pairing, at least in the Windward Islands.

4.3.3. Shifting settlement patterns

Having examined the potentially synchronic pattern of settlement pairs in the foregoing section, the logical diachronic corollary of this analysis is that of shifting settlement patterns through time. As mentioned above, there is every likelihood that the large time blocks with which archaeologist are forced to work in the absence of more precise chronological control conceal considerable short-term diachronic dynamism. However, for now, the only clear chronological markers are at the level of local complexes which mostly correlate with overarching (sub)series and can subsequently be translated into early and late phases of the Early and Late Ceramic Age. Developments from phase to phase will now be examined, and some hypothetical connections between neighbouring or proximate settlements will be drawn inspired by instances of micro-scale mobility documented in South American ethnography. This is not to paint an overly static, localised picture of the occupation history of the region in pre-colonial times, for naturally the dynamics of fission and fusion can play out at the micro-regional or regional scale as well as at the local scale (*cf.* David and Kramer 2001; Kowalewski 2008). Indeed, one of the tenets of this thesis is that socio-cultural developments need in no way be restricted to the confines of a single island. For that reason, these hypothetical settlements relationships drawn on the basis of proximity will be tested on the basis of material culture assemblage similarity in Chapter 6. But for now, a micro-mobility perspective.

Grenada

There are a number of possible mobility patterns on Grenada (see figure 4.10). One is that of a settlement with an early phase Early Ceramic Age component representing the parent community of a late phase Early Ceramic Age settlement. Such may be the case for either GRE-03 or GRE-34 and GRE-02 (although the former option is the more likely), for GRE-07 and GRE-09, GRE-10 and GRE-45/46, and GRE-01 or GRE-38 and GRE-37 (although the former is once again more likely). GRS-43 is of course part of the Grenadines technically, but on account of its proximity to Grenada, and the absence of Early Ceramic Age components on Ile de Ronde, the inhabitants of the Ile de Ronde settlement could only have come from elsewhere. As such, Ile de Ronde may have been settled from Grenada (*e.g.* GRE-01 or GRE-38) or from its neighbouring Grenadines Island to the north, Carriacou, during the early phase of the Late Ceramic Age. The second pattern is that of occupation ceasing at a settlement, making it likely that the population relocated elsewhere or merged with an existing nearby settlement. Such could be the case with GRE-02 and GRE-03 and GRE-34 at some point during the early phase of the Late Ceramic Age, and with GRE-37 and either GRE-01 or GRE-38 during the early phase of the Late Ceramic Age. The third pattern is the single component settlement that either represents a migration from another island or region or a splitting off from a parent settlement in the vicinity. As explained above, the latter will be assumed for now. In that respect, GRE-13 may represent a late phase Late Ceramic Age offshoot from GRE-01, and GRE-21 may have split off from either GRE-45/46 or GRE-39. GRS-63 on the Grenadine island Ile de Caille may also represent a late phase Late Ceramic Age offshoot from one of the settlements along the north coast of Grenada, or from Ile de Ronde.

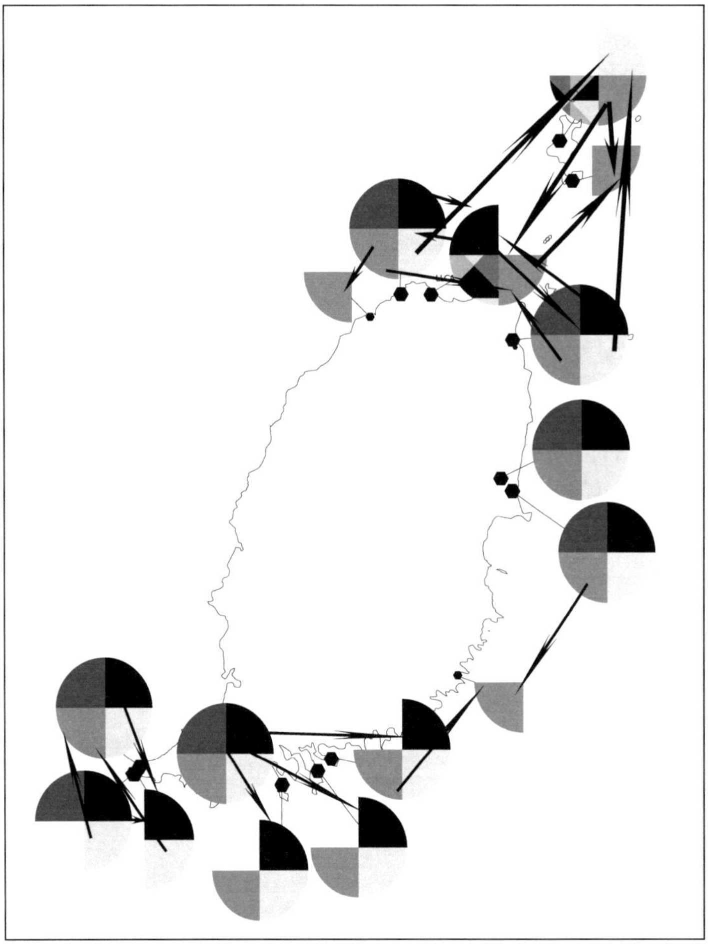

Figure 4.10. Grenada settlement occupation histories and hypothetical cases of settlement mobility.

Figure 4.11. The Grenadines settlement occupation histories and hypothetical cases of settlement mobility.

The Grenadines

From south to north, numerous potential mobility patterns are evident (see figure 4.11). GRS-63 may have split off from GRS-43 during the late phase of the Late Ceramic Age, and GRS-43 may itself represent an offshoot from one of the earlier settlements on the neighbouring island of Carriacou (*i.e.* GRS-32 or GRS-40). The possibility that Ile de Caille and Ile de Ronde may have been settled from Grenada was discussed above. On Carriacou, the late phase Early Ceramic Age populations of GRS-35 and GRS-37 presumably merged with those of the longer-lasting settlements GRS-32, GRS-40 or GRS-31. The inhabitants of GRS-41 may have merged with those of GRS-29 during the late phase of the Early Ceramic Age, only for a number of splits to occur at GRS-29 during the late phase of the Late Ceramic Age (GRS-41 and GRS-36). Although less likely, GRS-36 may also represent a late phase Late Ceramic Age offshoot from GRS-31. On Cannouan, GRS-21 and GRS-23 may have been settled around the same time, or either settlement may have split off from the other at some point during the late phase of the Early Ceramic Age. Whatever the case may be, the population of GRS-21 presumably merged with that of GRS-23 during the late phase of the Early Ceramic Age, after which a late phase Late Ceramic Age split occurred back to the GRS-21 location. An identical situation pertains to Bequia, where GRS-11 and GRS-15 exhibit the exact same pattern as GRS-21 and GRS-23.

St. Vincent

St. Vincent is the most densely settled island of the Windward Islands in terms of its area and the number of settlements and their longevity (see figure 4.12). There is a heavy concentration of early phase Early Ceramic Age settlements along the southern coast, which presumably served as parent communities for late phase Early Ceramic Age settlements such as SVI-18, SVI-30, SVI-37, SVI-40, SVI-57 and SVI-80. Apparently, SVI-18 was abandoned during the early phase of the Late Ceramic Age, in favour of SVI-46 or SVI-90 perhaps. The location was then reoccupied during the late phase of the Late Ceramic Age, a phase during which SVI-18 may itself have formed a donor community SVI-86. In the south-east, SVI-107 may represent either an unsuccessful initial settlement whose inhabitants later merged with SVI-30 or SVI-57, or an unsuccessful split off from either of the aforementioned communities. On the east coast, SVI-88 may have split off from SVI-19 during the late phase of Early Ceramic Age or even represent the in-migration of the population of SVI-19, before the SVI-19 location was occupied again during late phase Late Ceramic Age times, presumably from SVI-88. SVI-41 was apparently abandoned temporarily during the early phase of the Late Ceramic Age, perhaps in favour of SVI-50, before the location was reoccupied in the following phase. In the north, SVI-32 presumably served as a parent community from which SVI-68/69, SVI-62 and perhaps SVI 34 split off during the late phase of the Early Ceramic Age. The population of SVI-48 presumably merged with that of SVI-83 or SVI-40 during the late phase of the Early Ceramic Age. The population of SVI-57 presumably merged with that of SVI-90 after the early

Figure 4.12. St. Vincent settlement occupation histories and hypothetical cases of settlement mobility.

phase of the Late Ceramic Age. In the west, SVI-08 may have been contemporaneous with SVI-100 and SVI-36, but was apparently unoccupied during the early phase of the Late Ceramic Age, perhaps having been abandoned temporarily in favour of the location of SVI-36, SVI-100 or SVI-80, before being reoccupied during the following phase from one of the aforementioned settlements. The community of SVI-100 apparently merged with that of either SVI-36, SVI-80 or SVI-14 during the early phase of the Late Ceramic Age.

St. Lucia

There are a number of clear patterns on St. Lucia (see figure 4.13). The first concerns Late Ceramic Age offshoots from late phase Early Ceramic Age settlements (SLU-36 from SLU-117, SLU-42 from SLU-91, SLU-85 from SLU-70 and SLU-120 from SLU-119). There is also the probable case of a settlement fissioning into two new settlements (SLU-143 splits into SLU-96 and SLU-97) at some point during the early phase of the Late Ceramic Age. Similarly, inhabitants of SLU-24 appear to abandon the site and merge with either SLU-13 or SLU-67 during the early phase of the Late Ceramic Age, before activity is once again registered at SLU-24 during late pre-Colonial or early Colonial times. While SLU-112 prob-

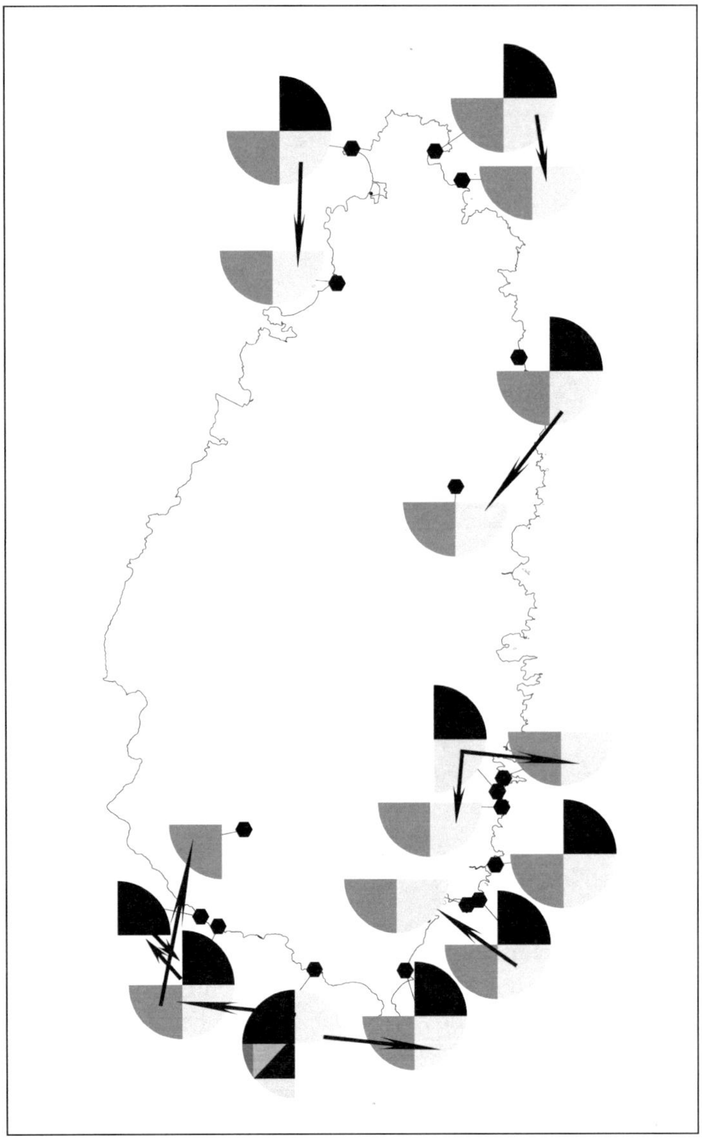

Figure 4.13. St. Lucia settlement occupation histories and hypothetical cases of settlement mobility.

ably represents a late phase Late Ceramic Age offshoot from SLU-13, it is unclear whether SLU-09 also represents a short-lived offshoot from SLU-13, or rather whether SLU-13 may itself represent an offshoot from or the continuation of SLU-09.

Martinique

The most remarkable pattern on Martinique is that of the absolute predilection of early phase Early Ceramic Age settlers for the north-east coast. However, it would appear that at some point during the late phase of the Early Ceramic Age, this part of the island was abandoned entirely, while around the same time settlement commenced out of the blue on the opposite coast (see figure 4.14). Although it is impossible to say with certainty, it is not farfetched to hypothesize that the seven communities on the east coast moved to the west coast, where eight late phase Early Ceramic Age communities consolidate into five multi-component settlements over time. The single component settlements MAR-37, MAR-53 and MAR-05 may represent short-lived offshoots from neighbouring settlements, or perhaps even initial locations settled from the east coast, before the more successful, long-lasting locations were exploited. It is possible that one or more north-east coast communities made their way to the south as well, setting in motion late phase Early Ceramic Age settlement of that part of the island. MAR-81 appears to have played a highly significant role in the subsequent settlement of the rest of the south-east, potentially representing the parent community of early phase Late Ceramic Age MAR-71 and MAR-34, as well as the late phase Late Ceramic Age communities of MAR-82, MAR-73 and MAR-13, before it was

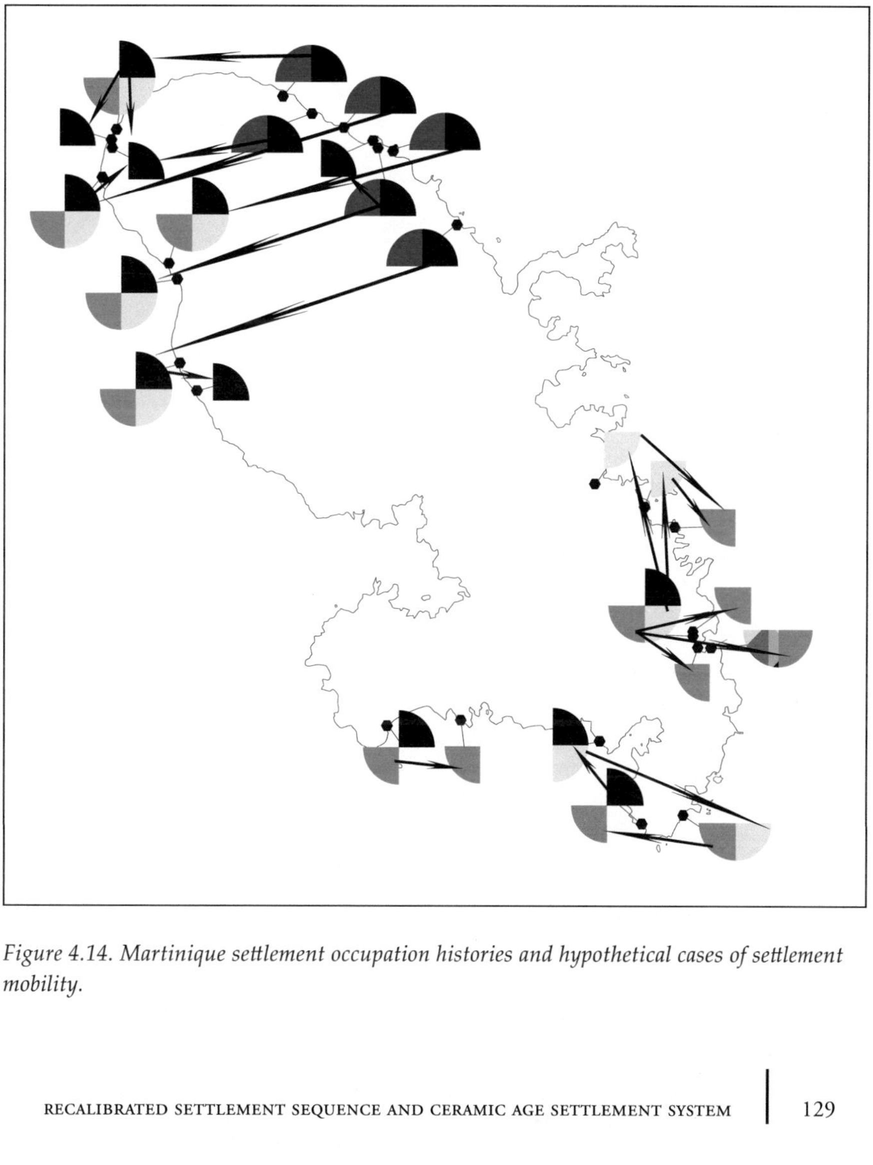

Figure 4.14. Martinique settlement occupation histories and hypothetical cases of settlement mobility.

ultimately eclipsed by MAR-73 in late pre-Colonial/early Colonial times. In the south, MAR-116 may represent an offshoot from MAR-33, although it is unclear what happened to the inhabitants of MAR-33 during the early phase of the Late Ceramic Age. MAR-09 and MAR-48 may be linked in the sense that MAR-48 may have been inhabited first, before the community relocated to MAR-09 during the late phase of the Early Ceramic Age, after which the MAR-09 community established itself at MAR-12 during early phase of the Late Ceramic Age. MAR-12 may then have been abandoned during the late phase of the Late Ceramic Age for the MAR-48 locality.

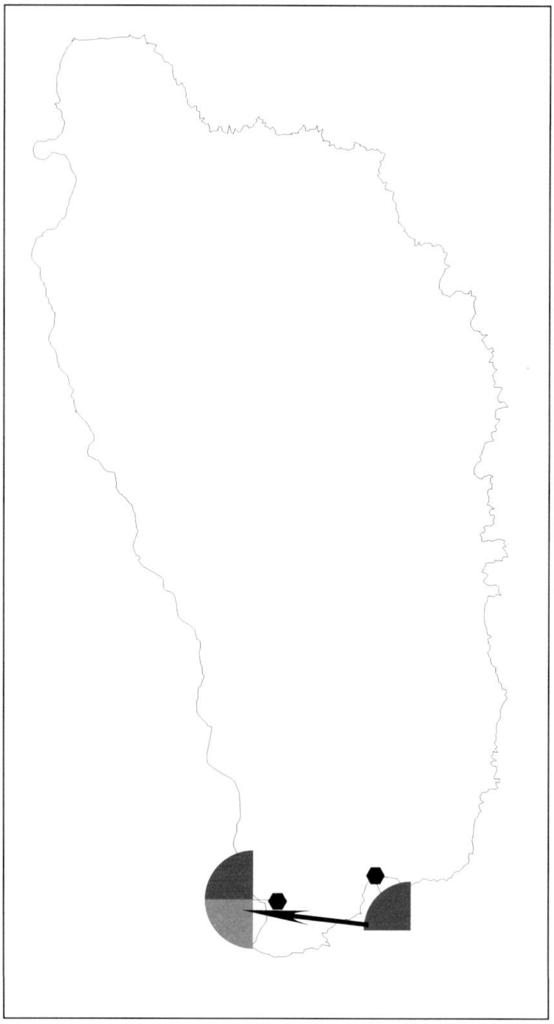

Figure 4.15. Dominica settlement occupation histories and hypothetical cases of settlement mobility.

Dominica

There is evidence of just two settlements on Dominica for the time being, both dating to the Early Ceramic Age (see figure 4.15). DOM-21 and DOM-56 may have been contemporaneous settlements, before the community at DOM-21 merged with that of DOM-56, or DOM-21 may represent a short-lived offshoot from DOM-56. It remains uncertain what happened to these communities during the late phase of the Early Ceramic Age and the early phase of the Late Ceramic Age.

Barbados

Many settlements on Barbados are inhabited through three consecutive phases, but the two-component settlements and the one single-component settlement can be regarded as offshoots of or donors to neighbouring settlements (see figure 4.16). Along the north-east coast, BAR-67 may have split off from BAR-16, and BAR-21 may in turn have fissioned from BAR-67. Alternatively, BAR-21 could be an offshoot from BAR-37, which itself may be an offshoot from BAR-39 or BAR-67. BAR-40 may likewise have split from BAR-39, or may represent half of

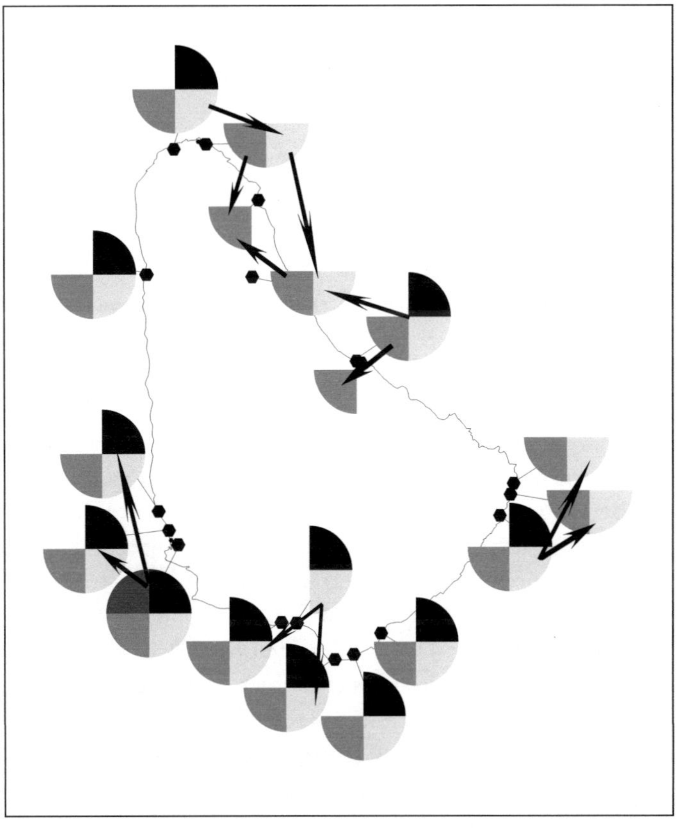

Figure 4.16. Barbados settlement occupation histories and hypothetical cases of settlement mobility.

a settlement pair (see section 4.3.2). In the south-east, BAR-66 may represent the parent community of BAR-61 and BAR-62. Along the south coast, the population of BAR-09 may have merged with that of BAR-72, or more likely, BAR-56.

General patterns

Reviewing the above, a number of general patterns come to the fore. Firstly, there are multi-component sites that endure for (much of) the length of the Ceramic Age, suggesting that these were stable, central places of continuous settlement, or at the very least of periodic re-occupation. Neighbouring single-component or multi-component settlements may represent parts of a community that fissioned from a parent community. Then there are the multi-component settlements that are missing one or more occupation phases, suggesting the arrival at, departure from and return to the initial settlement location. This phenomenon ties in with that of neighbouring single-component or multi-component settlements that presumably represent a migrating community. There are also single-component or multi-component settlement that merge with another, more long-lived community, and communities that abandon one locale in favour of a new one. The main assumption underlying these discerned patterns is that a community does not simply die out, but will move on and be perpetuated elsewhere. Of course, the potential remains for pioneer settlement independent of a parent community on the same island or in the same area, or for community mobility that does not adhere to the nearest neighbour/proximity principal. As explained above, these hypothetically drawn relationships will be evaluated on the basis of shared ceramic (decorative) traits in Chapter 6.

4.3.4. Settlement/use of Windward Island islets

Not only the larger islands of the Windwards, but also its many islets have yielded evidence of habitation sites, indicating that these islets were clearly not being passed over for settlement (see also Hofman *et al.* 2004). Reviewing the data, it is clear that the Amerindians were more resourceful than the Bullens (who proposed that these spots were too dry for settlement) had estimated. Indeed, only the very smallest islets have thus far failed to yield evidence of settlement, and even these may have been utilized for various other activities or as a stop-offs during long sea voyages (Bérard and Vidal 2003). And yet, exactly the limited area of islets, in combination with a certain ruggedness or relative inaccessibility, can result in islets following entirely different natural and/or historical trajectories than islands, which can support more species of flora and fauna (that may or may not compete with one another).[62] This is illustrated by the timing of the settlement or use of the majority of Windward islets, which starts during the late phase of the Early Ceramic Age (Gros Ilet, Martinique; Praslin Island, St. Lucia; Young's Island, St. Vincent; Caliviny Island, Grenada) and really picks ups during the Late Ceramic Age (Ilet Cabrits, Ilet Hardy, Ilet Madame, Ilet Sapotille, Martinique;

---

62 Resources that occur on the surface of the islet are being considered here, rather than resources surrounding it.

Pigeon Island, Praslin Island, Frigate Island, St. Lucia; Young's Island, St. Vincent; Petit Martinique, Ile de Ronde, Ile de Caille, Ile à Quatre, Grenadines; Caliviny Island, Grenada). A number of additional islets (Maria Island Major, Rat Island, St. Lucia; Petit Nevis, Isle à Quatre and Battowia, Grenadines; Culpepper Island, Barbados) have yielded non-diagnostic (ceramic) remains. It is worthwhile to explore the various roles that (settlements on) small islands or islets could have assumed, either distinct from or complementarily to (settlements on) larger islands (Bright 2006; see also Keegan *et al.* 2008).

Many of the islets located (just) offshore some of the larger Windward Islands such as St. Lucia and Martinique have poetic name such as Ramier Island (Columba squamosa – Scaly-naped pigeon), Frigate Island (Fregata magnificens – Magnificent Frigatebird), Pigeon Island (Columba sp. - Pigeon), Ilet à Aigrettes (Egreta thula – Snowy Egret), Ilet Burgaux (Cittarium pica – West Indian Crown Conch), which refer overtly to the specific resource that occur(ed) in abundance or in isolation there. Frigate birds nowadays nest only on offshore islets, wary as they are of predators. Their less sophisticated neighbour to the north, the Audubon's Shearwater (Puffinus lherminieri), has proven remarkably easy prey for humans from Archaic times to the present (Hofman *et al.* 2006). Other (nesting) birds that may have attracted Amerindians' attention are Brown Pelicans (Pelecanus occidentalis), Doves (Columbina sp. or Zenaida sp.) and Boobies (Sula sula) among others.[63] One or two of the Windward islets harbour specific lizard (*e.g.* Whiptail lizard -Cnemidophorus vanzoi) and snake (Fer-de-Lance - Bothrops caribbaeus, Couresse or St. Lucia Racer - Leimadophis ornatus, Cribo - Clelia clelia) populations, although it is unsure to how long ago their presence there dates. Furthermore, certain islets are to this day visited by turtles in order to lay their eggs, which would have represented two sources of food coming into close reach of Amerindians living along the coast of the main islands. Finally, some islets offered considerable collecting and offshore fishing potential, making them small but rich resource patches, extending as it were the outreach or catchment area of resource-exploiting Amerindians.[64] It is important to consider however that such islets may have attracted not just Amerindians from adjacent or nearby communities, but also those from a considerable distance away.[65]

Benoît Bérard, archaeologist on Martinique, has suggested (Bérard, personal communication 2005) that islets offshore Martinique were increasingly visited by Amerindians over the course of the pre-Colonial period. This is reflected by the overwhelmingly late pre-Colonial character of the material remains found on the islets, as well as by the nature of the remains (see also Bérard and Vidal 2003).

63 See *e.g.* John (2004) for a comprehensive overview of the habitats of migrant bird populations on St. Lucia and the appendices in Newsom and Wing (2004) for an overview of bird remains encountered at archaeological sites throughout the Caribbean.

64 De Waal (2006:117) has suggested that the marine resources around the islands of Petite Terre attracted settlers from the larger island of Guadeloupe over time, and in the Leeward Islands, Dog Island, north-west of Anguilla, is purported to have fulfilled such a role (Haviser 1991:134).

65 The prime example of this phenomenon would be Long Island, off the north-east coast of Antigua. Flint from Long Island has found its way throughout the Lesser Antilles, presumably through a combination of direct exploitation at the source and down-the-line exchange (Van Gijn 1993).

Bérard hypothesizes that over time, settlements lost their central role in all aspects of life. Various tasks were now carried out at different locations, for instance at fishing stations or temporary activity sites away from the main settlement. Bérard bases his idea on the reduction in the amount of lithic and shell debitage at Suazan Troumassoid settlement sites on Martinique compared to earlier sites, coevally with a proliferation of activity areas that in some cases can be determined to be late pre-Colonial, in other cases only suspected (Bérard, personal communication 2005). Similar patterns of (food-processing) activities taking place on offshore islets/cays have been attested for the Los Roques archipelago off the coast of central Venezuela (Antczak and Antczak 2006) and parts of the Jardines del Rey archipelago off the northern coast of Cuba (Calvera Rosés *et al.* 2005).

While many of the offshore islets are close to shore, there are examples throughout the Windwards that occur quite isolatedly. One can imagine that such rocky outcrops could serve as markers for navigation. Accessible islets could also serve as stop-off sites should adverse weather conditions preclude travel for instance. Also, the Grenadines chain offer perhaps the most comfortable sailing of the entire Lesser Antilles, certainly in terms of intervisibility and distance. Considering Grenada to be the first real navigational challenge for Amerindians voyaging from South America via Trinidad and Tobago or directly from the coast of Paria, the Grenadines would have certainly facilitated swift, secure travel onwards.

It is quite remarkable that of the relatively few sites that have yielded Cayo remains, two are located just opposite each other across the channel between Grenada and the southernmost Grenadines, namely the Sauteur's site on Grenada and an as yet undefined site on Ile de Ronde (see also Chapter 3). We have already established that connections between communities across sea passages are to be expected (see Chapter 2), and seen from this perspective, islets can be expected to represent logical extensions of a community or group territory. Elaborating upon this theme, it is illuminating to briefly consider modern day fishing practices in the study area. In Laborie Bay, southern St. Lucia for instance, cays and reefs are visited repeatedly by fishermen and given names by them: Go Lou (Big Heavy?), Mirikel Papèl, Lilèt Mèl (Blackbird islet), Kay Nwè (Black Cay), Kay Tiyo (underground water pipe), Kay Tòti (type of sea turtle), Kay Ati/Kay Koko (coconut), Kay Kén (may be the name of local fisherman), Lapo Patat (Sweet Potato Skin), Twa Lanm (Three Waves), Kay Mayòt (strong), Bwizan Pwent-la, La Pas (trouble, problem), Kawèt (type of sea turtle), Kay Koupé (cut, chopped) and Bwizan Kawèt are just some examples (CANARI 2003; Hutchinson *et al.* 2000).[66] The assignation of names and qualities to individual reef areas and cays illustrates that contemporary topography is not limited to terrestrial environments only, an observation that may be of value in considering past conceptions of topography as well.

66 Some of these translations are courtesy of Winston Phulgence, Saint Lucia. Others are drawn from Frank ed. (2001).

4.4. Windward Island settlement system: an (ethno)historical perspective

Having drawn on ethnographic information to complement archaeological data, all that remains is to implement (ethno)historical accounts, to potentially arrive at a more meaningful (re)construction of Caribbean Amerindian settlement and lifeways (*cf.* Harris 2001). Fortunately, we can draw profitably on the many (ethno)historical sources describing Amerindian life in the Windward Islands from the late 16th to the early 18th century, as highlighted in Chapter 2 (see also Verrand 2001).

Regarding non-descript pottery scatters and isolated (clusters of) individual lithic artefacts, once (ethno)historical accounts are perused, these phenomena begin to take shape as potential material reflections of small farming huts or shelters, land-clearing activities and garden maintenance, and perhaps the felling of trees for the purpose of manufacturing canoes or other endeavours. The Anonymous of Carpentras describes the long-winded, collective nature of such a logging expedition:

> *"Étant de retour, se contentant d'avoir remarqué un arbre, n'ayant peur qu'on lui dérobe, se repose encore quelque temps. Et puis s'en va par tout le village, et bien souvent en quelques autres, pour prier tous les hommes et garçons qui vont passer leur susdit degré de lui aller aider à couper l'arbre pour faire sa pirogue, chose qui lui est incontinent accordée, et à ces fins ceux qui ont des haches les aiguisent, et ceux qui n'en ont point lui en demandent et il leur en baille [...] Étant arrivées au lieu, celui qui les y mène les ayant tous fait reboire, les prie derechef l'un après l'autre de vouloir couper un tel arbre qu'il montre avec le doigt [...] lorsque le lieu où doit être coupé l'arbre est trop éloigné du village, et qu'il faut presque une journée pour y aller, joint que les arbres sont si gros, qu'il faut bien du temps à l'abattre, alors ils font porter leur lit de coton pour y coucher, et ne s'en reviennent que l'arbre ne soit coupé"* (Anonyme de Carpentras 2002:213).[67]

Once the tree has been chopped down, all return to their village(s). Some time after, a number of them will return with the canoe-builder to help him burn and hollow out the tree trunk until it takes rough shape, a process that can take as much as three weeks. Having accomplished this, all return to the village, to engage in a bout of copious eating and drinking (*caouynage*) at the expense of

---

67 "Having returned, satisfied with having selected a tree, and not fearing that another would rob him of it, he rests a while. And then, he goes around the whole village, and oftentimes around several others as well, to ask all the men and boys who have to go through the aforementioned initiation to come and help him chop down the tree to make his canoe, something which is directly agreed to and to this end, those who have axes sharpen them, and those who don't request them of him and he gives them one [...] Having arrived at the site, he who has brought them there, having made them all have drinks anew, asks them again one after the other to cut a certain tree which he points out [...] when the place where the tree is to be cut is very far from the village, and requires nearly a day's travel to reach, as well as when the trees are so large, that it will take a considerable time to chop it down, then they carry their cotton hammock along to sleep in, and don't return until the tree has been cut down".

the "contractor". A while later, the men return to the forest, to assist in carrying the canoe to the village. Once the canoe has been brought to the intended spot, the contractor thanks all his helpers by putting on another grand caouynage, after which he finishes working the canoe at his leisure (Anonyme de Carpentras 2002:213-215).

Regarding Amerindian settlements in the Windward Islands, one of the first to comment upon it was John Nicholl, who noted the following for St. Lucia:

> *"The Next morning we went ashore with all our weak men, where there was [sixe]*[68] *or seven houses planted by a pleasant fresh water River, which Captain Sen-Johns bought for a Hatchet of an Indian Captain called Anthony [...]"* (Jesse 1966:50).

A fellow crewmember describes another Amerindian settlement at a nearby bay as follows: *"halfe a dosen of Indian houses very pleasantly scituated upon the top of a hill, with a fresh water River at the foot of the same hill"* (Turner 1905-07:353). Anthony's village itself was reported to lie on the far side of a spit of land, just back from the beach. These Amerindian villages have been tentatively relocated along the south-eastern coastline of St. Lucia (Bullen 1966). Further, a map drawn up by Thomas Jefferys in 1770 depicts three Amerindian structures midway up along the eastern coast, near modern day Anse Louvet. All these settlements were within sight of the coast, at both low and higher elevations. A 1658 map of Martinique by Sanson (Bodington 2005) also depicts a number of Amerindian settlements, one near Anse Figuier along the southern coast, the other near present-day Le Vauclin along the south-eastern coast. A 1665 map by Blondel also depicts the latter Carib locality (Verrand 2001: figure 1). Interestingly, the former locality harbours a large Late Ceramic Age Amerindian site. Allaire (1977:88) further suggests that the toponyms Paquemar, Macabou, Simon, François and Vauclin may all have referred to Amerindian chiefs.

Father Breton lived among the Amerindians of Guadeloupe and Dominica for many years and relates under the heading icábanum (home, dwelling):

> *"Les Sauvages n'ont que fort peu de bois abattus au lieu où ils demeurent, savoir la place d'une carbet, et de quelques maisonettes à l'entour, et ce à dessein, afin que les Européens ne puissent les connaître ni surprendre; c'est pour le même motif que la plupart s'établissent au vent des Iles, parce que les mers y sont rudes, les terres fort élevées, et de difficile accès; néanmoins c'est toujours auprès des rivières" (Breton 1999:140).*[69]

68 Jesse mistakenly transcribes 'five' instead of 'sixe', see the original 1607 manuscript by Nicholl (British Library shelfmark 278.a.4).

69 "The Caribs have only a very small clearing at the place where they live, which is a place for the Carbet and some smaller houses around it. This is planned so the Europeans will not be able to know about them or capture them by surprise. It is for the same reason that the greater part of them are established on the windward side of the island, because here the waves are rough and terrain is high and it is difficult to gain access to it. Nevertheless, they are always near rivers because they would not be able to forego water, either for drinking or for bathing" (McKusick and Vérin in Myers 1978:330).

And under Bouellélebou: *"c'est la cour, la place qui est entre le carbet et les cases; chacun nettoie devant la sienne […]"* (Breton 1999:45).[70]

Father Le Breton, in an extremely valuable paragraph on Amerindian settlements and horti-cultural endeavour on St. Vincent, writes the following:

> *"Due to their customs, although they establish their centres or dwellings along the banks of watercourses and it would therefore seem much easier to cultivate especially the areas of soil spread around quite close to their buildings, they continue to do it in a different way. It is far from the sea, both on the slopes of hills and on flat ground, that they find it preferable to sow in the ground all the kinds of food crops, which I will list in a moment. They give two good reasons for this: 'It is quite clear', they say, 'that these places, on account of either the springs of running water they abound with, or the more abundant daily dew, or the proximity of the mountains from which the flow of the rains brings all fertility, provide harvests that are both more copious and pleasing to the palate'. As for the second reason, it pertains to the danger of destruction the community faces. 'Catastrophes!' they cry, 'Alas! We have known either the unbridled fury or the mortal hatred of our enemies all too often, to cultivate lands that are too close to our dwellings. As soon as we are able to escape from their hands, since all physical violence to persons is forbidden to them, in the first place they raze our homes to the ground and they completely ransack our fields to bring about our ruin, they sack and rampage over everything"* (Le Breton 1998).

A similar observation was made among Martiniquean Amerindians a century before:

> *"Lorsque nos Indiens veulent faire un jardin, ils choisissent un lieu fort haut et loin de la rivière […] Mais il arriva que pendant notre séjour il mourut la femme d'un capitaine, qui avait un jardin environ 500 pas proche de notre habitation, qui était chose rare d'en être si près […]" (Anonyme de Carpentras 2002:156-7).*[71]

And:

> *"[…] [I]l faut savoir qu'ils ont des jardins plein de manioc et autres racines jusques aux lieux plus écartés dans les hautes montagnes, expressément pour s'y retirer à une nécessité comme aussi des petites cabanes, de sorte que menant là leurs femmes et captifs qui ont apporté des vivres, ils vont quérir de la racine pour faire de la cassave" (Anonyme de Carpentras 2002:213).*[72]

---

70 "Here is a yard between the carbet and the other houses. Each one cleans the area of it in front of his own house […]" (McKusick and Vérin in Myers 1978:330).

71 "When our Indians want to establish a garden, they choose a place quite high up and far from the river. But it just so happened that the wife of a chief died during our stay, who had a garden some 500 feet away from our settlement, which was a rare thing, being so close".

72 "One should know that they have gardens full of manioc and other root crops up to the most remote places in the high mountains, on purpose to retire there when necessary, as well as small huts, so that taking along their wives and captives who have carried their victuals, they go searching for the root to make cassava".

A somewhat intermediary position was taken by Nicholl, who speaks of a garden of potatoes, *"round like a Bower, encompassed with a green Bank, located under a mile from Antonio's house"*, but also mentions encountering for the next two or three miles many more gardens full of *"Cassada, Potatoes, Tobacco, Cotton-wool-trees, and Guava trees"* (Bullen 1966:53; Nicholl 1607).

Thus all three observers highlight subsistence-related activities taking place deep inland, far-removed from the settlements (though Nicholl also notes gardens close to the settlement), observations that are potentially of great value in interpreting the pre-Colonial site pattern and settlement systems in the Windward Islands.[73] What is additionally interesting about Le Breton's account is the emphasis he places on the dispersed settlement pattern adopted by the independent-minded Amerindians, to which the undulating, concertina-like coastline of many of the Windwards was highly suited:

> *"Then the fortunate complicity of the country astonishingly encourages the people's frenzy for total independence. In fact the island which "dips" at each step and is riddled with bays and hollows, offers each father of a family the opportunity to choose without difficulty his ideal site or property, far from any foreign constraint and completely safe - because there was only one entrance to his estate and only by sea - to lead his life exactly as he pleases, with his wife, children and dear ones [...]"* (Le Breton 1998).

It would seem from his words that many of the early Colonial Amerindian settlements represented household hamlets rather than settlements consisting of multiple agglomerated household groups. Of course, it must be noted that Le Breton's is a late source, and the observations contained within may reflect the thinning out of Amerindian population by European encroachment.

But not all early Colonial period Amerindian settlements were coastal in nature, though most early visitors dared not venture beyond the shoreline on these dangerous, little-known islands. A few intrepid adventurers did though, and they noted settlements in inland locations as well. The Earl of Cumberland (Cumberland 1905), visiting Dominica in 1596, was taken quite some way upstream to the settlement of a Dominican chief. Thomas Gage (1758), who stopped off at Guadeloupe in 1625, also visited an Amerindian settlement quite some distance from the shore.

The use of small islands or islets, attested archaeologically above, also comes up quite frequently in (ethno)historical accounts. Referring to Grenada and the Grenadines, Rochefort (1666:7) states: *"There is good fishing all about it, and the Inhabitants have also good fishing and hunting in and about three little Islands, called the Granadines, lying North-East from it"*. Of Bequia, Rochefort (1666:8) says: *"[...] inasmuch as it is not furnish'd with fresh water, it is not much frequented, unless it be by some Caribbians of St. Vincent's, who sometimes go thither a fishing, or to dress some small Gardens they have up and down there for their diversion"*. Admiral Dirck Symonsz. reported the same nearly forty years earlier, in 1628: *"Het Eylandt is on-*

---

73 Allaire (1991:719) also pointed out the potential overlap in gardening practices between the Island Carib and the Late Ceramic Age inhabitants of the islands.

bewoondt, doch de Wilde van S. Vincent kommen daer dickmaels om eenighe vruchten te teelen ende te plucken"[74] (De Laet 1932:54). Even earlier, Thomas Maynarde writes of Marie-Galante in 1595:

> *"There the Generall went on shore in his barge, and by chance met a Canoa of Dominicans, to the people whereof he gave a wastcoate of flanell and an hankerchiefe; and they gave him such fruits as they had, and the Dominicans rowed to Dominica againe. They came thither to fetch some fruits which they sowe and plant in divers places of that Island which they keepe like gardens"* (Hulme and Whitehead 1992:56; Myers 1978:328).

According to De Laet (1630:39), Amerindians from Dominica would also occasionally visit the island of Nevis, although he neglects to mention why. Finally, though just north of the region under study, Breton writes of the little islands Les Saintes below Guadeloupe:

> *"Les Sainctes sont les plus belles, où les Savages mesme ont encore quelques jardins à coton. Les habitans de Guadelouppe y vont varer et tourner de la tortue. Ils y vont chasser aussy avec un baton au tuërou [...]"*[75] (Breton 1978:32).

In conclusion then, even in colonial times, no clear settlement patterning can be deduced from the data at our disposal, representing a seamless transition from the situation during the pre-Colonial period. It would seem that coastal locations were preferred because they are reported more frequently, but this could easily be put down to an observational bias on the part of hurried and wary European visitors. Further, the (ethno)historical sources, though potentially biased and not necessarily an accurate reflection of pre-Colonial activity, do afford us with valuable insights into the range of activities undertaken by Colonial–period Amerindians at least as well as into their use and traversing of land- and seascapes.

4.5. Concluding remarks

More than a decade ago, Watters and Petersen (1992:12) suggested that the search for general rules governing settlement location of Amerindians may be futile, as no clear patterns had as yet emerged for settlement patterns among islands or within the region. The current overview has done little to change this outlook, and there is no trend to be discerned for instance from a random, widespread, through clustered, infilling, to regular distribution of settlements (*cf.* Keegan 1992:227-228). Even if general patterns had emerged, these would have to have been treated with the utmost scepticism, precisely due to the arbitrary, opportunistic nature of sampling/surveying techniques adopted haphazardly by Caribbean archaeologists over the last decades (see also Chapter 3).

---

74 "The island is uninhabited, yet the Savages of St. Vincent go there frequently to plant and harvest certain fruits".

75 "Les Saintes are the most pretty, where the Savages still have some gardens for growing cotton. The inhabitants of Guadeloupe go there to flip turtles on their backs. They also go there to hunt the tuërou (a local bird) with a stick".

Of course there are more or less desirable locations on every island, but in general, the islands are so small that the majority of their terrestrial and marine resources are within a day's travel away from any point. Provided a number of general conditions were met, such as access to water (not a problem on well-watered volcanic islands or on limestone islands with stores of underground water and the option of digging wells in the dunes) and a number of key resources (be they marine, coastal or terrestrial) were within reach, most spots on the island would have been easily inhabitable and were indeed inhabited. On a more general note, numerous archaeological studies into settlement patterns have demonstrated that while environment and subsistence are an important factor in settlement, these factors are not all-determining. As such, many of the patterns and changes in such patterns detected across the Windward Islands likely reflect local demographic trends or community decisions as much as they do shifts in adaptation or climatic events. The dispersion of settlements in this manner is suggestive of Flannery and Coe's (1968) contagious distribution pattern, whereby all settlements are in a similar environmental setting and all utilize the surrounding environments in a similar way. This is contrary to Flannery and Coe's "symbiotic" distribution pattern, whereby settlements are spread over different environments with trade and interaction among them (Haviser 1989:5). The identification of a contagious settlement pattern is suggestive of relatively self-sufficient local communities. A symbiotic distribution pattern on the other hand is generally considered to reflect a chiefdom level of organization.

A side-by-side comparison of islands' settlement histories revealed the insight the Grenada and St. Vincent in particular demonstrated a high degree of settlement continuity. The examination of cultural components present at various settlements suggested various patterns through time, such as the potential abandonment of one settlement for another, the potential fissioning of settlements or instances of community cycling between communities over time. Of course, there is no way to accurately gauge the true extent of community or group mobility, as at the current resolution we can only pick up one instance of the phenomenon, which may mask a much higher frequency. Taking recourse to (ethno)historical accounts offers unique insights into Amerindian lifeways, although the degree to which these insights can be unproblematically projected back in time is debatable. However, if nothing else, it adds a very human dimension to the perspective on the data-set.

The implications of the Windward Island settlement system will be discussed in more detail in Chapter 7. In the following chapter, material connections between sites and the diversity of stylistic influences will be addressed on the basis of the distribution of ceramic (decorative) traits throughout the Windward Islands.

Chapter 5

CERAMIC (DECORATIVE) TRAIT DISTRIBUTION DURING THE LATE CERAMIC AGE: MULTI-SCALAR INTERACTION IN THE WINDWARD ISLANDS

5.1. Introduction

Having examined site patterns and general characteristics of the ceramic assemblages of the Windward Islands in the previous chapter, it is time to move on to a more detailed consideration of the distribution of a number of ceramic stylistic and morphological traits across the islands. As explained in Chapter 1, the basic tenets of interaction theory will be adhered to, while remaining entirely cognizant of the methodological issues surrounding the more far-reaching applications of the theory. A number of ceramic style phenomena – decoration modes, vessel forms and the styles themselves - will be studied at various scales: regional, micro-regional and local. Regional are those phenomena/developments that affect a number of sites in a given region and that are clearly related to phenomena/developments outside the region under study, or originate outside the region. Micro-regional phenomena or developments are those that occur at a number of sites across several islands that comprise a geographically bounded, recognised entity. Local refers to phenomena or developments that concern a limited number of sites on the same island. It must be emphasised that in order to keep the data-set manageable, a decorative mode, stylistic trait (attribute) or vessel type in general is considered, as opposed to individual specimens within such a mode. If discernable and quantitatively significant, subtypes will be distinguished within a decoration mode or stylistic attribute, but obviously, archaeological artefacts or stylistic expressions that are unique to just one or a few site assemblages may run the risk of being overlooked in such a general overview of the assemblages of all Windward Island sites. While this approach could undermine the local and micro-regional levels, it is deemed more germane to the underlying tenets of this research to seek out evidence for shared principles or interrelationships rather than unicity or isolation.

It goes without saying that differential research intensity, discussed in section 1.4, has a direct bearing on the assembled data-set. For this chapter, which aims merely to provide a simple overview of presence or absence of ceramic (decorative) traits, this bias is not so much of an issue, but it is important to keep in mind that traits may potentially have been more prevalent than has been determined thus far. For this chapter then, the data-set comprises 301 sites in all, with at least one (but potentially several or all three) of the following components: Troumassan Troumassoid, Suazan Troumassoid and Cayo. In the following chapter, where the data are quantified, an attempt is made to counter this bias somewhat by discussing only the data pertaining to settlements. Even then however, there are obvious differences between settlements that have seen large-scale excavation over numerous field seasons and those that for instance have merely been testpitted. However, addressing this bias more fully would render the data-set so small and divided as to make inferences almost meaningless in their limited scope. For that reason, it has been decided to lump together all settlements, in favour of sketching broad trends with a slight degree of unreliability.

Examples of heterogeneity and homogeneity in ceramic decoration modes in the Windward Islands will now be supplied on various scales of analysis, focussing on the Late Ceramic Age. As will be discussed below, the character of Early Ceramic Age ceramic assemblages and particularly the way they have been documented, preclude a detailed, specifying approach to their (sub)decoration modes. The data presented below are the outcome of study of the collections documented in the literature or seen and recorded by the author (see subchapter 2.5). Of course, the scalar categories in which certain traits are presently placed are subject to change as more materials surface, either from archaeological fieldwork, in new publications or online. However, while such a shift (*i.e.* a trait initially deemed local now turning out to be micro-regional) may affect the details, it does not detract from the basic value and tenets of this research, for as more materials are uncovered and a local trait becomes micro-regional, surely a new local trait will emerge in its place. In any case, as the trend will always be towards a style exhibiting a wider rather than a more limited distribution, it will always be in support of the argument of broader interaction between island communities within a given time period. Hypothetically speaking, it would of course be possible to detect a diachronic development entailing a relative drop in the geographical extent of interaction compared to other periods.

The treatment of the data is ordered into four sections: (1) background, which provides information regarding the appearance of a trait or ware in the archaeological literature; (2) details of decoration/composition, which discusses aspects of the decoration/manufacture of a given trait or ware; (3) distribution, which offers an overview of the spread of a given trait or ware across sites in the region, including a weighted distribution per island; and (4) stylistic similarities/dating, which aims to place a trait or ware within its (micro/macro-)regional developmental context, by determining the extent to which matching contemporaneous and/or antecedent but related stylistic traits can be recognized from a representative cross-section of sites throughout the macro-region.

5.2. The "Saladoid Veneer"

Before turning to a more detailed consideration of a number of decorative traits of the Late Ceramic Age at various geographic scales, the problem of the "Saladoid veneer" and its implications for the rest of this analysis must be discussed. First coined by Keegan (2001:238, 2004:42), the concept of "Saladoid veneer" refers to the apparent homogeneity in Saladoid ceramics, as represented by such general, region-wide decoration modes as white-on-red (WOR) painting and zoned-incised-crosshatching (ZIC), which in fact tend to obscure an as yet undetermined degree of material culture heterogeneity and divergent cultural development at a more local level (see also Hofman and Hoogland 2004:52). This line of thinking is entirely in keeping with the current perspectives on culture change and development as being not so much a result of uni-linear migration events, but rather as continuous, reticulate and in part attributable to diffusion and exchange as well as migration.

Having said that, how does one go about tackling this "veneer", exposing the alleged underlying heterogeneity? Unfortunately, that has proven nigh impossible, for a number of reasons. First and foremost, there is the pervasive, omnipresent veneer itself. There is no denying that at a superficial level of analysis, Early Ceramic Age assemblages show an uncanny uniformity over a long period of time (nearly a thousand years in fact) over a wide geographic area (from Trinidad tentatively to the south-eastern Dominican Republic [Rouse 1992]). In fact, decorative trait diffusion has occurred to such a degree across the islands that at first glance, there seems to be no evidence of micro-style zones or insular or regional variation. The ceramics evoke a sense of strong regional interdependency and of one extensive interaction sphere, which ties in with the ideology and social behaviour one would expect from pioneering communities (see also Hofman *et al.* 2007). Variability is encountered not at the level of decoration mode therefore, but rather at the level of the decoration motif or subtype of decoration mode and in exceptional cases at the level of unique vessels and artefacts, and this leads into the second problem, that of documentation. Whereas exceptional vessels and artefacts have a tendency to be remarked upon and noted, the same is not always the case for subtypes of decoration modes. While most publications dealing with Early Ceramic Age assemblages distinguish between Saladoid WOR and Saladoid ZIC, not many distinguish subtypes within WOR and ZIC. In fact not all decoration classified WOR is actually strictly speaking white-on-red; one also encounters white-and-red, besides different extremes of WOR such as a highly glossy variety and a chalky, powdery variety (both found on Martinique). Additionally, there is a great diversity in motifs depicted, ranging from abstract and geometric to more recognizably figurative. This problem essentially boils down to the type-variety approach versus modal approach issue discussed in Chapter 2, and the attention devoted to the technological as opposed to morphological details of pottery decoration. The problem is compounded by the general lack of (clear) photographs and illustrations of archaeological materials[76], leaving one to face either a lack of or low resolution information, or a skewed balance between high resolution information from one researcher and low resolution information from another.

Obviously this introduces a highly problematic bias into research that has nothing to do with the actual distribution of stylistic traits and everything to do with the manner and diligence of their documentation. A detailed study at the level of morphology or motifs, however desirable, was beyond the scope of this current research, which has out of necessity drawn mainly on in-depth literature study and cursory collections study across the Caribbean.

---

76 Although even the best photographs and illustrations sometimes do not permit the discerning of technological details of pottery decoration.

Even ignoring the problems posed by the "Saladoid veneer", there are good reasons to devote attention only to the Late Ceramic Age assemblages in this chapter. In general, the archaeological literature on Late Ceramic Age Windward Island assemblages is less ambiguous and more revealing concerning ceramic (decorative) traits than that centering on the Early Ceramic Age. Furthermore, Late Ceramic Age assemblages seem more conducive to studies at the level of subtypes of decoration, as decoration modes appear to be easier to break down into distinct yet clearly related subcategories. Variety in decorative traits is expressed mainly in morphology, rather than in technology or motifs, making it eminently observable and classifiable. Finally, the Late Ceramic Age is a highly interesting period at which to level questions concerning increasing social imbalance or inequality within the region (De Waal 2006; Hofman and Hoogland 2004; Knippenberg 2006). Having justified the selection of the Late Ceramic Age as the period under study, we now turn to the selection of ceramic decorative traits and their analysis.

5.3. Late Ceramic Age ceramic (decorative) traits

Having provided a general overview of ceramic developments in the Windward Islands during the Late Ceramic Age in Chapters 2 and 3, we now turn to a more detailed consideration of a number of ceramic (decorative) traits of the era at various geographic scales. The eleven traits considered are polychrome painting (Caliviny Polychrome), lugs, legs, legged griddles, support rings, anthropomorphic adornos, loom weights, finger indented rims, scratching, female statue(tte)s and Cayo ware. Taken together, these traits represent a good cross-section of Late Ceramic Age ceramic assemblages. Clearly, there are differences of type between the traits; some are decoration modes (polychrome painting), others are morphological or finishing attributes (legs, lugs, adornos, finger indented rims, scratching), and yet others are whole objects (support rings, female statuettes, loom weights, legged griddles). One trait (Cayo) actually represents an entire ware, though this particular ware is so rare and diagnostic that it can easily be treated as a singular ceramic (decorative) mode for the time being. Whereas initially these fundamentally different traits will be treated in similar fashion, their distinctive nature will ultimately be recognized by offsetting the decorative and morphological against each other, to determine whether there are any significant differences between the distribution or influence spheres of these two types of traits. The traits will now be examined in turn, and furnished with details on their research background, specifics about their decoration/composition, geographical distribution and stylistic similarities and dating.

5.3.1. Caliviny Polychrome

Background

Caliviny was first recognized by Bullen (1964) at sites on Caliviny Island just off the southern coast of Grenada. Bullen (1964, 1968) initially regarded it as a ware that could be placed within a chronological scheme, occurring in spatio-temporal terms between the Pearls/Simon (Saladoid) and Suazey (Suazan Troumassoid) wares, and tabulated it as such, despite stratigraphic evidence to the contrary.[77] However, by the time of Bullen and Bullen's publication on the archaeology of St. Vincent and the Grenadines, this position was becoming increasingly untenable, a fact they themselves acknowledged:

> *"Vessel fragments of the Caliviny series are frequently mixed with those of the Suazey series in the ground. Their relatively small number and much better quality suggest they may represent the ceremonial component of people having Suazey pottery as their domestic or kitchen ware"* (Bullen and Bullen 1972:142).

Petitjean Roget (1975) made a major contribution to the study of the Caliviny phenomenon, enumerating various islands on which the decoration mode had been found. Sutty (1983) describes the distribution of Caliviny ceramics as limited from Caliviny Island in the south to southern Martinique in the north, with a number of occurrences in between. Harris (1991; 2000) lists numerous occurrences of Caliviny Polychrome within assemblages from Barbados, but due to the syncopated structure of her contributions, it is hard to gain an overall impression of the characteristics of the ware. In fact, many no longer even recognize the existence of a Caliviny ware as such (*cf.* Boomert 1987a; Donop 2007), but rather consider the phenomenon as a decoration mode belonging to the Troumassoid series in general, or as representing a transitional ware comprising both Troumassan and Suazan Troumassoid characteristics. Therefore, rather than focussing on a general Caliviny ware, only the uniquely and highly recognizable decorative Caliviny Polychrome pottery will be examined to trace lines of contact and relations between communities throughout the southern Lesser Antilles, as it is universally accepted and its traits generally recognized and agreed upon. Unlike Cayo, with which it shares roughly the same geographical distribution, it occurs at a considerable number of sites per island, in some cases quite plentifully. It was presumably a highly valued ceramic ware, as the effort involved in attaining the paint pigments alone must have been considerable, let alone the successful execution of the polychrome design. Its limited distribution is intriguing, hinting at mechanisms underlying its spread that are different than those governing the wider distribution of contemporaneous Troumassoid ceramics.

Details decoration/composition

Bullen and Bullen (1972:142) state that Caliviny Polychrome typically occurs on casuela-shaped vessels, although open bowls, pedestal bowls and plates are known to carry the decoration as well. Generally, the vessels are red-painted all over, and additionally decorated with motifs in black on the section above the shoulder, keeling or halfway point. Occasionally, other colours such as buff, yellow/brown or purple are utilized as well. The black motifs fall into two general categories,

---

77 See for instance tables 1, 2, 4 and 5 in Bullen (1964), for evidence of total stratigraphic admixture of Suazey and Caliviny ceramics (see also Boomert 1987). If anything, Caliviny sherds are most numerous in the uppermost excavation levels, suggesting a development that took place during the late phase of the Late Ceramic Age, rather than the preceding period.

curvilinear (scrolls) and linear (geometric shapes or parallels). Vessel surfaces tend to be finished through burnishing, yielding a glossy, and smooth exterior, and sometimes interior as well (figure 5.1).

Distribution

The Caliviny Polychrome decoration mode has been encountered at 60 sites on 12 islands, from Barbados to Martinique (see figure 5.2).

Stylistic similarities/dating

The Bullens considered the Caliviny ware in general to be either an indigenous development within the Lesser Antilles, for lack of similarities or antecedents in Venezuelan pottery (Bullen and Bullen 1972:17), or as influenced by Ostionoid pottery of the Greater Antilles. In fact, at one point, Bullen noted similarities in terms of burnishing, rim modifications and temper materials to the Bay series of the Virgin Islands (Bullen 1964:48). This underscores not only the wide reach of this so-called series, but also the artificiality of the Troumassan and Mamoran divide between Windward and Leeward Island assemblages. Regarding the polychrome ware and its black painted designs, the Bullens (1972:165) pointed to the occurrence of black spiral or scroll motifs on just one Dabajuroid potsherd from the Henriquez site on Aruba, dated around AD 1200 give or take 100 years, but immediately acknowledged the possibility of it representing trade ware. Given the lack of clear antecedents elsewhere, the use of black and red paint in earlier periods, and the possibility that the casuela shape evolved out of the Saladoid bell-jar

Figure 5.1. Caliviny Polychrome ware, all from Caliviny Island, Grenada. Not to scale.

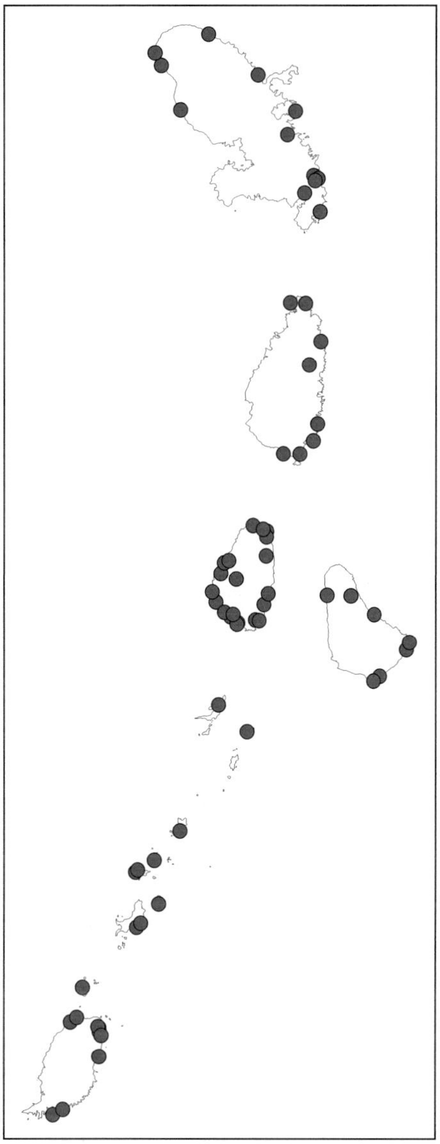

Figure 5.2. Distribution of Caliviny Polychrome throughout the Windward Islands: Barbados: Chancery Lane, Sam Lords, Greenland, Peak Bay, Heywoods/Port St. Charles, Silver Sands, Hillcrest (Site A); Grenada: Pearls (Petitjean Roget 2007), Caliviny Island 1, Caliviny Island 3, Westerhall Point 2, Simon Beach, Savanne Suazey, Calabasse, Big David Bay, Dusquene, River Antoine, High Bluff; Grenadines: Ile de Ronde (Ile de Ronde), Sabazan, Grand Bay (Carriacou), Petit Martinique (Petit Martinique), Chatham Bay, Miss Pierre (Union Island), Mayreau Beach/Saline Bay (Mayreau), Grand Bay (Cannouan), Banana Bay (Baliceaux), Industry Estate (Bequia); St. Vincent: Arnos Vale Field, Spring, Petit Bordel, Owia 2, Lot 14, North Mt. Wynn Bay, Buccament West/Cave, Fitz-Hughs, Hermitage, New Sandy Bay, Flour Mill, Mount Pleasant, Fancy, Espagnol Point South, South Union, Cumberland Ravine, Stubbs, Red Cross Hut, Petit Bordel, Indian Bay, Government House; St. Lucia: Giraudy, Lavoutte, Pigeon Island, Grande Anse, Massacare, Black Bay, La Ressource, Point de Caille, Saltibus Point; Martinique: Macabou, L'Esperance, A-Tout-Risque. Note: islands are not in exact geographical location. The same applies to all maps hereafter.

Caliviny Polychrome	*Sites with trait*	*Total sites*	*Weighted distribution percentage*
Barbados	7	52	13.46
Grenada	11	32	34.38
Grenadines	10	34	29.41
St. Vincent	21	66	31.82
St. Lucia	9	53	16.98
Martinique	3	44	6.82
Dominica	0	20	0

Table 5.1. Weighted distribution of Caliviny Polychrome per island.

form[78], they concluded that Caliviny Polychrome was a local development (Bullen and Bullen 1972:17, 165). However, the Caliviny black scrolls or linear decorations also recall the Santa Marta style of Curaçao and ceramics from Ceru Noka on Aruba, both local Dabajuroid ceramic traditions (Du Ry 1960; Van Heekeren 1963). Indeed, black painted designs are in general very frequent among assemblages of the Dabajuroid and Valencioid series of Venezuela (Allaire 1977:341; Antczak and Antczak 2006: figure 273; Rouse and Cruxent 1969). McKusick (1960:118) also refers to Rouse's suggestion that a number of his Fannis style sherds from St. Lucia may be traded pottery from coastal Venezuela related to the Dabajuroid horizon. Additionally, the Great Courland Bay site on Tobago has yielded a small number of sherds bearing typical Caliviny black painted designs, which could be local imitations of the style, but could also represent pieces of trade ware (Boomert 2007b:figure 8; Boomert and Kameneff 2005). Petitjean Roget (1993) mentions a Caliviny Polychrome vessel found at the Morel site on Guadeloupe (figure 5.3).

According to the weighted distribution data (table 5.1), Caliviny Polychrome is most prevalent on Grenada, St. Vincent and the Grenadines, and becomes a progressively weaker occurrence further north and east, which is what one would somewhat expect from a mainland South America influence. The issue of dating has yet to be resolved definitively, but it would appear that Caliviny Polychrome occurs throughout Troumassoid assemblages, albeit somewhat more frequently in later, Suazan Troumassoid assemblages, placing it broadly at the interface between the early and late phases of the Late Ceramic Age.

5.3.2. Troumassoid lugs

Background

The plethora of Late Ceramic Age vessel lugs were first detailed in depth by McKusick (1960), who determined square and pinched lugs on St. Lucia to be a trait of his Choc and Fannis styles. Bullen (1964, 1965) and Bullen and

78 But casuela-shaped vessels are also common on Tobago (Boomert 2007b: figures 3, 8, 13 and 14; Boomert and Kameneff 2005) and on the Virgin Islands (Bullen 1962) during the Late Ceramic Age, which could support both the argument of local development and of influence from elsewhere.

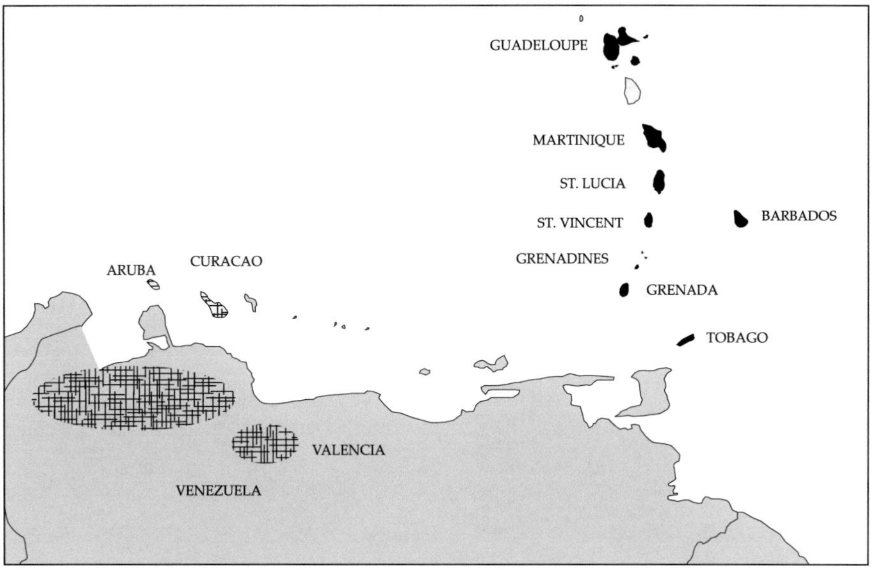

Figure 5.3. Distribution of Caliviny Polychrome throughout the Caribbean (black) and stylistic similarities (hatching). The same convention applies to all Caribbean distribution maps hereafter.

Bullen (1972) also recognized the phenomenon on Grenada, St. Vincent and the Grenadines, initially considering these lugs as belonging mainly to their so-called Caliviny series, although a number of lugs was attributed to the Saline (Bullen 1964: plate XV-2, 3, 4) and Suazey series (Bullen 1964: plate XXIII-8). The Saline series is now recognized as Troumassan Troumassoid, which explains the similarity of its lugs to the Caliviny and Suazey Rim Modified types (Bullen and Bullen 1972:143, 145). Allaire (1977) also devoted attention to lugs or rim modifications, finding them to occur in his L'Espérance, Paquemar and Macabou complexes. Finally, Harris (1991) depicted and described various different types of lugs for post-Saladoid Barbadian assemblages.

Details decoration/composition

A number of different types of lugs can be distinguished. First the flat, tabular lug, which can be rectangular, trapezoidal or even bat-shaped, and occurs plain, perforated or decorated with linear incisions (*cf.* Bullen and Bullen 1972: Caliviny Rim Modified subtype 3). Second is that of the horn- or mound-shaped lug, which does not extend very far from the rim, and can be pointy or rounded (*cf.* Bullen and Bullen 1972: Caliviny Rim Modified subtypes 1 and 5). A third category is the double horned lug, whose horns jut out in opposing directions, and are generally tubular or modelled in the round (Bullen 1964: plate XVII; *cf.* Bullen and Bullen 1972: Caliviny Rim Modified subtype 2). Fourth is the peg-shaped lug, which is cylindrical and terminates in a flat surface (figure 5.4).

The Bullens also distinguish another two subtypes, a concave, ear-like appendage and a rounded notch in the lip, the former of which I group with mound-shaped lugs, the latter of which is not adopted in this research as it does not occur

Figure 5.4. Various lug-types, clockwise from top left: double horned, mound-shaped, horn-shaped (all Savanne Suazey, Grenada), tab-shaped (Lavoutte, St. Lucia) and peg-shaped (Pigeon Island, St. Lucia). Not to scale.

frequently enough to be classed as a subtype. Another oft-occurring lug is that formed by the anthropomorphic adorno, but this subtype will be treated separately from lugs, as an individual decoration trait, with various subtypes.

Distribution

Thus far, vessel lugs have been reported for 62 sites on thirteen islands (figure 5.5). Of these 62 site occurrences, eight are of undetermined form. Trapezoidal, tab- or bat-shaped lugs are known from 24 sites on nine islands (figure 5.6). Horn- or mound-shaped lugs are known from 37 sites on ten islands (figure 5.7). Double-horned lugs are known from 19 sites on nine islands (figure 5.8). Finally, peg-shaped lugs are known from ten sites on four islands (figure 5.9).

Stylistic similarities/dating

Bullen's earliest recorded Caribbean vessel lugs are the 'Lugged' and 'Horned' decoration modes of his Botany, Bordeaux, Hull, Magens and Bay series of the Virgin Islands (1962), which in many cases are remarkably similar to the lugs and horns of the Windward Islands. Horn-shaped lugs are also known from Guadeloupe (Roseau Arrière Plage, personal observation). Tab-shaped lugs have been recorded on La Désirade (Hofman *et al.* 2004:figure 16), R. Bullen and A. Bullen (1966, 1974) found evidence of 'Caliviny' traits in the Cupecoy Bay complex on St. Martin (see also Haviser 1987), specifically of mound-shaped rim modification, and the Spring Bay 3 site on Saba has yielded double-horned lugs

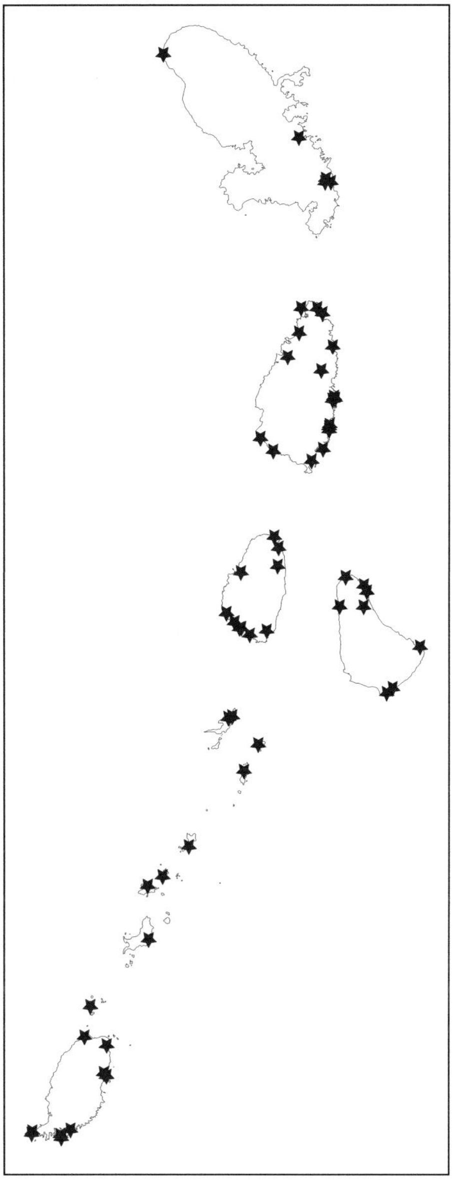

Figure 5.5. Distribution of vessel lugs throughout the Windward Islands: Barbados: Cluffs (Site A), Silver Sands, Pico Teneriffe, Cuckhold, East Point, Chancery Lane, Greenland, Heywoods/Port St. Charles; Grenada: Pearls, Black Point, Savanne Suazey, Big David Bay, Simon Beach, Salt Pond 1, Westerhall Point 2, Westerhall Point 3, Caliviny Island 1, Caliviny Island 2, Caliviny Island 3, Caliviny Island 4; Grenadines: Ile de Ronde (Ile de Ronde), Miss Pierre (Union), Grand Bay (Carriacou), Grand Bay (Cannouan), Mayreau Beach/Saline Bay (Mayreau), Rosemary/L'Ansecoy Bay (Mustique), Banana Bay (Baliceaux), Park Point, Industry Estate (Bequia); St. Vincent: Fitz-Hughs, Red Cross Hut, Stubbs, Lot 14, New Sandy Bay, Camden Park, Kingstown Post Office, Owia 1/2, Buccament West/ Cave, Arnos Vale Swamp; St. Lucia: Saltibus Point, Trou Zambé, La Ressource, Giraudy, Lavoutte, Comerette Point, Choc Point, Caraibe Point, Praslin Island, Sans Soucis, Pigeon Island, Frigate Island, Grande Anse, Massacare, Troumassée, Micoud Beach, Anse Touloulou; Martinique: Paquemar, L'Esperance, Anse Belleville, Macabou, A-Tout-Risque.

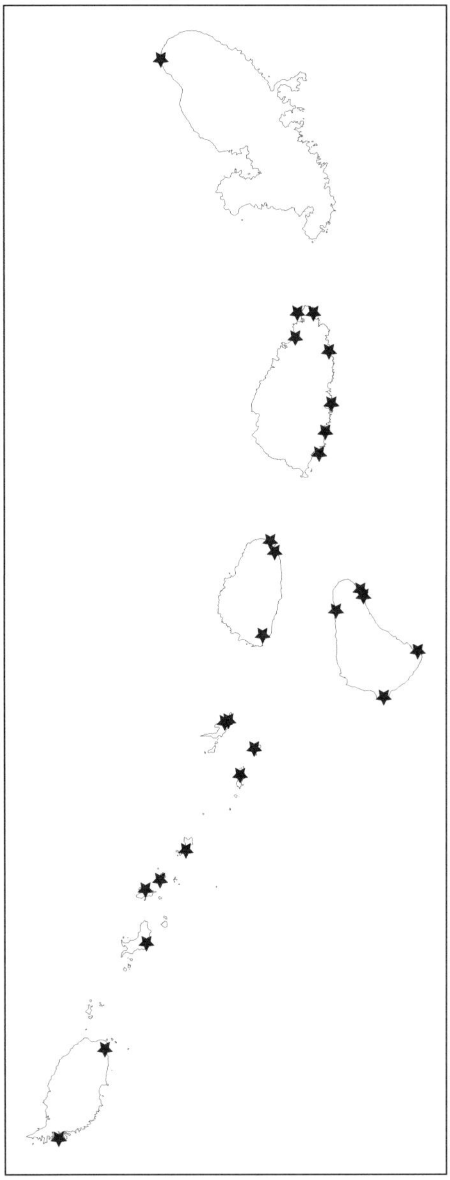

Figure 5.6. Distribution of trapezoidal, tab- or bat-shaped lugs throughout the Windward Islands: Barbados: Cluffs (Site A), Silver Sands, Pico Teneriffe, Cuckhold, East Point, Heywoods/Port St. Charles; Grenada: Savanne Suazey, Caliviny Island 3; Grenadines: Grand Bay (Carriacou), Grand Bay (Cannouan); Banana Bay (Baliceaux); Park Point (Bequia); St. Vincent: Owia 1/2, New Sandy Bay, Red Cross Hut; St. Lucia: Lavoutte, Frigate Island, Massacare, Pigeon Island, Grande Anse, Choc Point, Saltibus Point; Martinique: Anse Belleville.

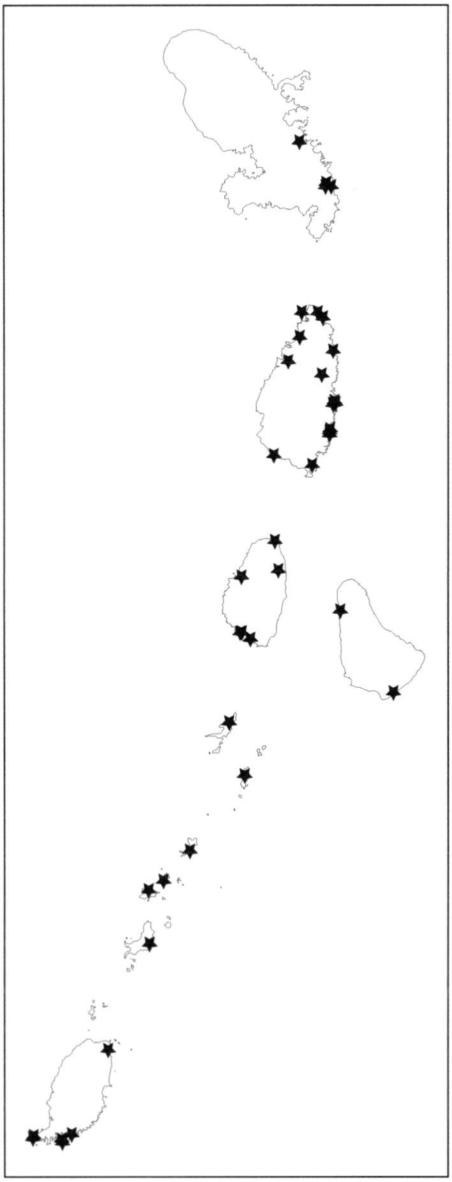

Figure 5.7. Distribution of horn- or mound-shaped lugs throughout the Windward Islands: Barbados: Chancery Lane, Greenland; Grenada: Westerhall Point 2, Salt Pond 1, Savanne Suazey, Caliviny Island 3; Grenadines: Grand Bay (Carriacou), Grand Bay (Cannouan); Mayreau Beach (Saline Bay) (Mayreau); Park Point (Bequia); Rosemary/L'Ansecoy Bay (Mustique); St. Vincent: Owia 1/2, Fitz-Hughs, Arnos Vale Swamp, Red Cross Hut, Lot 14, Camden Park; St. Lucia: Giraudy, Grande Anse, Lavoutte, Anse Touloulou, Choc Point, Massacare, Comorette Point, Pigeon Island, Sans Soucis, Troumassée, Praslin Island, Trou Zombé, Frigate Island, La Ressource; Martinique: Paquemar, L'Esperance, Macabou, A-Tout-Risque.

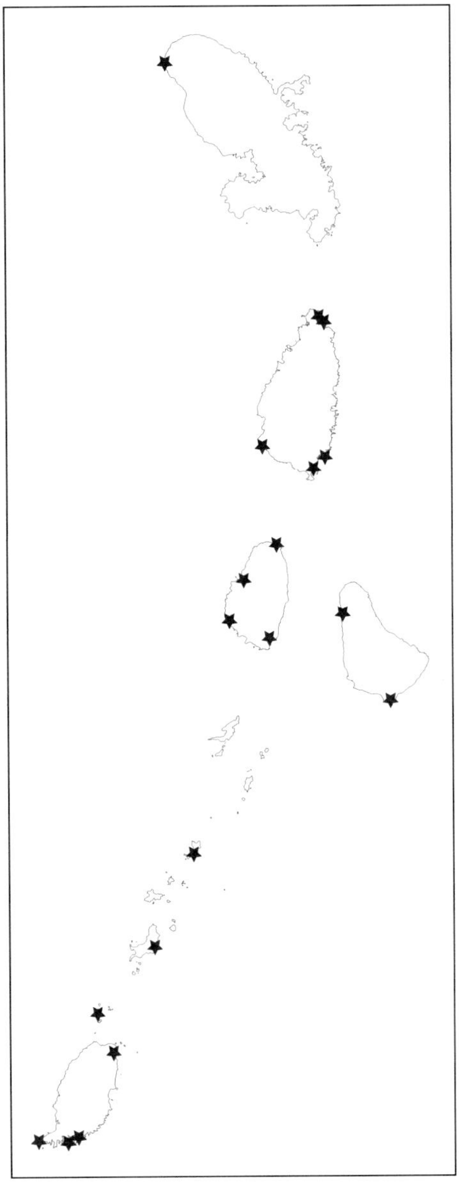

Figure 5.8. Distribution of double-horned lugs throughout the Windward Islands: Barbados: Silver Sands, Heywoods / Port St. Charles; Grenada: Westerhall Point 2, Savanne Suazey, Caliviny Island 3, Salt Pond 1; Grenadines: Grand Bay (Carriacou), Mayreau Beach (Saline Bay) (Mayreau); Ile de Ronde (Ile de Ronde), Industry Estate (Bequia); St. Vincent: New Sandy Bay, Fitz-Hughs, Buccament West/Cave, Stubbs; St. Lucia: Saltibus Point, Giraudy, Lavoutte, Caraibe Point; Martinique: Anse Belleville

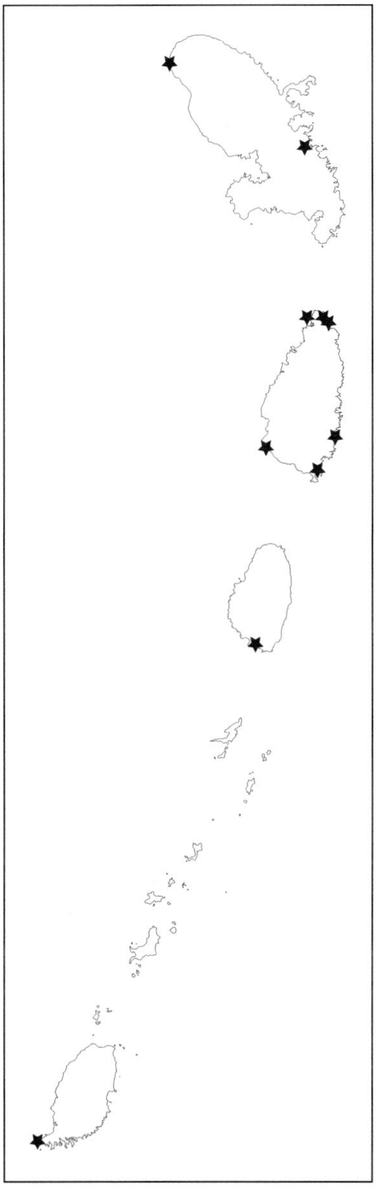

Figure 5.9. Distribution of peg-shaped lugs throughout the Windward Islands: Grenada: Salt Pond 1; St. Vincent: Kingstown Post Office; St. Lucia: Giraudy, Lavoutte, Micoud Beach, Comorette Point, Pigeon Island, Caraibe Point; Martinique: L'Esperance, Anse Belleville.

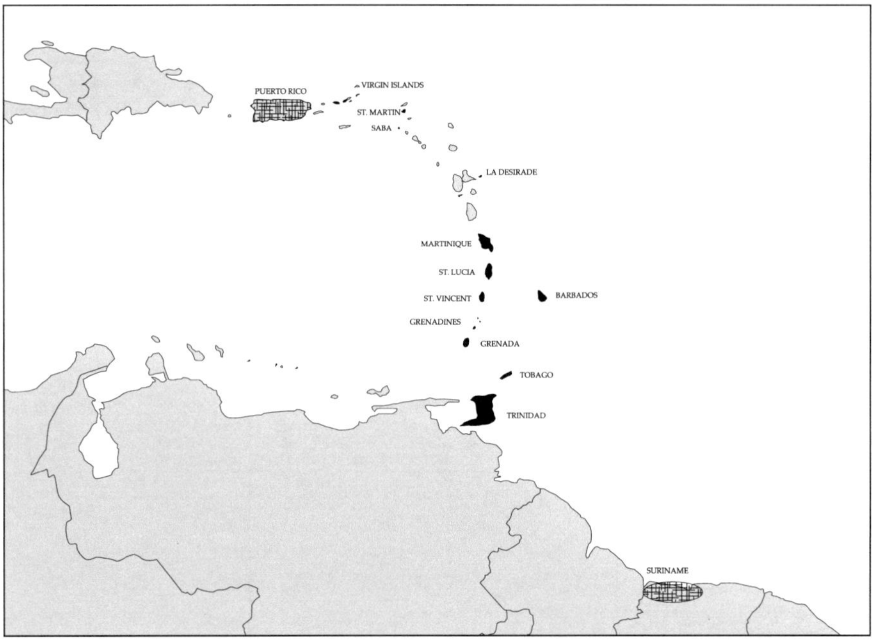

Figure 5.10. Distribution of lugs throughout the Caribbean and stylistic similarities.

(Hofman 1993:figure 36). Trapezoidal, bat-shaped, mound-shaped and double-horned lugs are a feature of Tobago's Golden Grove complex found at Golden Grove and Lovers' Retreat (Boomert 2005: figures 8 and 9; Harris 1980). They also feature in the Plymouth complex of Tobago at the site of the Great Courland Bay (Boomert and Kameneff 2005: figure 2) and furthermore extend to the Bontour complex of Trinidad (Boomert 1985:109-110 and figures 12, 13 and 14; Boomert 2007b:149-150). As Harris (1980:537) detailed, horned, double-horned or bat-head lugs are characteristic of Puerto Rican early Ostionoid ceramics and the Arauquinoid Hertenrits II ceramics of Suriname (see also Boomert 1980: figure 15 and Versteeg 2003:figure 6.23) (see also figure 5.10). Boomert points to additional general stylistic similarities with Arauquinoid complexes of Arauquín, Matraquero, Camoruco in the Middle Orinoco area, Macapaima near the Orinoco-Caroní junction, Mon Repos of coastal Guyana and Valencia in the Central Venezuelan coastal zone (Boomert 1985:98).

According to the weighted distribution data (table 5.2), vessel lugs are most prevalent on Grenada, St. Lucia and the Grenadines (in order of prevalence), and at most slightly more than half as prevalent on other islands. The issue of dating has yet to be resolved for the various subtypes specifically, but it would appear that Troumassoid vessel lugs occur throughout Troumassoid assemblages, albeit in varying degrees of prevalence.

Vessel lugs	*Sites with trait*	*Total sites*	*Weighted distribution percentage*
Barbados	7	52	13.46
Grenada	12	32	37.5
Grenadines	9	34	26.47
St. Vincent	10	66	15.15
St. Lucia	16	53	30.19
Martinique	5	44	11.36
Dominica	0	20	0

Table 5.2. Weighted distribution of vessel lugs per island.

5.3.3. Scratched ware

Background

Scratched ware has, like WOR and ZIC for Saladoid, become Caribbean archaeology shorthand for Suazan Troumassoid ware. Scratching is undoubtedly highly diagnostic for this latest pre-Colonial subseries, but this strong connection has in the past led to misconceptions concerning late prehistoric finer ware (previously ascribed to the earlier Troumassan Troumassoid subseries, now recognized as potentially representing a fine-ware component among Suazan assemblages). Also, it appears that on some islands scratched ware occurs within assemblages predating the Suazan Troumassoid, as reported by Rouse (cited in Goodwin 1979:301), Goodwin (1979:300-301) and Boomert (2005:40, figure 10). Finally, recent excavations at the sites of Woodford Hill (Dominica) and Argyle (St. Vincent) appear to point to commingling of scratched ware with Cayo ceramics, suggesting that the trait held over from the Suazan Troumassoid. However, in the absence of radiocarbon dates for Cayo sites in the Windward Islands, this remains a tentative assumption.

Details decoration/composition

There are various types of scratched ware, suggesting that a number of different procedures were undertaken to achieve the desired surface finish. Scraping resulted in the least coarse finish: striations were probably a by-product of temper material being dragged across the vessel surface. Scratching appears to represent intentional striation, which was often carried out in a number of overlapping directions, probably using local grasses. In some cases, the overlapping striations may represent the joining together of separate pieces of clay to form a vessel base (Jacobson 2002). Gouging or 'corrugating' (Allaire 1977) is a very rough form of surface finishing, which results in large, deep striations and a very uneven finish (figure 5.11). It has been suggested that in some instances, scratching may have been applied to the vessel surface to allow for better adhesion of slip or paint (Drewett and Harris 1991:181). Be that as it may, the overwhelming majority of scratched ware exhibits no evidence of the erstwhile application of slip or paint. Donop (2007:14) hypothesizes that scratching or unfinished scraping may have benefited a vessel's initial manufacture, improved a vessel's cooking performance (see also Boomert and Kameneff 2005:462), and made these larger, heavier vessels easier to hold.

Distribution

Suazan Troumassoid scratched ware has been encountered at 98 sites on 13 islands, from Barbados up to and including Dominica (figure 5.12).

Stylistic similarities/dating

North of the Windward Islands, scratched pottery has turned up in minimal quantities on the Virgin Islands (R. Bullen 1970:150), Saba (De Josselin de Jong 1947: plate III-18 and IV-33/36; Hofman 1993), at the Cupecoy Bay site on St. Martin (R. Bullen 1970:150; R. Bullen and A. Bullen 1966: plate B; Bullen and Bullen 1974: figure 3g-h), on Nevis (Wilson 2006: figure 4.19), at the Indian Creek, Winthorpe's West, Marmora Bay, Freeman's Bay and Mill Reef sites on Antigua (DeMille *et al.* 1999; Hoffman 1963 in R. Bullen 1970:150; Rouse 1976; Rouse and Faber Morse 1999), at Anse à l'Eau, Anse à la Gourde, Morel, Pointe

Figure 5.11. Scratched ware, demonstrating finer, multidirectional striations as well as cruder gouging (top right) from St. Pierre, Martinique (bottom left), Pigeon Island (top row) and Caraibe Point (bottom right), St. Lucia. Not to scale.

Figure 5.12. Distribution of Suazan Troumassoid scratched ware throughout the Windward Islands: Barbados: Chancery Lane, Heywoods/Port St. Charles, Sam Lords, Peak Bay, Silver Sands, Cuckhold, Laycock Bay, Hillcrest (Site B); Grenada: Caliviny Island 1, Caliviny Island 2, Caliviny Island 3, Caliviny Island 5, Westerhall Point 1, Westerhall Point 2, Westerhall Point 3, Simon Beach, Savanne Suazey, Pearls, Calabasse, Big David Bay, Chemin Bay, Salt Pond 1; Grenadines: Chatham Bay, Belmont Pond, Miss Pierre, Frigate Island (Union), Mt. Pleasant, Great Breteche Bay, Dover, Sabazan, Grand Bay (Carriacou), Grand Bay, Carenage (Cannouan), Mayreau Beach/Saline Bay (Mayreau), Isle à Quatre (Isle à Quatre), Industry Estate, Park Point (Bequia), Banana Bay (Baliceaux); St. Vincent: Arnos Vale Field, Arnos Vale Swamp, Queensbury, Petit Bordel, Owia 1/2, Texaco Tank, Lot 14, Stubbs, North Mt. Wynn Bay, Young's Island, Questelles School, Buccament West/Cave, Camden Park, Fitz-Hughs, Hermitage, New Sandy Bay, Careenage, Flour Mill, Mount Pleasant, Fancy, Espagnol Point South, Cumberland Ravine, Indian Bay, Colonarie, Coconut Oil Factory, Carib Piece, North Union, Government House; St. Lucia: Micoud Beach, Caraibe Point, Comerette Point, Giraudy, Lavoutte, Pigeon Island, Frigate Island, Park Estate, Anse Violon, Frigate Island Trail 1, La Ressource, Choc Point, Micoud Fannis Garden, Gayabois, Hope Estate, Massacare, Grand Anse, Saltibus Point; Martinique: Anse Charpentier, Anse Trabaud, Saint-Pierre Centre, Pointe de la Prairie/Cap Est, Paquemar, Macabou, A-Tout-Risque, Anse Couleuvre, Le Coin; Dominica: Walkers Rest, Toulaman River, La Plaine, Sophia Bay, Eden 1.

Helleux and several other sites on Guadeloupe (Bullen and Bullen 1973; De Waal 2006: Appendix 2; Hofman *et al.* 2001; Hoogland 1995), at the Grande Anse site on Terre de Bas, Les Saintes and at Morne Cybèle 2, À l'Escalier and Anse Petite Rivière on La Désirade (De Waal 2006: Appendix 3; Hofman 1995).

To the south, the Lovers' Retreat site on Tobago has yielded quite some scratched ware (R. Bullen 1970:150), as have Golden Grove (Boomert 2005:figure 10; Harris 1976) and, more recently, the Crown Point (Kameneff and Merlin 1994) and Great Courland Bay sites (Boomert 2007b:figures 15 and 16; Boomert and Kameneff 2005). Given the perceived scarcity of stylistic parallels to the north, Bullen (1970) looked to the south for possible origins of the scratched pottery of the Suazan Troumassoid series. However, Venezuela yielded nothing similar (Cruxent and Rouse 1982) and Trinidad also turned up a blank, despite rumours of findings of scratched ware in the south-east (R. Bullen 1970:150; Bullen and Bullen 1976. Bullen did not discount that the scratched ware and, by extension, Suazan Troumassoid pottery, originated further south in the delta of the Orinoco or in the Guianas, but provided no tangible evidence for his hypothesis, which rested purely on his desire to correlate the ware with the Island Carib who supposedly originated in these parts. However, all evidence currently points to a local Lesser Antillean development for this particular decorative/functional trait (see also figure 5.13).

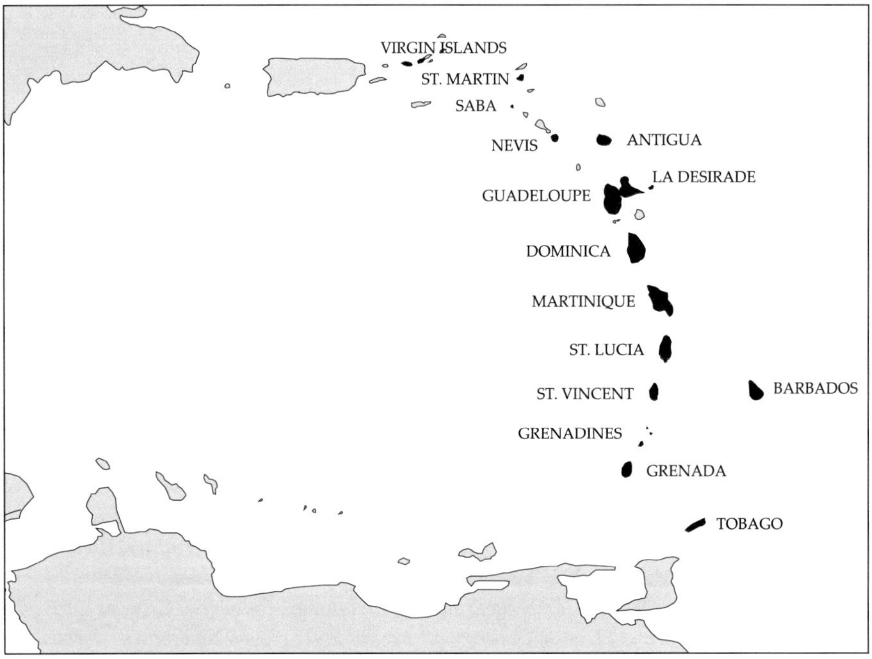

Figure 5.13. Distribution of scratched ware throughout the Caribbean and stylistic similarities.

Scratched ware	Sites with trait	Total sites	Weighted distribution percentage
Barbados	8	52	15.38
Grenada	14	32	43.75
Grenadines	16	34	47.06
St. Vincent	28	66	42.42
St. Lucia	18	53	33.96
Martinique	9	44	20.45
Dominica	5	20	25

Table 5.3. Weighted distribution of scratched ware per island.

According to the weighted distribution data (table 5.3), scratched ware is very prevalent throughout the Windward Islands, though significantly less so on Martinique, Dominica and Barbados. The issue of dating has yet to be resolved definitively, but it would appear that scratched ware occurs predominantly in Suazan Troumassoid assemblages in the Windward Islands, although it has been found in earlier assemblages both north and south of the Windward Islands in very limited quantities, and tentatively in later assemblages as well.

5.3.4 Troumassoid anthropomorphic modelling

Background

It has long been noted by many researchers that the Late Ceramic Age seems to see a proliferation of human imagery in ceramic form, particularly in the form of anthropomorphic adornos. While these do indeed make up a sizeable portion of the ceramic inventory of the period, it may not be wholly accurate to speak of a great and sudden shift towards the depiction of humanoid features in ceramics. It must not be forgotten that earlier Saladoid pottery was also laden with anthropomorphic imagery, albeit sometimes of a more abstract or transformational nature. Rather, post-Saladoid assemblages are perhaps better characterized as having jettisoned their fused anthropo-zoomorphic, fantastical imagery, in favour of more generalised, simplified anthropo– and zoomorphic imagery.

Details decoration/composition

A number of different types of anthropomorphic imagery can be distinguished. First is the rather flat adorno or appendage, which has simply gouged out eyes and mouth, sometimes supplemented with some modelling and/or linear incisions running from the eyes down the cheeks (*cf.* Bright 2007: figure 3). Second is the flattish or cylindrical adorno or appendage, which rather than having excised decoration, actually exhibits modelled appliqué in its eyes, nose and/or mouth. These adornos have a rather bulbous appearance and an owl-like countenance (*cf.* Drewett 2004: Fig. 8:64/65). These two aforementioned types mainly served as either straight or backward-bent rim-appendages, and are occasionally found as diametrically opposed pairs. Some are further elaborated by means of modelled, pierced ears, raising the possibility that these heads were once embellished with some form of pendant or ring. A third type of face is that which one finds on vessel walls or legs, often comprising coffee-bean eyes and a 'MacDonalds' arch over the eyes, the middle foot of which extends down towards the mouth, in effect forming the nose (*cf.* Bullen and Bullen 1968: Fig. 5 m-t; Drewett 2004: Fig. 8:66) (see also figure 5.14).

A separate category of anthropomorphic representation is that of very rudimentary eyes, nose and sometimes mouth carved onto a curious artefact category which is invariably termed loom weight or pestle (*cf.* Grouard *et al.* 2007). Regardless of their functional interpretation, some of these statuettes are either perforated or have been furnished with horns projecting from the tops as if to aid in suspension. While the foregoing has described some typical characteristics

Figure 5.14. Anthropomorphic adornos types 1 (left, Lavoutte), 2 (centre, Massacare) and 3 (right, Lavoutte), all from St. Lucia. Not to scale.

Figure 5.15. Anthropomorphic pestles/loom weights, fine and crude (from left to right Pigeon Island and Caraibe Point, St. Lucia and Martinique). Not to scale.

of ceramic human representations, it is almost impossible to maintain a rigorous typology of the various traits. In practice, the various ways of demarcating a face are used interchangeably in different contexts. Thus one finds very rudimentary, gouged rim appendages alongside highly elaborated, modelled and appliquéd ones. Conversely, besides the rather crude, roughly modelled clay loom weights or statues, there are much more finely worked specimens too. The exaggerated eyebrow arch and coffee-bean eyes are also not restricted exclusively to vessel walls, but appear on appendages as well, albeit less markedly (figure 5.15).

Distribution

Troumassoid anthropomorphic adornos have been encountered at 42 sites on ten islands, from Grenada up to and including Dominica (figure 5.16). However, the exact distribution of the various subtypes differs considerably. Type 1 features at 21 sites on six islands (figure 5.17). Type 2 occurs at eleven sites on five islands (figure 5.18). Type 3 can be found at eleven sites on six islands (figure 5.19). Anthropomorphic or undecorated pestles or loom weights are found at thirteen sites on six islands (figure 5.20).

Stylistic similarities/dating

The phenomenon of anthropomorphic modelling occurs outside the Windward Islands as well (see figure 5.21). Flat, head-shaped lugs with gouged facial features are seen as far north as western Puerto Rico, where they feature within the Ostionan Ostionoid subseries assemblages (*cf.* Rouse 1992: figure 23b) and are furthermore relatively common on Guadeloupe (*cf.* Delpuech *et al.* 1993: figure 9; Romon and Chancerel 2003:35). They have also been found at Hope Estate on St. Martin, Morne Cybèle on La Désirade (Hofman 1995: figures 6 and 7) and Grande Anse on Terre de Bas (Hofman 1995: figure 3). They also occur in the Hertenrits culture (Boomert 1980: figures 14 and 15; Rostain and Versteeg 2004: figure 4), but despite exhibiting the same basic features, these specimens look distinctly different.

Concerning the modelled, highly plastic adornos defined as type 2 above, there is some similarity between those from Grenada and the Grenadines (formerly classed as Caliviny by Bullen and Bullen (1972) and Petitjean Roget (2002)) and the adornos of the Matraquero and Arauquín styles (Cruxent and Rouse 1982: plates 79, 80). A similar, plastic human head rim adorno has turned up at the Lovers' Retreat site on Tobago (Harris 1980: plate 19). Highly identical specimens are also found far to the north, however, among Ostionoid assemblages on the Virgin Islands (Bullen 1964; Bullen and Bullen 1972), *i.e.* the Cinnamon Bay site, St. John's (Bullen 1962: plate 16b), and the Magens Bay site, St. Thomas (Hatt 1924: figure 4i).

Type 3 anthropomorphic representations that emerge out of vessel walls are already encountered in Saladoid ceramic assemblages across the Lesser Antilles and Puerto Rico, and carry over into Troumassan and Suazan Troumassoid assemblages, their stylistic execution shifting in tandem with the successive ceramic traditions. As far as stylistic similarities are concerned, the resemblance between

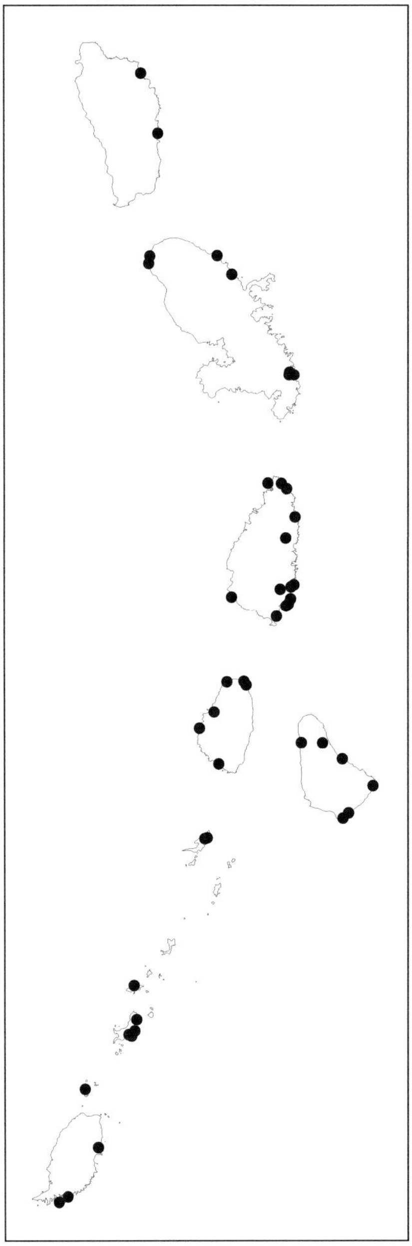

Figure 5.16. Distribution of Troumassoid anthropomorphic adornos throughout the Windward Islands: Barbados: Silver Sands, Chancery Lane, Heywoods/Port St. Charles, Hillcrest (Site A), Greenland, Palmetto Bay; Grenada: Caliviny Island 3, Westerhall Point 2, Pearls; Grenadines: Sabazan, Dover, Dumfries, Grand Bay (Carriacou), Park Point, Industry Estate (Bequia), Miss Pierre (Union), Ile de Ronde (Ile de Ronde); St. Vincent: Fitz-Hughs, Wallilibou, Espagnol Point South, Owia 1, Quashie Point; St. Lucia: Lavoutte, Pigeon Island, Giraudy, Canelles Point, Caraibe Point, Grande Anse, Comerette Point, La Ressource, Vierge Point 1, Massacare, Troumassée, Saltibus Point, Pointe de Caille; Martinique: Macabou, Paquemar, A-Tout-Risque, Anse Belleville, Galba; Dominica: Saint-Sauveur 1.

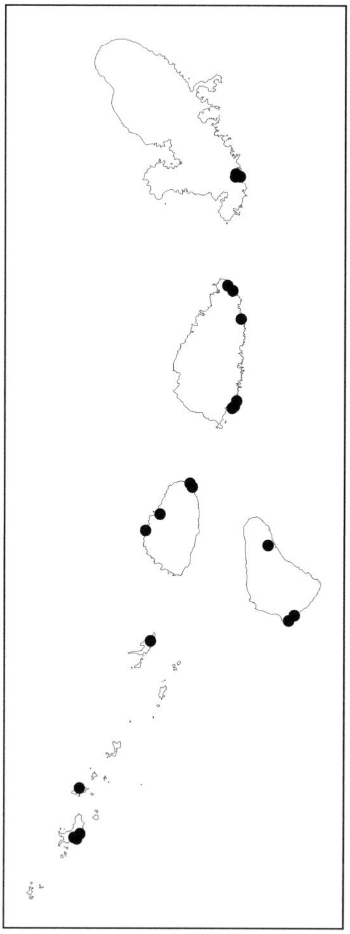

Figure 5.17. Distribution of Troumassoid anthropomorphic adorno type 1 throughout the Windward Islands: Barbados: Silver Sands (Drewett ed. 1991: plate 18, figure 49-158, figure 54-196), Palmetto Bay (Drewett ed. 1991: figure 30-15, plate 15), Chancery Lane; Grenadines: Grand Bay, Dumfries (Petitjean Roget 2002: figure 9), Sabazan (Petitjean Roget 2002: figure 41/43) (Carriacou), Miss Pierre (Union) (Petitjean Roget 2002: figure 145), Park Point (Bequia); St. Vincent: Espagnol Point South, Owia 1, Wallilibou, Quashie Point, Fitz-Hughs; St. Lucia: Saltibus Point, Lavoutte, Comerette Point, Massacare, Grande Anse, Pointe de Caille; Martinique: Macabou, Paquemar.

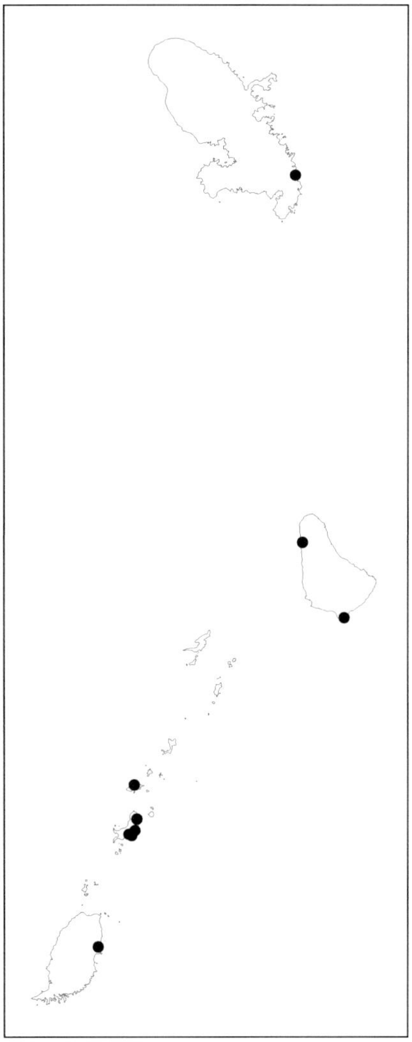

Figure 5.18. Distribution of Troumassoid anthropomorphic adorno type 2 throughout the Windward Islands: Barbados: Heywoods/Port St. Charles (Drewett ed. 1991: figure 61-317, plate 15; Harris 2000: figure 45-64-5), Silver Sands (Drewett ed. 1991: figure 54-197; Harris 2000: figure 37-28, 33); Grenada: Caliviny Island 3 and Westerhall Point 2 (Bullen 1964: plate XXII-1/3), Pearls (Bullen 1964: plate XII-1, Petitjean Roget 2002: figure 32); Grenadines: Dover (Petitjean Roget 2002: figure 40/51), Grand Bay (Petitjean Roget 2002: figure 53) (Carriacou), Chatham Bay (Union), Park Point (Bequia); Martinique: Macabou, Paquemar.

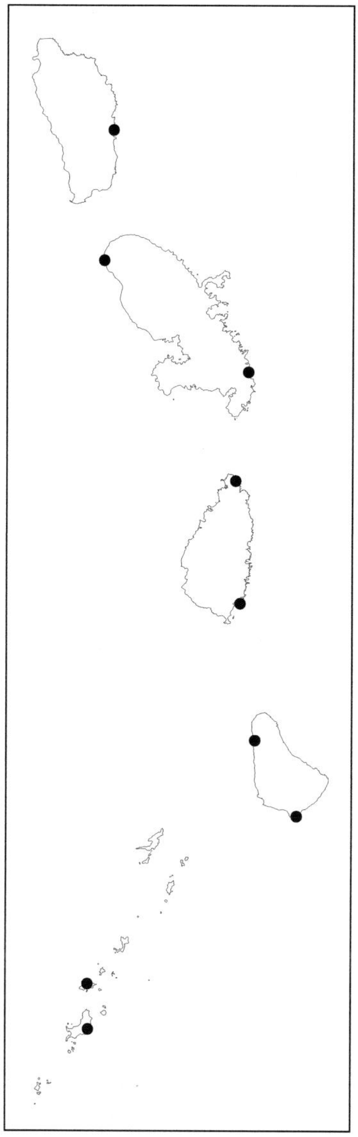

Figure 5.19. Distribution of Troumassoid anthropomorphic adorno type 3 throughout the Windward Islands: Barbados: Heywoods/Port St. Charles (Harris 2000: figure 45-66), Silver Sands (Drewett ed. 1991: figure 52-174; Harris 2000: figure 38-37); Grenadines: Sabazan (Carriacou), Chatham Bay (Union: Petitjean Roget 2002: figure 3); St. Lucia: Lavoutte, Saltibus Point, Point de Caille; Martinique: Anse Belleville (Conservation du Musée Départmental d'Archéologie 1991: figure C14), Macabou, Galba (Pinchon 1952 : plate XXX-6); Dominica: Saint-Sauveur 1 (Evans 1968: figure2-h).

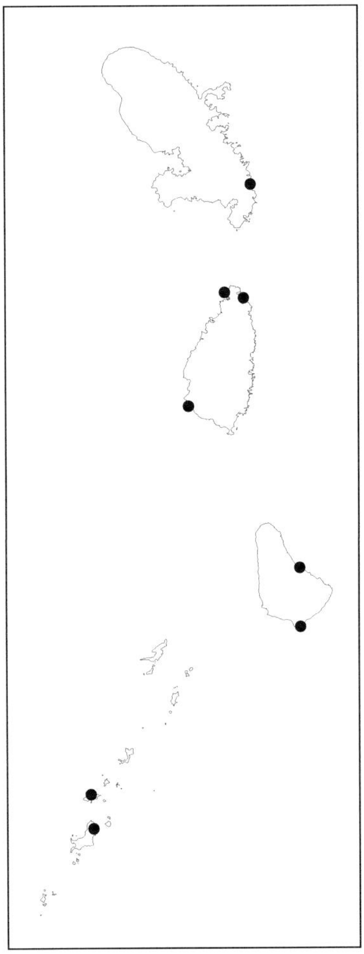

Figure 5.20. Distribution of Troumassoid anthropomorphic or undecorated poestles/loom weights throughout the Windward Islands: Barbados: Sam Lords, Silver Sands (Drewett ed. 1991: figure 54-207, 208), Hillcrest (Site A) (Drewett ed. 1991: figure 58-296); Grenada: Savanne Suazey (Bullen 1964: plate XXII-7), Caliviny Island 2, Caliviny Island 3 (Bullen 1964: plate XXI-6/7); Grenadines: Miss Pierre (Union), Dover (Carriacou: Petitjean Roget 2002: figure 52); St. Lucia: Caraibe Point, Comerette Point, Pigeon Island; Martinique: Ilet Madame, Paquemar (Mattioni and Nicolas 1972:66), Macabou.

the vessel faces from Arauquín, Venezuela (Cruxent and Rouse 1982: plate 76, 1 and 3) and that from Heywoods/Port St. Charles, Barbados (Drewett 2004: figure 8-66) was so notable as to have already been remarked upon. Vessel wall faces are also a typical trait of Valencioid and Dabajuroid assemblages, where they are often found along the upper portion of composite vessels (Antczak and Antczak 2006: figures 243-245; Cruxent and Rouse 1982: plate 68; Dijkhoff 1997: figure B-28). Closer to home, they also feature in Tobago's Plymouth complex at the Great Courland Bay site (Boomert 2007b: figures 4, 5 and 10; Boomert and Kameneff 2005: figure 3).

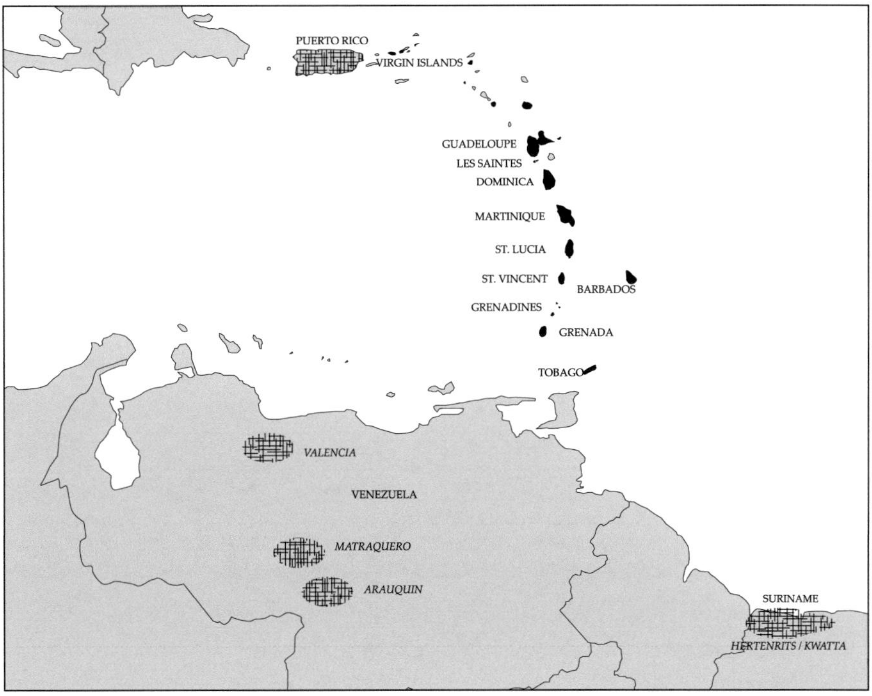

Figure 5.21. Distribution of anthropomorphic adornos and loomweights / pestles throughout the Caribbean and stylistic similarities.

Specimens similar to the anthropomorphic pestles/loom weights of the Windward Islands have been encountered on Guadeloupe (Pointe Helleux, Hoogland and Hofman 1995; Hofman *et al.* 2004:figure 5) and Terre-de-Bas (Grande Anse, Hofman 1995; Hofman *et al.* 2004:figure 4) to the north and Great Courland Bay, Tobago to the south (Boomert 2007b:figure 11). On the South American mainland, similar pestle artefacts are known from the Arauquinoid Hertenrits (Boomert 1980: figure 18; Versteeg 2003: figure 6.32) and Kwatta (Versteeg 2003: figure 7.15) assemblages in the Guianas (see also Versteeg 2003: figure 7.39).

Though not treated as a separate category, adornos bearing exaggerated eyebrow ridges deserve some discussion as these have been found among assemblages on Guadeloupe (Delpuech *et al.* 1993: figure 68). Even further afield, similarly styled but not identical adornos are found in the Valencia, Arauquín, Matraquero, and Guarguapo styles of Venezuela (Allaire 1977:340; Cruxent and Rouse 1982: figures 79-2, 80-23, 99-22). All but Arauquín (which starts halfway through period III) are relatively late styles, namely period IV or V in the Cruxent and Rouse terminology, suggesting a date of after AD 1000 at the earliest for these adornos (Cruxent and Rouse 1982:34; Rouse and Cruxent 1969:20, 91). This would seem to suggest that this decorative trait diffused from the mainland to the Windward Islands sometime after AD 1000, or possibly a little earlier if one takes into account early Arauquín developments. That the eyebrow ridge-phenomenon is a

Anthropomorphic adornos	Sites with trait	Total sites	Weighted distribution percentage
Barbados	6	52	11.54
Grenada	3	32	9.38
Grenadines	9	34	26.47
St. Vincent	5	66	7.58
St. Lucia	11	53	20.75
Martinique	4	44	9.09
Dominica	1	20	5

Table 5.4. Weighted distribution of anthropomorphic adornos per island.

Anthropomorphic pestles / loom weights	Sites with trait	Total sites	Weighted distribution percentage
Barbados	3	52	5.77
Grenada	2	32	6.25
Grenadines	2	34	5.88
St. Vincent	0	66	0
St. Lucia	3	53	5.66
Martinique	3	44	6.82
Dominica	0	20	0

Table 5.5. Weighted distribution of anthropomorphic pestles/loom weights per island.

wide ranging one indeed can be seen from some of the figurines or statuettes from Marajó Island, which also exhibit the feature (Palmatary 1950: plate 39; Roosevelt 1991).

According to the weighted distribution data (table 5.4), Troumassoid anthropomorphic adornos are most prevalent on the Grenadines and St. Lucia, and significantly less so on other islands. Interestingly enough, they are least common on St. Vincent, which is sandwiched between the two highest values for the trait. Anthropomorphic pestles/loom weights are most prevalent on Martinique, followed by Grenada and St. Lucia, the Grenadines, and Barbados (table 5.5). They do not occur at all on St. Vincent or Dominica.

The absence of anthropomorphic adornos at the Suazan Troumassoid type site Savanne Suazey led Bullen to conclude that this decorative trait should be dated to early post-Saladoid times, rather than his Suazey period (Bullen 1964:31). However, at many other sites, the adornos feature prominently in the later Troumassoid assemblages, suggesting Savanna Suazey should be regarded as the exception rather than the rule.

5.3.5. Troumassoid female statues

Background

Petitjean Roget was the first to call attention to the phenomenon of female figurines or statues in Suazan Troumassoid assemblages (Petitjean Roget 1993, 2003, 2005:44, 2007). They seem to be an exclusively Late Ceramic Age trait then, although one so-called caraïbe female statuette described by Petitjean Roget (1978a: plate 17-O.24) for the L'Adoration site on Martinique must date to Early Ceramic Age times, if the site's date as reported thus far is valid. Kirby (1978:66) suggested that the phenomenon of kneeling female figurines could be representations of the use of ritual enemas, known from the Maya area.

Details decoration/composition

There is no fixed stylistic template for the female figurines known from the Windwards Islands, and they differ greatly in form, style and dimensions. In general though, they appear to conform to one of two general principles, *i.e.* seated or kneeling women. Breasts are generally represented through modelling, whereas the female genitalia are portrayed by means of incision and occasionally perforation. The Lavoutte specimen appears exceptional both in terms of its size and the characteristic of the canopy or plateau above its head (figure 5.22).

Figure 5.22. Female statuettes from Lavoutte, St. Lucia. Not to scale.

Distribution

Suazan Troumassoid female statues have been encountered at twelve sites on seven islands, from Barbados up to and including Martinique (see figure 5.23).

Stylistic similarities/dating

Female statues occur outside the Windwards as well (figure 5.24). They have been encountered sparingly to the north, for instance at the Tourlourous site on Marie-Galante (Chancerel 2005: figure 4.9). However, standing female statuettes feature quite regularly in Cuban Meillacan assemblages (Portuondo Zúñiga 1995). To the south, female statues have been reported for Great Courland Bay and an unidentified site on Tobago (Boomert 2007b: figure 11; Boomert and Kameneff 2005:462) and for an unrecorded site (Ayubi 1990:fig. 64) and Tanki Flip (Dijkhoff 1997: figure 80) on Aruba. Turning to the mainland, the Arauquinoid culture (Rostain and Versteeg 2004: figure 6B) in general and Hertenrits in particular (Boomert 1980: figure 19-2; Rostain and Versteeg 2004: figure 6A; Versteeg 2003: figure 6.34; Versteeg and Rostain 2005:24) exhibit the phenomenon, as does the Santarém complex (part of the late prehistoric Amazonian Incised and Punctate Horizon) and Marajoaroid of coastal Brazil (Roosevelt 1991: figure 1.22; Roosevelt 1999). The series most notable for its female statues and standing figurines is however the Central Venezuelan Valencioid, dated to Cruxent and Rouse's Period IV, or 1150-1500 AD (Rouse and Cruxent 1969:100). The Los Roques archipelago has yielded hundreds of sitting or standing female figurines in varying degrees of elaboration (Antczak 1995; Antczak and Antczak 2006).

Regarding the seated figurines, particularly the Lavoutte "canopied idol" (Bullen and Bullen 1970), numerous researchers have already pointed out the marked similarities with Greater Antillean Taíno wooden and ceramic seated statues (Allaire 1990; Hofman *et al.* 2008). The canopy or plateau atop the St. Lucian specimen recalls the trays or dishes on top of a number of wooden cemí idols, and is typically associated with the preparing and inhaling of cohoba. One remarkable difference between the statues from the two areas concerns the sex of those represented. In Taíno material culture, the seated are invariably male, often with an erect phallus, whereas most ceramic figurines of the Lesser Antilles and mainland South America represent women. Petitjean Roget (2005:44) regards the rise of female idolatry in the Lesser Antilles as coeval with a rise in phallic statuary, and suggests a realignment of society and perhaps a response to lengthy drought in the region (see also Chapter 2). Petitjean Roget ascribes the female (and male) statues to the post-Saladoid period in general, potentially tracing their roots back to the late Saladoid (Petitjean Roget 1993). However, in the absence of securely dated find contexts, it appears safer to date these artefacts slightly later and classify them as Suazan Troumassoid.

Although weighted distributions mean little with such low numbers, the weighted distribution data (table 5.6) indicate that female statues are most prevalent on St. Lucia, followed by Grenada, Martinique and the Grenadines, Barbados and St. Vincent. Dominica has yielded none thus far.

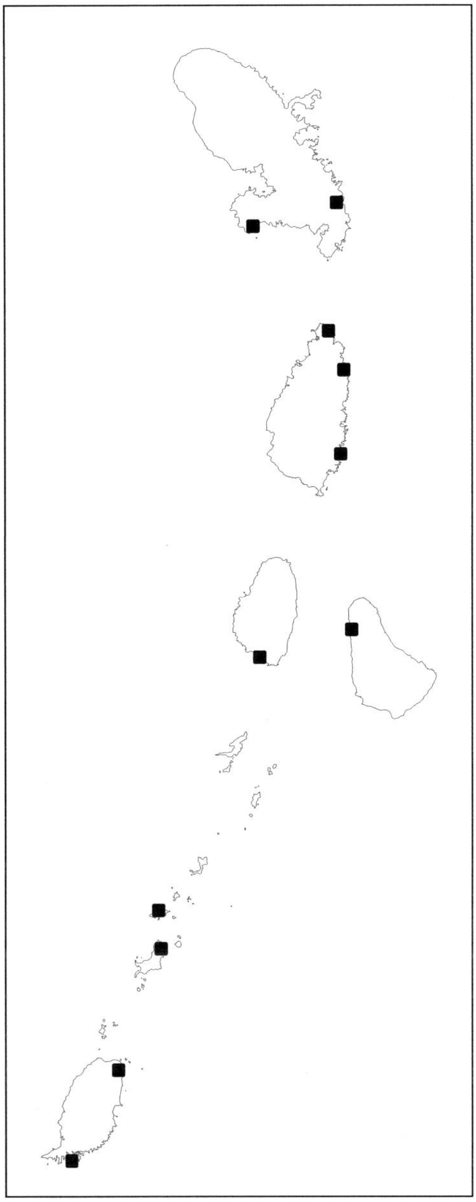

Figure 5.23. Distribution of female statues throughout the Windward Islands: Barbados: Heywoods/Port St. Charles (Harris 2007b); Grenada: Caliviny Island 3 (Bullen and Bullen 1968a: figure 5a), Savanne Suazey (Petitjean Roget 2002:46); Grenadines: Dover (Carriacou) (Petitjean Roget 1996: figure 33), Miss Pierre (Union Island) (Petitjean Roget 2005: figure 10); St. Vincent: Arnos Vale Field (Bullen and Bullen 1972:plate XXII-b); St. Lucia: Lavoutte, Massacare, Grande Anse, Giraudy; Martinique: Diamant (Petitjean Roget 1978: plate 104-O52), Paquemar (Pinchon 1952: plate XXX-7).

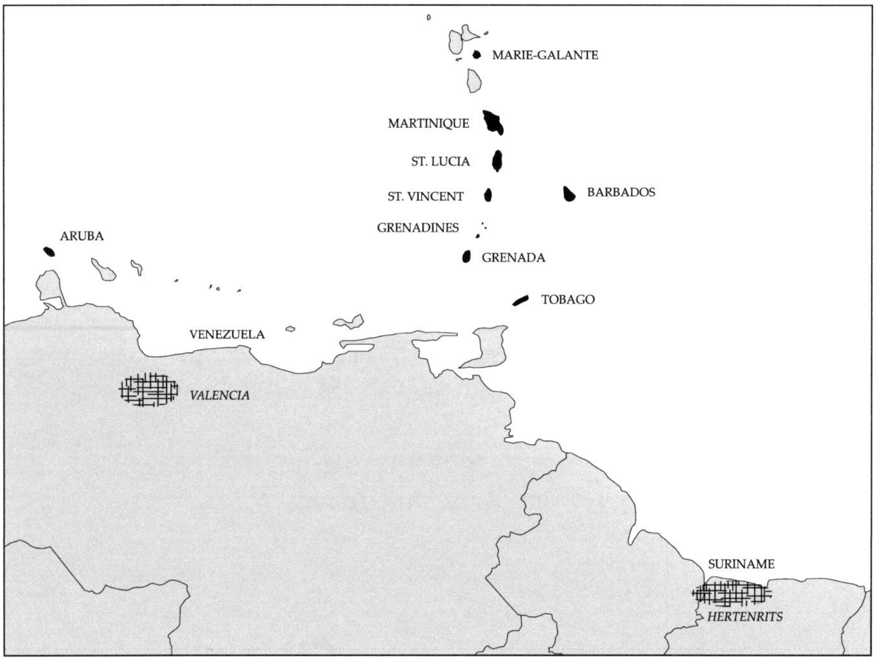

Figure 5.24. Distribution of female statues throughout the Caribbean and stylistic similarities.

Female statues	*Sites with trait*	*Total sites*	*Weighted distribution percentage*
Barbados	1	52	1.92
Grenada	2	32	6.25
Grenadines	2	34	5.88
St. Vincent	1	66	1.52
St. Lucia	4	53	7.55
Martinique	2	44	4.55
Dominica	0	20	0

Table 5.6. Weighted distribution of female statues per island.

5.3.6. Suazan Troumassoid rim indentation

Background

At the micro-regional scale, rim punctation or indentation is one of the most widespread and characteristic decoration modes applied to Suazan Troumassoid ceramics. Late Ceramic Age assemblages across the Windward Islands, Tobago and Guadeloupe exhibit the trait, although there is considerable diversity in the exact manner and manifestation of the indentation. First recognized by Fewkes (1914:675) on St. Kitts, the trait was subsequently recorded by Lovén (1935:281; as finger-pressure-made-ware), Barton (1953:51-53), McKusick (1960:36, 149),

Haag (1964; as Fannis Finger Punctate), and Bullen (1964), who gave it its lasting name of Suazey Finger Indented. It has since become the defining decoration mode for the Suazan Troumassoid subseries, along with scratching, and is found on every Windward Island in some form or fashion. Finger indented rims occur to this day among Afro-Caribbean folk pottery assemblages (*cf.* Hofman and Bright 2004)

Details decoration/composition

Bullen and Bullen (1972:145) enumerated five different subtypes within the overarching decoration mode for St. Vincent and the Grenadines alone: single row on top of lip, single row at edge of lip, single row across top of lip made with a rod-like tool, very deeply indented with excess paste pushed outward, double row, and long indents with major axis parallel to side of vessel. The most common indentation is indeed a single band of fingertip indentations running along the top of the rim of the vessel (type 1). Alongside these single-row decorations, there are also more complex modes that consist of two or even three rows of indentations (type 2). However, indentations in the form of small neat circles on rims also occur, presumably accomplished by using a circular stick-like implement (type 3). Another indentation is more aptly described as a form of filleting or notching, accomplished by pressing something that tapers into the rim, either held perpendicularly or at an angle (type 4). A slightly different but related decoration mode

Figure 5.25. Five types of rim indentation, clockwise from top left: fingernail indentation (Peak Bay, Barbados), multiple rows of finger indentation (Chancery Lane, Barbados), single row of finger indentation (Praslin Island, St. Lucia), notched or filleted indentation (Grande Anse, St. Lucia) and circular or punctuated indentation (Comerette Point, St. Lucia). Not to scale.

is that of fingernail indentation, often in two or more bands running parallel to one another along the top of the vessel (type 5). In all cases, while the method of execution may be similar, the force or precision with which the decoration is applied varies from one instance to the next, as does the size of the indentation (see also figure 5.25).

Distribution

Suazan finger indented rims have been encountered at 95 sites on 12 islands, from Barbados to Martinique (figure 5.26). However, the exact distribution of the various subtypes differs considerably. In so far as the subtype has been specified in the literature or encountered in collections, these will now be examined in turn. A single row of fingertip indentations is perhaps the most common mode, featuring at 42 sites on eight islands (figure 5.27). Multiple rows of fingertip indentations are rarer, featuring at seventeen sites on four islands (figure 5.28). Small, round indentations or punctations on rims occur at four sites on three islands (figure 5.29). Filleting or notching can be found at eight sites on four islands (figure 5.30). Finally, fingernail indentation is found at nine sites on three islands (although the Saltibus Point specimen is arguably of a slightly different type, the nail imprints having been placed perpendicular to the rim, rather than parallel), making it the most restricted in terms of island distribution of the various subtypes (figure 5.31).

Stylistic similarities/dating

Rim finger(nail) indentation appears to be a phenomenon occurring mainly in the insular Caribbean, and then principally between Tobago (Golden Grove: Harris 1976:150; Lovers' Retreat: Harris 1980:530; Great Courland Bay: Boomert 2007b:figure 2; Boomert and Kameneff 2005:462) and Guadeloupe (figure 5.32). According to Boomert and Kameneff (2005), the decoration mode reached its creative peak on Barbados, which may be either indicative of or, by the same token, the result of the geographically marginal position of the island. The phenomenon has been firmly ascribed to the Suazan Troumassoid subseries, whose date range differs from island to island, but can at least be characterized with certainty as representing the late phase of the Late Ceramic Age.

Looking to mainland developments during this period, McKusick (1960:158) noted that finger indentation occurred sporadically along the northern coast of South America, but saw its greatest manifestation in Suriname and the lower Amazon region. Finger punctation along vessel rims has also been reported for the Late Ceramic Age Guarita/Amazonian Polychrome complex of the Central Amazon (Petersen *et al.* 2003:255-256). It is intriguing to note that punctation or indentation in general is a common feature of both the Valencioid series of Central Venezuela (Rouse and Cruxent 1969) and the period IV and V Guarguapo and Apostadero styles of the Arauquinoid of the Lower Orinoco region (Cruxent

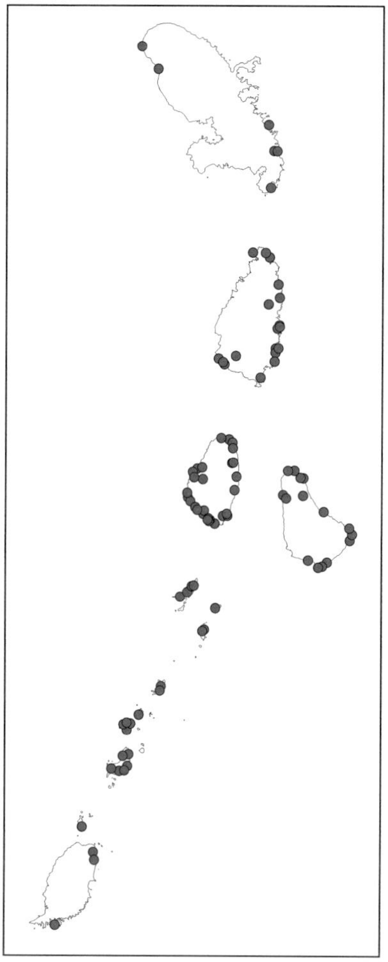

Figure 5.26. Distribution of Suazan finger indented rims throughout the Windward Islands: Barbados: Chancery Lane, Sam Lords, Peak Bay, Heywoods/Port St. Charles, Maxwell, Silver Sands, Cuckhold, South Point, Chandler Bay (Site A), Sandy Hill, Greenland, East Point; Grenada: Savanne Suazey, Calabasse, Caliviny Island 3; Grenadines: Chatham Bay, Belmont Pond, Miss Pierre, Frigate Island (Union), Plantain Bay, Rosemary/L'Ansecoy Bay (Mustique), L'Esterre, Great Breteche Bay, Dover, Sabazan, Sparrow Bay, Grand Bay (Carriacou), Grand Bay, Carenage (Cannouan), Mayreau Beach/Saline Bay (Mayreau), Mitchell, Paget Farm, Industry Estate, Park Estate (Bequia), Banana Bay (Baliceaux), Ile de Caille (Ile de Caille); St. Vincent: Arnos Vale Field, Kingstown Post Office, Rutland Vale, Petit Bordel, Owia 1/2, Copeland, Texaco Tank, Lot 14, Stubbs, North Mt. Wynn Bay, Questelles School, Arnos Vale Swamp, Buccament West/Cave, Fitz-Hughs, New Sandy Bay, Careenage, Flour Mill, Mount Pleasant/Rawacou, Fancy, Troumaka Bay, Espagnol Point South, Cumberland Ravine, Indian Bay, Government House, Friendly; (continued next page) St. Lucia: Saltibus Point, Pointe de Caille, Micoud Beach, Grande Anse, Vierge Point 1, Massacare, Praslin Island, Micoud Point, La Ressource, Caraibe Point, Canelles Point, Comerette Point, Giraudy, Lavoutte, Pigeon Island, Frigate Island, Trou Zambé, Choiseul Catholic Church, Louvet River, Ridge South of Anse John, Park Estate; Martinique: Diamant, Usine Simon, Saint-Pierre Centre, Anse Trabaud, Macabou, A-Tout-Risque, Anse Belleville, Pointe de la Prairie/Cap Est.

Figure 5.27. Distribution of single row of finger indentation throughout the Windward Islands: Barbados: Chancery Lane, Heywoods/Port St. Charles; Greenland; Grenada: Caliviny Island 3, Savanne Suazey; Grenadines: Miss Pierre (Union), Rosemary / L'Ansecoy Bay, Plantain Bay (Mustique), Grand Bay (Carriacou), Mayreau Beach/Saline Bay (Mayreau), Industry Estate (Bequia); St. Vincent: Mount Pleasant/Rawacou, Orange Hill 2, Grand Sable, Owia 1/2, Arnos Vale Field, Buccament West/Cave, New Sandy Bay, Kingstown Post Office, Espagnol Point South, Indian Bay; St. Lucia: Saltibus Point, Caraibe Point, Massacare, Comerette Point, Giraudy, Lavoutte, Pigeon Island, La Ressource, Louvet River, Ridge South of Anse John, Park Estate, Micoud Point, Trou Zambé, Grande Anse; Martinique: Saint-Pierre Centre, Anse Trabaud, Macabou, A-Tout-Risque, Anse Belleville, Pointe de la Prairie/ Cap Est.

Figure 5.28. Distribution of multiple rows of finger indentation throughout the Windward Islands: Barbados: Chancery Lane, Heywoods/Port St. Charles, Silver Sands. Grenadines: Rosemary/L'Ansecoy Bay (Mustique); Grand Bay (Carriacou); St. Vincent: Cumberland Ravine, North Mt. Wynn, Espagnol Point South, Fancy, Mount Pleasant/Rawacou, Arnos Vale Field, Owia 1/2, Brighton Beach 1, Copeland, Buccament West/Cave, New Sandy Bay.

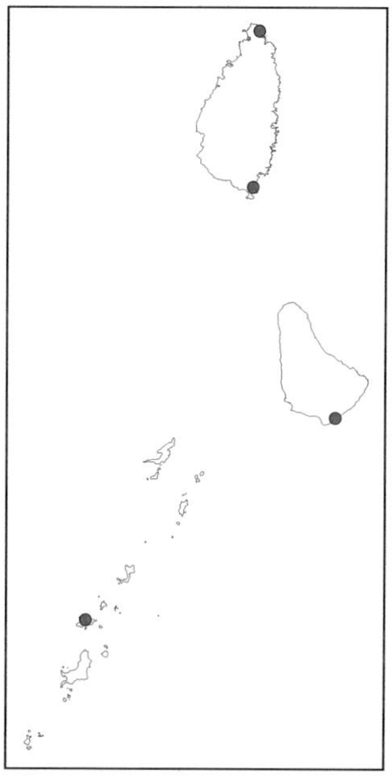

Figure 5.29. Distribution of round indentations or punctations throughout the Windward Islands: Barbados: Chancery Lane; Grenadines: Miss Pierre (Union); St. Lucia: Comerette Point, Giraudy.

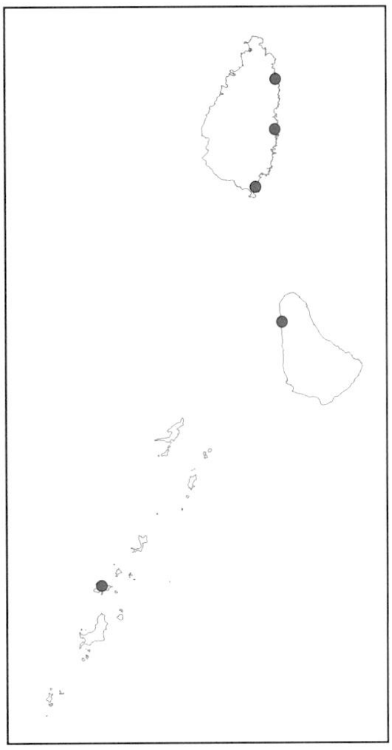

Figure 5.30. Distribution of filleting or notching throughout the Windward Islands: Barbados: Heywoods/Port St. Charles; Grenadines: Miss Pierre (Union); St. Vincent: Mount Pleasant/ Rawacou; St. Lucia: Grande Anse, Praslin Island, Giraudy, La Ressource, Pointe de Caille.

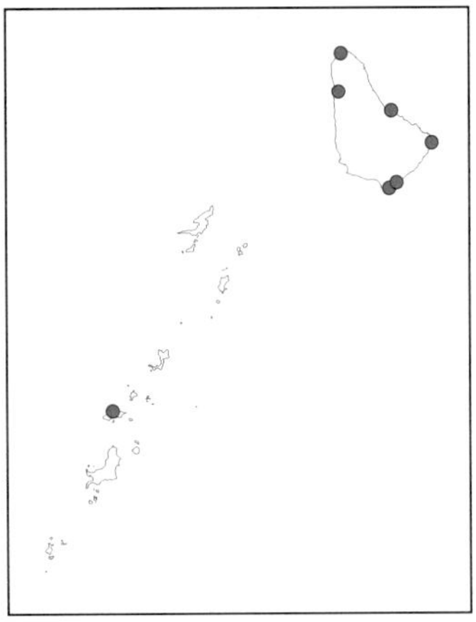

Figure 5.31. Distribution of fingernail indentations throughout the Windward Islands: Barbados: Silver Sands, Peak Bay, Heywoods/Port St. Charles, Chancery Lane, Gouldings Green and Hillcrest (Site B); Grenadines: Miss Pierre (Union); St. Lucia: Choiseul Catholic Church, Saltibus Point.

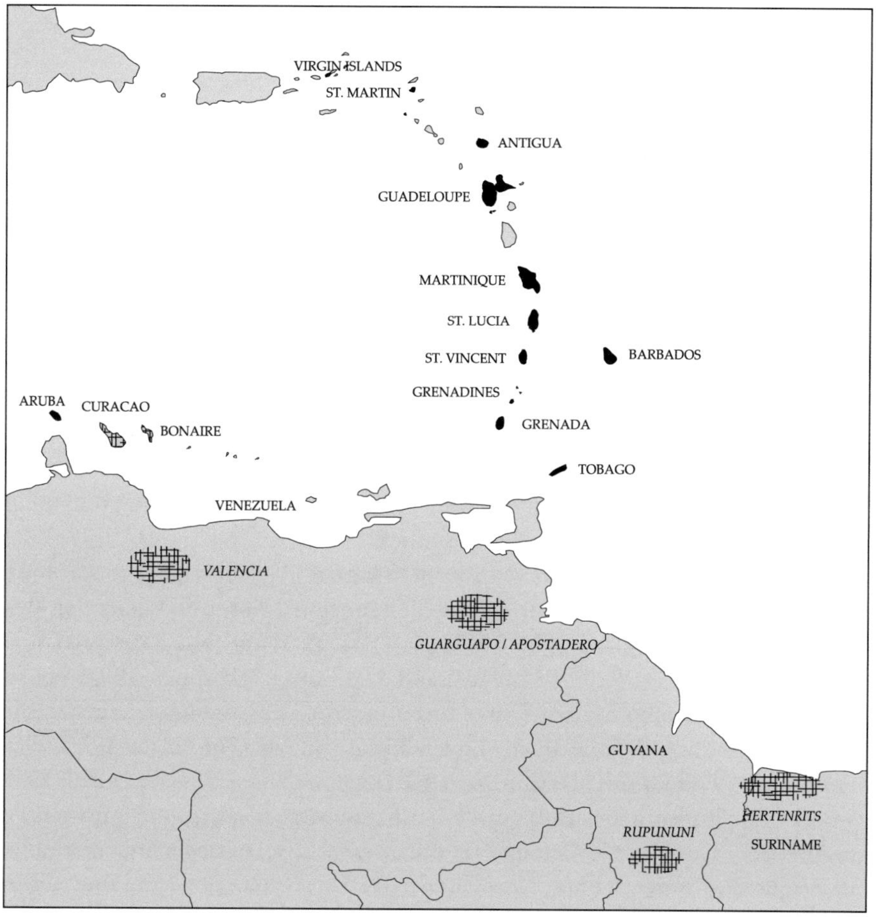

Figure 5.32. Distribution of finger indentation throughout the Caribbean and stylistic similarities.

and Rouse 1982: plates 99 and 104)[79]. Fingerprinting and rim corrugations have also been recorded for the Dabajuroid series on the Dutch ABC-islands (Ayubi 1990:132), although in the absence of illustrations or further description, these phenomena cannot be unequivocally related to the Lesser Antillean finger indentations. Fingernail indentation has been recorded at Tanki Flip, Aruba, but in this case, the decoration does not run along the top of the rim, but rather along the side of the vessel's rim segment (Dijkhoff 1997:figure B-1). The same holds for the notched or fingertip-indented rims recorded in Arauquinoid assemblages at the Hertenrits site, Suriname (Geijskes 1964:59; Versteeg 2003: figure 6.21). Furthermore, rim indentation is also reported for the late Colonial Taruma and Rupununi phase assemblages in Guyana (Evans and Meggers 1960: plate 47-e and 63-i, j, k), which postdate the Suazan Troumassoid subseries considerably.

79 Although the punctation is not found on rims but usually as appliqué strips along the neck or walls of vessels.

Rim indentation	Sites with trait	Total sites	Weighted distribution percentage
Barbados	14	52	26.92
Grenada	3	32	9.38
Grenadines	21	34	61.76
St. Vincent	29	66	43.94
St. Lucia	19	53	35.85
Martinique	8	44	18.18
Dominica	0	20	0

Table 5.7. Weighted distribution of rim indentation per island.

Besides, given the general absence of frequency tables of decorative traits in the archaeological literature, it is difficult to determine whether these mainland (rim-) indented sherds represent incidental trade wares or whether this decoration mode was produced locally in substantial quantities.

There is also the rare occurrence of rim indentation in the islands to the north of the Windwards, as attested by the Bay Lip Punctated rim from Cinnamon Bay, St. John, Virgin Islands (Bullen 1962: plate IX-m), round punctations in rims at Spring Bay 1b, 1c, Kelbey's Ridge 2 and The Bottom (Hofman 1993: figures 22h, 34, 57h, 64 and 68), two Suazey finger indented lips and one punctated rim from Cupecoy Bay, St. Martin (R. Bullen and A. Bullen 1966: plate A-9; Bullen and Bullen 1974: figure 2-i), some possible finger indented rims from Mill Reef, Antigua (R. Bullen 1970:150), two rim sherds with small, round punctations at Anse à la Gourde, Guadeloupe (Hofman *et al.* 2001), finger indentation at Montagne des Petites Salines, Guadeloupe (De Waal 2006:190), and one fingernail-impressed rim sherd from Grande Anse, Terre des Bas, Les Saintes (Hofman 1995: figure 5). However, available evidence points overwhelmingly to rim indentation being a local late phase Late Ceramic Age innovation, perhaps inspired by or, considering the relatively late dates of similar modes on the mainland, rather inspiring the general trend towards punctation and indentation on the mainland. It is tempting to link this possible historic diffusion to the destabilizing influence of European presence in the region, but concrete proof is lacking.

According to the weighted distribution data (table 5.7), Suazan Troumassoid rim indentation is most prevalent on the Grenadines, followed at some distance by St. Lucia and St. Vincent, again followed at some distance by Barbados and Martinique. Grenada has the most limited presence and Dominica none at all.

5.3.7. Vessel legs

Background

Vessel legs are a common feature of the late Troumassan and Suazan Troumassoid subseries, arising at more or less the same point in time as footed griddles and annular or pedestal bases (Allaire 1977; Rouse 1992). Lovén was one of the first to remark upon them, referring to them as clay feet, and reported such vessel legs from Barbados (1935:258) and St. Vincent (1935:263-4). Barton (1953:47, 57-58) reported tubular and shouldered vessel legs from Barbados. Their occurrence on St. Lucia was discussed at length by McKusick (1960), and Allaire (1977) later described specimens from Martinique. In the discussion that follows, griddle legs will be distinguished from vessel legs, as they relate to an entirely different vessel type. It may therefore be more interesting to treat them as a separate category, to potentially highlight differences between assemblages. Another related but technically different ceramic feature is the pot-rest or support ring, first described by Bullen and Bullen (1972: plate V-i-k), and named Lavoutte support ring. These are likewise not included in the category of vessel legs and will be discussed separately, as they are not attached to the main vessel, but rather to a subsidiary vessel of their own. The literal leg, often with a modelled foot and toes, is not included in this category, both because it is primarily a Saladoid phenomenon and because it is usually not a vessel support pur sang, but part of a modelled, non-functional entity. Its different status is highlighted by its red-painted, burnished state.

Details decoration/composition

At present, three different types can be discerned among vessel legs. The first type is that of the strictly tubular leg or the tubular leg that tapers towards its extremity. The second type is that of the inward keeling legs, termed 'shouldered' by Harris (1991), that seem to have been provided with knee or elbow joints. The third type of leg is only found on Barbados, Martinique and St. Lucia, and has the interesting addition of an appliqué knob on the upper, outer part of the leg. It must be assumed that these additions represent knees or elbows. The first type is usually roughly executed, *i.e.* scratched, scored and unpainted, often exhibiting at the surface the coarse temper materials utilized in its manufacture. The other two types are generally smoothed to a degree, although coarsely finished examples are known as well (see figure 5.33).

Griddle legs are generally flat, wide and U- or V-shaped. They come in all degrees of finishing, from coarse and crude to smoothed or even incised and perforated all the way through (figure 5.34).

The so-called Lavoutte support ring occurs either as a hollow cylinder or, more frequently, as a ringed stand, usually resting on three legs. It is generally rather crudely executed, in much the same manner as Suazan Troumassoid plainware. Decoration is wholly absent, if one discounts scarification or scratching that is probably an epiphenomenon of manufacture rather than an intentional decorative trait (see figure 5.35).

Distribution

Thus far, vessel legs in general have been encountered at 44 sites on seven islands (figure 5.36). Of these 44 site occurrences, eleven are of unknown form. Tubular and tapering vessel legs are relatively common among the Suazan Troumassoid assemblages of Barbados and St. Lucia in particular, and occur sparingly on three other Windward Islands as well, at 25 sites in total (figure 5.37). The jointed or

Figure 5.33. Tubular/tapering leg from Micoud, St. Lucia (left), shouldered or jointed leg from Chancery Lane, Barbados (centre) and an appliquéd leg from Heywoods, Barbados (right). Not to scale.

Figure 5.34. V-shaped griddle foot from Lavoutte (left) and U-shaped griddle foot from Comerette Point (right), St. Lucia. Not to scale.

shouldered legs are far less common, however, depending on how strictly one formulates "jointed" (*i.e.* whether an appliqué representing a joint suffices or whether only a keeling point will do). This keeling type of leg is restricted in occurrence to thirteen sites on three islands (figure 5.38). Turning to the modelled appliqué variety, we see an even more marginal distribution: seven sites on the same three islands (figure 5.39).

Figure 5.35. Ringed stands from Anse Trabaud (left) and Diamant (right), Martinique, demonstrating both crude and fine finishing. Not to scale.

Legged or footed griddles are relatively common, and the data at present permit no significant distinction to be drawn between the U-shaped and V-shaped types. Both types appear to occur interchangeably and with equal frequency at 70 sites on nine islands. However, only on Barbados are the rims of footed griddles occasionally decorated with finger indentation (Bullen and Bullen 1972:147; Drewett ed. 1991:71) (figure 5.40).

The support ring mentioned briefly above is altogether rarer. Thus far it has been encountered at 21 sites on nine islands (figure 5.41).

Stylistic similarities/dating

Linné (1929:111-17) detailed the distribution of so-called tripod vessels across North, Central and South America, of which the occurrences near Lake Valencia and Trujillo (Venezuela) are presumably of most relevance to this study. Lovén mentions the discovery of vessel legs in the Barima region of Guyana (1935:244), Venezuela and Central America (1935:264). They are also present in the Tanki Flip assemblage, Aruba (Dijkhoff 1997: figure 74). Barton (1953:47), pointing out that clay feet are a common occurrence in Central American cultures, suggested that the trait may have originated in that area and diffused south-eastwards along the South American coastline as far as Guyana, and thence up to Barbados. This explained to him why the trait was not found on Trinidad. Again concerning mainland similarities, McKusick established that bowl legs had not been reported from the Amazon, the Guianas, Trinidad and most of eastern Venezuela (McKusick 1960:154-155). Nevertheless, the Punta Arenas style of Cumaná, eastern Venezuela, was proposed as the most likely mainland origin of the vessel shape, although the possibility of independent origin was also advanced (McKusick 1960:155-156; see also Rouse and Cruxent 1982:257; figure 5.42). McKusick reports a crude legged bowl for St. Croix and legs and a tripod bowl for Puerto Rico (McKusick 1960:143), but dismisses the latter two instances as too dissimilar to the Lesser Antillean type. Lovén also points to Puerto Rico (1935:285). Another

Figure 5.36. Distribution of vessel legs throughout the Windward Islands: Barbados: South Point, Chancery Lane, Sam Lords, Peak Bay, Heywoods/Port St. Charles, Greenland, The Landlock, Cuckhold, Sandy Hill, Silver Sands, Hillcrest (Site A), Speightstown; Grenada: Caliviny Island 3; Grenadines: Grand Bay (Carriacou), Grand Bay (Cannouan); St. Vincent: Stubbs, Buccament West/Cave, Mount Pleasant/Rawacou, Government House; St. Lucia: Above Anse John, Micoud Beach, Caraibe Point, Massacare, Comerette Point, Trou Zambé, Giraudy, Troumassée, Lavoutte, Choc Point, Pigeon Island, Grande Anse, Frigate Island, La Ressource, Praslin Island, Londonderry 1, Vierge Point 1, Canelles Point, Saltibus Point, Pointe de Caille, Park Estate; Martinique: Anse Trabaud, Macabou, Paquemar, A-Tout-Risque.

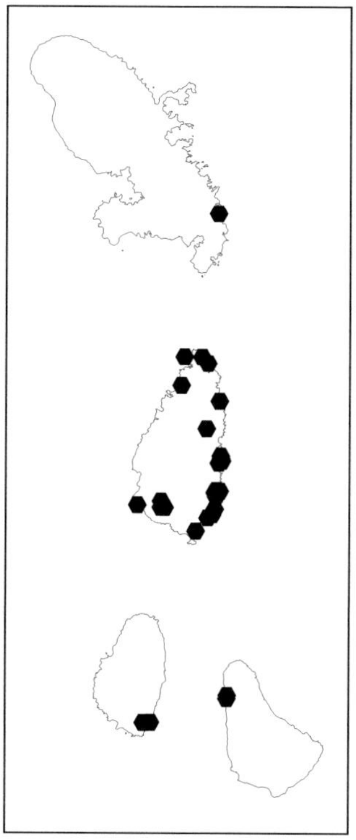

Figure 5.37. Distribution of tubular and tapering vessel legs throughout the Windward Islands: Barbados: Sandy Hill, Heywoods/ Port St. Charles, Speightstown; St. Vincent: Stubbs, Mt. Pleasant; St. Lucia: Micoud Beach, Troumassée, Caraibe Point, Comerette Point, Giraudy, Choc Point, Lavoutte, Grande Anse, Pigeon Island, Frigate Island, Praslin Island, Vierge Point 1, Canelles Point, Saltibus Point, Pointe de Caille, La Ressource, Park Estate, Londonderry 1, Trou Zambé; Martinique: Macabou, Paquemar.

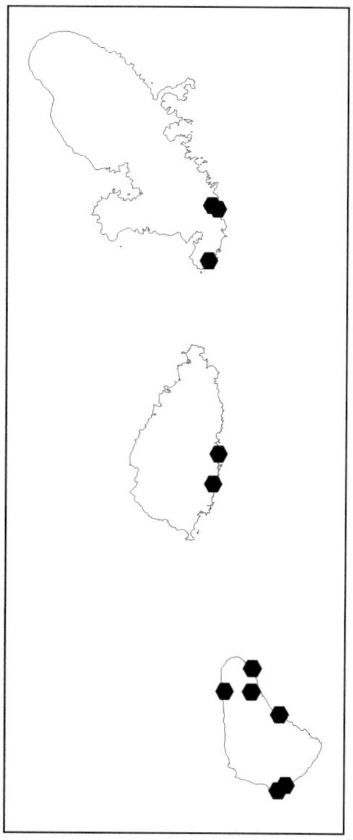

Figure 5.38. Distribution of jointed or shouldered vessel legs throughout the Windward Islands: Barbados: Chancery Lane, Heywoods/Port St. Charles, Greenland, Silver Sands, Sandy Hill, The Landlock, Cuckhold, Hillcrest (Site A); St. Lucia: Micoud Beach, Trou Zambé; Martinique: Anse Trabaud, Macabou, Paquemar.

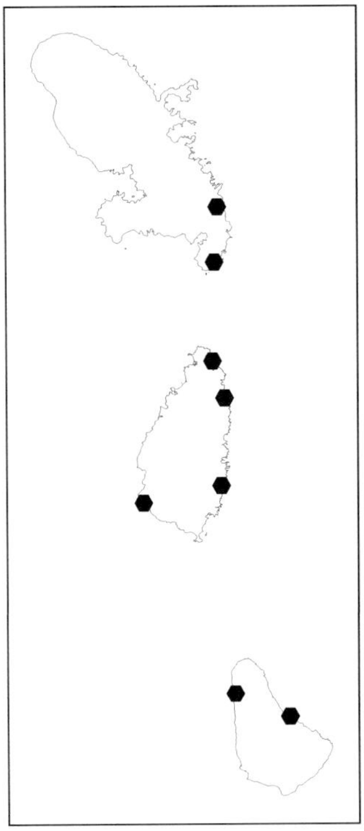

Figure 5.39. Distribution of modelled appliqué vessel legs throughout the Windward Islands: Barbados: Heywoods/Port St. Charles, Hillcrest (Site A); St. Lucia: Micoud Beach, Caraibe Point, Comerette Point, Grande Anse; Martinique: Paquemar.

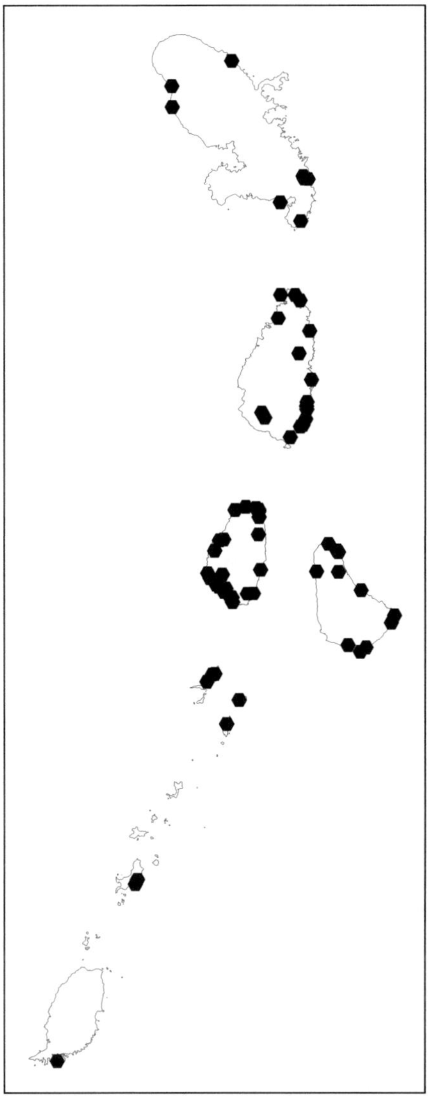

Figure 5.40. Distribution of griddle legs throughout the Windward Islands: Barbados: Chancery Lane, Sam Lords, Indian Mound, Peak Bay, Heywoods/Port St. Charles, Greenland, Sandy Hill, Cuckhold, Silver Sands, Little Welches, Hillcrest (Site A); Grenada: Caliviny Island; Grenadines: Sabazan, Grand Bay (Carriacou), Rosemary/L'Ansecoy Bay (Mustique), Mitchell, Industry Estate, Park Estate (Bequia), Banana Bay (Baliceaux); St. Vincent: Arnos Vale Field, Queensbury, Red Cross Hut, Petit Bordel, Owia 1/2, Lot 14, Stubbs, Windsor Forest, Young's Island, Questelles School, Arnos Vale Swamp, Buccament West/Cave, Camden Park, Fitz-Hughs, New Sandy Bay, Mt. Pleasant, Fancy, Espagnol Point South, Espagnol Point North, Cumberland Ravine, Indian Bay, South Union, Government House; St. Lucia: Micoud Beach, Massacare, Comerette Point, Choc Point, Giraudy, Lavoutte, Grande Anse, Pigeon Island, Troumassée, Troumassée River North, Canelles Point, La Ressource, Londonderry 1, Park Estate, Frigate Island, Saltibus Point, Pointe de Caille, Gayabois, Hope Estate, Eastern Nature Trail 6; Martinique: Macabou, Anse Charpentier, Saint-Pierre Centre, Anse Trabaud, Anse Figuier, Paquemar, A-Tout-Risque, Le Coin.

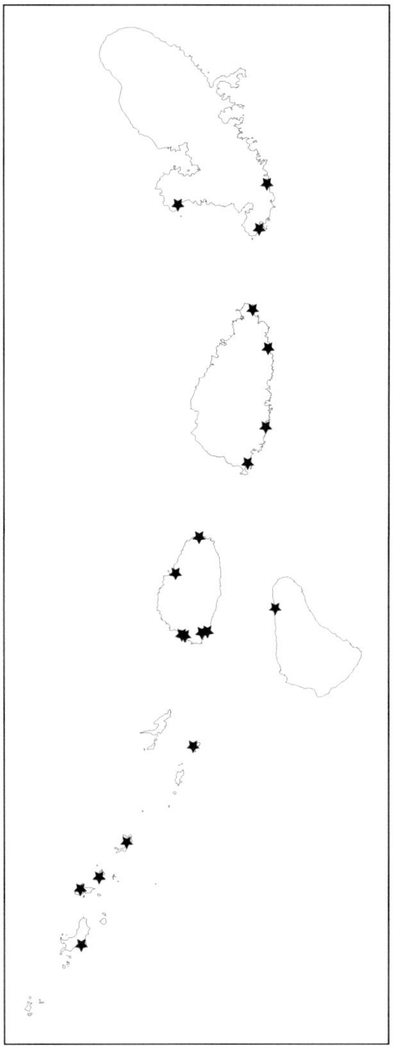

Figure 5.41. Distribution of support rings throughout the Windward Islands: Barbados: Heywoods/Port St. Charles (Drewett ed. 2000:fig. 41, no. 49); Grenadines: Sabazan (Carriacou; Bullen and Bullen 1972:14), Chatham Bay (Union Island; Bullen and Bullen 1972: plate V-i-k), Mayreau Beach/Saline Bay (Mayreau; Bullen and Bullen 1972: plate VIII-j), Carenage Bay (Cannouan; Bullen and Bullen 1972:32), Banana Bay (Baliceaux; Bullen and Bullen 1972); St. Vincent: Mt. Pleasant/Rawacou, Coconut Oil Factory, Arnos Vale Swamp, Fancy, Stubbs, Fitz-Hughs (Bullen and Bullen 1972: plate XXX-k); St. Lucia: Micoud Beach (McKusick 1960:117), Lavoutte (Bullen and Bullen 1970: figure 9), Grande Anse (Bullen and Bullen 1968), Giraudy (Bullen et al. 1973), La Ressource, Saltibus Point; Martinique: Anse Trabaud, Diamant, Macabou.

vessel leg has been recovered from Spring Bay 1b on Saba (Hofman 1993: figure 32g).

The footed griddle, with its U-shaped or V-shaped legs, occurs on a number of Leeward Islands: at a great number of sites on Guadeloupe (De Waal 2006: Appendices 2-4), on Désirade and Terre-de-Bas (Hofman 1995; Hofman *et al.* 2004: figures 10/11), Antigua (Faber Morse and Rouse 2001; Healy *et al.* 2005; Murphy n.d.; Rouse and Faber Morse 1999), St. Eustatius (Josselin de Jong 1947: plate XI-10), and St. Martin (Bonnissent 2005:43). It has also been reported to the south, at the Lovers' Retreat and Great Courland Bay sites on Tobago (Boomert 2007b: figure 12; Boomert and Kameneff 2005). While legged vessels and ornamental statue legs are common throughout a number of mainland, particularly west Venezuelan, assemblages, there seems to be no mainland precursor to the footed griddle so typical of the late phase of the Late Ceramic Age in the Windward Islands, making it highly likely that this trait represents a local innovation (*cf.* McKusick 1960:156).

Concerning tripod support rings, Lovén (1935:264) recorded a specimen for St. Croix, and Anse à la Gourde has apparently yielded one too (personal communication Hofman, 2008).

According to the weighted distribution data (table 5.8), vessel legs are most prevalent on St. Lucia, only half as prevalent on Barbados, then half as prevalent as that on Martinique, and half as prevalent again on the Grenadines and St. Vincent, and finally half as prevalent once more on Grenada. Dominica once again draws a blank. Griddle legs are most prevalent on St. Lucia, followed by St. Vincent. Martinique, the Grenadines and Barbados follow at considerable distance, and Grenada brings up the rear. Dominica once again draws a blank (table 5.9). Support rings (table 5.10) are most prevalent on the Grenadines, and ever less so on St. Lucia, St. Vincent and Martinique. Barbados has the most limited presence, and they are absent from Dominica.

As to dating, vessel legs in the Windward Islands have been firmly placed by McKusick (1960) within his Choc and Fannis styles and by Allaire (1977) within his Paquemar and Macabou styles, or late Troumassan and Suazan Troumassoid subseries. This gives them a rough date of between AD 850 and 1500. Footed griddles occur in Troumassan Troumassoid assemblages (Mill Reef, Troumassée B and Paquemar complexes), but predominate in Suazan Troumassoid assemblages (Macabou, Plymouth), dating them to most of the Late Ceramic Age. Support rings appear to be a strictly Suazan Troumassoid feature, dating them to the late phase of the Late Ceramic Age.

5.3.8. Cayo

Background

Cayo ceramics were first discovered at the New Sandy Bay site in northeastern St. Vincent, and named after the Amerindian name for the area (Kirby 1974). Following in the footsteps of Kirby, the Bullens made mention of aberrant pottery amid Suazan Troumassoid assemblages at the sites of Biabou and, alerted by

Vessel legs	*Sites with trait*	*Total sites*	*Weighted distribution percentage*
Barbados	12	52	23.08
Grenada	1	32	3.13
Grenadines	2	34	5.88
St. Vincent	4	66	6.06
St. Lucia	21	53	39.62
Martinique	4	44	9.09
Dominica	0	20	0

Table 5.8. Weighted distribution of vessel legs per island.

Griddle legs	Sites with trait	Total sites	Weighted distribution percentage
Barbados	10	52	19.23
Grenada	1	32	3.13
Grenadines	7	34	20.59
St. Vincent	23	66	34.85
St. Lucia	19	53	35.85
Martinique	8	44	18.18
Dominica	0	20	0

Table 5.9. Weighted distribution of griddle legs per island.

Support ring	*Sites with trait*	*Total sites*	*Weighted distribution percentage*
Barbados	1	52	1.92
Grenada	0	32	0
Grenadines	5	34	14.71
St. Vincent	6	66	9.09
St. Lucia	6	53	11.32
Martinique	3	44	6.82
Dominica	0	20	0

Table 5.10. Weighted distribution of support rings per island

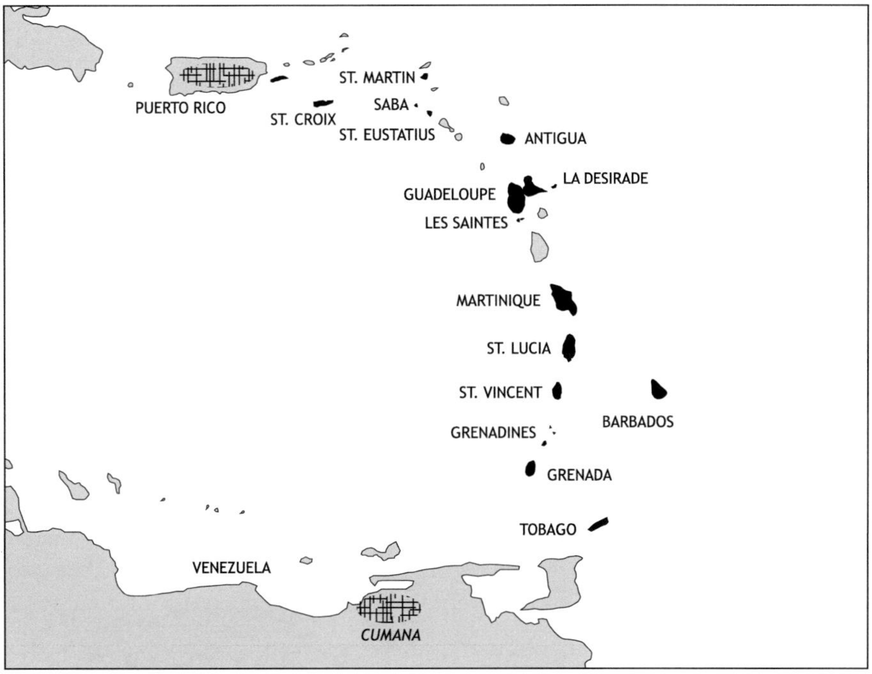

Figure 5.42. Distribution of vessel legs throughout the Caribbean and stylistic similarities.

Kirby, at New Sandy Bay, but did not ascribe these to a separate style or ware (Bullen and Bullen 1972:44, 162). If anything, a number of traits we would now deem Cayo were subsumed by them either under their Caliviny or Suazey series or their Peasant Ware category. Although Cayo finds were subsequently reported on Dominica (Petitjean Roget 1978) and alluded to on Martinique (Allaire 1984), the ware did not receive thorough treatment until the mid 1980s, when Boomert (1986) discussed the Cayo phenomenon from both (ethno)historical and archaeological angles, arriving at the first convincing reconstruction of provenience, chronology and typology of the Cayo ware.[80] In the past, the Suazan Troumassoid subseries ceramics were ascribed by some to the historically reported Island Caribs or Kallinago (*cf.* Bullen and Bullen 1972:166; Kirby 1980), but these ideas were firmly dismissed by Allaire (1984) and later by Boomert (1986, 1995). They concluded that not Suazan Troumassoid but Cayo pottery in fact represented the latest ceramic assemblage in the Windward Islands, making it the likely archaeological signature of the Island Carib. It is expected that the Leiden University excavation of the Cayo settlement of Argyle on St. Vincent (2009/2010) will provide conclusive answers as to dating and stylistic affiliations. What is presently known about Cayo ceramics is discussed briefly below.

80 Although Boomert may have been a little over-zealous in including in his definition of Cayo those types earlier called Peasant Ware and Savanne Plain (Bullen 1964; Bullen & Bullen 1972). As of yet, there has been little revisiting of Bullen's original data-set, and many of his determinations and classifications are intuitive at best and therefore unreliable.

Details decoration/composition

Kirby (1974:61) describes the pottery as mainly of quite fine paste, although in some cases, the paste contained a large amount of quartz. Kirby (1974:62-3) identified the following vessel shapes: large and small open-mouthed closed bowls, cauldrons with bevelled rims, casuelas, deep bowls, a large open container, double-globular bowls and the rather typical straight-necked vessels with a globular body and outflaring rims. Rims are rounded or flattened on the inside, resulting in a bevel. In some cases a "feather" or everted edge remains, or has evidently been removed, leaving tell-tale traces. Some rims are fashioned in the shape of a succession of arches (personal communication Boomert, June 2010). Surface finishing consisted of scratching, scraping and smoothing. Surface decoration includes punctation, modelled appliqué strips, both straight and curved, some of which are notched, red slip, anthropomorphic, zoomorphic and abstract lugs or appendages (figure 5.43). Incised decoration is also turning up ever more frequently, as are scratched surfaces and the trait of footed griddles (personal communication Boomert, June 2010). These may potentially be hold-overs from the Suazan

Figure 5.43. Cayo vessels from Woodford Hill, Dominica (top), and from Argyle, St. Vincent (bottom). Not to scale.

Troumassoid, although in the absence of radiocarbon dates, the possibility of contemporaneity cannot be ruled out. Not all stylistic features ascribed by Kirby to the Cayo ware can be upheld however. In particular, his anthropomorphic and bat-shaped lugs or twin appendages have since been recognized first as being diagnostic of the Caliviny style (*i.e.* Bullen and Bullen 1972) and subsequently of Troumassan Troumassoid pottery (Boomert 2005). Boomert enumerated more or less the same decorative traits as Kirby, but arrived at a more formal inventory of temper (*cf.* his discovery of *kwepi*) and vessel shapes (Boomert 1986: figures 3-6).

Distribution

Cayo ceramics have been encountered at nineteen sites on six of the Windward Islands (see figure 5.44).

At the majority of the sites, the Cayo remains are incidental; the 152 sherds reported by Boomert for the sites on St. Vincent represent the overwhelming majority of the total share of Cayo ceramics known for the Windward Islands and Guadeloupe. Furthermore, while a number of sites on St. Vincent may be said to harbour a Cayo component, the finds on other islands occur so infrequently among the established ceramic series as to be merely categorized as Cayo ware or Cayo ceramics. The two complete vessels found at Woodford Hill Bay (Dominica) form the only exception in both respects. Concerning the general distribution of Cayo ceramics across the islands, it is intriguing that none have so far been discovered on Barbados, an island that has received considerable archaeological attention in the last two decades. Also, while it should come as no surprise to see the phenomenon become increasingly widespread in terms of geographic distribution (*i.e.*, recent finds on Guadeloupe), it does strike one as odd that these ceramics remain so under-represented relative to the rest of the ceramic assemblage at sites.

Stylistic similarities/dating

Just north of the research area, Cayo ceramics have turned up on Guadeloupe (Richard 2002, 2003; see also Hofman and Bright 2004 and Hofman *et al.* 2007). Other than that, we find ourselves in the realm of stylistic similarity for instance with the Tainan styles in Camaguey and Damajayabo, the White Marl complex on Jamaica, the late Ostiones of Puerto Rico and the Botany Bay complex of St. Thomas (Kirby 1974) (figure 5.45). On the basis of dubious cultural stratigraphy, he hypothesized that the Cayo potters in time made their way up the island chain into the Greater Antilles (Kirby 1974:63). The Bullens never recognized the Cayo ware themselves, but replicated Kirby's findings and correlated the sherds with those of the Ostiones, Santa Elena and Esperanza styles of Puerto Rico (Bullen and Bullen 1972: 66). Boomert was unable to second Kirby's conclusions regarding cultural stratigraphy, and instead considered the Cayo phenomenon to postdate rather than pre-date the appearance of Suazan Troumassoid ceramics. While Boomert acknowledged that a small component of the ware (what he termed vessel form 4 and its notched fillet decoration; Boomert 1986:54) showed similarities with Greater Antillean Ostionoid ceramics (albeit the later Chican rather than

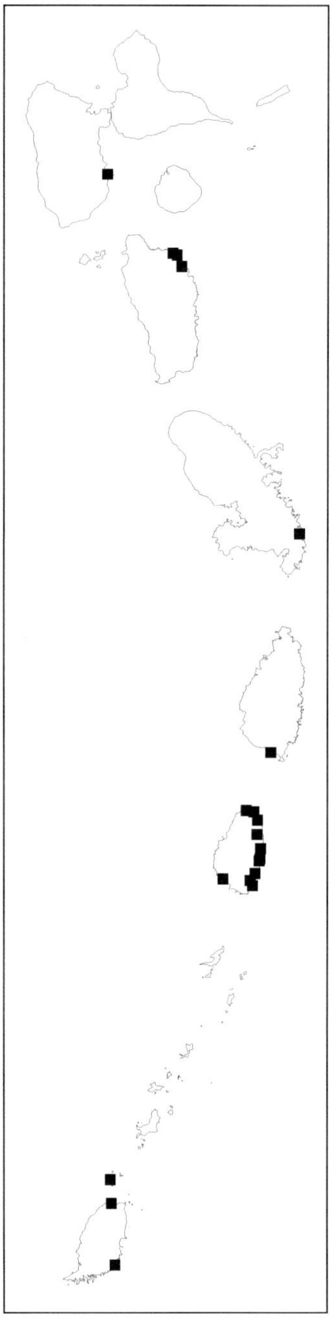

Figure 5.44. Distribution of Cayo throughout the Windward Islands: Grenada: Sauteurs Bay, Galby Bay (Cody Holdren 1998); Grenadines: Ile de Ronde (Ile de Ronde) (Petitjean Roget 2002); St. Vincent: Mount Pleasant/Rawacou, New Sandy Bay, Owia 2, Spring, Friendly, Fancy, Camden Park, Lot 14, Argyle 1, Sans Souci, Grand Sable; St. Lucia: Black Bay; Martinique: Macabou; Dominica: Woodford Hill Bay, Melville Hall 2 (B), Eden 1 (Boomert 2009; Honychurch n.d.).

earlier Ostionan and other components suggested by Kirby), he considered the overwhelming majority of the ceramics to show close resemblances to the Koriabo ceramics of the Guianas. The radiocarbon dating of the Koriabo complex on the mainland to between AD 750 and 1500, and the occurrence of Taíno-style material amongst assemblages of Cayo ceramics on St. Vincent led Boomert to tentatively date the occurrence of Cayo ceramics in the Windward Islands to between AD 1250 and the contact period (Boomert 2004:256). Certain decorative traits of Cayo such as punctation show stylistic similarities to sherds from the Kwatta and Barbakoeba cultures of Surinam (see Rostain and Versteeg 2004: figures 8 and 10).

There are only two possible hypotheses regarding Cayo's origins: either Cayo represents a trade ware from the Greater Antilles or the mainland of South America (*cf.* Boomert 1986) or, particularly with a view to Cayo seeming to be an amalgam of stylistic influences from the Greater Antilles and the South American mainland, it represents small-scale local production entailing imitation of ceramics from other regions. Given the late pre-Colonial/early Colonial period date of the ware, it is worth considering the possible role that Taíno refugees (Farr 1995; Sued-Badillo 1978; see also Oliver 2008) or Carib raids on Taíno settlements (Figueredo 1978; Allaire 1987; see also Hofman *et al.* 2008) may have played in the transmission of Greater Antillean stylistic traits to Lesser Antillean ceramic assemblages. The South-American Koriabo similarities may be attributed to the general ethnic affiliation between the Island Carib and the Amerindians of mainland South America attested by predominantly French (ethno)historical documents (see also Chapter 2, section 2.5). In general, the late phase of the Late Ceramic Age period is characterized by extensive to-ing and fro-ing between communities within the wider Caribbean macro-region, encompassing the Greater Antilles, the Lesser Antilles and mainland South America (Hofman *et al.* 2007).

According to the weighted distribution data (table 5.11), Cayo is most prevalent on St. Vincent, followed by Dominica and Grenada. The Grenadines, St. Lucia and Martinique harbour just one site with Cayo each, and Barbados draws a blank.

The issue of dating has yet to be resolved definitively, but it would appear that Cayo ceramics initially occur alongside Suazan Troumassoid ceramics but subsequently outlasts the latter and carry on into Colonial times, albeit retaining several Suazan Troumassoid traits, as folk pottery similarly appears to do (*cf.* Hofman and Bright 2004).

5.4. Concluding remarks

Having discussed in detail the distribution of a number of ceramic stylistic and morphological traits across the Windward Islands and elucidated various patterns and stylistic parallels and/or influences, the following chapter will submit selected ceramic (decorative) traits to a quantitative, network-style analysis through the application of graph-theory, to measure degree of connectedness between assemblages of the Windward Island settlements on the basis of number of shared ceramic (sub)traits.

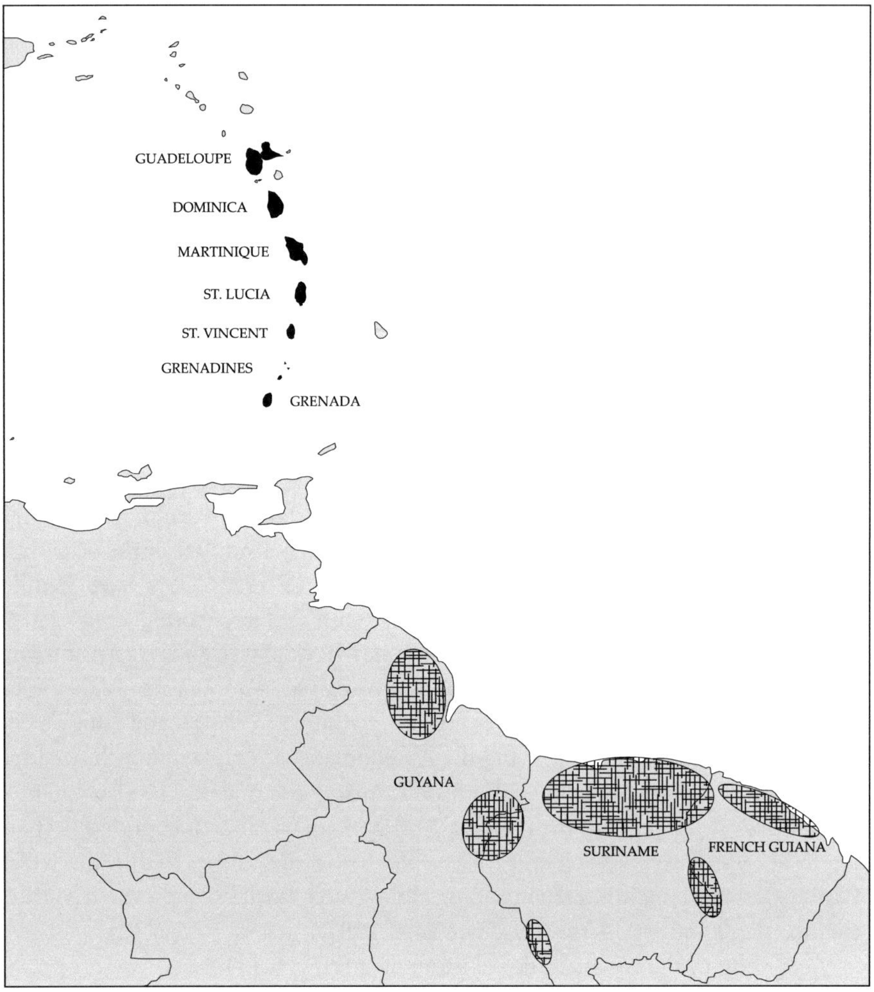

Figure 5.45. Distribution of Cayo throughout the Caribbean and stylistic similarities.

Cayo	*Sites with trait*	*Total sites*	*Weighted distribution percentage*
Barbados	0	52	0
Grenada	2	32	6.25
Grenadines	1	34	2.94
St. Vincent	11	66	16.67
St. Lucia	1	53	1.89
Martinique	1	44	2.27
Dominica	3	20	15

Table 5.11. Weighted distribution of Cayo per island.

Chapter 6

A GRAPH-THEORETICAL APPROACH TO LATE CERAMIC AGE WINDWARD ISLAND CERAMIC ASSEMBLAGES

6.1. The sharing of traits

The previous chapter has provided an overview of the distribution of ceramic (decorative) traits throughout the Windward Islands and beyond, but it is possible to make further inferences on the basis of the data-set at hand. Starting point remains the belief that a higher degree of stylistic homogeneity between site assemblages equates to a higher degree of inter-community interaction (see also Chapter 2). Terrell (2008:80-81) recently advocated that rather than endlessly debating the relative insularity of island(er)s (Rainbird 2007; Terrell *et al.* 1997; Anderson 2004b, 2006; see also Erlandson 2008), it is time to move on to more specific, detailed and quantifiable analyses of pre-Colonial social networks through the application of graph-theory among other approaches. Taking Terrell's lead, this chapter tabulates, quantifies and compares the ceramic trait data from Chapter 5 through simple graph-based approaches at ever higher resolutions.

Firstly, by comparing number of ceramic (decorative) traits shared between site assemblages, it should be possible to come to a crude ranking of sites in the sense of network analysis (see Broodbank 2002:202-207 for basic forays in this direction within Cycladic archaeology), from those with a greater number of trait overlaps shared to those with a lesser (or no) overlap in traits. However, before examining the sharing of traits between assemblages, we can first examine the number of ceramic (decorative) traits present in a given assemblage, to gain an impression of the relative (*i.e.* wide or narrow) elaboration of stylistic repertoire and its (potentially) non-uniform distribution across the archipelago. One would expect to see more traits exhibited at settlement sites, where a wide range of activities is expected to have taken place, requiring a larger arsenal of specific vessel types or meriting stylistic elaboration. Such places could be deemed possible 'hubs', as opposed to more ephemeral, single or limited activity sites, which could be regarded as 'peripheral nodes'. It must be noted that initially, only general traits are included in the analysis, rather than subtraits. The ten traits considered are polychrome painting (Caliviny Polychrome), lugs, legs, legged griddles, support rings, anthropomorphic adornos, loom weights, finger-indented rims, scratching and female statue-(tte)s. The fact that the traits potentially range from decorative to functional (although it can be difficult to make such a distinction in some cases) does not invalidate the comparison, as it is the range of traits characterizing Late Ceramic Age ceramic assemblages that is under review here, rather than offsetting individual traits against one another. The sites of the early and late phases of the Late Ceramic Age are considered in unison, for the simple reason that many ceramic (decorative) traits cannot be unequivocally assigned to either one or the other phase, and indeed may have featured in assemblages throughout the entire Late Ceramic Age. An unfortunate outcome of this hazy view of typochronology is that it is beyond the scope of this analysis to offset the early and late phase of the Late Ceramic Age; in other words, no potential shifts in degree of stylistic elaboration or changes in configurations and intensity of interaction can be teased out from the rather long Late Ceramic Age. For this and the following analyses, the choice has been made to only incorporate settlement data as opposed to including data from all sites, to correct for inadvertent biases in traits counts as a result of varying research intensity. As mentioned before, it is highly likely that a small number of sites now classified as pottery scatters may in fact represent settlement sites, but for now, this assumption cannot be substantiated.

The 111 Late Ceramic Age settlements break down over the individual islands as follows: Barbados (18), Grenada (14), the Grenadines (18), St. Vincent (27), St. Lucia (16), Martinique (17) and Dominica (1). Making an arbitrary subdivision of these settlements into those exhibiting one to three traits, four to seven traits and eight traits or more, it appears that twelve settlements were large hives of activity during the Late Ceramic Age, as their ceramic assemblages exhibit an extensive stylistic and morphological repertoire. It is surprising to note that of these twelve major settlements, half are on St. Lucia, whereas the remaining six are spread over Barbados (two), Martinique, Grenada, St. Vincent and the Grenadines (one each). Forty-three settlements fall within the middle bracket and exhibit a fair amount of ceramic variety. The pattern is somewhat different than the upper bracket, with St. Vincent (fourteen settlements) best represented, followed by the Grenadines (eight settlements), St. Lucia (eight settlements), Martinique and Barbados (five settlements each) and finally Grenada (three settlements). The lower bracket, consisting of 56 settlements yielding rather limited ceramic assemblages, breaks down as follows: St. Vincent (twelve settlements) is again best represented, followed by the Martinique and Barbados (eleven settlements each), Grenada (ten settlements), the Grenadines (eight settlements), St. Lucia (two settlements) and finally Dominica (one settlement).

This analysis of number of ceramic (decorative) traits characterizing an assemblage has yielded the additional insight that as many as eight sites now classified as just pottery scatters purely on the basis of number of sherds recovered (*i.e.* fewer than 200) may in fact represent settlements, as the stylistic/morphological variability that their limited assemblages exhibit (*i.e.* four or more decorative/morphological traits present) far surpasses expectations for non-settlement sites or activity areas. These sites are Caraibe Point (SLU-33), Cumberland Ravine (SVI-25), Petit Bordel (SVI-76) and Owia 1 (SVI-68)), Industry Estate (GRS-10, Bequia) and Cuckhold (BAR-23). Conversely, a great number of settlement sites (n=56) exhibits a rather circumscribed stylistic repertoire, which can generally be attributed to limited excavation or lack of information on the particulars of a given settlement's material assemblage as recorded in the archaeological literature (see also Appendix 1).

We now turn to a comparison of the number of ceramic (decorative) traits shared between assemblages, to come to a rough indicator of inter-site connectivity. On a general level, the same ten traits as above can be considered, namely

Caliviny Polychrome, lugs, legs, legged griddles, support rings, anthropomorphic adornos, loom weights, finger-indented rims, scratching and statue(tte)s. However, not enough distinction can be made between settlements at the level of trait, as too many assemblages have at least one subtype of every trait. Therefore, a higher resolution will be sought after, by comparing the sharing of subtraits. These analyses should go some way in positing stronger and weaker interaction ties between very roughly contemporaneous settlements, as well as investigating at which geographical scale stylistic communication was shared most.

A different method than that of the trait list utilized above must be applied to enable such an inter-site comparison to be made. Therefore, the basics of graph-theory will be adhered to by plotting data in a so-called adjacency matrix or square binary matrix, in which each site is positioned along the x- and y-axes, giving it a row and column of its own (*cf.* Hage and Harary 1991:20-21, Hage and Harary 1996; Irwin 1974; Scott 2005:63-69). Entries in the individual cells represent the number of (sub)types of ceramic (decorative) traits shared between the sites off-set against one another. Naturally, where a site encounters itself in the matrix, a value of 0 is recorded.

6.2. The sharing of subtraits

Regarding the sharing of subtraits, the four categories of legs, lugs, anthropomorphic adornos and finger indentation can be studied at a higher resolution than the other trait categories thanks to the various recognized and described subtypes of these traits, and will be discussed in turn. The first step in the analysis was to offset the sites against one another along the x- and y-axes, grouped by island, and to tally the number of shared subtraits.[81] This yielded an initial value per site that provided an indication of degree of stylistic elaboration in a settlement's assemblage, as well as a degree of connectivity with other sites. Thus, at first glance, one can get an impression of which settlements represented well-connected nodes and stylistic hives of activity, and which settlements were rather more peripheral with stylistically restricted assemblages.

The second step was to determine the degree of connectivity between sites on the same island, and then off-set that value against the connectivity with sites throughout the rest of the Windwards in general, to evaluate the assumption that (stylistic) interaction was stronger within the confines of a single island than outside them. In order to do that, first the weighted average sharing percentage between sites on one island was calculated. This involved calculating the percentage present of a hypothetical 100% connected situation. One attains this percentage by equating the sum value of a totally connected situation with 100%. By subsequently dividing 100% by this sum value, and multiplying the outcome by the actually present sum value, one arrives at an individual island's connectedness percentage. The same procedure is then carried out for the rest of the sites, yield-

81 Obviously a subtrait within a settlement's assemblage had to have been defined precisely in the archaeological literature or recognised through the author's own study of collections for the settlement to be included in this analysis. Regrettably, many archaeologists do not elaborate upon their description of general ceramic decorative traits, which means that many settlements that featured in earlier stages had to be left out at this stage of the analysis.

ing the connectedness percentage of a given island with the rest of the sites on other islands.

A third step was to compare the average weighted connectivity of sites of one island with sites on all other islands in turn, to determine whether stronger and weaker inter-island connections could be recognized. A subsidiary motive was to test the assumption that geographic proximity would translate into a higher degree of interaction between islands. Furthermore, it is hypothesized that the wide disparity in number of settlement assemblages yielding a certain (sub)trait and in average sharing values may indicate where a certain sub(trait) developed and from where it consequently spread to other settlements and islands.

Finally, the analysis was raised to a higher resolution by examining a number of settlements individually, focusing on some connectivity-values that may go unnoticed or be skewed at the level of the island. This is a highly necessary step to take, as there is absolutely no justification for treating contemporary geographic entities as culturally relevant units of analysis, as has been elaborated upon in Chapter 1. In this way then, we can move on from the general trends and insights yielded by an archaeology of islands, towards the more dynamic perspective afforded by an archaeology of island communities.

Vessel legs

Of the 111 settlements attributable to the Late Ceramic Age, 34 share the general trait of vessel legs between them. However, we only have further details on subtype of vessel leg at our disposal for 24 settlements. This analysis incorporates three defined subtypes of vessel leg.

First an overview of the tabulated data per island. The six settlements on Barbados yielded a sum value of 34 out of a potential total of 90 (6 x 5 x 3), which makes for a connectedness percentage of 37.78 (100 / 90 x 34). The rest of the sites yielded a sum value of 66 out of a potential 324 (18 x 6 x 3), which results in a connectedness percentage of 20.37 (100 / 324 x 66). This indicates that sites on Barbados share many more subtraits with each other than with the rest of the Windward Island sites. The three settlements on Martinique yielded a sum value of 8 out of a potential total of 18 (3 x 2 x 3), which makes for a connectedness percentage of 44.44 (100 / 18 x 8). The rest of the sites yielded a sum value of 60 out of a potential 189 (21 x 3 x 3), which results in a connectedness percentage of 31.75 (100 / 189 x 60). This indicates that sites on Martinique share more subtraits with each other than with the rest of the Windward Island sites. The thirteen settlements on St. Lucia yielded a sum value of 162 out of a potential total of 468 (13 x 12 x 3), which makes for a connectedness percentage of 34.62 (100 / 468 x 162). The rest of the sites yielded a sum value of 96 out of a potential 429 (11 x 13 x 3), which results in a connectedness percentage of 22.38 (100 / 429 x 96). This indicates that sites on St. Lucia share more subtraits with each other than they do with the rest of the Windward Island sites. The two settlements on St. Vincent yielded a sum value of 2 out of a potential total of 6 (2 x 1 x 3), which makes for a connectedness percentage of 33.33 (100 / 6 x 2). The rest of the sites yielded a sum value of 34 out of a potential 132 (22 x 2 x 3), which results in a connectedness percentage of 25.76 (100 / 132 x 34). This indicates that sites on

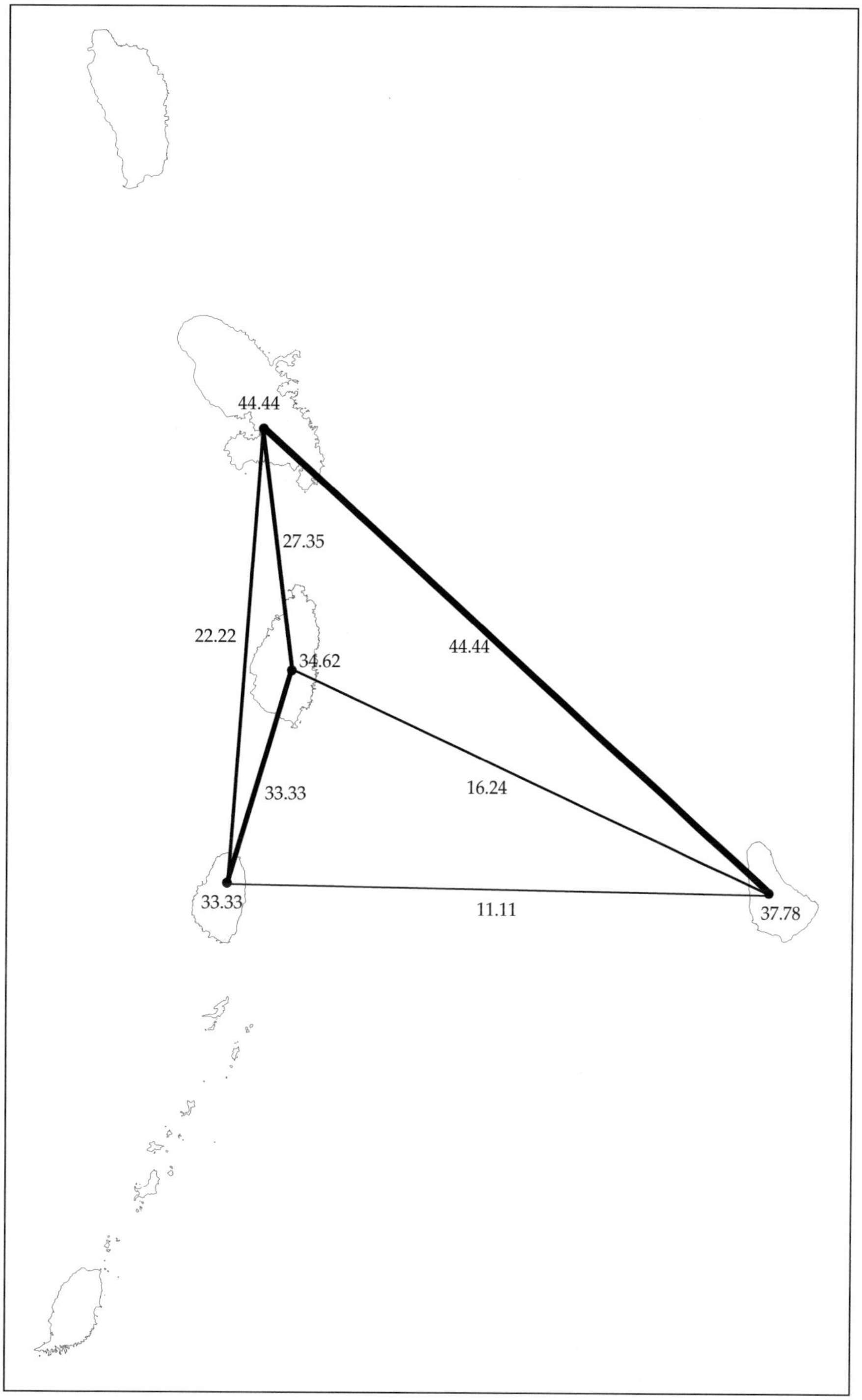

Figure 6.1. Inter-island connectivity on the basis of degree of sharing of vessel leg sub-types between settlement assemblages. Line thickness represents weight of connectivity (connectivity value in mm x 2).

	Barbados	*St. Vincent*	*St. Lucia*	*Martinique*
Barbados	**37.78**	11.11	16.24	44.44
St. Vincent	11.11	**33.33**	33.33	22.22
St. Lucia	16.24	33.33	**34.62**	27.35
Martinique	44.44	22.22	27.35	**44.44**

Table 6.1. Inter-island connectivity for trait of vessel legs (%).

St. Vincent share more subtraits with each other than they do with the rest of the Windward Island sites.

Moving on to specified inter-island connectivity for vessel legs (see also table 6.1 and figure 6.1), Barbados connects strongly to Martinique, with a connectivity value of 24 out of a potential 54 (6 x 3 x 3), or a percentage of 44.44 (100 / 54 x 24), more strongly in fact than sites on Barbados connect with each other. However, this strong connection was lost in the overview of all Windward Island sites, mitigated as it was by the weak connections with St. Lucia (38 of a potential 234, giving a percentage of 16.24) and St. Vincent (4 out of a potential 36, giving a percentage of 11.11). Martinique's strong connection with Barbados is likewise diluted by weaker connections with St. Lucia (32 of a potential 117, giving a percentage of 27.35) and St. Vincent (4 of a potential 18, giving a percentage of 22.22). St. Lucia's connection with St. Vincent (26 of a potential 78, giving a percentage of 33.33), only slightly weaker than between sites on St. Lucia itself, is again mitigated even weaker connections to Martinique and Barbados.

Taking the sites individually, Heywoods/Port St. Charles (BAR-38), Paquemar (MAR-81) and Micoud Beach (SLU-97) have the highest shared trait value (32), Silver Sands (BAR-70), Greenland (BAR-37), Chancery Lane (BAR-12) and Macabou (MAR-73) share the lowest value (9). That yields an average value of 20.5, of which the overwhelming majority of the settlements falls short.

It is interesting to note that Grenada and the Grenadines do not feature here. As is detailed in Chapter 5, the occurrences of vessel legs on these islands were three of the eleven that were not further specified in the literature, resulting in their exclusion from this analysis. This low number of occurrences in general suggests though that vessel legs were not a common part of the stylistic repertoire of communities on these islands.

Vessel lugs

Of the 111 settlements attributable to the Late Ceramic Age, 49 share the general trait of vessel lugs between them. However for only 44 settlements do we have further details on subtype of vessel lug at our disposal. This analysis incorporates four defined subtypes of vessel lug.

First an overview of the tabulated data per island. The five settlements on Barbados yielded a sum value of 10 out of a potential total of 80 (5 x 4 x 4), which makes for a connectedness percentage of 12.5 (100 / 80 x 10). The rest of the sites yielded a sum value of 138 out of a potential 780 (39 x 5 x 4), which results in a connectedness percentage of 17.69 (100 / 780 x 138). This indicates that sites on Barbados share more subtraits with the rest of the Windward Island sites than with each other. The four settlements on Grenada yielded a sum value of 26 out of a potential total of 48 (4 x 3 x 4), which makes for a connectedness percentage of 54.17 (100 / 48 x 26). The rest of the sites yielded a sum value of 206 out of a potential 640 (40 x 4 x 4), which results in a connectedness percentage of 32.19 (100 / 640 x 206). This indicates that sites on Grenada share considerably more subtraits with each other than they do with the rest of the Windward Island sites. The eight settlements in the Grenadines yielded a sum value of 48 out of a potential total of 224 (8 x 7 x 4), which makes for a connectedness percentage of 21.43 (100 / 224 x 48). The rest of the sites yielded a sum value of 258 out of a potential 1152 (36 x 8 x 4), which results in a connectedness percentage of 22.4 (100 / 1152 x 258). This indicates that sites in the Grenadines share slightly fewer subtraits with each other than they do with the rest of the Windward Island sites. The five settlements on Martinique yielded a sum value of 14 out of a potential total of 80 (5 x 4 x 4), which makes for a connectedness percentage of 17.5 (100 / 80 x 14). The rest of the sites yielded a sum value of 160 out of a potential 780 (39 x 5 x 4), which results in a connectedness percentage of 20.51 (100 / 780 x 160). This indicates that sites on Martinique share more subtraits with the rest of the Windward Island sites than they do with each other. The twelve settlements on St. Lucia yielded a sum value of 146 out of a potential total of 528 (12 x 11 x 4), which makes for a connectedness percentage of 27.65 (100 / 528 x 146). The rest of the sites yielded a sum value of 360 out of a potential 1536 (32 x 12 x 4), which results in a connectedness percentage of 23.44 (100 / 1536 x 360). This indicates that sites on St. Lucia share more subtraits with each other than they do with the rest of the Windward Island sites. The ten settlements on St. Vincent yielded a sum value of 48 out of a potential total of 360 (10 x 9 x 4), which makes for a connectedness percentage of 13.33 (100 / 360 x 48). The rest of the sites yielded a sum value of 264 out of a potential 1360 (34 x 10 x 4), which results in a connectedness percentage of 19.41 (100 / 1360 x 264). This indicates that sites on St. Vincent share more subtraits with the rest of the Windward Island sites than they do with each other.

Moving on to specified inter-island connectivity for vessel lugs (see also table 6.2 and figure 6.2), Barbados connects more strongly to every other island than it does internally. However, the general connectivity value with other islands of 17.69 masks considerable variability in individual island connections. Barbados's strongest connection is with Grenada (22 of a potential 80, giving a percentage of 27.5), followed by the progressively weaker connections with the Grenadines (30 of a potential 160, giving a percentage of 18.75), St. Lucia (44 of a potential 240, giving a percentage of 18.33), St. Vincent (31 of a potential 220, giving a percentage of 14.09) and Martinique (13 of a potential 100, giving a percentage of 13). For Grenada, the picture is rather more homogenous, and values cluster more closely around the Windward Island average of 32.19; the island is connected most strongly with St. Lucia (69 of a potential 192, giving a percentage of 35.94) and the Grenadines (44 of a potential 128, giving a percentage of 34.38), followed by the progressively weaker connections with Martinique (24 of a po-

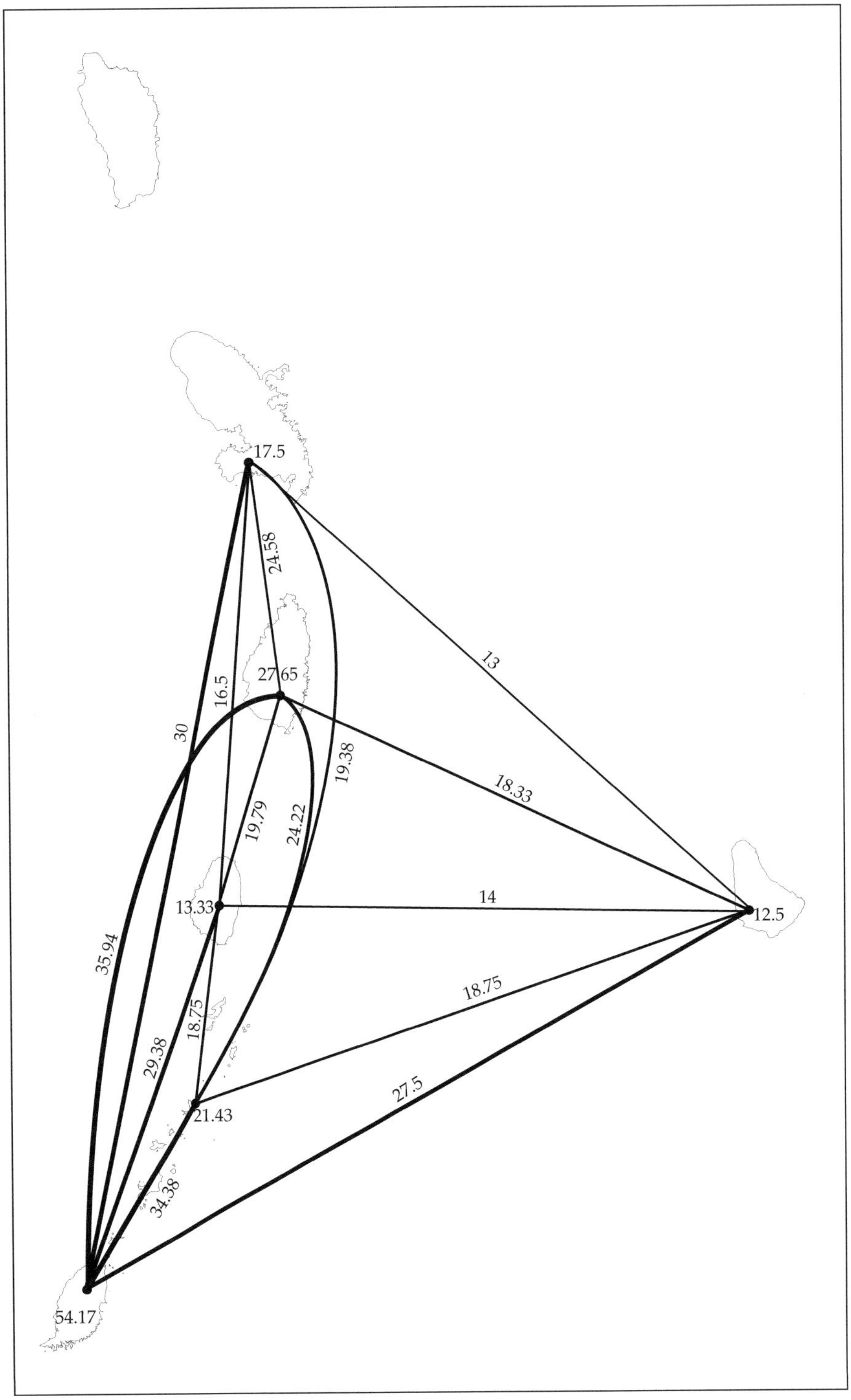

Figure 6.2. Inter-island connectivity on the basis of degree of sharing of vessel lug sub-types between settlement assemblages. Line thickness represents weight of connectivity (connectivity value in mm x 2).

	Barbados	Grenada	Grenadines	St. Vincent	St. Lucia	Martinique
Barbados	**12.5**	27.5	18.75	14.0	18.33	13
Grenada	27.5	**54.17**	34.38	29.38	35.94	30
Grenadines	18.75	34.38	**21.43**	18.75	24.22	19.38
St. Vincent	14.0	29.38	18.75	**13.33**	19.79	16.5
St. Lucia	18.33	35.94	24.22	19.79	**27.65**	24.58
Martinique	13	30	19.38	16.5	24.58	**17.5**

Table 6.2. Inter-island connectivity for trait of vessel lugs (%).

tential 80, giving a percentage of 30), St. Vincent (47 of a potential 160, giving a percentage of 29.38), and Barbados (22 of a potential 80, giving a percentage of 27.5). Seen from the perspective of the Grenadines, the value of 22.4 for connectedness with all other Windward Islands again masks some variability, particularly the considerably higher connectivity values with Grenada just established (44 of a potential 128, giving a percentage of 34.38) and with St. Lucia (93 of a potential 384, giving a percentage of 24.22). The connectivity values for Barbados (30 of a potential 160, giving a percentage of 18.75), Martinique (31 of a potential 160, giving a percentage of 19.38) and St. Vincent (60 of a potential 320, giving a percentage of 18.75) all fall slightly below the Windward Island general average. Turning to Martinique, great heterogeneity again underlies the Windward Island average of 20.51. Surprisingly perhaps, Martinique connects most strongly with Grenada (24 of a potential 80, giving a percentage of 30) and least strongly with Barbados (13 of a potential 100, giving a percentage of 13). Connection values of the other islands fall within these two extremes: 24.58 for St. Lucia (59 of a potential 240), 19.38 for the Grenadines (31 of a potential 160) and 16.5 for St. Vincent (33 of a potential 200). In its Windward Island average, St. Lucia's strong connection with Grenada (69 of a potential 192, giving a percentage of 35.94) is significantly dragged down by weak connections with Barbados (44 of a potential 240, giving a percentage of 18.33) and St. Vincent (95 of a potential 480, giving a percentage of 19.79). Connections with the Grenadines and Martinique are close to the average, at 24.22 (93 of a potential 384) and 24.58 (59 of a potential 240) respectively.

Taking the sites individually, Lavoutte (SLU-91) has the highest shared trait value (73), Kingstown Post Office (SVI-48) and Micoud Beach (SLU-97) share the lowest value (8). That yields an average value of 40.5, of which the majority of the settlements falls short.

Anthropomorphic adornos

Of the 111 settlements attributable to the Late Ceramic Age, 33 share the trait of anthropomorphic adornos between them. However we only have further details on subtype of anthropomorphic adorno at our disposal for 32 settlements. This analysis incorporates three defined subtypes of anthropomorphic adorno.

First an overview of the tabulated data per island. The six settlements on Barbados yielded a sum value of 24 out of a potential total of 90 (6 x 5 x 3), which makes for a connectedness percentage of 26.67 (100 / 90 x 24). The rest of the sites yielded a sum value of 125 out of a potential 468 (26 x 6 x 3), which results in a connectedness percentage of 26.71 (100 / 468 x 125). This indicates that sites on Barbados share more or less the same number of subtraits with the rest of the Windward Island sites as they do with each other. The three settlements on Grenada yielded a sum value of 6 out of a potential total of 18 (3 x 2 x 3), which makes for a connectedness percentage of 33.33 (100 / 18 x 6). The rest of the sites yielded a sum value of 27 out of a potential 261 (29 x 3 x 3), which results in a connectedness percentage of 10.34 (100 / 261 x 27). This indicates that sites on Grenada share many more subtraits with each other than they do with the rest of the Windward Island sites. The seven settlements in the Grenadines yielded a sum value of 35 out of a potential total of 126 (7 x 6 x 3), which makes for a connectedness percentage of 27.78 (100 / 126 x 35). The rest of the sites yielded a sum value of 126 out of a potential 525 (25 x 7 x 3), which results in a connectedness percentage of 24 (100 / 525 x 126). This indicates that sites in the Grenadines share more subtraits with each other than they do with the rest of the Windward Island sites. The four settlements on Martinique yielded a sum value of 8 out of a potential total of 36 (4 x 3 x 3), which makes for a connectedness percentage of 22.22 (100 / 36 x 8). The rest of the sites yielded a sum value of 86 out of a potential 336 (28 x 4 x 3), which results in a connectedness percentage of 25.6 (100 / 336 x 86). This indicates that sites on Martinique share more subtraits with the rest of the Windward Island sites than they do with each other. The nine settlements on St. Lucia yielded a sum value of 72 out of a potential total of 216 (9 x 8 x 3), which makes for a connectedness percentage of 33.33 (100 / 216 x 72). The rest of the sites yielded a sum value of 151 out of a potential 621 (23 x 9 x 3), which results in a connectedness percentage of 24.32 (100 / 621 x 151). This indicates that sites on St. Lucia share many more subtraits with each other than they do with the rest of the Windward Island sites. The three settlements on St. Vincent yielded a sum value of 6 out of a potential total of 18 (3 x 2 x 3), which makes for a connectedness percentage of 33.33 (100 / 18 x 6). The rest of the sites yielded a sum value of 57 out of a potential 261 (29 x 3 x 3), which results in a connectedness percentage of 21.84 (100 / 261 x 57). This indicates that sites on St. Vincent many more subtraits with each other than they do with the rest of the Windward Island sites.

Moving on to specified inter-island connectivity for anthropomorphic adornos (see also table 6.3 and figure 6.3), Barbados's relatively high general connectivity average with the rest of the Windward Islands (26.71) masks its very weak connection with Grenada (6 of a potential 54, giving a percentage of 11.11). Connections with all other islands yield values above the average, starting with the Grenadines (34 of a potential 126, giving a percentage of 26.98) and rising steadily through St. Vincent (15 of a potential 54, giving a percentage of 27.78) and Martinique (21 of a potential 72, giving a percentage of 29.17) to St. Lucia (49 of a potential 162, giving a percentage of 30.25). Departing from Grenada, the general Windward Island average of 10.34 is highly misleading, masking as it does

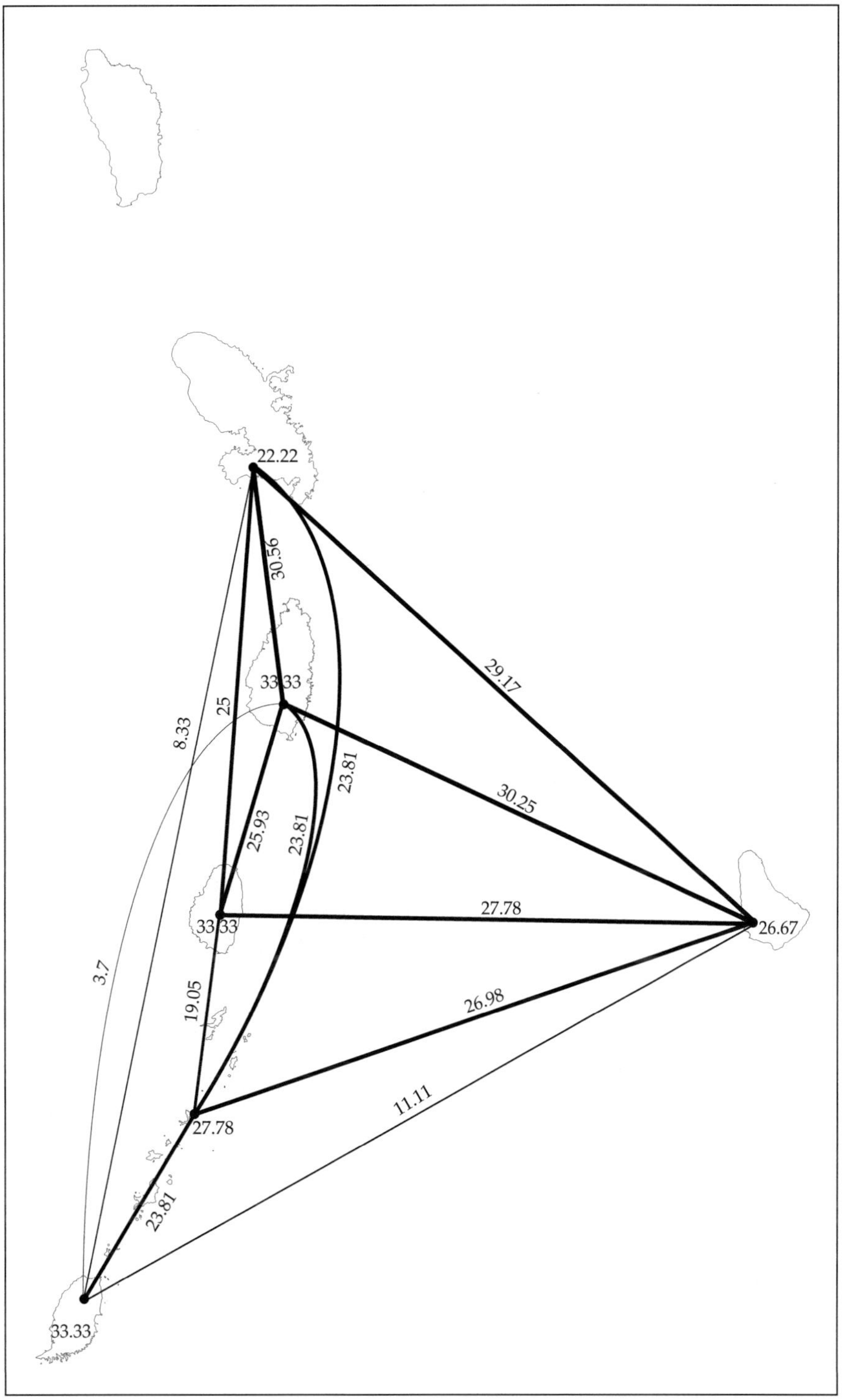

Figure 6.3. Inter-island connectivity on the basis of degree of sharing of anthropomorphic adorno sub-types between settlement assemblages. Line thickness represents weight of connectivity (connectivity value in mm x 2).

	Barbados	Grenada	Grenadines	St. Vincent	St. Lucia	Martinique
Barbados	**26.67**	11.11	26.98	27.78	30.25	29.17
Grenada	11.11	**33.33**	23.81	0	3.7	8.33
Grenadines	26.98	23.81	**27.78**	19.05	23.81	23.81
St. Vincent	27.78	0	19.05	**33.33**	25.93	25
St. Lucia	30.25	3.7	23.81	25.93	**33.33**	30.56
Martinique	29.17	8.33	23.81	25	30.56	**22.22**

Table 6.3. Inter-island connectivity for the trait of anthropomorphic adornos (%).

the strong connection with the Grenadines (15 of a potential 63, giving a percentage of 23.81) and the total lack of a connection with St. Vincent (0 of a potential 27, giving a percentage of 0). Connection with Barbados (6 of a potential 54, giving a percentage of 11.11) is slightly stronger than one would suspect from the general average, whereas connections with Martinique (3 of a potential 36, giving a percentage of 8.33) and St. Lucia (3 of a potential 81, giving a percentage of 3.7) are much weaker. Seen from the Grenadines, the general Windward Island average (24) is spot on for Grenada (15 of a potential 63, giving a percentage of 23.81), Martinique (20 of a potential 84, giving a percentage of 23.81) and St. Lucia (12 of a potential 63, giving a percentage of 23.81). It slightly masks the relatively stronger connection with Barbados (34 of a potential 126, giving a percentage of 26.98) and the relatively weaker connection with St. Vincent (12 of a potential 63, giving a percentage of 19.05), however. Martinique's general average connectivity with the rest of the Windward Islands (25.6) is reasonably accurate for the Grenadines (20 of a potential 84, giving a percentage of 23.81) and St. Vincent (9 of a potential 36, giving a percentage of 25), but does not do justice to the stronger connections with Barbados (21 of a potential 72, giving a percentage of 29.17) and St. Lucia (33 of a potential 108, giving a percentage of 30.56), and masks the weak connection with Grenada (3 of a potential 26, giving a percentage of 8.33). Similarly, St. Lucia's general average connectivity with the rest of the Windward Islands (24.32) is reasonably accurate for the Grenadines (45 of a potential 189, giving a percentage of 23.81) and St. Vincent (21 of a potential 81, giving a percentage of 25.93), but does not do justice to the stronger connections with Barbados (49 of a potential 162, giving a percentage of 30.25) and Martinique (33 of a potential 108, giving a percentage of 30.56), and masks the weak connection with Grenada (3 of a potential 81, giving a percentage of 3.7). From the perspective of St. Vincent, the lack of a connection with Grenada and the relatively weak connection with the Grenadines (12 of a potential 63, giving a percentage of 19.05) somewhat mitigate the stronger connections with Martinique (9 of a potential 36, giving a percentage of 25), St. Lucia (21 of a potential 81, giving a percentage of 25.93) and particularly Barbados (15 of a potential 54, giving a percentage of 27.78).

Taking the sites individually, Silver Sands (BAR-70) has the highest shared trait value (43), whereas Westerhall Point 2 (GRE-45), Pearls (GRE-29), Caliviny Island 3 (GRE-07), Ile de Ronde (GRS-43), Anse Belleville (Le Precheur) (MAR-02), Canelles Point (SLU-32) and Troumassée (SLU-143) all share the lowest value (11). That yields an average value of 27, of which the overwhelming majority of the settlements falls short.

Finger indentation

Of the 111 settlements attributable to the Late Ceramic Age, 64 share the trait of finger indentation between them. However, for only 44 of that number do we have further details on subtype of finger indentation at our disposal. This analysis incorporates five defined subtypes of finger indentation: single row, multiple rows, round indents, filetted indents and fingernail indented.

First an overview of the tabulated data per island. The six settlements on Barbados yielded a sum value of 32 out of a potential total of 150 (6 x 5 x 5), which makes for a connectedness percentage of 21.33 (100 / 150 x 32). The rest of the sites yielded a sum value of 157 out of a potential 1140 (38 x 6 x 5), which results in a connectedness percentage of 13.77 (100 / 1140 x 157). This indicates that sites on Barbados share many more subtraits with each other than with the rest of the Windward Island sites. The two settlements on Grenada yielded a sum value of 2 out of a potential total of 10 (2 x 1 x 5), which makes for a connectedness percentage of 20 (100 / 10 x 2). The rest of the sites yielded a sum value of 74 out of a potential 420 (42 x 2 x 5), which results in a connectedness percentage of 17.62 (100 / 420 x 74). This indicates that sites on Grenada share slightly more subtraits with each other than they do with the rest of the Windward Island sites. The six settlements in the Grenadines yielded a sum value of 32 out of a potential total of 150 (6 x 5 x 5), which makes for a connectedness percentage of 21.33 (100 / 150 x 32). The rest of the sites yielded a sum value of 232 out of a potential 1140 (38 x 6 x 5), which results in a connectedness percentage of 20.35 (100 / 1140 x 232). This indicates that sites in the Grenadines share slightly more subtraits with each other than they do with the rest of the Windward Island sites. The six settlements on Martinique yielded a sum value of 30 out of a potential total of 150 (6 x 5 x 5), which makes for a connectedness percentage of 20 (100 / 150 x 30). The rest of the sites yielded a sum value of 198 out of a potential 1140 (38 x 6 x 5), which results in a connectedness percentage of 17.37 (100 / 1140 x 198). This indicates that sites on Martinique share slightly more subtraits with each other than they do with the rest of the Windward Island sites. The ten settlements on St. Lucia yielded a sum value of 86 out of a potential total of 450 (10 x 9 x 5), which makes for a connectedness percentage of 18.67 (100 / 450 x 84). The rest of the sites yielded a sum value of 289 out of a potential 1700 (34 x 10 x 5), which results in a connectedness percentage of 17 (100 / 1700 x 289). This indicates that sites on St. Lucia share slightly more subtraits with each other than they do with the rest of the Windward Island sites. The fourteen settlements on St. Vincent yielded a sum value of 228 out of a potential total of 910 (14 x 13 x 5), which makes for a connectedness percentage of 25.05 (100 / 910 x 228). The rest of the sites yielded a sum value of 389 out of a potential 2100 (30 x 14 x 5), which results in a connectedness percentage of 18.52 (100 / 2100 x 389). This indicates that sites on St. Vincent share more subtraits with each other than they do with the rest of the Windward Island sites.

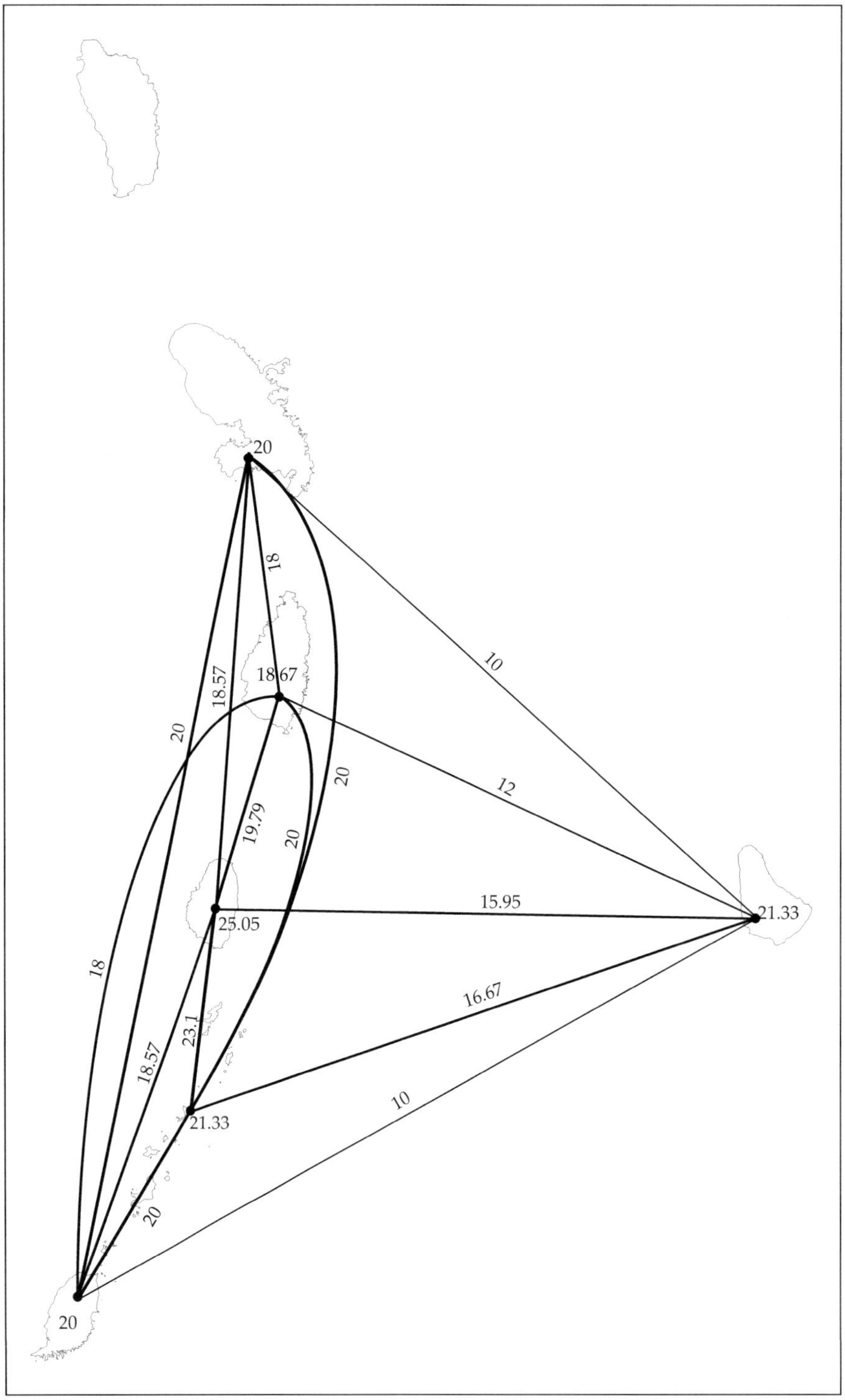

Figure 6.4. Inter-island connectivity on the basis of degree of sharing of finger indentation sub-types between settlement assemblages. Line thickness represents weight of connectivity (connectivity value in mm x 2).

	Barbados	Grenada	Grenadines	St. Vincent	St. Lucia	Martinique
Barbados	**21.33**	10	16.67	15.95	12	10
Grenada	10	**20**	20	18.57	18	20
Grenadines	16.67	20	**21.33**	23.1	20	20
St. Vincent	15.95	18.57	23.1	**25.05**	17.29	18.57
St. Lucia	12	18	20	17.29	**18.67**	18
Martinique	10	20	20	18.57	18	**20**

Table 6.4. Inter-island connectivity for the trait of finger indentation (%).

Moving on to specified inter-island connectivity for finger indentation (see also table 6.4 and figure 6.4), Barbados's general connectivity value with the rest of the Windward Islands (13.77) is the result of the averaging out of the stronger connections with St. Vincent (67 of a potential 420, giving a percentage of 15.95) and the Grenadines (30 of a potential 180, giving a percentage of 16.67) with the weaker connections with Grenada (6 of a potential 60, giving a percentage of 10), Martinique (18 of a potential 180, giving a percentage of 10) and St. Lucia (36 of a potential 300 giving a percentage of 11.85). Grenada's general connectivity value with the rest of the Windward Islands (17.62) turns out to be too low for most of the other islands, as a result of the mitigating effect of the weak connection with Barbados (6 of a potential 60, giving a percentage of 10). St. Lucia (18 of a potential 100, giving a percentage of 18), St. Vincent (26 of a potential 140, giving a percentage of 18.57) and Martinique and the Grenadines (both 12 of a potential 60, giving a percentage of 20) all connect more strongly with Grenada. The Grenadines' general connectivity value with the rest of the Windward Islands (20.35) is very close to the mark for Grenada (9 of a potential 60, giving a percentage of 20), St. Lucia (60 of a potential 300, giving a percentage of 20) and Martinique (36 of a potential 180, giving a percentage of 20), but averages out the somewhat weaker connection with Barbados (30 of a potential 180, giving a percentage of 16.67) and the somewhat stronger connection with St. Vincent (97 of a potential 420, giving a percentage of 23.1). Martinique has stronger individual connections with most of the other Windward Islands than its general average of 17.37 suggests, mitigated as these stronger values are by the weak connection with Barbados (18 of a potential 180, giving a percentage of 10). Thus connections with St. Lucia (54 of a potential 300, giving a percentage of 18), St. Vincent (78 of a potential 420, giving a percentage of 18.57), Grenada (12 of a potential 60, giving a percentage of 20) and the Grenadines (36 of a potential 180, likewise giving a percentage of 20) are all higher than the general average. St. Lucia's general average connection with other Windward Islands (17) matches the specified values of St. Vincent (121 of a potential 700, giving a percentage of 17.29), Grenada (18 of a potential 100, giving a percentage of 18) and Martinique (54 of a potential 300, giving a percentage of 18) quite well. However, it masks the weak connection with Barbados (36 of a potential 300, giving a percentage of 12) and does not do justice to the relatively strong connection with the Grenadines (60 of a potential 300, giving a percentage of 20). From the perspective of St. Vincent, the connection values with Grenada (26 of a potential 140, giving a percentage of 18.57) and Martinique (78 of a potential 420, giving a percentage of 18.57) match the general average (18.52) almost exactly. However, the strong connection with the Grenadines (97 of a potential 420, giving a percentage of 23.1) is lost due the averaging with the weaker connections of St. Lucia (121 of a potential 700, giving a percentage of 17.29) and Barbados (67 of a potential 420, giving a percentage of 15.95).

Taking the sites individually, Heywoods/Port St. Charles (BAR-38) has the highest shared trait value (63), Point de Caille (SLU-119), Hillcrest (Site B) (BAR-40) and Peak Bay (BAR-62) share the lowest value (6). That yields an average value of 34.5, exceeded by the overwhelming majority of the settlements.

6.3. Comparison between traits

Comparing the outcome of the four traits, it can be remarked that no homogenous picture emerges. One of the questions that one could address with the foregoing analysis is that of the relationship between geographical location and connectivity. As such, the geographical isolation of Barbados, located some 150 km east of the Windward Island chain, is borne out in higher internal connections for some traits (finger indentation and vessel legs, bar an exceptionally strong connection with Martinique) but not others (vessel lugs and anthropomorphic adornos). Grenada, at the southern end of the Windward Island chain, has a stronger internal connection when it comes to vessel lugs and anthropomorphic adornos, but is more or less equally connected externally and internally for the trait of finger indentation (bar a much weaker connection with Barbados). Martinique, despite being the northernmost representative of the Windward Islands in the absence of Dominica, exhibits stronger external rather than internal connections for the trait of vessel lugs (bar weaker connections with Barbados and St. Vincent) and anthropomorphic adornos (bar a weak connection with Grenada). It has a stronger internal connection for vessel legs though, bar an equally strong connection with Barbados. The picture is more ambivalent for the trait of finger indentation. The Grenadines either have weaker external connections (anthropomorphic adornos and finger indentation, bar a slightly stronger connection with St. Vincent) or display a more ambivalent pattern (vessel lugs). St. Vincent demonstrates one stronger external connections (lugs) and three stronger internal rather than external connections (vessel legs, bar an equally strong connection with St. Lucia, finger indentation and anthropomorphic adornos). St. Lucia finally shows strong internal connections for the traits of vessel legs, vessel lugs (although the connection value with Grenada is considerably stronger than the internal value) and anthropomorphic adornos and one more ambivalent connection for the trait of finger indentation. Summarising then, on a general level, the geographically peripheral Barbados and Grenada exhibit a measure of isolation, with a number of strong internal connections. The inverse is not necessarily the case though: the intermediate islands of St. Vincent and St. Lucia demonstrate a higher degree of internal rather than external connectivity. The Grenadines and Martinique do seem to exhibit the degree of externality that would be expected given their intermediacy.

What of a possible relation between degree of connectivity and geographical adjacency or proximity? By utilising the approach taken above and analysing the outcome, it is possible to test the assumption that island communities interacted more strongly with neighbouring or more proximate island communities than they did with further-flung island communities.

Considering the inter-island connectivity data (tables 6.1 through 6.4), it rapidly becomes apparent that there is very little correlation between a strong connection and neighbouring islands, or even such as thing as a steady fall-off rate in relation to increasing distance. Of the many possible combinations of neighbouring islands, in only seven cases was the connection value higher than with more distant islands. Concerning a fall-off of connectivity as distance increases, there a few tantalising inklings, but even these are generally spoiled by one or more islands not conforming to such a pattern. In the overwhelming majority of cases, strength of connection does not correlate to geographical proximity. It can be safely concluded that interaction was intensive during this period throughout the entire Windwards, though the degree of interaction varied per ceramic (decorative) trait across alternating constellations of islands.

One final question that can be addressed at island level concerns the position of the Grenadines. Taken together as a single unit above for ease of analysis and to ensure a sample of decent size, the eighteen settlements in the Grenadines are in actual fact distributed over eight small islands. Considering the limited dimensions of these islands, it is interesting to see whether small island communities demonstrated a high degree of internal connectivity, suggesting that they relied more strongly on each other and were in effect relatively self-supporting, or whether they maintained an inordinate degree of contact with communities on larger islands. As discussed above, the Grenadines as a whole connect equally with other islands or more strongly than they do with each other, with just two exceptions. This could be a result of their intermediate position as much as of their alleged dependence on larger neighbours. However, examining them on a site by site basis per trait yields some interesting patterns. For anthropomorphic adornos for instance, Ile de Ronde (GRS-43), Dover (GRS-29) and Chatham Bay (GRS-56) connect with three sites on Grenada, but not with any of the three sites on St. Vincent. Miss Pierre (GRS-61) and Sabazan (GRS-40) do not connect to the three sites on Grenada, but to all three sites on St. Vincent. Grand Bay (GRS-31; Carriacou) and Park Point (GRS-15) connect equally to all six sites. For finger indentation, every site in the Grenadines is connected to at least one site on each other island, the main difference being in strength of connectivity. Grand Bay, Miss Pierre and Rosemary/L'Ansecoy Bay (GRS-51) have the highest connection values, and demonstrate markedly stronger connections with Barbados (all three sites), St. Vincent (Grand Bay on Carriacou and Rosemary/L'Ansecoy) and St. Lucia (only Miss Pierre). For lugs, little in the way of remarkable patterning shows up. All Grenadines sites connect with at least one site on every other island, and once again the main difference lies in strength of connectivity. Grand Bay (Carriacou), Park Point, Mayreau Beach/Saline Bay (GRS-46) and Grand Bay (GRS-23; Cannouan) connect more strongly with sites on other islands, as was already evident from their higher overall connection value. Overall, what is clear from the foregoing is that most settlements in the Grenadines did not exhibit inordinately strong connections with settlements on other islands, and that stronger connections do not necessarily follow from closer proximity, suggesting that geographical distance is of no consequence for intensity of contact, at least not at this scale. This mirrors the findings at the Windward Islands scale.

Finally, we turn to a consideration of a number of individual, highly connected settlements, which lends the analysis an even higher resolution. Thus, for the trait of vessel legs, the strongest individual connections are those between Heywoods/Port St. Charles (BAR-38) and Paquemar (MAR-81)/Micoud Beach (SLU-97) and between Micoud Beach and Paquemar (three of three subtraits shared). The connection between proximate Micoud Beach and Paquemar is perhaps to be expected, but the strong connections between a settlement on Barbados and one on Martinique and one on St. Lucia are more surprising. For the trait of vessel lugs, there are no 100% connections, but a number of settlements share three out of four subtraits: Salt Pond 1 (GRE-34) and Giraudy (SLU-67), Salt Pond 1 and Lavoutte (SLU-91), Savanne Suazey (GRE-38) and Caliviny Island 3 (GRE-07), Savanne Suazey and Grand Bay (GRS-31), Savanne Suazey and Lavoutte, Caliviny Island 3 and Grand Bay, Caliviny Island 3 and Lavoutte, Grand Bay and Lavoutte, Lavoutte and Anse Belleville (Le Precheur) (MAR-02), Lavoutte and Pigeon Island (SLU-117) and Lavoutte and Giraudy. For the trait of anthropomorphic adornos, the strongest connection – three out of three subtraits shared - is that between Silver Sands (BAR-70) and Macabou (MAR-73). For the trait of finger indentation, there are no 100% or even 80% connections, but a number of settlements share three out of five subtraits: Heywoods/Port St. Charles and Chancery Lane (BAR-12), Heywoods/Port St. Charles and Miss Pierre (GRS-61), Heywoods/Port St. Charles and Mount Pleasant/Rawacou (SVI-57) and Miss Pierre and Giraudy.

6.4. Testing settlement dynamics through analysis of shared ceramic traits

In section 4.3.3 of this dissertation, numerous hypothetical cases of settlement mobility were outlined on the basis of occupation/abandonment of proximate settlements from phase to phase. These suggestions remained hypothetical in the absence of any corroborating evidence for a relation between the settlements, other than the likelihood of a relation on the basis of their very proximity to one another. Having identified the Late Ceramic Age ceramic (decorative) traits present in each settlement's assemblage, it is now possible to evaluate the proposed Late Ceramic Age settlement connections on the basis of the principle that the more traits are shared, the more likely that there was a relationship. Naturally, only the relationships between settlements with at least one overlapping component can be tested for assemblage similarity.

Grenada

The hypothetical early phase Late Ceramic Age link between GRE-02/GRE-03 and GRE-34 finds some corroboration in the form of the presence of the general trait of lugs shared between GRE-03 and GRE-34, though not by GRE-02. GRE-02/GRE-03 do not share GRE-34's scratching, but this may have been a later development. There are no other traits present, making further corroboration or dispelling impossible. In the late phase of the Late Ceramic Age, the hypothetical split of GRE-13 from GRE-01 is corroborated by the shared presence of Caliviny Polychrome, though GRE-13 does not share GRE-01's presence of lugs or scratching. GRE-21's split from either GRE-45/46 or GRE-39 is not convincingly upheld by examining the shared ceramic traits, as GRE-21 fails to share four and three traits with GRE-45/46 and GRE-39 respectively. GRE-37 cannot be clearly linked to any of the suggestions, as it fails to match three, five and three traits with GRE-01, GRE-38 and GRS-43 respectively.

Grenadines

Regarding the hypothesized early phase Late Ceramic Age link between GRS-43 on Ile de Ronde and either Grenada's GRE-01 or GRE-38 or Carriacou's GRS-32 or GRS-40, the argument is more convincing for Grenada, considering the two traits shared with GRE-01 (though two traits are not shared) and the two traits including one subtrait shared with GRE-38 (though a further four traits are not shared). Having said that, two traits are shared with GRS-40 as well (a further five are not), whereas there are five traits not shared between GRS-32 and GRS-43. For the late phase of the Late Ceramic Age, GRS-63 on Ile de Caille appears not to have split off from GRS-43 or GRE-01 (four traits are not shared), but more likely – though not convincingly - from GRE-37 (one trait not shared) or GRE-38 (one trait shared, four not). As to GRS-41 and GRS-36 on Carriacou splitting from GRS-29, the ceramic assemblages are not very supportive, showing five traits not shared (GRS-36) and one trait shared and four not (GRS-41). GRS-36 was also hypothesized to have possibly split from GRS-31, but on the evidence of seven counts of non-shared traits, this seems even more unlikely. On Cannouan, the hypothetical split of GRS-21 from GRS-23 is supported by the sharing of two traits (although a further four traits do not match up). Finally, on Bequia, GRS-11 is hypothesized to have split from GRS-15, but with five counts of non-shared traits, this is not borne out by the ceramic assemblages.

St. Vincent

The community of SVI-100 apparently merged with that of either SVI-36, SVI-80 or SVI-14 during the early phase of the Late Ceramic Age. It is difficult to judge whether one shared (sub)trait with SVI-36 outweighs the seven traits not shared though. Perhaps fewer traits not shared, such as the two not shared with SVI-80, make for a stronger case in this instance. Either way, the six traits not shared with SVI-14 appear to rule out this connection. The alleged merging of SVI-57 with SVI-90 appears to be conclusively underscored by the sharing of six traits (one trait not shared). Turning to the late phase of the Late Ceramic Age, SVI-36 may have represented the parent community of SVI-08, although the seven non-shared traits do not bode particularly well. The hypothesized relationship between SVI-19 and SVI-88 yields three non-shared traits, SVI-41 and SVI-50 have one trait in common and four non-shared traits, and SVI-46 to SVI-92 have two traits but do not share a further two traits. Finally, comparison between SVI-18 and SVI-86 reveals two non-shared traits, and the hypothesized split off of SVI-20 from SVI-03 is materialized in just one shared trait and five non-shared ones.

St. Lucia

In the early phase of the Late Ceramic Age, SLU-36 is hypothesized to have split from SLU-117. With four traits shared and three non-shared traits, a link seems credible. The relationship between SLU-91 and SLU-42 is equally credible, with six traits shared and four non-shared traits. The split from SLU-70 of SLU-85 certainly seems to borne out by trait comparison, with eight traits shared, and just one not shared. As for SLU-143 representing a parent community to SLU-96 and SLU-97, with four traits shared and four not, and three traits shared and four not shared respectively, a link with either seems credible. The hypothesized split from SLU-119 of SLU-120 seems to be corroborated by assemblage comparison, with five traits shared and three not. The link between SLU-24 and SLU-67 appears unlikely upon inspection of their assemblages (eight non-shared traits) whereas the link between SLU-24 and SLU-13 is neither corroborated nor invalidated (one non-shared trait). Moving to the late phase of the Late Ceramic Age, the alleged split from SLU-13 to SLU-112 is marked by four traits not shared.

Martinique

In the early phase of the Late Ceramic Age, MAR-12 is hypothesized to have split off from MAR-09, a link which is not borne out by assemblage comparison (five non-shared traits). MAR-81 is postulated to have served as parent community of MAR-71 and MAR-34, which is not reflected as such in the number of shared traits between assemblages (one shared, seven not and seven not shared respectively). Turning to the late phase of the Late Ceramic Age, the link between MAR-33 and MAR-116 is not necessarily expressed by the sharing of traits (three not shared). Concerning the hypothesized split from MAR-12 to MAR-48, we are faced with five non-shared traits. Finally, what of the alleged role of parent community to MAR-82, MAR-73 and MAR-13 played by MAR-81? Interestingly, MAR-82, the closest community to MAR-81 shows the least degree of matching, with seven traits not shared. MAR-13 (five traits shared, four traits not) and

MAR-73 (six traits shared, four not) both suggest a higher degree of interaction. The latter two settlements show an extremely large degree of overlap incidentally (seven traits shared, many even to the level of subtrait, one trait not shared).

Barbados

The hypothesized early phase Late Ceramic Age split from BAR-16 of BAR-67 does not materialize in shared traits (four not shared). BAR-37 presumably represents an offshoot of either BAR-39 (four shared traits, three not shared) or BAR-67 (three traits shared, thee not shared), or perhaps from both considering the assemblage comparison. Of the two potential split offs from BAR-66, BAR-62 (five traits shared, one not) is far more likely than BAR-61 (seven traits not shared). Concerning the merging of BAR-09 with BAR-72 or BAR-56, the material is equivocal, with one trait not shared between BAR-09 and BAR-56, and two traits not shared between BAR-09 and BAR-72. Turning to the late phase of the Late Ceramic Age, as far as BAR-21 is concerned, a split from BAR-67 (three non-matches) is more likely than from BAR-37 (six non-matches), but still not convincing. BAR-39 representing a parent community to BAR-40 also seems questionable, in the face of seven non-matches between ceramic traits.

Dominica cannot be evaluated, as its settlements date to the Early Ceramic Age only.

6.5. Concluding remarks

This chapter provided a graph-theoretical analysis of the sharing of a number of Late Ceramic Age ceramic (decorative) traits by settlements in the Windward Islands, through the application of graph-theory. In so doing, it tested a number of assumptions in the realm of insularity, interaction and settlement dynamics. In the final chapter, the results of the analyses carried out in all foregoing chapters are placed within an overall narrative of diachronic developments in the Windward Islands and evaluated for the insights they provide in the realm of social organization.

Chapter 7

A MULTI-SCALAR APPROACH TO WINDWARD ISLAND INTER- AND INTRA-ISLAND INTERACTION AND SOCIAL ORGANIZATION

In this final chapter, a brief overview will be given of the outcomes of the research presented within this dissertation, followed by a discussion of the multi-scalar approach to Late Ceramic Age dynamism and social organization in the Windward Islands on the basis of the twinned and intertwined data-set of sites and ceramic site assemblages. As such, settlement dynamics and the distribution of ceramic (decorative) traits are examined at the local, micro-regional and regional scale. Finally, a reconstruction of Windward Island Amerindian settlement and intra- and inter-insular relationships is provided, a narrative that will be punctuated with Ceramic Age data from the Leeward Islands, in order to discern more parallel trends or divergent developments throughout the Lesser Antilles. This endeavour represents a first step in understanding the developments in the Windward Islands as influenced by and influencing other parts of the greater Caribbean area or Caribbeanscape (Rodríguez Ramos 2010). The chapter charts the development of the region through time from an avenue connecting mainland South America to the Leeward Islands and the Greater Antilles to a region that came into its own during the Late Ceramic Age, one that maintained diverse ties with communities in various parts of the mainland and was ultimately to prove the most resilient to European endeavour in the early Colonial period. This chapter will be rounded off by drawing some final conclusions, suggesting a number of follow-up avenues with future research potential and highlighting a number of problems that remain to be addressed in future research.

7.1. Recapitulation and results of dissertation research

The main research problems of the dissertation research were introduced in Chapter 1, namely defining the variegated interactions of Amerindian communities both within the Windward Islands as well as between the Windward Islands and neighbours to the north and south, and ascertaining how Windward Island society was organised socially through time. The current state of research in the Caribbean into social complexity is such that there are a great number of conditioning factors at play such as ethnographic analogies and (ethno)historical information, as well as imbalances in archaeological research conducted throughout the region. Furthermore, it is apparent that various archaeological proxies for complexity are adhered to by Caribbean archaeologists, some more valid or successful than others. This study departs from a theoretical framework and approach that draws on tenets of site pattern archaeology, interaction theory, graph-theoretical analysis and multi-scalarity. The data-set at hand has been collated from a variety of sources, ranging from archaeological and anthropological literature and (museum) collections to archaeological survey and excavation.

The concept of islandscape and developments in the field of island archaeology are believed to be of considerable importance for the present study; indeed several facets of island archaeology appear highly applicable to Windward Island archaeology. In turn, Windward Island archaeology can (and in some cases already does) contribute to the general field of island studies in many respects, for instance in the form of research on transported or domesticated landscapes, the transition from Archaic to Ceramic culture, aspects of voyaging and inter-island interactions, and adaptation of coastal or riverine societies to insular settings. Particular attention has been devoted to the maritime orientation of Windward Island communities, which would have enabled and encouraged them to seek out and maintain interactions with neighbouring communities near and far. This leads seamlessly into the necessity of abandoning the island as unit of analysis, or rather, as only unit of analysis. In this dissertation, sites and the archipelago form additional units of analysis within a multi-scalar approach. Also, the dissertation takes an explicit inter-unit approach, comparing sites, islands and even regions. In order to ground discussions of the Windward Islandscape, a geographical, environmental, archaeological and (ethno)historical perspective on the island group was given. The established archaeological narrative served as a baseline against which new findings and updated analyses of the data-set could be offset (Chapter 2).

The two main data-sets (archaeological sites and their ceramic assemblages) that have been analysed for the present study were introduced in Chapter 3, and past classificatory and typochronological approaches to these data within the (wider) study area were detailed. This historiography makes clear where the data-set came from and what biases may be present that have affected collections or observations, essentially predetermining the data. In this respect, the distinction between modal and type-variety approaches to ceramic classification has had great ramifications for the interpretation of ceramic (decorative) traits, rendering them either regionally comparable or micro-regionally/locally distinctive. The updated account of site distributions and the distribution of ceramic styles in the study area provided per island underlined that some islands have seen much more intensive and professional archaeological study (and curation of finds) than others, introducing a regrettable but unavoidable bias to the data-set.

The re-examination of the Windward Island sequence of settlement on the basis of recalibrated radiocarbon dates makes clear that Early Ceramic Age settlement of the islands remains difficult to get a handle on (Chapter 4). In the absence of additional early dates, one can only hypothesize about potential early yet undetected settlement, and conclude for now that most islands were indeed skipped over, in favour of the Leeward Islands and Puerto Rico. The Late Ceramic Age dates are more satisfying in the sense that they provide firm evidence of continual occupation throughout the period, with numerous dates extending into Colonial times, raising expectations of a link with the (ethno)historically documented Island Carib. Reconsideration of site periodisation yielded the insight that Windward Island occupation was remarkably stable over time, bar a minor dip during the early phase of the Late Ceramic Age. Despite the best efforts of various archaeologists, there is no apparent patterning in site location. By defining a settlement system for the region by drawing on archaeology, ethnography and (ethno)history, enigmatic pottery scatters or individual lithic finds discovered away from settlement sites were interpreted as possible hamlets, activity areas related to wood clearing or canoe-building and subsistence-related activities such as planting fields, hunting and foraging. The pattern of settlement pairs and clustered settlements was interpreted as multi-generational shifting occupation or community fissioning and it was ascertained that islets or isles played a much greater role in Windward Island society than previously considered. Furthermore, specific patterns in cultural components present across neighbouring settlements were interpreted as representing various instances of settlement or community mobility, such as fissioning, fusing and oscillating between proximate settlement locations.

The overview of ceramic (decorative) trait distribution during the Late Ceramic Age (Chapter 5) proved the first step towards elucidating intra- and inter-island community interaction in the Windward Islands. By implementing the multi-scalar approach, local ceramic innovations could be distinguished from traits shared within the micro-region or even throughout the Lesser Antilles. Furthermore, by expanding the comparative scope to the Greater Antilles and the South American mainland, possible stylistic influences from more distant regions could be suggested. The main outcome of this comparison was that while Windward Island communities certainly developed a localized stylistic identity, they remained open to a host of wide-ranging contacts, either having an influence on or being influenced by developments outside the micro-region. In particular, the Windward Islanders appear to have consciously realigned themselves with their erst-while homeland, albeit in an ever more cosmopolitan and wide-ranging manner. Weighted distribution counts suggest that in some cases, certain islands may have functioned as prime nodes for the introduction and further dissemination of traits, but the patterning does not carry over to multiple traits, suggesting incipient differentiation amidst a high degree of autonomy. The graph theoretical network analysis undertaken in Chapter 6 merely underscored these suppositions, but rendered them quantifiable, hard inferences about distribution frequencies of ceramic decorative traits and – somewhat less hard - degrees of connectivity between islands and, significantly, individual communities. By taking the resolution up a notch to the settlement site level, we have perhaps come as close as we can get to Amerindian social organization and interaction at the community level. The multiple and varied outcomes of the analysis of four traits merely underscored the dynamic character of relationships between various Windward Island communities. The application of the ceramic trait distribution analysis to the instances of settlement mobility hypothesized in Chapter 4 yielded the insight that in many cases, there is a very weak correlation between proximity and specific material culture homogeneity. This would appear to provide yet another independent line of evidence against the study of islands as analytical units, arguing instead for an archipelagic approach (*cf.* Hofman *et al.* in press).

Attributes Island	Cayo	Caliviny P.	Lugs	Legs	Legged G.	Support Ring	Anthrop. adorno	Loom weight	Finger indent.	Scratch.	Statues
Barbados	0	7	8	12	11	1	6	3	12	8	1
Grenada	2	11	12	1	1	0	3	2	3	14	2
Grenadines	1	10	9	2	7	5	8	2	21	16	2
St. Vincent	11	21	10	4	23	6	5	0	25	27	1
St. Lucia	1	9	17	21	20	6	13	3	21	18	4
Martinique	1	3	5	4	8	3	5	3	8	9	2
Dominica	3	0	0	0	0	0	1	0	0	5	0
Total	19	61	61	44	70	21	41	13	90	97	12

Table 7.1. Distribution of ceramic (decorative) traits over Windward Island assemblages.

Having provided an overview of the research carried out and discussed in this dissertation, the next section will synthesize the results obtained from analysis of the two main data-sets utilized in this study - namely settlements and ceramic site assemblages - in a multi-scalar fashion.

7.2. A multi-scalar approach to Late Ceramic Age dynamism and social organization in the Windward Islands

As was outlined in Chapter 1, it was deemed useful to take a multi-scalar approach (*cf.* Curet 2005; Hofman 1993; Parkinson 2006) to the study of archaeological data from the Windward Islands, particularly the distribution of decorative traits. It is straightforward enough to discuss settlement data from a multi-scalar perspective (Windward Islands region, individual Windward Islands, parts of individual islands). However, it initially proved confounding to apply a tripartite scale to ceramic (decorative) traits, as it readily became apparent that in some cases, the unit of analysis should not be the trait but rather the sub-trait of decoration. For this reason, the presentation of the results in multi-scalar fashion has been defrayed until this final section of the dissertation, where the data overview is not bound by strictures of category. The following section will draw a number of conclusions from Windward Island settlement patterning discussed in chapter 4 and the distribution of ceramic (decorative) traits throughout the Windwards and beyond discussed in chapter 5 (see also table 7.1). For the sake of symmetry, the discussion will centre on the Late Ceramic Age only.

7.2.1. Late Ceramic Age scales

Regional

In general, settlement in the Windward Islands during the Late Ceramic Age has two faces. As detailed in section 4.2, at first glance the early phase of the Late Ceramic Age appears to herald a population slump compared to the previous period, with site tallies dropping significantly. However, when site type is factored into the equation, the picture becomes more balanced, suggesting only a slight decline in population. Alternatively, the more concentrated site pattern could represent a shift in lifeways entailing less roaming and a less extensive use of the landscape, and consolidation of settlement, perhaps attributable to enhanced knowledge of the environment and adaptation to island life. Whatever the case, both site and settlement tallies increase significantly again during the late phase of the Late Ceramic Age, suggesting either a return to Early Ceramic Age wide-ranging lifeways, a demographic increase, or increasing settlement mobility.

Turning to ceramic assemblages, on the face of it, many Late Ceramic Age ceramic (decorative) traits seem just as widespread and homogenous as those of the Early Ceramic Age. On a general level, some Troumassoid traits (such as scratching or finger indentation) occur almost as frequently and widely during the Late Ceramic Age as do certain Saladoid traits (ZIC and WOR) during the Early Ceramic Age. Looking closer, however, it becomes evident that there is one major difference governing decorative trait distribution now: very few traits can confidently be said to originate or occur in mainland South America. In most cases, stylistic influences from the mainland or Greater Antilles are detectable, but exact parallels are absent. The one exception is Cayo ware, micro-regionally distributed throughout the Windward Islands (and on Guadeloupe), which has clear antecedents in the coastal and inland parts of the Guianas. Being a late pre-Colonial or possible early Colonial period ceramic ware, its mainland origins come as no surprise to those familiar with the oral history of the Island Caribs, who claimed to have arrived from the mainland and wrested possession of the Windward Islands from their prior inhabitants at some unspecified time in the past (Verrand 2001:103-104; see also Chapter 4).

Other decoration modes or vessel shapes classed as regional fall within the next category, that of regionally distributed and exhibiting stylistic influence from the mainland or Greater Antilles. This applies to single-row finger indented rims (type 1), gouged adornos (type 1), modeled adornos (type 2), tubular vessel legs (type 1), trapezoidal or bat-shaped lugs (type 1), horn or mound-shaped lugs (type 2) and double-horned lugs (type 3). The distribution of these decorative traits is perhaps indicative of a degree of independence from the Saladoid cultural straitjacket of earlier times, but at the same time an indication of the enduring connectedness with the South American "homeland". Although the first Ceramic Age island inhabitants had long since migrated away from the coasts and rivers of the mainland, ties were never severed. Indeed interplay between Windward Islanders in particular and mainlanders must have been a constant throughout the pre-Colonial era (Hofman *et al.* in press). While the Windward Island stylistic canon was no longer dominated by South American developments, it retained certain vestigial characteristics while remaining open to influences, and the loose similarities exhibited by decorative traits reflect this new-found independence and flexibility.

The final category of regionally distributed decoration modes or vessel shapes are the logical outcome of this emancipation from stylistic constraints: regional distribution without South American mainland influence. Here belong the griddle legs, scratched ware and small round indentations on rims (indentation type 3), which are evidently insular innovations.

Micro-regional

Moving down a scale, settlement at the level of individual Windward Islands presents a number of interesting patterns. Firstly, as discussed in section 4.2, only the islands of St. Vincent and Grenada harbour four-component settlements and many more three-component settlements, making them the region's long-term settlement centres. Regarding settlement territories, it is unsurprising to note that during the early phase of the Early Ceramic Age, settlements tend to cluster close together in specific parts of islands. From the late phase of the Early Ceramic Age onwards, other parts of islands become infilled, and clustering perhaps becomes less of a conscious choice but rather an unavoidable consequence of an expanding population in a circumscribed environment. What is remarkable is that after a period of relatively sparse initial colonization, the number of settlements rises dramatically to a tally which does not increase significantly in later periods. This suggests that the islands reached some sort of settlement equilibrium quite early on in the Ceramic Age, bar a possible slight demographic wobble during the early phase of the Late Ceramic Age. Of course, in the absence of extensive information on many settlements, it cannot be ascertained whether the specific characteristics of settlements changed over time (*i.e.* size, longevity, structure).

Evidence of more localized spheres of interaction are the ceramic (decorative) traits with a micro-regional distribution, exhibiting mainland influence. To this category belong female statuettes, vessel wall human faces (adorno type 3), faces on pestles or loom weights and Caliviny Polychrome. What is particularly interesting is how communities on the same restricted set of islands incorporated stylistic influences from such a wide area, from Dabajuroid cultures in the west to Arauquinoid cultures in the east. In a departure from the greater micro-regional heterogeneity and the development of micro-style zones commonly ascribed to this era, it would appear that Windward Island communities were actually branching out in terms of social interactions and becoming great purveyors and synthesizers of (material) cultural developments taking place along the entire northeastern seaboard of South America. Alternatively, Windward Island communities may have been responsible for the spread of certain decorative modes or techniques to the mainland. Either way, these islanders were keeping their ears close to the ground and their eyes firmly fixed on other cultural horizons, both near and distant.

At the same time, some developments apparently did not spread further than the limits of the micro-region (or to only one or two outliers) and had no stylistic antecedent or parallel on the mainland: double-row finger indented rims (type 2), notched or filleted rims (type 4), peg-shaped lugs (type 4), support rings, fingernail rim indentation (type 5) and jointed and modeled appliqué vessel legs (types 2 and 3). These examples show that the idea of micro-style zones should not be abandoned, merely that it needs complementing with an archipelagic/mainland perspective that does justice to the full reach of Late Ceramic Age Windward Islanders.

Local

At the local scale, the settlement phenomena of settlement pairs and settlement micro-mobility require discussing. As outlined earlier (section 4.3.2), most of the Windward Islands exhibit the phenomenon of settlement pairs, and occasionally as many as four settlement sites are found in close proximity to one another. In the absence of more detailed information about the dimensions of these sites and more extensive excavation, it seems a bridge too far to label those settlements that are attributed to the same phase as contemporaneous, literally paired communities. It is perhaps safer for now or even more justifiable to regard these neighbouring communities as the successive habitational footprints of a generationally shifting population. And what to make of those proximate settlements that belong to markedly different cultural phases? In section 4.3.3, these settlement configurations were examined from a settlement micro-mobility perspective. Admittedly, there is no a priori reason to assume that proximity should be regarded as a relevant factor in settlement mobility, but ethnographic analogies suggest that generally, groups will not move further than necessary, though more frequently than one might have anticipated. Thus patterns in proximate settlements inhabited throughout successive phases were examined, particularly when a settlement appeared to be abandoned in favour of a new nearby settlement. Given the settlement intensity on some islands during the Ceramic Age, a multitude of potential patterns arose, although the proximity argument narrowed down the choices. Partly to once more test the proximity argument, these hypothesized instances of micro-mobility are tested on the basis of ceramic assemblage similarities below (section 7.2.3). What this initial exercise has indubitably proved is that there was a significant degree of single-period, fresh settlement or reoccupation of earlier settlements throughout the Ceramic Age, besides a significant amount of long-lived settlement spanning much of the period under study here. It is highly likely that stable, long-lasting settlements represented parent communities of various offshoots in the vicinity, gradually accruing more importance as communities inhabiting them weathered the vicissitudes of time and society in general. Of course, it is possible that even these multi-component settlements in fact saw a succession of abandonments and reoccupations, but this is impossible to gauge on the basis of evidence presently at hand. Be that as it may, just the fact that people returned to these locations time and again suggests a form of continuity and attachment to place and tradition.

Turning to ceramic (decorative) traits, the local scale is perhaps impossible to define within the current approach, and is in any case highly dependent on the definition of local to which one adheres. As defined in chapter 5, a local phenomenon is one that is limited to a number of sites on the same island. None of the traits or even subtraits discussed above falls within this category, but there may be traits that are so unique as to not have been included in the analysis because they do not form a recognized (sub)category. Alternatively, potential distinction may be expressed at a higher level of resolution than that adopted for this analysis, so that variability of a trait may have been masked by inclusion in an undiscriminating (sub)category. Be that as it may, the general conclusion one can draw from the approach utilized above is that many ceramic (decorative) traits exhibit a high degree of similarity throughout the region at a basic level of resolution, and within the micro-region at a more discerning level of resolution. So although local, slight variations on a theme may have been somewhat lost in the mix, there is a clear underlying stylistic canon governing the general expression of ceramic (decorative) traits within the Windward Islands. This is suggestive of a relatively tight-knit society interacting constantly within the Windward Islands region (potentially including the islands of Guadeloupe and Tobago) and maintaining frequent contacts with communities further afield.

7.2.2. Weighted distribution and possible place of origin for (sub)traits

Analysis of the weighted distributions of the traits under consideration in some cases just underscores the quantitative data (*i.e.* trait found at many sites or trait found at few sites). In other cases, however, weighted tallies provide a different picture than the strictly numerical tallies; for instance a trait found at five sites on St. Lucia is a less impressive statistic than a trait found at five sites on Grenada, considering that the former island has yielded many more sites than the latter. This weighted information therefore provides a reliable determination of how common or rare the occurrence of a certain subtrait is on an island. Taking the weighted distribution one step further, once could argue that islands with a higher relative share of a (sub)trait across their assemblages may represent the place(s) of origin of a certain subtrait. If a subtrait is known or suspected to originate from outside the region, then the higher relative frequency may indicate where a trait was initially or most heavily introduced to the area from outside. Furthermore, if a number of islands exhibit high relative occurrences of the (sub)trait, these could potentially represent core constituents of an interaction sphere.

Caliviny Polychrome and scratched ware are most strongly present on Grenada, the Grenadines and St. Vincent. Vessel lugs and female statues are most frequent on Grenada, the Grenadines and St. Lucia. Finger indentation and support rings are most prevalent on the Grenadines, St. Vincent and St. Lucia. Anthropomorphic adornos are most frequent on the Grenadines and St. Lucia. Griddle legs occur most on St. Vincent and St. Lucia. Cayo is most prevalent on St. Vincent and Dominica, not surprisingly the very islands that maintained the greatest Island Carib presence deep into Colonial times. Vessel legs are most prevalent on St. Lucia and Barbados. Anthropomorphic pestles/loom weights exhibit no clear peaks in distribution, only two lows, *i.e.* their total absence on St. Vincent and Dominica. It is surprising to see that Martinique does not seem to be a high ranking island when it comes to relative frequency of (sub)traits throughout its Late Ceramic Age assemblages. Barbados and Dominica are also fairly peripheral, only figuring as prime nodes in one (sub)trait distribution pattern (see also figure 7.1). In conclusion then, despite frequencies shifting per trait, the Grenadines (seven times), St. Vincent (six times) and St. Lucia (seven times) most often exhibit the highest weighted distribution values for decorative (sub)traits in general. This would seem to suggest that this cluster of islands represented the stylistic heartland of the Windward Island archipelago, or at least the region where stylistic behaviour attained its greatest spread across the islands.

7.2.3. Settlement dynamics tested through analysis of shared ceramic traits

In section 4.3.3 of this dissertation, numerous hypothetical cases of settlement mobility were outlined on the basis of occupation/abandonment of proximate settlements from phase to phase. In section 6.4, corroborating evidence was sought for these hypothetical suggestions of a relation between settlements, other than the likelihood of a relation on the basis of their very proximity to one another.

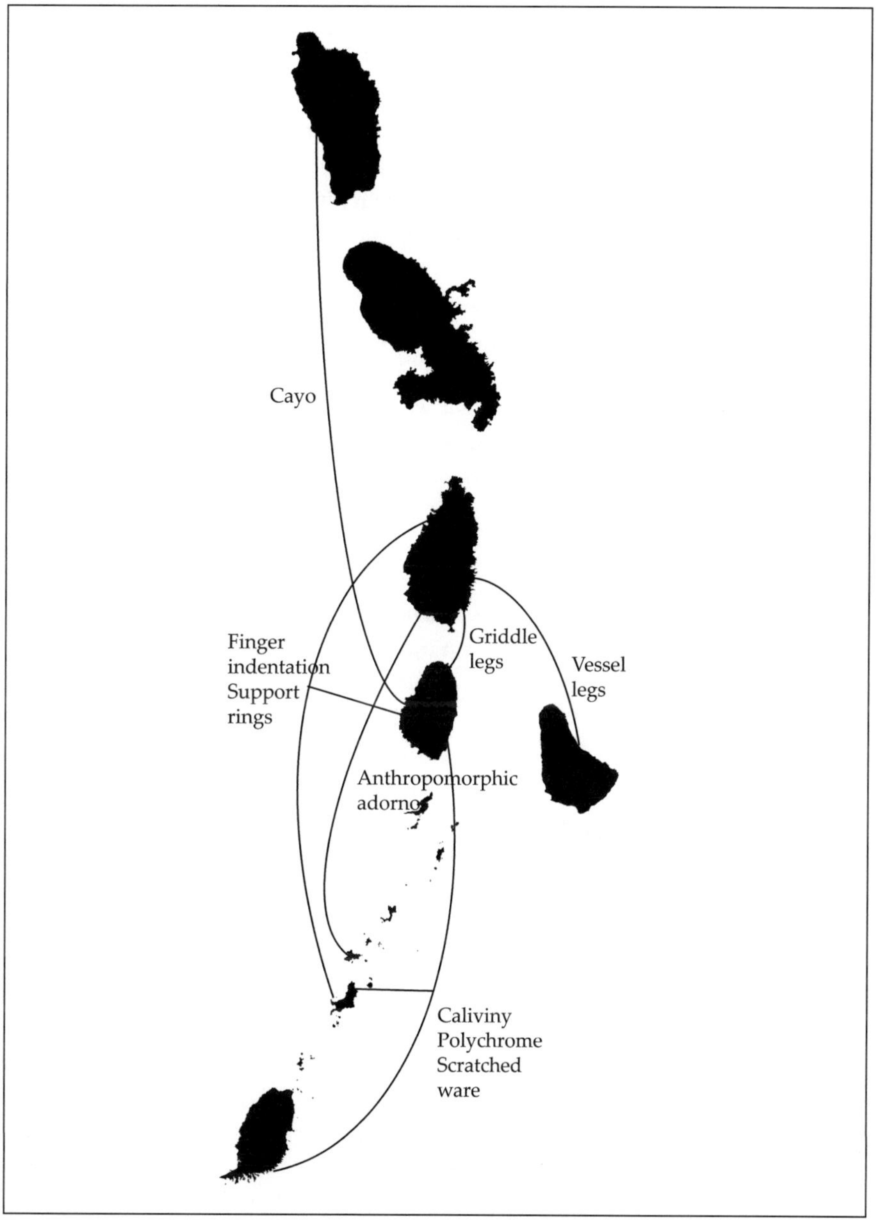

Figure 7.1. Spheres of highest weighted distribution of various (sub)traits.

Having identified the Late Ceramic Age ceramic (decorative) traits present in each settlement's assemblage in Chapter 5, it was possible to evaluate the proposed Late Ceramic Age settlement connections on the basis of the principle that the more traits are shared, the more likely that there was a relationship. This exercise revealed that there was less overlap between ceramic assemblages than might be expected on the basis of proximity. Even more surprisingly perhaps were the cases of islands with only two settlements that exhibit little to no similarity in assemblages. Of course, this must be partly attributed to the vicissitudes of time and the arbitrariness of excavation or publication. However, it remains possible that highly distinctive communities lived side-by-side, maintaining that distinctiveness precisely in the face of (intensive) interaction. Indeed, this hypothesis appears to be underscored by the outcome of the network analyses undertaken in the previous section, which showed that the strongest trait connections were often to be found between settlements on different islands. Having said that, this finding does nothing to detract from the approach developed here, it merely suggests that the geographic scale at which comparisons between site assemblages are effected should not be dictated by principles of proximity. Rather, in an archipelagic setting such as the Windward Islands, a multi-island perspective should be maintained.

Ultimately, positive or strong connections point only to an elevated degree of similarity between ceramic assemblages. This can be taken as a proxy for stronger social connections or interaction, but it would be a bridge too far to attach concepts like ethnicity or kinship to these results. Frequent trading encounters could equally be responsible for the dissemination of similar (sub)traits throughout the archipelago. More attention to the actual manufacturing characteristics and provenance studies may go some way in resolving this issue (*cf.* Descantes *et al.* 2008; Isendoorn *et al.* 2008). Furthermore, interaction may actually prove to be better gauged by studying very different characteristics of the ceramic assemblage, such as decisions that are made at an earlier stage of the manufacturing process rather than specific modelling or decorative characteristics (*cf.* Stark *et al.* 2000). Negative outcomes or weak connections on the other hand need not mean that there was little to no social interaction between communities, but do suggest that what interaction there was had an extremely limited impact on the material under study. It furthermore suggests that for whatever reason, material cultural differences were maintained (perhaps along with divergent identities or distinct ethnicities), and that there was very limited structural transmission of (the technique of producing) specific ceramic (decorative) traits between communities.

What the foregoing analysis has provided, however, is a solid means of testing certain hypotheses regarding interaction and exchange in an archipelagic setting. That the results are not homogenous across the board does nothing to dispel the validity of the approach or discredit the site sample, but merely accentuates the variability and pluriformity inherent in Windward Islanders' lifeways and interconnections between communities in general. The main outcome of these analyses has been that geographical distance in no way equates to intensity of interaction or a rough social distance. Furthermore, the limited homogeneity displayed across settlement assemblages suspected to be linked by instances of micro-mobility need not invalidate the hypothesis. In some cases, we may be witnessing subtle diachronic differences within ceramic repertoires that do not stand out within the large time periods currently in use. For whatever reason, contacts may not have been maintained between parent community and spin-off, resulting in a markedly distinctive ceramic repertoire, or a decisive break in pottery manufacture and decoration may have been implemented, even in the face of ongoing contacts. It is even possible, or even likely, that pottery manufacture was far from standardised within a community, the consequence of which is that any shift in community composition (departure or arrival of an individual, family or group) could have a dramatic impact on the ceramic repertoire.

Of course we also cannot overlook the simple fact that we may be missing many settlements in the archaeological record[82], some of which may have formed more convincing links in the chain that is the sequence of settlement micro-mobility. Also, as discussed above, it seems safe to dismiss propinquity once and for all as a guiding principle, and to cast a wider net when it comes to comparing site assemblages. Furthermore, there is great potential – indeed perhaps even a need - for further elaborating this approach in the Caribbean to cover the Early Ceramic Age, as well as additional ceramic traits, different aspects of the material culture assemblage, or even societal traits, such as has been carried out in Papua New Guinea for example (Moore and Romney 1994; Welsch *et al.* 1992).

7.2.4. Windward Island social organization

Reviewing the archaeological evidence, it is extremely difficult to characterize the social organization of Windward Island society. Undoubtedly, it falls somewhere between band and chiefdom level as defined by Service (1971), or Johnson and Earle's local group or village-level society (Johnson and Earle 1987:101-159), but considering that the utility of these static types is being increasingly questioned (*cf.* Chapman 2003), it is probably more productive to pursue other avenues such as determining level of craft specialization, status differences, and acquisition or exchange of exotic materials and social valuables. In the words of Saitta and McGuire (1998:335): "[…] *organizational complexity is to be found in any society and* […] *our task is to illuminate the nature and transformative potential of that complexity*". For now, it seems safest to deem leadership (if present) as temporary or situational, and societal differences expressed in heterarchical fashion rather than hierarchically (*cf.* Rautman 1998). Departing from the archaeological record, as highlighted earlier, site patterns across the Windward Islands do not suggest any form of hierarchy, other than the basic typological distinction between settlement sites, (temporary) activity areas and the like, and on the basis of settlement number, population levels appear to have remained reasonably stable through time, suggesting an absence of spiraling population growth or other demographic events place that would have occasioned a response in the form of societal reorganization.[83] The possibility that the Windward Islands may have absorbed settlers from the Leeward Islands during the late phase of the Late Ceramic

82 Either completely undiscovered sites, or sites identified as *e.g.* pottery scatters in the absence of more thorough archaeological testing.

83 However, information on settlement dimensions (if even present) was not utilized in this study.

Age is intriguing. Kowalewski points out that collapse in and abandonment of one area can spark population growth or greater centralization in another area (Kowalewski 2008:236), but as yet, such a process is not detectable in the archaeological record of the Windwards.[84] As became evident in chapters 4 and 6, there is great variation in cultural components present at settlements that can be explained by hypothesizing a range of population dynamics in the realm of settlement mobility such as initial colonization, abandonment, fissioning and fusing. Unfortunately, as yet, dating resolution is still not at the level to afford more than only rudimentary insight into occupation and abandonment, and is still nowhere near the generational time-scale we would ideally adopt, especially if we consider ethnographic case studies from the tropical lowlands of South America as relevant analogies for our pre-Colonial Caribbean societies and desire to make use of them as such. Furthermore, in most cases, material corroboration for the hypothesized settlement links was ambiguous if not absent, although this may not invalidate the link, merely the assumption that material homogeneity should necessarily be expected from neighbouring or proximate communities.

As far as the distribution of ceramic (decorative) traits is concerned, superficially, one could be lulled into belief in a "Troumassoid Veneer", considering the widespread sharing of a number of traits throughout the Windward Islands or indeed the Lesser Antilles as a whole. However, on the basis of other traits or at the level of subtraits, subtle inter-island and inter-community differences come to the fore. As discussed above and in Chapter 5, the differences are articulated at a number of scales, starting with the regional scale. A few ceramic traits that are either distributed throughout the region (Windward and Leeward Islands) or harbour influences or represent parallel developments of mainland traits underscore that at a more abstract level, Windward Island communities participated actively in a wider Circum-Caribbean culture area during late pre-Colonial times (Allaire 1990; Boomert 2000; Hofman *et al.* 2008). Cayo ceramics are somewhat ambiguous in this regard, clearly demonstrating stylistic parallels with Koriabo ceramics from Suriname, yet present only within the Windward Island micro-region and on Guadeloupe. Until remains turn up on islands where they are thus far absent, this phenomenon must be interpreted as somewhat exclusive, either pointing to special, restricted contact lines, or limited direct affiliation or even migration. However, traits expressed at the micro-regional level with no exact parallels elsewhere evidence that while Windward Island communities at times spoke a material lingua franca, there was certainly such a thing as a micro-regional identity, comprising local communities dispersed across the Windward Island archipelago that shared knowledge, practices and material culture, and that no doubt relied upon one another for survival, maintaining intensive trading and exchange networks, cementing alliances through inter-community marriage and operating as a collective in times of warfare (see also Hofman *et al.* 2007). The distribution of Caliviny Polychrome, female statuettes, vessel wall faces and anthropomorphic loom weights or pestles underwrites the cosmopolitan, outward-looking nature of

84 As pointed out earlier, Curet (2005) has suggested such a process taking place in certain parts of Puerto Rico, and a similar process may be responsible for the alleged depopulation of many of the Leeward Islands during the late phase of the Late Ceramic Age (see also Chapter 1).

communities within the Windward Islands, as they appear to purvey and rework stylistic influences from various mainland areas. That Windward Islanders were not just synthesizers but innovators is proved by traits expressed at the micro-regional scale without parallels outside the micro-region itself. Various rim indentations (fingernail, notched and double/triple rows), peg-shaped lugs, vessel legs (jointed and 'knee-capped') and tripod support rings all appear to be exclusively Windward Island in distribution (bar one or two exceptions).

On the basis of weighted distribution of ceramic (decorative) (sub)traits, it can be concluded that Martinique, Barbados and Dominica were quite peripheral islands and that the triumvirate of the Grenadines, St. Vincent and St. Lucia formed the stylistic heartland of the Windward Islands in terms of elaboration and relative frequency. These findings are echoed at the site level for St. Lucia, which harboured six large hives of activity in terms of stylistic elaboration. The Grenadines, St. Vincent and St. Lucia also account for the lion's share of medium hives of activity (see also section 6.1). This in turns leads one to surmise that interaction between these islands was greater than between other islands. However, individual settlement connectivity at the level of individual traits (see also section 6.3) confounds these general observations, with a strong connection appearing between Grenada and St. Lucia, as well as medium connections between St. Lucia and Martinique and Barbados and Martinique. Only the medium strong connection between the Grenadines and St. Lucia supports the heartland hypothesis advanced above. Of course, it is unknown to what degree possible temporal differences, effaced by the treatment of the Late Ceramic Age as one great time period, might be affecting our view. On the face of current evidence however, the lack of strong patterning in one direction or another across multiple lines of evidence or scales of analysis is highly suggestive of relatively autonomous communities operating within certain broad shared parameters, but in the main expressing themselves independently or communally, but free from cultural or geographical strictures. Once more, it has become apparent that in many respects, the island is not the appropriate unit of analysis in archipelagic settings, particularly when kinship ties might well result in shifting constellations of multi-island community groups (*cf.* Chapters 2 and 3; see also different lines of research into human mobility and potential kinship such as Booden *et al.* 2008 and Laffoon and De Vos 2010). It is still a bridge too far to tease out community-level ties with communities in the wider region, given the lack of quantifiable data and the confounding potential for indirect procurement/down-the-line exchange within the Windward Islands of either an artefact exhibiting a certain trait or even the manufacturing know-how of the trait itself. However, it is safe to pinpoint the range of potential connections between Windward Island communities as a whole and mainland, Leeward Island and Greater Antillean groups.

As can be gathered from this dissertation as a whole, the role of the Windward Islands has varied through time from open conduit or avenue for developments from mainland South America to further north, through island filter or funnel to independent entity with strong affiliations to various mainland cultures and communities. As such, Saladoid culture epitomizes the lifeline model stretching from South America to the Greater Antilles in Early Ceramic Age times, Troumassan

Troumassoid can be regarded as the breakdown of interregional hegemony and the waning of Saladoid stylistic influence, and Suazan Troumassoid could be seen as representing reconfiguration of Windward Island Society and the rise of local hegemonies or interaction spheres (*cf.* Hofman *et al.* 2007, in press). Despite following reasonably similar trajectories during the Early Ceramic Age and early phase of the Late Ceramic Age, Leeward Island communities were later increasingly caught up in the Taíno influence sphere and apparently became somewhat depopulated, whereas Windward Island communities manifested themselves ever more prominently within the region, and came to lean increasingly towards numerous South American influence spheres. The flexibility and resourcefulness exhibited by Windward Islanders over more than 1500 years afforded them a considerable measure of success in maintaining themselves in their archipelago, until they too ultimately succumbed to the unrelenting onslaught of European enterprise in the Caribbean.

7.2.5. Early Colonial period Windward Island social organization: a postscript

In early Colonial times, the rivalry and heightened tension provoked by the presence and actions of various European nations - documented in numerous (ethno)historical accounts - strike one as characteristic of a predominantly egalitarian society, with fluctuating, temporary leadership among groups at most and an extremely complex but kin-bound web of social relationships that bridged many a water passage. I would like to suggest that the concept of chieftain cycling might apply to this period (and potentially earlier periods too, although this conjecture necessitates further research). The concept is analogous to that of chiefdom cycling (Anderson 1994; Redmond *et al.* 2008), but at the community level of chieftains rather than at the society wide level of the chiefdom. In the case of chiefdom cycling, regional volatility is the key issue, involving the temporary domination of one paramount chief and regional political centralization, before political dissolution allows for a power vacuum and rise of a rival paramount chiefdom (*cf.* Redmond *et al.* 2008). Anderson characterizes this process as the oscillation between simple and complex chiefdoms, with chiefdoms undergoing cycles of emergence, expansion, collapse and reconstitution. The emergence and rise to domination would most likely hinge upon several factors including population growth, denser settlement patterns, construction or intensification of monumental architecture, intensified agricultural production and production of surplus, specialized craft production, prestige goods exchange between paramount centers and distribution of valuables to vassals and allies (Redmond *et al.* 2008:111). I would argue that chieftain cycling revolves around personal status vulnerability. As such, aspiring leaders find themselves forced to constantly renegotiate and reaffirm their status and concomitant claims to power. This strikes a chord with a recent modification of the chiefdom instability/cycling model by Blitz (1999, 2009), who visualizes prehistoric Mississippian political dynamics in terms of fission-fusion of social groups. Such a model of flexibility and constant realignment would appear to better match the shifting settlement patterns of certain islands in pre-Colonial times as well as the heterogeneous ceramic trait distributions discussed in the foregoing chapters (see Chapters 4 through 6), than the Big-Man model with its emphasis on surplus production and centripetal dynamics or a chiefdom model with its essential aspects of institutionalized leadership, permanent status differences, settlement hierarchies and overarching control over various aspects of manufacture, distribution and exchange (see Chapter 1).

However, it is highly likely that Windward Island Amerindian social organization underwent substantial restructuring in response to colonial enterprise (see Hulme 1986:67 for parallel thinking in the domain of ethnicity). Though the banding together of kin-related groups in the Lesser Antilles for the purpose of raiding may have been a feature of pre-Contact Amerindian society, it was probably intensified post-AD 1492, both to opportunistically take advantage of weakened Taíno groups, as well as in violent reaction to Spanish encroachment and slaving expeditions. Cody (1995:316) has raised the possibility of two Kallinago networks in operation in the larger area at this time: a northern network comprising Dominica, Guadeloupe and some of the Leewards, and a southern network comprising Martinique, St. Lucia, St. Vincent and Grenada. A different but related development that may have taken place post-AD 1600 in particular is that of the apparent stockpiling of victuals – in other words creating of surplus - in order to trade with mainly French, Dutch, English and Portuguese ships for desirable goods (see for example various passages in De Laet 1931 and De Laet 1932). Later still, access to prestigious trade goods and political maneuvering between warring European factions may have afforded enterprising Amerindian chiefs every opportunity to acquire distinction, prestige and, in the long run, power, allowing them to rise above their counterparts (*cf.* Gasson 2000, who describes a similar process in northern South America).

7.3. Windward Island Amerindian settlement and diachronic intra- and inter-insular relationships

Although contemporary archaeological theory rightly emphasizes the role of internal stimuli in society's socio-political development, external stimuli cannot be discounted, particularly not when geographic and cultural settings prevail that are extremely conducive to interregional, cross-cultural contact. To properly evaluate and put into perspective the material and socio-political development in the Windward Islands, it is therefore necessary to take a wider view, and offset local developments against those taking place coevally in adjacent regions. As Allaire has pointed out:

> *"The geographical unity of the Caribbean, as opposed to the Mediterranean, is a phenomenon that has been largely ignored by archaeologists, even within the context of the circum-Caribbean theory. The task may have appeared as amounting to an idle collage of disjuncted [sic] local sequences of unrelated prehistoric peoples and cultures with little more than a documentary interest to offer. Yet the potential for a more comprehensive ap-*

proach is enticing and well worth exploring but without any preconceived ideas about distant interaction or claims of trans-Caribbean contacts, which have been occasionally raised but which are more often spurious and unsubstantiated by facts" (Allaire 1999:675-676).

Indeed, similarities in material culture provide some idea of how far afield one should cast a comparative net: Windward Island culture appears to have been influenced by the cultures of the Greater Antilles, the Leeward Islands, Trinidad and the Venezuelan and Guianan coastal areas (see also Chapter 5). Taken together, these territories form what has been termed by Allaire (1999:674) the Caribbean area proper (see the recent NWO research programme Communicating Communities, for thinking along similar lines and heuristically positing the existence of pan-Caribbean mobility and exchange networks[85]). By utilizing an archipelagic approach, the gamut of stylistic influences and their full extent have become visible (see also Chapter 5). Although the Windward Islands certainly saw autochthonous developments on a micro-regional scale, there were presumably continual waves of influence from the Greater Antilles, the Leeward Islands and various parts of the South American mainland, which left their mark heterogeneously on communities across the archipelago. These various influences will be examined from a multi-scalar perspective in section 7.3. The following section will provide an overview of diachronic developments in the realm of settlement and material culture developments in the Windward Islands offset by similar, coeval developments in the Leeward Islands[86], to determine micro-regional divergence as well as regional parallels.

From mainlanders to islanders: Early Ceramic Age occupation of the Windward Islands (400 BC–AD 700)

All of the Windward Islands saw occupation at some point in time during this long Early Ceramic Age period, although the precise timing differed from island to island (see also Chapter 4 and Appendix 2). Indeed, only Martinique has thus far yielded convincing evidence backed by readiocarbon dating of intensive settlement during the early phase of the Early Ceramic Age. However, by the end of the early phase of the Early Ceramic Age, most of the islands were occupied, and well occupied by the following phase, with 99 settlements distributed (unequally) over them. St. Vincent and Martinique (and to a lesser degree St. Lucia) exhibit a rather dense settlement pattern compared to the rest of the Windward Islands, with numerous 3km radius settlement territories overlapping one another. This would seem to suggest that (parts of) the former islands were the prime target for colonizing groups from the mainland and saw the most intensive settlement or that there was a high degree of residential mobility on these islands in particular. A combination of the two explanations is also possible: if these islands received more settlers than other islands, then in time social or environmental thresholds

85 http://archaeology.leiden.edu/research/ancient-america/caribbean/communicating/

86 Ideally, developments in the Greater Antilles and in coastal areas of the South American would be considered in detail as well, but unfortunately, this falls beyond the scope of the current research.

would have been reached sooner and more frequently, resulting in a denser archaeological settlement pattern. Furthermore, the first hesitant settlement or use of Windward islets takes place during the late phase of the Early Ceramic Age, *i.e.* Gros Ilet (Martinique), Praslin Island (St. Lucia), Young's Island (St. Vincent) and Caliviny Island (Grenada). As mentioned in Chapter 4, the clustered dispersion of settlements in the Windward Islands during the Early Ceramic Age is suggestive of Flannery and Coe's (1968) 'contagious' distribution pattern, whereby all settlements are in a similar environmental setting and all utilize the surrounding environments in a similar way. The identification of such a contagious settlement pattern is suggestive of relatively self-sufficient local communities.

In terms of material culture, this period is dominated by the Saladoid series, which was distributed from mainland South America to (parts of) the Greater Antilles. Despite its apparent broad homogeneity, there was significant local variation between Saladoid assemblages throughout the region, as demonstrated by a multitude of slightly differing local complexes or styles. As such, the Saladoid "veneer" is in urgent need of stripping (see also section 5.2). For instance, the Barrancoid series, whose impact was so considerable on Trinidad and Tobago and the South American mainland, was highly attenuated in the Windward Islands. Indeed, it is found on only a number of the Windward Islands, and even then mainly in the form of rare, obviously traded or introduced items (*cf.* Conservation du Musée Départmental d'Archéologie, 1991:48). No trace of Barrancoid is found further north, suggesting a natural fall-off curve. A certain degree of homogeneity remains expected though in this early phase, considering the vulnerability of initial colonising groups and hence the vital importance of maintaining a lifeline with the homeland(s) (Hofman *et al.* 2007, in press). In that respect, there are numerous additional material connections between the Windward Islands and South America. Unionidae or naiads, freshwater mussels that can only have come from Trinidad or the South American mainland, have turned up at a number of sites on Martinique (Dizac and Grande Anse des Salines) and throughout the Lesser Antilles (St. Martin, Guadeloupe, Trinidad and Tobago) (Bérard 2006a; Serrand 2001, 2007; see also Hofman *et al.* 2007). Mainland iconography on Windward Island materials is another telling indicator: jaguars, king vultures, peccaries and various rodents underscore the continuing continental affiliations of the Windward islanders (Hofman *et al.* in press). Connections with the Leeward Islands are evident in the form of Long Island flint and worked St. Martin greenstone (Hofman *et al.* 2007:253).

By and large, the same scenario for settlement as in the Windward Islands appears to hold true for the Leeward Islands. These islands too were occupied at various points in time, with St. Martin (*e.g.* Hope Estate: Hofman and Hoogland 1999) and Montserrat (*e.g.* Trants: Reed and Petersen 2001) seeing perhaps the earliest settlement in the area, followed by the likes of St. Eustatius (*e.g.* Golden Rock: Versteeg and Schinkel eds 1992) and Antigua (Rouse and Faber Morse 1999). St. Martin eventually numbered five sites in total during what Bonnissent (2008:figure 478) has termed the Néoindien ancien (500 BC – 960 AD). On Nevis, Wilson (1989:435-437 and figure 4) found just two sites dating the Early

Ceramic Age, while on Anguilla there are just three: two settlements and a cave site (Crock 2000:20). However, the Saladoid sites on these latter two islands all date to the late phase of the Early Ceramic Age. In the Guadeloupean Pointe des Châteaux micro-region there are a few large short-lived villages during the late phase of the Early Ceramic Age, presumably not coevally inhabited and thus a demonstration of shifting settlement. The Anse à la Gourde site seems to be the exception, as it appears to have been settled continuously throughout much of the Ceramic Age. Activities centred around large settlements. These villages were dispersed, relatively distant, but evenly distributed without clustering (De Waal 2006:106-108, 110-112).

Hegemony disrupted: divergent developments in the islands during the early phase of the Late Ceramic Age (AD 700-1000)

During the early phase of the Late Ceramic Age, there is a sharp decrease in the number of sites in the Windward Islands, although this alleged population slump can be qualified somewhat by bringing site type into the equation (see also section 4.2). Whereas the site tally drops from 232 to 167, the decrease in settlements is less pronounced: from 99 to 84. General trends are elusive, but whereas settlement intensity on St. Vincent and Martinique drops considerably, there is still a fair degree of clustering in the settlements that remain, particularly on St. Vincent and a number of the Grenadines. Also, whereas Dominica yields no settlements for this period, a number of other islands see settlements appear in previously ignored areas (Martinique's south-east coast and northern St. Lucia). Furthermore, settlement or use of Windward islets really picks ups during the Late Ceramic Age: Ilet Cabrits, Ilet Hardy, Ilet Madame and Ilet Sapotille (Martinique), Pigeon Island, Praslin Island and Frigate Island (St. Lucia), Young's Island (St. Vincent), Petit Martinique, Ile de Ronde, Ile de Caille and Ile à Quatre (Grenadines) and Caliviny Island (Grenada) all see (continued) occupation or use.

In the Leeward Islands, site tallies generally increased during the Late Ceramic Age, like on Nevis, where the site tally increases from two to seventeen (Wilson 1989:436). On Anguilla the tally rises to fourteen settlements, not counting other smaller sites (Crock 2000:20). The number of sites on St. Martin increased from five to seventeen during the Néoindien récent, between AD 740 and 1600 (Bonnissent 2008:fig. 478). On Guadeloupe, occupation was consolidated and intensified, visible in the increase number of settlements especially after AD 1000. Settlement mobility may have been higher than before, yielding a denser settlement pattern, though there is also the possibility of site succession and fissioning. There is a greater diversity in site type, and activities are less centralised in settlements but rather more spread out across landscape (De Waal 2006:115-117). Settlements are evenly distributed but increase in number, resulting in shorter inter-settlement distances and smaller territories, though there is still little clustering. De Waal (2006:121) elucidates a settlement hierarchy, with Anse à la Gourde representing the central settlement.

This period is characterized by a significant development in the realm of material culture: the transition from the Saladoid series to a Troumassan Troumassoid subseries. As detailed in section 3.3, this development may have been somewhat overstated, considering the many late Saladoid hold-overs present in Troumassan Troumassoid assemblages. As such, contradictorily, the break between Troumassan and Suazan Troumassoid seems at times just as great as that between Saladoid and Troumassan Troumassoid. However, through time, Saladoid features wane and a convincingly new series arises. Interestingly enough, on the face of it, many Late Ceramic Age decorative traits seem just as widespread and homogenous as those of the Early Ceramic Age. Upon closer inspection, however, it becomes evident that there is one major difference: very few Late Ceramic Age Windward Island ceramic (decorative) traits can confidently be said to originate or occur outside the Lesser Antilles. In many cases, stylistic influences from the mainland (or possibly even the Greater Antilles) are detectable, but exact parallels are absent, underlining the divergent trajectory taken by Windward Island society during this period. However, emancipation from the strictures of overarching stylistic canons did not entail a complete severing of continental ties. On the contrary, the somewhat one-dimensional mainland links of the Early Ceramic Age are replaced by potential interactions with a panoply of communities, from Dabajuroid communities in western Venezuela to Arauquinoid communities in coastal Suriname (see also section 5.4.1). As many of the Late Ceramic Age ceramic traits examined in Chapter 5 date to the (transition between early and) late phase of the Late Ceramic Age, these will be discussed in more detail under the next heading.

Concerning material culture in the Leeward Islands, the late Saladoid of the early phase of the Late Ceramic Age gave way to the Mamoran Troumassoid subseries, which, like Troumassan Troumassoid in the Windwards, clearly exhibits Ostionoid influences from the Virgin Islands and the Greater Antilles as well as Arauquinoid influences from Trinidad and the mainland. About midway through this period, numerous site assemblages in the northern Leeward Islands such as Kelbey's Ridge 2, Saba (Hoogland and Hofman 1993, 1999), Baie Rouge, St. Martin (Henocq and Petit 1995), Sandy Hill and Shoal Bay East, Anguilla (Crock and Petersen 2004) and Smoke Alley, St. Eustatius (Versteeg 1998) begin to demonstrate a Chican Ostionoid component (Kelbey's Ridge 2) or at least yield a number of Chican artefacts. In a highly localized, divergent development further south, ceramics from Morne Cybèle and Morne Souffleur, La Désirade, dated to the late 15th century, exhibit local Suazan Troumassoid features combined with possible mainland elements (Hofman 1995a; Hofman, Delpuech, Hoogland and De Waal 2004).

Coming up between Greater Antillean and Venezuelan chiefdoms: the late phase of the Late Ceramic Age (AD 1000–1500)

On the whole, the Windward Islands seem to have been most extensively occupied and utilized during the late phase of the Late Ceramic Age: the number of sites rises to 252 of which 100 represent settlements (see also section 4.2). Martinique regains some of its former settlement intensity, but Barbados, St. Lucia and St. Vincent exhibit particularly dense settlement patterns during this late phase. St. Lucia and St. Vincent settlements show a high degree of overlap in terms of territory, once more suggesting either a high number of contemporaneous settlements or a relatively high degree of residential mobility compared to the preceding period. Also, as mentioned above, numerous Windward islets have yielded evidence of Late Ceramic Age occupation or exploitation.

In contrast to the population surge during the early phase of the Late Ceramic Age in the Leeward Islands, there appears to have been a possible depopulation of these islands, bar St. Kitts, Antigua and Nevis, in the centuries prior to the arrival of Europeans in the area. De Waal (2006:124-128) reports much lower number of settlements, smaller settlements, and presumed low settlement mobility for her Guadeloupean micro-region. Settlements were located at great distances from each other, had large territories, and a preference arose for well-defensible locations. The landscape appeared to be less intensively used and activities were more centralised at settlements again. Various hypotheses have been proposed to explain this phenomenon, ranging from resource depletion and Amerindians fleeing other Amerindians to disease, Taíno encroachment and subsequent absorption of Leeward Island inhabitants into either Greater Antillean, Windward Island or mainland South American society and Spanish slave raids during the early 16th century (see also section 1.2 and 4.1). Whatever the case, European settlers pouring into the region from the seventeenth century onwards reported most of the Leeward Islands to be (recently) deserted (Coppier 1645). Until the widespread availability of radiocarbon dates however, the matter will not be resolved. Wilson has spoken not so much of depopulation, as he has of Elenan Ostionoid ceramics (later reclassified as Mamoran Troumassoid ceramics) on Nevis not being supplanted by a later style (Wilson 1989:436), suggesting either a population on the decline or an extremely conservative one. However, he also points to Suazan Troumassoid influences on the assemblage (Wilson 1989:436), suggesting that there may have been a residual population that incorporated a number of stylistic innovations/adaptations after all.

Material culture in this period is characterized foremost by the rise of the Suazan Troumassoid subseries, which in many ways represents a continuation of the Troumassan Troumassoid subseries, but also introduces numerous innovations, that appear to be both local and non-local in origin (see also Chapter 5). At an as yet undetermined point in time, certain sites in the Windward Islands begin to exhibit Cayo ceramics, which have been linked to the Koriabo ceramic tradition of Surinam and Guyana. There are numerous additional telling material indicators that Windward Island society was caught up in developments both to the north and south. A range of Taíno-like artefacts has been found at sites in the Windwards, from vomiting spatulae (Sutty 1991) and a canopied standing figurine – albeit ceramic - (Bullen and Bullen 1968; Hofman and Hoogland 2009) to duhos (Honychurch n.d.) and large threepointers (see also Hofman *et al.* 2008). Additionally, a number of potentially Taíno artifacts have been recovered in the Windward Islands in the past, including a cotton idol and a wooden turtle effigy

(Du Tertre 1667 [II]:369-370; Ober 1899). According to Allaire (1977:342), the ceramic assemblage of the Macabou site exhibited numerous Chicoid features, including a winged motif, a large circle and dot motif, and the gutter running from the eyes of certain anthropomorphic adornos. Lavoutte on St. Lucia has yielded similar motifs (Bullen and Bullen 1968). A range of Late Ceramic Age ceramic (decorative) traits demonstrate similarities with traits found in other areas both continental and insular, *i.e.* vessel legs, specific rim indentations, certain anthropomorphic adornos and female statuettes, suggesting, if not firmly proving a degree of inter-communication (see also Chapter 5).

Conclusions Windward Islands settlement pattern and ceramic assemblage developments

Though undoubtedly somewhat biased by the less distinctive nature of the Troumassan Troumassoid material assemblage, the view of Ceramic Age settlement in the Windward Islands suggests a pattern of initial influxes of settlers from the mainland (Early Ceramic Age), followed by a period of relative stasis, when migration to the Windwards was perhaps not great enough to offset possible onward migration to the Leeward Islands or even further afield (early phase of the Late Ceramic Age). Considering the late phase Late Ceramic Age settlement evidence for the Leeward Islands, it somehow seems unconvincing that a society allegedly moving towards a form of social stratification would suddenly collapse in the following period, with people instead heading towards a different, chiefdom society. Rather, instead of consolidation, perhaps the early phase Late Ceramic Age dense settlement actually reflects a period of incipient instability, with much societal unrest, fissioning and realignment, ultimately seguing into the collapse/abandonment signalled in the late phase. This instability may well be related to the climate change attested for this time period by Petitjean Roget (2005) and Blancaneaux (2009). Seen from that perspective, the apparent population growth in the Windward Islands may represent not just internal growth and renewed influxes from the South American mainland, but also migration from Leeward Island communities. A similar hypothesis has been advanced by Curet (2005) to account for the coeval circumstances of population rise in Puerto Rico, increasing Taíno stylistic influence in the Leeward Islands, and the apparent depopulation of the region (see also Chapter 1).

Placing developments in ceramic assemblages of the Windwards and Leewards side by side yields numerous insights. Firstly, in many cases, differences between the two areas can be seen as of degree rather than of kind, at least until the late phase of the Late Ceramic Age. Though not discussed here, vessel morphology and (supposed) function do not differ greatly. This suggests that while community identity may have been varyingly constructed and expressed throughout the two regions, there may have been a degree of shared identity. In contrast, the Greater Antillean material culture assemblages took on an entirely different face during the Late Ceramic Age, presumably under the influence of the earlier (Archaic) inhabitants, a process exacerbated by continued mainland South American impulses being withheld or absorbed by intermediate Lesser Antillean communities. There are indubitably differences in aspects of specific decoration and modeling though, as is apparent from the various distribution maps for specific ceramic traits (Chapter 5). Certain traits rarely occur outside the Windwards, some are stylistically quite different, and others do not occur at all. Another important finding in this respect is that assemblages on Guadeloupe and Tobago featured eight out of the twelve analysed ceramic (decorative) traits, while Dominica assemblages featured only three. Although research bias has certainly contributed to this skewed perspective, it seems that in retrospect parts of or rather, certain communities on Guadeloupe and Tobago formed part of the Windward Islands interaction sphere, or at the very least represented significant transitional areas between the Windward islands and regions further north and south.

7.4. Future Research

There is enough potential for continuing the research undertaken here in the future, for instance by examining Early Ceramic Age ceramic trait distribution in the Windward Islands, or by expanding the examination of site patterns and distribution of ceramic trait distribution to the Leeward Islands. Another approach could be to expand the graph-theory analysis to include additional ceramic traits, different aspects of material culture such as lithics, shell and bone, or to tackle completely different traits such as for instance faunal remains, settlement characteristics and burials. Of course much work remains to be done and we are still a long way off from even a partial understanding of the dynamics and social organization of the multitude of ethnic groups in the Windward Island archipelago and the Greater Caribbean, of their shifting alliances and of mobility and exchange between prehistoric Amerindian communities. However, I believe that the present study of site patterns and distribution of ceramic (decorative) traits has proven a suitable avenue to broaching these topics, and, through recourse to other lines of evidence, has gone some way in unraveling the entangled threads that are the prehistoric Amerindian lifeways.

Bibliography

Adovasio, James M., and David Pedler, 2005: The peopling of North America. In *North American Archaeology*. Timothy R. Pauketat and Diana DiPaolo Loren (eds):30-55. Blackwell Studies in Global Archaeology. Malden [etc.]:Blackwell Publishing.

Allaire, Louis, 1974a: Paquemar revisited. *Proceedings of the 5th International Congress for the study of pre-Columbian cultures of the Lesser Antilles*. St. John's: The Antigua Archaeological Society:117-126.

Allaire, Louis, 1974b: An archaeological reconnaissance of St. Kitts, Leeward Islands. *Proceedings of the 5th International Congress for the study of pre-Columbian cultures of the Lesser Antilles*. St. John's: The Antigua Archaeological Society:158-161.

Allaire, Louis, 1977: *Later prehistory in Martinique and the Island Caribs: problems in ethnic identification*. PhD thesis, Yale University.

Allaire, Louis, 1980: On the historicity of Carib migrations in the Lesser Antilles. *American Antiquity* 45:238-245.

Allaire, Louis, 1984: A reconstruction of early historical Island Carib pottery. *Southeastern Archaeology* 3:121-133.

Allaire, Louis, 1985: Changements lithiques dans l'archéologie de la Martinique. *Proceedings of the 10th International Congress for Caribbean Archaeology*. Louis Allaire and Francine-M. Mayer (eds):299-310. Montréal: Centre de recherches caraïbes, Université de Montréal.

Allaire, Louis, 1987: Some comments on the ethnic identity of the Taino-Carib frontier. *Ethnicity and Culture*. Reginald Augier, Margaret F. Glass, Scott MacEachern and Peter H. McCartney (eds):127-133. Calgary: Archaeological Association, University of Calgary.

Allaire, Louis, 1989: Volcanic chronology and the early Saladoid occupation of Martinique. In *Early Ceramic population lifeways and adaptive strategies in the Caribbean*. Peter E. Siegel (ed.):147-169. BAR International Series 506. Oxford: Archaeopress.

Allaire, Louis, 1990: *Prehistoric Taino Interaction with the Lesser Antilles: the View from Martinique*. Paper presented at the 55th Annual Meeting of the Society for American Archaeology, Las Vegas, Nevada.

Allaire, Louis, 1991: Understanding Suazey. *Proceedings of the 13th Congress of the International Association for Caribbean Archaeology (2)*. Edwin N. Ayubi and Jay B. Haviser (eds):715-728. Reports of the Archaeological-Anthropological Institute of the Netherlands Antilles, No. 9. Willemstad: Archaeological-Anthropological Institute of the Netherlands Antilles.

Allaire, Louis, 1994: Historic Carib site discovered! *University of Manitoba St. Vincent Archaeological Project Newsletter*:1-3.

Allaire, Louis, 1997: The Caribs of the Lesser Antilles (Ch.18). In *The Indigenous People of the Caribbean*, Samuel M. Wilson (ed.):179-185. Gainesville [etc.]: University Press of Florida.

Allaire, Louis, 1999: Archaeology of the Caribbean Region (Ch.8). In *The Cambridge History of the Native Peoples of the Americans, vol. 3, South America. Part 1*. Frank Salomon and Stuart B. Schwartz (eds):668-733. Cambridge: Cambridge University Press.

Allaire, Louis, 2003: Agricultural societies in the Caribbean: the Lesser Antilles. In *General History of the Caribbean vol. 1, Autochthonous Societies.* Jalil Sued-Badillo (ed.):195-227. Cambridge: UNESCO Publishing /Macmillan.

Allaire, Louis, and David T. Duval, 1995: St. Vincent revisited. *Proceedings of the 15th Congress of the International Association for Caribbean Archaeology.* Ricardo A. Alegría and Miguel Rodríguez (eds):255-262. San Juan: Centro de Estudios Avanzados de Puerto Rico y el Caribe/Fundación Puertorriqueña de las Humanidades/Universidad del Turabo.

Allaire, Louis, Olivier Kayser, and Nathalie Vidal, 2002: *L'occupation amérindienne tardive de la Martinique.* Online resource. http://www.ouacabou.org/octard.php, accessed 6 June 2007.

Allaire, Louis, and Mario Mattioni, 1983: Boutbois et le Godinot: deux gisements acéramiques de la Martinique. *Proceedings of the 9th International Congress for Caribbean Archaeology.* Louis Allaire and Francine-M. Mayer (eds):27-38. Montreal: Centre de recherches caraïbes, Université de Montréal.

Anderson, Atholl, 2004a: Entering uncharted waters. *Colonization of unfamiliar landscapes: the archaeology of adaptation.* Marcy Rockman and James Steele (eds):169-89. London & New York: Routledge.

Anderson, Atholl, 2004b: *Islands of Ambivalence. Voyages of Discovery: the Archaeology of Islands.* Scott M. Fitzpatrick (ed.):251-273. Westport:Praeger.

Anderson, Atholl, 2006: Islands of exile: ideological motivation in maritime migration. *Journal of Island and Coastal Archaeology* 1(1):33-47.

Anderson, David G., 1994: *The Savannah River Chiefdoms: Political Change in the Late Prehistoric Southeast.* Tuscaloosa: The University of Alabama Press.

Anonyme de Carpentras, 2002 [1618-1620]: *Un flibustier français dans la Mer des Antilles, 1618-1620: relation d'un voyage infortuné fait aux Indes occidentales par le capitaine Fleury avec la description de quelques îles qu'on y rencontre, recueillie par l'un de ceux de la compagnie qui fit le voyage.* Jean-Pierre Moreau (ed.). Paris: Éditions Payot & Rivages.

Antczak, María M., 1995: Insights on the prehistoric Anthropomorphic figurines of los Roques, Venezuela. *Proceedings of the 16th Congress of the International Association for Caribbean Archaeology (2).* Conseil Régional de la Guadeloupe-Mission Archéologique et du Patrimoine (ed.):100-104. Basse Terre: Editions du Ponant.

Antczak, María M., and Andrzej Antczak, 2006: *Los ídolos de las islas prometidas: arqueología prehispánica del archipiélago de Los Roques.* Caracas: Editorial Equinoccio.

Århem, Kaj, 1996: *Makuna, an Amazonian people.* SANS Papers in Social Anthropology. Göteborg: Göteborg University.

Arnold, Dean A., 1989 [1985]: *Ceramic theory and cultural process.* New Studies in Archaeology. Cambridge: Cambridge University Press.

Ayubi, Edwin N., 1990: The Study of the Aesthetic Aspects of the Pre-Columbian Pottery of Aruba, Curaçao and Bonaire. *Proceedings of the 11th Congress of the International Association for Caribbean Archaeology.* Agamemnon Gus Pantel Tekakis, Iraida Vargas Arenas and Mario Sanoja Obediente (eds):128-140. San Juan: La Fundación Arqueológica, Antropológica E Historica De Puerto Rico/La Universidad De Puerto Rico/Recato De Rio Piedras/United States Department Of Agriculture/Forest Service.

Baker Littman, Sherri, 2003: Quaternary sea level change in the Caribbean: the implications for archaeology. *Proceedings of the 19th Congress of the International Association for Caribbean Archaeology (1)*. Luc Alofs and Raymundo A.C.F. Dijkhoff (eds):58-64. Publications of the Archaeological Museum Aruba 9. Oranjestad: Museo Arqueologico Aruba.

Barrau, J., and C. Montbrun, 1978: La mangrove et l'insertion humaine dans les écosystemes insulaires des Petites Antilles – le cas de la Martinique et de la Guadeloupe. *Social Science Information* 17(6):897-919.

Barton, Guy T., 1953: *The prehistory of Barbados*. Bridgetown: Advocate Co.

Beets, Cay J., Simon R. Troelstra, Pieter M. Grootes, Marie-Josee Nadeau, Klaas van der Borg, Arie F.M. de Jong, Corinne L. Hofman and Menno L.P. Hoogland, 2006: Climate and pre-Columbian settlement at Anse à la Gourde, Guadeloupe, northeastern Caribbean. *Geoarchaeology* 3:271-280.

Bennell, Maureen, 2002: An archaeological survey of Holetown Fort, Barbados. *Journal of the Barbados Museum and Historical Society* 48:12-28.

Bérard, Benoît, 2000: Sainte-Marie: Anse Charpentier. *Bilan Scientifique 1999 DRAC/SRA Martinique*:20. Fort-de-France: Ministère de la Culture et de la Communication.

Bérard, Benoît, 2001a: Le Lorrain: Vivé. *Bilan Scientifique 2000 DRAC/SRA Martinique*: 18-20. Fort-de-France: Ministère de la Culture et de la Communication.

Bérard, Benoît, 2001b: Le Néolithique de la Martinique dans son contexte Antillaise. *Bilan Scientifique 2000 DRAC/SRA Martinique*:13-15. Fort-de-France: Ministère de la Culture et de la Communication.

Bérard, Benoît, 2002: De l'occupation précéramique de la Martinique. *Archéologie précolombienne et coloniale des Caraïbes – Actes des Congrès Nationaux des Sociétés Historiques et Scientifiques, 123ème Antilles-Guyane (Fort-de-France–Schoelcher, 4-11 avril 1998, Guadeloupe 11-17 avril 1998)*. André Delpuech, Jean-Pierre Giraud and Albert Hesse (eds):55-66. Paris: Éditions du CTHS.

Bérard, Benoît, 2004: *Les premières occupations agricoles de l'arc antillais, migration et insularité: le cas de l'occupation saladoïde ancienne de la Martinique*. BAR International Series 1299 / Paris Monographs in American Archaeology. Oxford: Archaeopress.

Bérard, Benoît, 2006a: Sainte-Anne: Grande Anse des Salines. *Bilan Scientifique 2003 DRAC/SRA Martinique*:17-19. Fort-de-France: Ministère de la Culture et de la Communication.

Bérard, Benoît, 2006b: Le Néolithique de la Martinique dans son contexte antillais. *Bilan Scientifique 2003 DRAC/SRA Martinique*. Fort-de-France: Ministère de la Culture et de la Communication: 22-23.

Bérard, Benoît, 2006c: Le Carbet: Boutbois. *Bilan Scientifique 2003 DRAC/SRA Martinique*:9-11. Fort-de-France: Ministère de la Culture et de la Communication.

Bérard, Benoît, 2006d: Le Carbet: Godinot. *Bilan Scientifique 2003 DRAC/SRA Martinique*:12-13. Fort-de-France: Ministère de la Culture et de la Communication.

Bérard, Benoît, 2008: Lithic technology: a way to more complex diversity in Caribbean archaeology. In *Crossing the Borders: New Methods and Techniques in the Study of Archaeological Materials from the Caribbean*. Corinne L. Hofman, Menno L.P. Hoogland and Annelou van Gijn (eds):90-100. Tuscaloosa: The University of Alabama Press.

Bérard, Benoît, and Jean-Pierre Giraud, 2000: Le Lorrain: Vivé. *Bilan Scientifique 1999 DRAC/SRA Martinique*:15-17. Fort-de-France: Ministère de la Culture et de la Communication.

Bérard, Benoît and Nathalie Vidal, 2002: Le site précolombien de La Pointe au Marigot, Martinique. *Archéologie précolombienne et coloniale des Caraïbes – Actes des Congrès Nationaux des Sociétés Historiques et Scientifiques, 123ème Antilles-Guyane (Fort-de-France–Schoelcher, 4-11 avril 1998, Guadeloupe 11-17 avril 1998).* André Delpuech, Jean-Pierre Giraud and Albert Hesse (eds):95-109. Paris: Éditions du CTHS.

Bérard, Benoît, and Nathalie Vidal, 2003: Essai de géographie amérindienne de la Martinique. *Proceedings of the 19th Congress of the International Association for Caribbean Archaeology (1).* Luc Alofs and Raymundo A.C.F. Dijkhoff (eds):22-35. Publications of the Archaeological Museum Aruba 9. Oranjestad: Archaeological Museum Aruba.

Bérard, Benoît, Jean-Pierre Giraud and James Petersen, 2005: *Opération Sud-Dominique 2005. Rapport de Terrain*, Ministère Français de Affaires Etrangères. Online resource: http://www.ouacabou.org/dominique_2005, accessed 23 September 2007.

Berman, Mary J., and Deborah M. Pearsall, 2000: Plants, people, and culture in the prehistoric central Bahamas: a view from the Three Dog site, an early Lucayan settlement on San Salvador Island, Bahamas. *Latin American Antiquity* 11(3):219-239.

Binford, Lewis R., 1980: Willow smoke and dogs' tails: hunter-gatherer settlement systems and archaeological site formation. *American Antiquity* 45(1):4-20.

Binford, Lewis R., 1982: The archaeology of place. *Journal of Anthropological Archaeology* 1:5-31.

Binford, Lewis R., 2002: *In pursuit of the past: decoding the archaeological record.* Berkeley: University of California Press.

Bintliff, John, Phil Howard and Anthony Snodgrass, 1999: The Hidden Landscape of Prehistoric Greece. *Journal of Mediterranean Archaeology* 12(2):139-168.

Blancaneaux, Annabella F., 2009: *Contribution à l'étude de la disparition de la culture salaoïde aux Petites Antilles: corrélation préhistorique possible entre climat et culture.* Unpublished Ph.D. dissertation, Université des Antilles et de la Guyane / Université de soutenance / Centre d'études et de recherches caraïbéennes, Pointe-à-Pitre, Guadeloupe.

Blitz, John H., 1999: Mississippian Chiefdoms and the Fission-Fusion Process. *American Antiquity* 64(4):577-592.

Blitz, John H., 2009: New Perspectives in Mississippian Archaeology. *Journal of Archaeological Research* 18:1-39.

Bodington, Jeff, 2005: The mapping of Martinique and Guadeloupe to 1800. *Mapforum* 8:46-50.

Bonnissent, Dominique, 2003: Modifications des paleo-environnement et occupations Amerindiennes de l'île de Saint-Martin. *Bilan Scientifique 2002.* Service Régional de l'Archéologie. Basse-Terre: Direction Régionale des Affaires Culturelles de Guadeloupe:54-59.

Bonnissent, Dominique, 2005: La Céramique du Site Postsaladoïde de Baie Aux Prunes (Plum Bay): Les Implications Chronologiques et Géographiques (Saint-Martin, Petites Antilles). *Proceedings of the 20th Congress of the International Association for Caribbean Archaeology (1).* Clenis Tavárez María and Manuel A. García Arévalo (eds):41-48. Santo Domingo: Museo del Hombre Dominicano and Fundación García Arévalo.

Bonnissent, Dominique, 2008: *Archéologie précolombienne de l'île de Saint-Martin, Petites Antilles (3300 BC - 1600 AD).* Ph.D. dissertation, Université Aix-Marseille I - Université de Provence, Marseille.

Bonnissent, Dominique, P. Bertran, D. Galop, D. Imbert, C. Stouvenot, 2007: Chronologie des occupations précolombiennes de l'île de Saint-Martin (Petites Antilles) et relations avec les paléoenvironnements. *Proceedings of the 21st Congress of the International Association for Caribbean Archaeology.* Basil Reid, L. Antonio Curet and Henri Petitjean Roget (eds):20-30. St. Augustine: University of the West Indies.

Booden, Matthijs, Raphaël G.A.M. Panhuysen, Menno L.P. Hoogland, Hylke N. de Jong, Gareth R. Davies, and Corinne L. Hofman, 2008; Tracing human mobility with 87Sr/86Sr at Anse à la Gourde, Guadeloupe. In *Crossing the Borders: New Methods and Techniques in the Study of Archaeological Materials from the Caribbean.* Corinne L. Hofman, Menno L.P. Hoogland and Annelou L. van Gijn (eds):214-225. Tuscaloosa: The University of Alabama Press.

Boomert, Arie, 1980: Hertenrits: an Arauquinoid complex in north west Suriname (part 1). *Archaeology and Anthropology* 3(2):68-104.

Boomert, Arie, 1985: The Guayabitoid and Mayoid series: Amerindian culture history in Trinidad during late prehistoric and protohistoric times. *Proceedings of the 10th Congress of the International Association for Caribbean Archaeology.* Louis Allaire and Francine-M. Mayer (eds):93-148. Montréal: Centre de recherches caraïbes, Université de Montréal.

Boomert, Arie, 1986: The Cayo Complex of St. Vincent: Ethnohistorical and Archaeological Aspects of the Island Carib Problem. *Antropológica* 66:3-68.

Boomert, Arie, 1987a: Notes on Barbados prehistory. *The Journal of the Barbados Museum and Historical Society* 38(1):8-43.

Boomert, Arie, 1987b: Gifts of the Amazons: "Green Stone" Pendants and Beads as Items of Ceremonial Exchange in Amazonia and the Caribbean. *Antropológica* 67:33-54.

Boomert, Arie, 1995: Island Carib archaeology. In *Wolves from the Sea.* Neil. Whitehead (ed.):1-26. Leiden: KITLV Press.

Boomert, Arie, 2000: *Trinidad, Tobago and the Lower Orinoco interaction sphere: an archaeological/ethnohistorical study.* Ph.D. Dissertation, Faculty of Archaeology, Leiden University, Leiden. Alkmaar: Cairi Publications.

Boomert, Arie, 2002: Amerindian-European Encounters on Tobago (1498-ca. 1810). *Antropológica* 97/98:71-207.

Boomert, Arie, 2003: Raptorial birds as icons of shamanism in the prehistoric Caribbean and Amazonia. *Proceedings of the 19th Congress of the International Association for Caribbean Archaeology (2).* Luc Alofs and Raymundo A.C.F. Dijkhoff (eds):121-157. Publications of the Archaeological Museum Aruba 9. Oranjestad: Museo Arqueologico Aruba.

Boomert, Arie, 2004: Koriabo and the Polychrome Tradition: the late-prehistoric era between the Orinoco and the Amazon mouths. In *Late Ceramic Age Societies in the Eastern Caribbean*. André Delpuech and Corinne L. Hofman (eds):251-266. Paris Monographs in American Archaeology 14/BAR International Series 1273. Oxford: Archaeopress.

Boomert, Arie, 2005: Golden Grove: a late-prehistoric ceramic complex of Tobago. *Leiden Journal of Pottery Studies (formerly: Newsletter Department of Pottery Technology)* 21:27-60.

Boomert, Arie, 2007a: *Exotics from Pearls, Grenada: A preliminary assessment.* Paper presented at the 21st Congress of the International Association for Caribbean Archaeology. Kingstown, Jamaica.

Boomert, Arie, 2007b: Plymouth: a late-prehistoric ceramic complex of Tobago. *Leiden Journal of Pottery Studies (formerly: Newsletter Department of Pottery Technology)* 23:121-158.

Boomert, Arie, 2009: *Searching for Cayo in Dominica.* Paper presented at the Twenty-third International Congress for Caribbean Archaeology, St. John's, Antigua, June-July 2009.

Boomert, Arie, and Alistair J. Bright, 2007: Island archaeology: in search of a new horizon. *Island Studies Journal* 2(1):3-26.

Boomert, Arie and Leonid Kameneff, 2005: Preliminary report on archaeological investigations at Great Courland Bay, Tobago. *Proceedings of the 20th Congress of the International Association for Caribbean Archaeology (2).* Clenis Tavárez María and Manuel A. García Arévalo (eds):457-468. Santo Domingo: Museo del Hombre Dominicano and Fundación García Arévalo.

Boucher, Philip P., 1992: *Cannibal Encounters: Europeans and Island Caribs, 1492-1763.* Johns Hopkins Studies in Atlantic History and Culture. Baltimore: The Johns Hopkins University Press.

Boucher, Philip P., 2002: The "Frontier Era" of the French Caribbean. In *Negotiated Empires: centers and peripheries on the Americas, 1500-1820.* Christine Daniels and Michael V. Kennedy (eds):207-234. New York and London: Routledge.

Bowser, Brenda, 2000: From Pottery to Politics: An Ethnoarchaeological Study of Political Factionalism, Ethnicity, and Domestic Pottery Style in the Ecuadorian Amazon. *Journal of Archaeological Method and Theory* 7(3):219-248.

Bradford, Margaret A.C., 2001a: *Caribbean perspectives on settlement patterns: the Windward Island study.* Ph.D. Dissertation, University of Iowa, Iowa City.

Bradford, Margaret A.C., 2001b: Windward Island Settlement Pattern Study update. *Proceedings of the 18th Congress of the International Association for Caribbean Archaeology.* L'Association Internationale d'Archéologie de la Caraïbe Région Guadeloupe (ed.):67-74. St. George.

Bradford, Margaret A.C., 2003: Caribbean perspectives on settlement patterns: the Windward Island study. *Proceedings of the 19th Congress of the International Association for Caribbean Archaeology (2).* Luc Alofs and Raymundo A.C.F. Dijkhoff (eds):109-120. Publications of the Archaeological Museum Aruba 9. Oranjestad: Archaeological Museum Aruba.

Branford, Eric, 1974: *Archaeological Secretary's report.* Unpublished manuscript.

Breton, Raymond, 1978 [1647]: *Relations de l'ile de la Guadeloupe.* Basse-Terre: Société d'histoire de la Guadeloupe.

Breton, Raymond, 1999 [1665]: *Dictionnaire Caraïbe-Français*. Paris: Karthala.

Bright, Alistair J., 2003: *Spatial dynamics and social development in the Northern Lesser Antilles: a pilot study based on settlement structure at the site of Anse à la Gourde, Guadeloupe*. MA Thesis, Leiden University, Leiden.

Bright, Alistair J., 2005: *Martinique survey 2005*. Online manuscript. Leiden: Leiden University. http://www.brightbriels.com/martinique2005report.pdf, accessed 8 October 2008.

Bright, Alistair J., 2006: *From lush expanses to barren rocks: Windward island and islet archaeology*. Paper presented at the 'Small Islands in the Caribbean' Symposium, 31st May 2006, Leiden University, Leiden.

Bright, Alistair J., 2007: Across the channel: southernmost Martinique and northern St. Lucia compared. *Proceedings of the 21st Congress of the International Association for Caribbean Archaeology (2)*. Basil Reid, L. Antonio Curet and Henri Petitjean Roget (eds):597-607. St. Augustine: University of the West Indies.

Bright, Alistair J. and Corinne L. Hofman, in press: L'occupation Amérindienne Tardive Des Îles du Vent (Antilles) et l'utilisation archéologique des sources ethnohistoriques. In *Villes et Sociétés urbaines en Amérique coloniale*, Bernard Grunberg (ed.). Cahiers d'Histoire de l'Amérique Coloniale, n°4. Paris: L'Harmattan.

Broodbank, Cyprian, 2002 [2000]: *An island archaeology of the Early Cyclades*. Cambridge: Cambridge University Press.

Bullen, Adelaide K., 1970: Case study of an Amerindian burial with grave goods from Grande Anse, St Lucia. *Proceedings of the 3rd International Congress for the study of pre-Columbian cultures of the Lesser Antilles*. Grenada:45-60.

Bullen, Adelaide K., and Ripley P. Bullen, 1966: Barbados, a Carib center. *Bajan* (Bridgetown, Barbados) 155:20-22.

Bullen, Adelaide K., and Ripley P. Bullen, 1970: The Lavoutte site, St Lucia: a Carib ceremonial center, in *Proceedings of the 3rd International Congress for the study of pre-Columbian cultures of the Lesser Antilles*. Grenada:61-86.

Bullen, Ripley P., 1962: *Ceramic Periods of St. Thomas and St. John Islands, Virgin Islands*. William L. Bryant Foundation, American Studies, Report No. 4. Orlando: Florida Technological University.

Bullen, Ripley P., 1964: *The archaeology of Grenada, West Indies*. Contributions of the Florida State Museum, Social Sciences, No. 11. Gainesville: Florida State Museum.

Bullen, Ripley P., 1965: Archaeological chronology of Grenada. *American Antiquity* 31(2):237-241.

Bullen, Ripley P., 1966: The First English Settlement on St. Lucia. *Caribbean Quarterly* 12(2):29-35.

Bullen, Ripley P., 1968: Some Arawak ceramic variations between Grenada, Barbados, St Lucia, and Eastern Trinidad. *Proceedings of the 2nd International Congress for the study of pre-Columbian cultures of the Lesser Antilles*. Ripley P. Bullen (ed.):81-86. St. Ann's Garrison: Barbados Musem.

Bullen, Ripley P., 1970: The archaeology of Grenada, West Indies, and the spread of ceramic people in the Antilles. *Proceedings of the Proceedings of the 3rd International Congress for the study of pre-Columbian cultures of the Lesser Antilles*. Grenada:147-152.

Bullen, Ripley P. and Adelaide K. Bullen, 1966: Three Indian sites on St. Martin. *Nieuwe West-Indische Gids* 44:137-143.

Bullen, Ripley P., and Adelaide K. Bullen, 1968a: Salvage archaeology at Caliviny Island, Grenada: a problem in typology. *Proceedings of the 2nd International Congress for the study of pre-Columbian cultures of the Lesser Antilles.* Ripley P. Bullen (ed.):31-43. St. Ann's Garrison: Barbados Museum.

Bullen, Ripley P., and Adelaide K. Bullen, 1968b: Barbados Archaeology: 1966. *Proceedings of the 2nd International Congress for the study of pre-Columbian cultures of the Lesser Antilles.* Ripley P. Bullen (ed.):134-144. St. Ann's Garrison: Barbados Museum.

Bullen, Ripley P., and Adelaide K. Bullen, 1972: *Archaeological Investigations on St. Vincent and the Grenadines, West Indies.* William L. Bryant Foundation, American Studies, Report No. 8. Orlando: Florida Technological University.

Bullen, Ripley P., and Adelaide K. Bullen, 1973: Stratigraphic tests at two sites on Guadeloupe. *Proceedings of the 4th International Congress for the study of pre-Columbian cultures of the Lesser Antilles.* Castries: St. Lucia Archaeological and Historical Society:192-196.

Bullen, Ripley P., and Adelaide K. Bullen, 1974: Inferences from cultural diffusion to Tower Hill, Jamaica, and Cupercoy Bay, St. Martin. *Proceedings of the 5th International Congress for the study of pre-Columbian cultures of the Lesser Antilles.* St. John's: The Antigua Archaeological Society:48-60.

Bullen, Ripley P., and Adelaide K. Bullen, 1976: Three stratigraphic tests along the eastern shore of Trinidad. *Proceedings of the 6th International Congress for the study of pre-Columbian cultures of the Lesser Antilles.* Ripley P. Bullen (ed.):28-34. Gainesville: Florida State Museum, University of Florida.

Bullen, Ripley P., Adelaide K. Bullen and Eric Branford, 1973: The Giraudy site, Beane Field, St Lucia. *Proceedings of the 4th International Congress for the study of pre-Columbian cultures of the Lesser Antilles.* Castries: St. Lucia Archaeological and Historical Society:199-214.

Bullen, Ripley P., Adelaide K. Bullen and E. Kirby, 1973: Dating the Troumassée decorated cylinder: a horizon style. *Proceedings of the 4th International Congress for the study of pre-Columbian cultures of the Lesser Antilles.* Castries: St. Lucia Archaeological and Historical Society:197-198.

Butt Colson, Audrey, 1973: Inter-tribal trade in the Guiana highlands. *Antropológica* 34:1-70.

Byrne, Bryan, and William F. Keegan, 2001: Structural analysis of Saladoid adornos from Grenada. *Proceedings of the 18th Congress of the International Association for Caribbean Archaeology*. L'Association Internationale d'Archéologie de la Caraïbe Région Guadeloupe (ed.):21-24. St. George.

Callaghan, Richard T., 2001: Ceramic Age seafaring and interaction potential in the Antilles: a computer simulation. *Current Anthropology* 42(2):308-313.

Callaghan, Richard T., 2007: Prehistoric Settlement Patterns on St. Vincent, West Indies. *Caribbean Journal of Science* 43(1):11-22.

Callaghan, Richard T., 2008: On the question of the absence of Archaic Age sites on Jamaica. *Journal of Island and Coastal Archaeology* 3:54-71.

Cambridge, T.C., 1967: *Report on visit to Tobago from 6th to 13th June, 1967.* Unpublished manuscript.

Calvera Rosés, Jorge, Roberto Valcárcel Rojas, Jago Cooper and Odalys Brito Martínez, 2005: Exploraciones arqueológicas en Jardines del Rey. *Gabinete de Arqueología* 4:203.

CANARI, 2003. *The Sea is our Garden: a report on a study of institutional and technical options for improving coastal livelihoods in Laborie, Saint Lucia.* CANARI Technical Report No. 322. 146 pp. Online resource, http://www.nrsp.org/database/documents/819.pdf. Accessed 9 October 2008.

Canner, Thomas, 1905-07 (1625): A Relation of the Voyage made to Virginia, in the Elizabeth of London, a Barke of fiftie tunnes by Captaine Bartholomew Gilbert, in the yeere 1603. Written by Master Thomas Canner, a Gentleman of Bernards Inne his companion in the same Voyage. In *Hakluytus Posthumus or Purchas his Pilgrimes; Contayning a History of the World, in Sea Voyages and Lande Travells, by Englishmen and Others*, S. Purchas (ed.), Vol. XVIII. Maclehose: Glasgow.

Cardona, Nicolás de, 1974[1632]: *Geographic and hydrographic descriptions of many Northern and Southern lands and seas in the Indies, specifically of the discovery of the kingdom of California (1632).* Translated and edited by W. Michael Mathes. Los Angeles: Dawson's Book Shop.

Carlson, Betsy and William F. Keegan, 2004: Resource depletion in the prehistoric northern West Indies. In *Voyages of Discovery: The Archaeology of Islands.* Scott M. Fitzpatrick (ed.):85–107. Westport: Praeger.

Carrington, Sean, Henry Fraser, John Gilmore and Addington Forde, 2004: *A-Z of Barbados heritage.* Oxford: Macmillan Caribbean.

Castres, Caillé de, 2002 [1694]: *De wilde ou les sauvages caribes insulaires d'Amérique.* Conseil Général de la Martinique / Musée Départemental d'Archéologie Précolombienne et de Préhistoire / Société d'Histoire de la Martinique / Société des Amis du Musée d'Archéologie. Fort-de-France: Caraïbe Ediprint.

Celma, Cecil (ed.), 1997: *L'archéologie à la Martinique – 60 anneés de passion et de recherches. Catalogue d' exposition avril-juin 1997.* Fort-de-France: Conseil Général de la Martinique / DRAC.

Chagnon, Napoleon A., 1997: *Yanomamö.* Case Studies in Cultural Anthropology, George and Louise Spindler (eds), Fort Worth [etc.]: Harcourt Brace College Publishers.

Champlain, Samuel, 1964[1859]: *Narrative of a voyage to the West Indies and Mexico in the years 1599-1602.* Translated by Alice Wilmere, Norton Shaw (ed.). New York: Burt Franklin, Publisher.

Chanca, Diego Alvarez, 1993: 'Letter' to the Mayor of Seville. In *Christopher Columbus's Discoveries in the testimonials of Diego Alvarez Chanca and Andrés Bernáldez.* Nuova Raccolta Colombiana Volume V. Luciano F. Farina and C.K. Zacher (eds):11-59. Roma: Istituto Poligrafico e Zecca dello Stato, Libreria dello Stato.

Chancerel, Gaëlle, 2005: La Céramique Du Site De Tourlourous à Marie Galante (Guadeloupe). *Proceedings of the 20th Congress of the International Association for Caribbean Archaeology (1).* Clenis Tavárez María and Manuel A. García Arévalo (eds):151-158. Santo Domingo: Museo del Hombre Dominicano y Fundación García Arévalo.

Chanlatte-Baik, Luis A., 1984: *Arqueología de Vieques.* Santo Domingo: Editora Corripio.

Chanlatte-Baik, Luis A., and Yvonne M. Narganes, 1980: La Hueca, Vieques: nuevo complejo cultural agroalfarero en la Arqueología Antillana. *Proceedings of the 8th International Congress for Caribbean Archaeology.* Suzanne M. Lewenstein (ed.):501-523. Anthropological Research Papers no. 22. Tempe: Arizona State University.

Chapman, Robert, 2003: *Archaeologies of complexity.* London and New York: Routledge.

Cherry, John F., 1984: The Initial Colonisation of the West Mediterranean Islands in the Light of Island Biogeography and Palaeogeography. *The Deya Conference of Prehistory: Early Settlement in the Western Mediterranean Islands and the Peripheral Areas.* William H. Waldren, Robert Chapman, James Lewthwaite and Rex-Claire Kennard (eds):7-23. British Archaeological Reports International Series 229. Oxford: British Archaeological Reports.

Chew, Sing C., 2001: *World Ecological Degradation: Accumulation, Urbanization, and Deforestation, 3000 B.C.-A.D. 2000.* Walnut Creek: AltaMira Press.

Chilton, Elizabeth, 2005: Farming and social complexity in the Northeast. In *North American Archaeology*, Timothy R. Pauketat and Diana DiPaolo Loren (eds):138-160. Blackwell Studies in Global Archaeology. Malden [etc.]:Blackwell Publishing.

Clarke, James, 1806: June 9, 1803. *Archaeologia: or, Miscellaneous Tracts, Relating to Antiquity* 15:406-408.

Cody, Annie, 1991: From the Site of Pearls, Grenada: Exotic Lithics and Radiocarbon Dates. *Proceedings of the 13th Congress of the International Association for Caribbean Archaeology (2).* Edwin N. Ayubi and Jay B. Haviser (eds):589-604. Reports of the Archaeological-Anthropological Institute of the Netherlands Antilles, No. 9. Willemstad: Archaeological-Anthropological Institute of the Netherlands Antilles.

Cody, Annie, 1995: Kalinago alliance networks. *Proceedings of the 15th Congress of the International Association for Caribbean Archaeology.* Ricardo A. Alegría and Miguel Rodríguez (eds):311-326. San Juan: Centro de Estudios Avanzados de Puerto Rico y el Caribe/Fundación Puertorriqueña de las Humanidades/Universidad del Turabo.

Cody Holdren, Annie, 1998: *Raiders and Traiders: Caraïbe Social and Political Networks at the Time of European Contact and Colonization in the Eastern Caribbean.* PhD Thesis. University of California, Los Angeles.

Columbus, Christopher, 1997: Libro Copiador, II. In *Accounts and letters of the second, third, and fourth voyages.* Nuova Raccolta Colombiana Volume VI Part 1. Luciano F. Farina (ed.):201-239. Roma: Istituto Poligrafico e Zecca dello Stato, Libreria dello Stato.

Conservation du Musée Départmental d'Archéologie, 1991: *Archéologie Martinique – Musée Départmental d'Archéologie, Fort-de-France. Guide des collections.* Trinité: Gondwana Editions.

Conzemius, Eduard, 1928: Ethnographical Notes on the Black Carib (Garif). *American Anthropologist*, New Series, 30(2):183-205.

Cooney, Gabriel, 2003: Introduction: seeing land from the sea. *World Archaeology* 35(3): 323-328.

Cooney, Gabriel, 2004: Neolithic worlds; islands in the Irish Sea (chapter 16). In *The Neolithic of the Irish Sea: materiality and traditions of practice*. Vicki Cummings and Chris Fowler (eds):145-159. Oxford: Oxbow Books.

Cooper, Jago, and Matthew C. Peros, 2010: The archaeology of climate change in the Caribbean. *Journal of Archaeological Science* 37(6):1226-1232.

Coppens, R., B. Guillet, R. Jaegy and P. Richard, 1979: Nancy natural radiocarbon measurements V. *Radiocarbon* 21(3):453-464.

Coppier, Guillaume, 1645: Chapître V: Des Isles Indoises, pays des sauvages. *Histoire et voyage des Indes occidentales et de plusieurs autres régions maritimes et esloignées*. Lyon: J. Hugeteau.

Craig, Nathan, and Napoleon A. Chagnon, 2006: Locational analysis of Yanomamö gardens and villages observed in satellite imagery. In *Archaeology and Ethnoarchaeology of Mobility*. Frédéric Sellet, Russell Graves and Pei-Lin Yu (eds):44-74. Tallahassee [etc.]: University Press of Florida.

Crock, John, 2000: *Interisland interaction and the development of chiefdoms in the Eastern Caribbean*. Ph.D. Thesis, University of Pittsburgh. Ann Arbor: UMI.

Crock, John G. and James B. Petersen, 2001: Stratified sites and storm events: the formation and destruction of beach sites in Anguilla, West Indies. *Proceedings of the 19th Congress of the International Association for Caribbean Archaeology (1)*. Luc Alofs and Raymundo A.C.F. Dijkhoff (eds):204-213. Publications of the Archaeological Museum Aruba 9. Oranjestad: Museo Arqueologico Aruba.

Crock, John G. and James B. Petersen, 2004: Inter-island exchange, settlement hierarchy, and a Taíno-related chiefdom on the Anguilla Bank, Northern Lesser Antilles. In *Late Ceramic Age Societies in the Eastern Caribbean*. André Delpuech and Corinne L. Hofman (eds):139-156. Paris Monographs in American Archaeology 14/BAR International Series 1273. Oxford: Archaeopress.

Cruxent, José M., and Irving Rouse, 1982[1958]: *Arqueología cronológica de Venezuela*. Ernesto Armitano Editor. Washington D.C.: Pan American Union.

Cumberland, The Earl of, 1905 [1625]: A briefe relation of the severall voyages undertaken by the Right Honourable, George, Earle of Cumberland in his owne person, or at his owne charge, and by his direction, collected out of the relations and journals of credible persons Actors therein. *Hakluytus Posthumus, or, Purchas his pilgrimes: contayning a history of the world, in sea voyages and lande travells by Englishmen and others*. Samuel Purchas (ed.):52-57. Glasgow: MacLehose.

Curet, L. Antonio, 1992a: House structure and cultural change in the Caribbean: three case studies from Puerto Rico. *Latin American Antiquity* 3(2):160-74.

Curet, L. Antonio, 1992b: *The Development of Chiefdoms in the Greater Antilles: A Regional Study of the Valley of Maunabo, Puerto Rico*. Ph.D. Dissertation. Arizona State University, Arizona.

Curet, L. Antonio, 1996: Ideology, Chiefly Power, and Material Culture: An Example from the Greater Antilles. *Latin American Antiquity* 7(2):114-131.

Curet, L. Antonio, 2002: The Chief is Dead, Long Live...Who? Descent and Succession in the Protohistoric Chiefdoms of the Greater Antilles. *Ethnohistory* 49(2): 259-280.

Curet, L. Antonio, 2003: Issues on the Diversity and Emergence of Middle-Range Societies of the Ancient Caribbean: a Critique. *Journal of Archaeological Research* 11(1):1-42.

Curet, L. Antonio, 2005: *Caribbean Paleodemography: Population, Culture History, and Sociopolitical Processes in Ancient Puerto Rico*. Tuscaloosa: The University of Alabama Press.

Curet, L. Antonio, Shannon L. Dawdy and Gabino La Rosa Corzo (eds), 2005: *Dialogues in Cuban Archaeology*. Tuscaloosa: The University of Alabama Press.

Curet, L. Antonio, and José R. Oliver, 1998: Mortuary Practices, Social Development, and Ideology in Precolumbian Puerto Rico. *Latin American Antiquity* 9(3):217-239.

Curet, L. Antonio, and Lisa M. Stringer, 2010: Introduction. In *Tibes: people, power, and ritual at the center of the cosmos*. L. Antonio Curet and Lisa M. Stringer (eds):1-18. Tuscaloosa: The University of Alabama Press.

Curet, L. Antonio, and Lisa M. Stringer (eds), 2010: *Tibes: people, power, and ritual at the center of the cosmos*. Tuscaloosa: The University of Alabama Press.

Curet, L. Antonio, Joshua M. Torres and Miguel Rodríguez, 2004: Political and social history of Eastern Puerto Rico: the Ceramic Age. In *Late Ceramic Age Societies in the Eastern Caribbean*. André Delpuech and Corinne L. Hofman (eds):59-85. Paris Monographs in American Archaeology 14/BAR International Series 1273. Oxford: Archaeopress.

Curtis, Jason H., and David A. Hodell, 1993: An isotopic and trace element study of Ostracods from Lake Miragoane, Haiti: a 10,500 year record of paleosalinity and paleotemperature changes in the Caribbean. In *Climate Change in Continental Isotopic Records*. Peter K. Swart, Kyger C. Lohmann, Judith McKenzie and S. Savin (eds):135-152. Geophysical Monograph 78. Washington D.C.: American Geophysical Union.

Curtis, Jason H., Brenner, Mark, and David A. Hodell, 2001: Climate Change in the Circum-Caribbean (Late Pleistocene-to-Present) and Implications for Regional Biogeography. In *Biogeography of the West Indies: Past. Present, and Future*, 2nd edition. Charles E. Woods and Florence E. Sergile (eds):35-54. Gainesville: Sandhill Crane.

David, Nicholas, and Carol Kramer, 2001: *Ethnoarchaeology in action*. Cambridge World Archaeology. Cambridge: Cambridge University Press.

Davis, Dave D., 1996: Revolutionary Archaeology in Cuba. *Journal of Archaeological Method and Theory* 3(3):159-188.

Davis, Dave D., 2000: *Jolly Beach and the Preceramic occupation of Antigua, West Indies*. Yale University Publications in Anthropology 84. New Haven: Department of Anthropology, Yale University/Division of Anthropology, Peabody Museum of Natural History, Yale University.

Davis, Dave D., and R. Christopher Goodwin, 1990: Island Carib origins: evidence and nonevidence. *American Antiquity* 55(1):37-48.

Davis, Dave, and Kevin Oldfield, 2003: Archaeological reconnaissance of Anegada, British Virgin Islands. *Journal of Caribbean Archaeology* 4:1-11.

DeBoer, Warren R., 1990: Interaction, Imitation, and Communication as Expr essed in Style: The Ucayali Experience. In *The Uses of Style in Archaeology,* Margaret Conkey and Christine Hastorf (eds):82–104. Cambridge: Cambridge University Press.

De Hostos, Alfonso, 1923: Three-Pointed Stone Zemi or Idols from the West Indies: An Interpretation. *American Anthropologist*, New Series, 25(1):56-71.

De Laet, Joannes, 1630: *Beschrijvinghe van West-Indien door Joannes de Laet. Tweede druk: In ontallycke placesen verbetert, vermeerdert, met eenige nieuwe caerten, beelden van verscheijden dieren ende planten verciert.* Leiden: Bonaventure & Abraham Elseviers.

De Laet, Joannes, 1931[1644]: *Iaerlyck Verhael van de Verrichtinghen der Geoctroyeerde West-Indische Compagnie in derthien Boecken. Eerste deel, boek I-III (1624-1626).* S.P. L'Honoré Naber (ed.). 's Gravenhage: Martinus Nijhoff.

De Laet, Joannes, 1932[1644]: *Iaerlyck Verhael van de Verrichtinghen der Geoctroyeerde West-Indische Compagnie in derthien Boecken. Tweede deel, boek IV-VII (1627-1630).* S.P. L'Honoré Naber (ed.). 's Gravenhage: Martinus Nijhoff.

DeFrance, Susan D., William F. Keegan and Lee A. Newsom, 1996: The archaeobotanical, bone isotope, and zooarchaeological records from Caribbean sites in comparative perspective. *Case studies in environmental archaeology.* Elizabeth J. Reitz, Lee A. Newsom and Sylvia J. Scudder (eds):289-304. New York & London: Plenum Press.

Delawarde, Jean-Baptiste, 1937: *Préhistoire Martiniquaise: les gisements du Prêcheur et du Marigot.* Fort-de-France: Imprimerie Officielle.

Delawarde, Jean-Baptiste, 1946: Préhistoire Martiniquaise: les gisements du Paquemar et de Vivé. *Martinique*, 6, Sept. 1946:53-60.

Delhaye, Pascale, 1995: Prêcheur: Anse Ceron. *Bilan Scientifique 1994 DRAC/SRA Martinique*: 16-17. Ministère de la Culture: Fort-de-France.

Delpuech, André, 2001: Historical archaeology in the French West Indies: recent research in Guadeloupe. In *Island Lives: Historical Archaeologies of the Caribbean*, Paul Farnsworth (ed.):21-59. Tuscaloosa: The University of Alabama Press.

Delpuech, André, 2004: Espaces naturels et territoires amérindiens dans la Caraïbe orientale. In *Late Ceramic Age Societies in the Eastern Caribbean.* André Delpuech and Corinne L. Hofman (eds):3-16. Paris Monographs in American Archaeology 14/BAR International Series 1273. Oxford: Archaeopress.

Delpuech, André, Christophe Henocq and Thierry l'Etang, 1993: *Presents Caraibes: 5000 ans d'histoire amérindienne.* PRIM: Basse-Terre.

Delpuech, André, and Corinne L. Hofman (eds), 2004: *Late Ceramic Age Societies in the Eastern Caribbean.* Paris Monographs in American Archaeology 14/BAR International Series 1273. Oxford: Archaeopress.

DeMille, Christy, A. Reg Murphy and Paul F. Healy, 1999: Preliminary Archaeological Investigations At Winthorpe's Bay, Antigua. *Proceedings of the 17th Congress of the International Association for Caribbean Archaeology.* John H. Winter (ed.):105-121. New York: Rockville Center/Molloy College.

Denevan, William M. (ed.), 1976: *The native population of the Americas in 1492.* Madison: University of Wisconsin Press.

Descantes, Christophe, Robert J. Speakman, Michael D. Glascock, and Matthew T. Boulanger (eds), 2008: An exploratory study into the chemical characterization of Caribbean ceramics: an introduction to a special volume of the Journal of Caribbean Archaeology in memory of James B. Petersen. *Journal of Caribbean Archaeology* Special Publication Number 2: An Exploratory Study into the Chemical Characterization of Caribbean Ceramics.

Devaux, Robert J., 1975: *Saint Lucia Historic Sites*. Castries: Saint Lucia National Trust.

Devaux, Robert J., 1976: Petroglyphs recently discovered at Stonefield, St. Lucia. *Proceedings of the 6th International Congress for the study of pre-Columbian cultures of the Lesser Antilles*. Ripley P. Bullen (ed.):213. Gainesville: Florida State Museum, University of Florida.

Devaux, Robert J., and P.M.D., 1984: *Belfond Estate*. Unpublished manuscript. Castries: St. Lucia National Trust.

De Waal, Maaike, 2006: *Pre-Columbian Social Organisation and Interaction interpreted through the study of settlement patterns. An archaeological case-study of the Pointe des Châteaux, La Désirade and les Îles de la Petite Terre Micro-region, Guadeloupe, French West Indies*. Ph.D. Dissertation. Faculty of Archaeology. Leiden University. Leiden.

D'Harcourt, Raoul, 1952: Collections archéologiques martiniquaises du Musée de l'Homme. *Journal de la Société des Américanistes de Paris* 41(2):353-373.

Di Piazza, Anne, and Eric Pearthree, 2001: Voyaging and basalt exchange in the Phoenix and Line archipelagoes: the viewpoint from three Mystery Islands. *Archaeology in Oceania* 36:146-152.

Dijkhoff, Raymundo A.C.F., 1997: *Tanki Flip/Henriquez: An early Urumaco site in Aruba*. Unpublished MA Thesis, Leiden University, Leiden.

Donop, Mark, 2007: A reanalysis of Ripley P. Bullen's Savanne Suazey ceramics. In *Proceedings of the 21st Congress of the International Association for Caribbean Archaeology*. Basil Reid, L. Antonio Curet and Henri Petitjean Roget (eds):9-19. St. Augustine: University of the West Indies, Trinidad.

Drewett, Peter L. (ed.), 1991: *Prehistoric Barbados*. London: Archetype Publications.

Drewett, Peter L., 1993: Excavations at Heywoods, Barbados, and the Economic Basis of the Suazoid Period in the Lesser Antilles. *Journal of the Barbados Museum and Historical Society* 38:113-137.

Drewett, Peter L. (ed.), 2000: *Prehistoric settlements in the Caribbean: fieldwork in Barbados, Tortola and the Cayman Islands*. London: Archetype Publications.

Drewett, Peter L., 2004: Post-Saladoid society on Barbados. In *Late Ceramic Age Societies in the Eastern Caribbean*. André Delpuech and Corinne L. Hofman (eds):215-230. Paris Monographs in American Archaeology 14/BAR International Series 1273. Oxford: Archaeopress.

Drewett, Peter L., 2007: *Above Sweet Waters: Cultural and natural change at Port St Charles, Barbados, c. 1750 BC – AD 1850*. London: Archetype Publications.

Drewett, Peter L., and Maureen Bennell, 2000: Settlement archaeology on Barbados II: The Port St Charles (Heywoods) Archaeological Rescue Project. In *Prehistoric settlements in the Caribbean: fieldwork in Barbados, Tortola and the Cayman Islands*, Peter L. Drewett (ed.): 27-50. London: Archetype Publications.

Drewett, Peter L., and Mary Hill Harris, 1991: The archaeological survey of Barbados; 1985-87. *Proceedings of the 12th Congress of the International Association for Caribbean Archaeology*. Linda S. Robinson (ed.):175-202. Fort-de-France: Association Internationale d'Archéologie de la Caraïbe, Martinique.

Dreyfus, Simone, 1976: Remarques sur l'organisation socio-politique des Caraïbes insulaires au XVIIème siècle. *Proceedings of the 6th International Congress for the study of pre-Columbian cultures of the Lesser Antilles*. Ripley P. Bullen (ed.):87-97. Gainesville: Florida State Museum, University of Florida.

Dreyfus, Simone, 1983/1984: Historical and political anthropological inter-connections: the multilinguistic indigenous polity of the "Carib" Islands and Mainland Coast from the 16th to the 18th century. *Antropológica* 59-62:39-55.

Du Puis, Mathias, 1972 [1652]: *Relation de l'establissement d'une colonie françoise dans la Gardeloupe, isle de l'Amérique et des moeurs des sauvages*. Basse-Terre: Société d'Histoire de la Guadeloupe.

Du Ry, C.J., 1960: *Notes on the pottery of Aruba, Curaçao and Bonaire*. Studies on the Archaeology of the Netherlands Antilles I. Willemstad: Natuurwetenschappelijke Werkgroep Nederlandse Antillen.

Du Tertre, Jean-Baptiste, 1654: *Histoire generale, des isles de S. Christophe, de la Guadeloupe, de la Martinique, et autres dans l'Amerique* [etc]. Paris: Jacques et Emmanuel Langlois.

Dubelaar, Cees N., 1995: *The Petroglyphs of the Lesser Antilles, the Virgin Islands and Trinidad*. Amsterdam: Foundation for Scientific Research in the Caribbean Region.

Duval, David T., 1994: *The 1993 University of Manitoba St. Vincent Site Survey: Preliminary Report Number 1 (Artifact Cataloguing)*. Report presented to the St. Vincent National Trust, St. Vincent and the Grenadines, June 1994. Online manuscript. http://www.davidtimothyduval.com/files/archaeology/SVG_Preliminary_Report_I.pdf, accessed 10 December 2007.

Duval, David T., 1996: *Saladoid Archaeology on St. Vincent, West Indies: Results of the 1993/1994 University of Manitoba Survey*. MA Thesis (Anthropology), Department of Anthropology, University of Manitoba.

Erlandson, Jon M., 2008: Isolation, interaction, and island archaeology. *Journal of Island and Coastal Archaeology* 3:83-86.

Erlandson, Jon M., and Madonna L. Moss, 1999: The systematic use of radiocarbon dating in archaeological surveys in coastal and other erosional environments. *American Antiquity* 64(3):431-443.

Espenshade, Chris, 2000: Reconstructing Household Vessel Assemblages and Site Duration at an Early Ostionoid Site from South-Central Puerto Rico. *Journal of Caribbean Archaeology* 1:1-22.

Etrich, Christine, 2007: Le Lorrain: Le Seguineau – Lotissement Caïali. *Bilan Scientifique 2005 DRAC/SRA Martinique*:15-17. Fort-de-France: Ministère de la Culture et de la Communication.

Evans, Clifford, 1968: Lack of archaeology on Dominica. *Proceedings of the 2nd International Congress for the study of pre-Columbian cultures of the Lesser Antilles*. Ripley P. Bullen (ed.):93-102. St. Ann's Garrison: Barbados Museum.

Evans, Clifford, and Betsy J. Meggers, 1960: *Archaeological investigations in British Guiana*. Washington: United States Government Printing Office.

Evans, J.D., 1973: Islands as laboratories for the study of culture process. Colin Renfrew (ed.), *The explanation of culture change: models in prehistory.* London: Duckworth.

Faber Morse, Birgit, 1989: Saladoid Remains and Adaptive Strategies in St. Croix, Virgin Islands. In *Early Ceramic population lifeways and adaptive strategies in the Caribbean.* Peter E. Siegel (ed.):29–41. BAR International Series 506. Oxford: British Archaeological Reports.

Faber Morse, Birgit, and Irving Rouse, 2001: The Mamora Bay period: the latest ceramic period

at the Indian Creek site, Antigua. *Proceedings of the 18th Congress of the International Association for Caribbean Archaeology.* L'Association Internationale d'Archéologie de la Caraïbe Région Guadeloupe (ed.):187-198. St. George.

Fabrizii-Reuer, Susanne, and Egon Reuer, 2006: *Die Gräber aus den „shell-middens" der präkolumbianischen Siedlung von Pointe de Caille, St. Lucia, West Indies.* Mitteilungen der Prähistorischen Kommission 58/Abhandlungen der Senckenbergischen Naturforschenden Gesellschaft 563. Wien: Verlag der Österreichischen Akademie der Wissenschaften.

Fairbridge, Rhodes W., 1976: Effects of Holocene Climatic Change on Some Tropical Geomorphic Processes. *Quaternary Research* 6:529-556.

Farr, Starr, 1995: Gender and Ethnogenesis in the Early Colonial Lesser Antilles. *Proceedings of the 15th Congress of the International Association for Caribbean Archaeology.* Ricardo A. Alegría and Miguel Rodríguez (eds):369-375. San Juan: Centro de Estudios Avanzados de Puerto Rico y el Caribe/Fundación Puertorriqueña de las Humanidades/Universidad del Turabo.

Fewkes, Jesse W., 1904: Prehistoric Culture of Cuba. *American Anthropologist* 6:585-598.

Fewkes, Jesse W., 1907: The Aborigines of Porto Rico and Neighboring Islands. In *25th Annual Report of the Bureau of American Ethnology to the Secretary of the Smithsonian Institution 1903-1904.* W.H. Holmes (ed.):3-220. Washington: Government Printing Office.

Fewkes, Jesse W., 1914: Relations of aboriginal culture and environment in the Lesser Antilles. *Bulletin of the American Geographical Society* XLVI(9):662-678.

Fewkes, Jesse W., 1915: Archaeology of Barbados. *Proceedings of the National Academy of Sciences* 1:47-51.

Fewkes, Jesse W., 1922: A Prehistoric Island Culture Area of America. In *34th Annual Report of the Bureau of American Ethnology to the Secretary of the Smithsonian Institution 1912-1913.* F.W. Hodge (ed.):35-271. Washington: Government Printing Office.

Figueredo, Alfredo E., 1978: The Virgin Islands as an historical frontier between the Tainos and the Caribs. *Revista/Review Interamericana* VIII(3):393-399.

Fitzpatrick, Scott M. (ed.), 2004: *Voyages of Discovery: The Archaeology of Islands.* Westport: Praeger.

Fitzpatrick, Scott M., 2004a: *Quo vadis* Caribbean Archaeology? The Future of the Discipline in an International Forum. *Caribbean Journal of Science* 40(3):281-290.

Fitzpatrick, Scott M., 2004b: Preface. In *Voyages of Discovery: The Archaeology of Islands*. Scott M. Fitzpatrick (ed.):xiii-xv. Westport: Praeger.

Fitzpatrick, Scott M., 2004c: Synthesizing island archaeology. In *Voyages of Discovery: The Archaeology of Islands*. Scott M. Fitzpatrick (ed.):3-18. Westport: Praeger.

Fitzpatrick, Scott M., 2006: A critical approach to 14C dating in the Caribbean: Using chronometric hygiene to evaluate chronological control and prehistoric settlement. *Latin American Antiquity* 17(4):389-418.

Fitzpatrick, Scott M., Jon M. Erlandson, Atholl Anderson and Patrick V. Kirch, 2007: Straw Boats and the Proverbial Sea: A Response to 'Island Archaeology: In Search of a New Horizon'. *Island Studies Journal* 2(2):229-238.

Fitzpatrick, Scott M., Quetta Kaye and Michiel Kappers, 2004: A radiocarbon sequence for the Sabazan site, Carriacou, West Indies. *Journal of Caribbean Archaeology* 5:1-11.

Fitzpatrick, Scott M., Michiel Kappers, Quetta P. Kaye, Christina M. Giovas, Michelle J. LeFebvre, Mary Hill Harris, Scott Burnett, Jennifer A. Pavia, Kathleen Marsaglia, James Feathers, 2009: Precolumbian settlements on Carriacou, West Indies. *Journal of Field Archaeology* 34(3):247-266.

Fitzpatrick, Scott M., and William F. Keegan, 2007: Human impacts and adaptations in the Caribbean Islands: an historical ecology approach. *Earth and Environmental Science Transactions of the Royal Society of Edinburgh* 98:29–45.

Flannery, Kent V. (ed.), 1976: *The Mesoamerican Village*. London [etc.]: Academic Press.

Flannery, Kent V., and Michael D. Coe, 1968: Social and economic systems in Formative Mesoamerica. In *New Perspectives in Archeology*, Sally R. Binford and Lewis R. Binford (eds):267-284. Chicago: Aldine.

Fock, Niels, 1963: *Waiwai: religion and society of an Amazonian tribe*. Nationalmuseets Skrifter, Etnografisk Række VIII. Copenhagen: The National Museum.

Foster, Byron, 1987: Celebrating autonomy: the development of Garifuna ritual on St. Vincent. *Caribbean Quarterly* 33(3/4):75-83.

Frank, David (ed.), 2001: *Kwéyòl Dictionary*. Castries: Ministry of Education, Government of Saint Lucia.

Friesinger, Herwig, 1986: Archäologische Ausgrabungen und Untersuchungen 1984 auf der Karibikinsel St. Lucia, West Indies. In *Grabungen und Forschungen auf St. Lucia 1984*. Friesinger, Herwig, Egon Reuer, Fritz Steininger and Peter Faupl (eds):5-32. Mitteilungen der Prähistorischen Kommission der Österreichischen Akademie der Wissenschaften XXIII. Vienna: Verlag der Österreichischen Akademie der Wissenschaften.

Friesinger, Herwig, Egon Reuer, Fritz Steininger and Peter Faupl (eds), 1986: *Grabungen und Forschungen auf St. Lucia 1984*. Mitteilungen der Prähistorischen Kommission der Österreichischen Akademie der Wissenschaften XXIII. Vienna: Verlag der Österreichischen Akademie der Wissenschaften.

Friesinger, Herwig, and Robert Devaux, 1983: *Vorbericht über die Österreichischen Ausgrabungen auf St. Lucia, Westindien*. Anzeiger der phil.-hist. Klasse der Österreichischen Akademie der Wissenschaften 120. Vienna: Verlag der Österreichischen Akademie der Wissenschaften.

Gage, Thomas, 1758: A journey of three thousand three hundred miles, through the mainland of South-America. *The Traveller, part 1*. Woodbridge: James Parker.

Gaspar, David Barry, 1979: Runaways in Seventeenth-Century Antigua, West Indies. *Boletín de Estudios Latinoamericanos y del Caribe* 26:3-13.

Gassón, Rafaël A., 2000: Quirípas and mostacillas: the evolution of shell beads as a medium of exchange in northern South America. *Ethnohistory* 47(3-4):581-609.

Gautier, Jeanne, 1974: Etude des pâtes céramiques de la Martinique précolombienne. *Proceedings of the 5th International Congress for the study of pre-Columbian Cultures in the Lesser Antilles*. St. John's: The Antigua Archaeological Society:133-139.

Geijskes, D.C., 1964: Arowaks in the prehistory of Surinam. *Proceedings of the 1st International Congress for the study of pre-Columbian cultures of the Lesser Antilles (1)*. Martinique:57-70.

Gell, Alfred, 1985: How to read a map: remarks on the practical logic of navigation. *Man*, New Series, Vol. 20(2):271-86.

Gillin, John, 1975 [1936]: *The Barama River Caribs of British Guiana*. Papers of the Peabody Museum of American archaeology and ethnology Vol. XIV, No. 2, Harvard University, Cambridge (Mass.). Millwood: Kraus Reprint Co.

Giraud, Jean-Pierre, 1996: Les Anses des Arlets: Petite Anse. *Bilan Scientifique 1995 DRAC/SRA Martinique*:14-15. Fort-de-France: Ministère de la Culture.

Giraud, Jean-Pierre, 2000: Le François: Cap Est/Pointe de la Prairie. *Bilan Scientifique 1999 DRAC/SRA Martinique*:15. Fort-de-France: Ministère de la Culture et de la Communication.

Giraud, Jean-Pierre, 2002: Histoire et problématiques de la recherche archéologique en Martinique. *Archéologie précolombienne et coloniale des Caraïbes – Actes des Congrès Nationaux des Sociétés Historiques et Scientifiques, 123ème Antilles-Guyane (Fort-de-France–Schoelcher, 4-11 avril 1998, Guadeloupe 11-17 avril 1998)*. André Delpuech, Jean-Pierre Giraud and Albert Hesse (eds):15-25. Paris: Éditions du CTHS.

Gmelch, George, and Sharon B. Gmelch, 1996: Barbados's Amerindian Past. *Anthropology Today* 12(1):11-15.

Gonzalez, Nancie L., 1988: *Sojourners of the Caribbean. Ethnogenesis and ethnohistory of the Garifuna*. Urbana and Chicago: University of Illinois Press.

Gonzalez, Nancie L., 1990: From Cannibals to Mercenaries: Carib Militarism, 1600-1840. *Journal of Anthropological Research* 46(1):25-39.

Goodwin, R. Christopher, 1979: *The prehistoric cultural ecology of St. Kitts, West Indies: a case study in island archaeology*. Ph.D. Dissertation, Arizona State University. Ann Arbor: University Microfilms Inc.

Goodwin, R. Christopher, 1980: Demographic change and the crab-shell dichotomy. *Proceedings of the 8th International Congress for the study of pre-Columbian cultures of the Lesser Antilles*. Suzanne M. Lewenstein (ed.):45-68. Anthropological Research Papers no. 22. Tempe: Arizona State University.

Gosden, Chris and Lesley Head, 1994: Landscape - a usefully ambiguous concept. *Archaeology in Oceania* 29:113-116.

Gosden, Chris and Christina Pavlides, 1994: Are islands insular? Landscape vs. seascape in the case of the Arawe Islands, Papua New Guinea. *Archaeology in Oceania* 29:162-171.

Gosselain, Olivier P., 1992: Technology and style: potters and pottery among Bafia of Cameroon. *Man*, N.S., 27:559-586.

Gros, Philippe, and Jean-Michel Martin, 1993a: Sainte-Anne: Cap Chevalier/Pointe à Pommes. *Bilan Scientifique 1992 DRAC/SRA Martinique*:53. Fort-de-France: Ministère de la Culture.

Gros, Philippe, and Jean-Michel Martin, 1993b: Sainte-Anne: Anse Trabaud. *Bilan Scientifique 1992 DRAC/SRA Martinique*:54. Fort-de-France: Ministère de la Culture.

Gros, Philippe, and Jean-Michel Martin, 1993c: Sainte-Anne: Pointe Marin. *Bilan Scientifique 1992 DRAC/SRA Martinique*:53. Fort-de-France: Ministère de la Culture.

Gros, Philippe, and Jean-Michel Martin, 1993d: Sainte-Luce: Anse Corps de Garde – Fond Banane. *Bilan Scientifique 1992 DRAC/SRA Martinique*:55. Fort-de-France: Ministère de la Culture.

Gros, Philippe, and Jean-Michel Martin, 1993e: Diamant: Terres Rouge. *Bilan Scientifique 1992 DRAC/SRA Martinique*:48. Fort-de-France: Ministère de la Culture.

Gros, Philippe, and Jean-Michel Martin, 1993f: Diamant: La Tete de Singe. *Bilan Scientifique 1992 DRAC/SRA Martinique*:49. Fort-de-France: Ministère de la Culture.

Gros, Philippe, and Jean-Michel Martin, 1993g: Diamant: Anse à l'Ane. *Bilan Scientifique 1992 DRAC/SRA Martinique*:52. Fort-de-France: Ministère de la Culture.

Grouard, Sandrine, Nathalie Serrand and Benoît Bérard, 2007: Le Vauclin – Macabou. *Bilan Scientifique 2005 DRAC/SRA Martinique*: 22-29. Fort-de-France: Ministère de la Culture et de la Communication.

Guarch-Delmonte, J. M., 2003: The first Caribbean people, Part I: The Palaeoindians in Cuba and the Circum-Caribbean. *General History of the Caribbean 1, Autochthonous Societies*. J. Sued-Badillo (ed.):93-118. Cambridge: UNESCO Publishing/Macmillan.

Gullick, Charles J.M.R., 1980: Island Carib traditions about their arrival in the Lesser Antilles. *Proceedings of the 7th International Congress for the Study of Pre-Columbian Cultures of the Lesser Antilles*. Jean Benoist, Francine-M. Mayer and Elisabeth Crosnier (eds):283-290. Montréal: Centre de Recherches Caraïbes of the Université de Montréal.

Gullick, Charles J.M.R., 1995: Communicating Caribness. In *Wolves from the Sea*, Neil. Whitehead (ed.):157-170. Leiden: KITLV Press.

Haag, William G., 1964: A comparison of Arawak sites in the Lesser Antilles (inc. Martinique, St Lucia). *Proceedings of the 1st International Congress for the study of pre-Columbian cultures of the Lesser Antilles (1)*. Martinique:10 & 2.

Haag, William G., 1965: Pottery typology in certain Lesser Antilles. *American Antiquity* 31(2):242-245.

Hackenberger, Steven, 1988: An Abstract of Archaeological Investigations by the Barbados Museum, 1986. *Journal of the Barbados Museum and Historical Society* 38(2):155-162.

Hackenberger, Steven, 1991: An Abstract of Archaeological Investigations by the Barbados Museum, 1986. *Proceedings of the 12th Congress of the International Association for Caribbean Archaeology*. Linda S. Robinson (ed.):163-173. Fort-de-France: Association Internationale d'Archéologie de la Caraïbe: Martinique.

Hage, Per, and Frank Harary, 1991: *Exchange in Oceania: a graph theoretic analysis*. Oxford [etc.]:Oxford University Press.

Hage, Per, and Frank Harary, 1996: *Island networks: communication, kinship, and classification structures in Oceania*. Structural analysis in the social sciences, Mark Granovetter (ed.). Cambridge [etc.]: Cambridge University Press.

Harlow, Vincent T., 1967[1925]: *Colonising expeditions to the West Indies and Guiana, 1623-1667*. Works issued by the Hakluyt Society, Second series, 56. Wiesbaden: Nendeln Kraus Reprint Limited.

Harrington, Mark, 1921: *Cuba before Columbus*. Indian Notes and Monographs 1(1-2). New York: Museum of the American *Indian,* Heye Foundation.

Harris, Mary H., 1991: Material Culture I – Pottery. In *Prehistoric Barbados*, Peter L. Drewett (ed.):37-100. London: Archetype Publications.

Harris, Mary H., 1993: The Barbados Archaeological Survey, 1985-1988. The pottery. *Proceedings of the 13th Congress of the International Association for Caribbean Archaeology (2)*. Edwin N. Ayubi and Jay B. Haviser (eds):524-540. Reports of the Archaeological-Anthropological Institute of the Netherlands Antilles, No. 9. Willemstad: Archaeological-Anthropological Institute of the Netherlands Antilles.

Harris, Mary H., 2000: Barbados material culture I – Pottery: technology and style. In *Prehistoric settlements in the Caribbean: fieldwork in Barbados, Tortola and the Cayman Islands*. Peter L. Drewett (ed.):51-102. London: Archetype Publications.

Harris, Mary H., 2007a: An introduction to the pottery of Carriacou. *Proceedings of the 21st Congress of the International Association for Caribbean Archaeology*. Basil Reid, L. Antonio Curet and Henri Petitjean Roget (eds):347-354. St. Augustine: University of the West Indies.

Harris, Mary H., 2007b: Prehistoric pottery from the sea and marsh edge deposits: the 1995 and 1997 excavations. In *Above Sweet Waters: Cultural and natural change at Port St Charles, Barbados, c. 1750 BC – AD 1850*. Peter L. Drewett (ed.):15-26. London: Archetype Publications.

Harris, Mary H., and Peter Drewett, 1995: Saladoid occupation at Hillcrest, Bathsheba, Barbados. *Proceedings of the 16th Congress of the International Association for Caribbean Archaeology (2)*. Conseil Régional de la Guadeloupe-Mission Archéologique et du Patrimoine (ed.):301-311. Basse Terre: Editions du Ponant.

Harris, Mary H., and Robert Hinds, 1995: Pottery from Maxwell, Barbados. *Proceedings of the 15th Congress of the International Association for Caribbean Archaeology*. Ricardo A. Alegría and Miguel Rodríguez (eds):511-522. San Juan: Centro de Estudios Avanzados de Puerto Rico y el Caribe/Fundación Puertorriqueña de las Humanidades/Universidad del Turabo.

Harris, Peter O'B., 1976: Excavation report on the ceramic site of Golden Grove, Tobago. *Proceedings of the 6th International Congress for the study of pre-Columbian cultures of the Lesser Antilles.* Ripley P. Bullen (ed.):145-157. Gainesville: Florida State Museum, University of Florida.

Harris, Peter O'B., 1980: Excavation Report: Lovers Retreat period IV, Tobago. *Proceedings of the 8th International Congress for the study of pre-Columbian cultures of the Lesser Antilles.* Suzanne M. Lewenstein (ed.):524-552. Anthropological Research Papers no. 22. Tempe: Arizona State University.

Harris, Peter O'B., 1993: A Paleo-Indian Stemmed Point from Trinidad, West Indies. *Proceedings of the 14th Congress of the International Association for Caribbean Archaeology,* Alissandra Cummins and Philippa King (eds):73-93. Bridgetown: Barbados Museum and Historical Society.

Harris, Peter O'B., 1995: Ethnotypology: the basis for a new classification of Caribbean pottery. *Proceedings of the 16th Congress of the International Association for Caribbean Archaeology (2).* Conseil Régional de la Guadeloupe-Mission Archéologique et du Patrimoine (ed.):345-356. Basse Terre: Editions du Ponant.

Harris, Peter O'B., 2001a: *Management of St. Lucia's archaeological heritage.* Unpublished manuscript.

Harris, Peter O'B., 2001b: A common format for basic archaeological data in Caribbean islands: Grenada as test example. *Proceedings of the 18th Congress of the International Association for Caribbean Archaeology.* L'Association Internationale d'Archéologie de la Caraïbe Région Guadeloupe (ed.):40-54. St. George.

Hatt, Gudmund, 1924: Archaeology of the Virgin Islands. *Proceedings of the 21st International Congress of Americanists.* Den Haag:29-50.

Haug, Gerald H., Detlef Günther, Larry C. Peterson, Daniel M. Sigman, Konrad A. Hughen and Beat Aeschlimann, 2003: Climate and the collapse of Maya civilization. *Science* 299:1731-1735.

Haviser, Jay B., 1987: *Amerindian cultural geography on Curaçao.* Ph.D. Dissertation, Faculty of Archaeology, Leiden University, Leiden.

Haviser, Jay B., 1988: *An archaeological survey of St. Martin – St. Maarten.* Reports of the Institute of Archaeology and Anthropology of the Netherlands Antilles, no. 7. Willemstad: Institute of Archaeology and Anthropology of the Netherlands Antilles.

Haviser, Jay B., 1989: A comparison of Amerindian insular adaptive strategies on Curaçao, in *Early Ceramic population lifeways and adaptive strategies in the Caribbean,* Peter E. Siegel (ed.):3-28. BAR International Series 506, Oxford: Archaeopress.

Haviser, Jay B., 1993: Preliminary Results of Test Excavations at the Hope Estate Site (SM-026), St. Martin. *Proceedings of the 13th Congress of the International Association for Caribbean Archaeology (2).* Edwin N. Ayubi and Jay B. Haviser (eds):647-666. Reports of the Archaeological-Anthropological Institute of the Netherlands Antilles, No. 9. Willemstad: Archaeological-Anthropological Institute of the Netherlands Antilles.

Haviser, Jay B., 1997: Settlement strategies in the Early Ceramic Age. In *The Indigenous People of the Caribbean.* Samuel M. Wilson (ed.):57-69. Gainesville [etc.]: University Press of Florida.

Haynes, Gary, 2005 [2002]: *The early settlement of North America: the Clovis Era*. Cambridge [etc]: Cambridge University Press.

Healy, Paul F., Erin Thornton, and Martin T. Fuess, 2005: The post-Saladoid faunal assemblage from the Coconut Hall site, Antigua, West Indies. *Proceedings of the 20th Congress of the International Association for Caribbean Archaeology (1).* Clenis Tavárez María and Manuel A. García Arévalo (eds):189-200. Santo Domingo: Museo del Hombre Dominicano y Fundación García Arévalo.

Heckenberger, Michael J., James B. Petersen and Eduardo Goés Neves, 1999: Village size and permanence in Amazonia: two archaeological examples from Brazil. *Latin American Antiquity* 10(4):353-376.

Heckenberger, Michael J., J. Christian Russell, Carlos Fausto, Joshua R. Toney, Morgan J. Schmidt, Edithe Pereira, Bruna Franchetto, Afukaka Kuikuro, 2008: Pre-Columbian Urbanism, Anthropogenic Landscapes, and the Future of the Amazon. *Science* 321:1214-1217.

Hegmon, Michelle, 1992: Archaeological Research on Style. *Annual Review of Anthropology* 21:517-536.

Heidke, James M., and Miriam T. Stark 2001: Early ceramics in southeastern Arizona: technology, iconography and function. *Eureka: the archaeology of innovation & science / Proceedings of the Twenty-Ninth Annual Conference of the Archaeological Association of the University of Calgary.* Roman Harrison, Milan Gillespie and Meaghan Peuramaki-Brown (eds):345-356. Calgary: The Archaeological Association of the University of Calgary.

Henocq, Christophe, and Francois Petit, 1995: Présentation de six sites archéologiques de Saint-Martin et de leur environnement. *Proceedings of the 16th Congress of the International Association for Caribbean Archaeology (1).* Conseil Régional de la Guadeloupe-Mission Archéologique et du Patrimoine (ed.):300-315. Basse Terre: Editions du Ponant.

Higgs, Eric, and Claudio Vita-Finzi, 1972: Prehistoric economies: a territorial approach. In *Papers in Economic Prehistory.* E. Higgs (ed.):27-36. Cambridge: Cambridge University Press.

Hilditch, Jillian Ruth, 2008: *Reconstruction of technological choice, social practice and networks of exchange from a ceramic perspective in the Middle Bronze Age Cyclades.* Unpublished Ph.D. dissertation, Department of Archaeology, University of Exeter, Exeter.

Hinds, Robert, and Mary Hill Harris, 1995: Pottery from Mustique. *Proceedings of the 15th Congress of the International Association for Caribbean Archaeology.* Ricardo A. Alegría and Miguel Rodríguez (eds):459-469. San Juan: Centro de Estudios Avanzados de Puerto Rico y el Caribe/Fundación Puertorriqueña de las Humanidades/Universidad del Turabo.

Hinds, Ronald, Bruce Jardine and Karl Watson, 2000: A Saladoid site on Spring Garden: a preliminary report. *Journal of the Barbados Museum and Historical Society* 46:90-105.

Hodder, Ian, 1982: *Symbols in action*. London: Routledge.

Hodell, David A., Jason H. Curtis, Antonia Higuera-Gundy, Mark Brenner, Michael W. Binford and Kathleen T. Dorsey, 1991: Reconstruction of Caribbean climate change over the past 10,500 years. *Nature* 352:790-793.

Hodell, David A., Mark Brenner, Jason H. Curtis and Thomas Guilderson, 2001: Solar forcing of drought frequency in the Maya lowlands. *Science* 292:1367-1370.

Hodges, Henry, 1995: *Artifacts - An Introduction to Early Materials And Technology*. London: Gerald Duckworth & Co Ltd.

Hoff, Berend J., 1995: Language contact, war, and Amerindian historical tradition. The special case of the Island Carib. In *Wolves from the Sea*, Neil. Whitehead (ed.):37-59. Leiden: KITLV Press.

Hofman, Corinne L., 1987: *Toponiemenstudie aan de hand van de woordenboeken van Père R. Breton*. Unpublished manuscript. Leiden: Faculty of Archaeology, Leiden University.

Hofman, Corinne L., 1993: *The Native Population of Pre-Columbian Saba. Part One. Pottery Styles and their Interpretations*. Ph.D. dissertation, Faculty of Archaeology, Leiden University, Leiden.

Hofman, Corinne L., 1995: Terre-de-Bas: Grande Anse. *Bilan Scientifique 1994*. Service Régional de l'Archéologie. Basse-Terre: Direction Régionale des Affaires Culturelles de Guadeloupe:34.

Hofman, Corinne L., 1999: Hope Estate: Pottery. *Archaeological investigations on St. Martin (Lesser Antilles). The sites of Norman Estate, Anse des Pères, and Hope Estate. With a contribution to the 'La Hueca problem'*. Corinne L. Hofman and Menno L. P. Hoogland (eds): 149-187. Archaeological Studies Leiden University 4. Leiden: Faculty of Archaeology, Leiden University.

Hofman, Corinne L., Arie Boomert, Alistair J. Bright, Menno L.P. Hoogland, Sebastiaan Knippenberg, and Alice V.M. Samson, in press: *Ties with the 'Homelands': archipelagic interaction and the enduring role of the continental American mainland in the pre-Columbian Lesser Antilles*. In *Islands in the Stream: Interisland and Continental Interaction in the Caribbean*, L. Antonio Curet and Mark W. Hauser (eds). Tuscaloosa: University of Alabama Press.

Hofman, Corinne L., and Eric M. Branford, 2009: *Lavoutte revisited: preliminary results of the 2009 rescue excavations at Cas-En- Bas, St. Lucia*. Paper presented at the 23rd Congress of the International Association for Caribbean Archaeology, Jolly Beach, Antigua.

Hofman, Corinne L., and Alistair J. Bright, 2004: From Suazoid to Folk Pottery: pottery manufacturing traditions in a changing social and cultural environment on St. Lucia. *New West Indian Guide* 78(1-2):73-104.

Hofman, Corinne L., Alistair J. Bright, Arie Boomert and Sebastiaan Knippenberg, 2007: Island rhythms: the web of social relationships and interaction networks in the Lesser Antillean archipelago between 400 BC and AD 1492. *Latin American Antiquity* 18(3):243-268.

Hofman, Corinne L., Alistair J. Bright and Menno L.P. Hoogland, 2006: Archipelagic resource procurement and mobility in the Northern Lesser Antilles: the view from a 3000-year-old tropical forest campsite on Saba, *Journal of Island and Coastal Archaeology* 1(2):145-164.

Hofman, Corinne L., Alistair J. Bright, William F. Keegan, and Menno L.P. Hoogland, 2008: Attractive ideas, desirable goods: examining the Late Ceramic Age relationships between Greater and Lesser Antillean societies. *Journal of Island and Coastal Archaeology* 3(1):17-34.

Hofman, Corinne L., André Delpuech, Menno L.P. Hoogland, and Maaike S. De Waal, 2004: Late Ceramic Age survey of the northeastern islands of the Guadeloupean archipelago. In *Late Ceramic Age Societies in the Eastern Caribbean*. André Delpuech and Corinne L. Hofman (eds):159-181. BAR International Series 1273. Oxford: Archaeopress.

Hofman, Corinne L., and Menno L.P. Hoogland (eds), 1999: *Archaeological investigations on St. Martin (Lesser Antilles). The sites of Norman Estate, Anse des Pères, and Hope Estate. With a contribution to the 'La Hueca problem'*. Archaeological Studies Leiden University 4. Leiden: Faculty of Archaeology, Leiden University.

Hofman, Corinne L., and Menno L.P. Hoogland, 2004: Social Dynamics and Change in the Northern Lesser Antilles. In *Late Ceramic Age Societies in the Eastern Caribbean*. André Delpuech and Corinne L. Hofman (eds):1-22. BAR International Series 1273. Oxford: Archaeopress.

Hofman, Corinne L., and Menno L.P. Hoogland, 2009a: *The Lavoutte Site (Cas-En- Bas), St. Lucia*. Manuscript on file, Faculty of Archaeology, Leiden University, Leiden.

Hofman, Corinne L., and Menno L.P. Hoogland, 2009b: *Interim Report on the Results of the 2009 (May and June) Rescue Excavations at the Lavoutte Site (Cas-En- Bas), St. Lucia*. Online resource, accessed 6 February 2010: http://media.leidenuniv.nl/legacy/lavoutte-interim-report-2009.pdf.

Hofman, Corinne L., Menno L.P. Hoogland, and André Delpuech, 1999: The presence of a Huecan assemblage on Guadeloupe: the case of Morel I. *Archaeological investigations on St-Martin (Lesser Antilles): the sites of Norman Estate, Anse des Pères and Hope Estate, with a contribution to the 'la Hueca problem'*. Corinne L. Hofman and Menno L.P. Hoogland (eds): 303-312. Archaeological Studies Leiden University 4. Leiden: Faculty of Archaeology, Leiden University.

Hofman, Corinne L., Menno L.P. Hoogland and André Delpuech, 2001: *Guadeloupe, Saint-François, Anse à la Gourde. Fouille programmée pluriannuelle 1995-2000, Rapport de synthèse 2000*. Saint-François/Leiden: Conseil Régional de la Guadeloupe/Municipalité de Saint-François/Direction Régionale des Affaires Culturelles de Guadeloupe/Maison René Ginouvès, E. P. 2063 Archéologie des Amériques/Leiden University, Faculty of Archaeology.

Hofman, Corinne L., Menno L.P. Hoogland and William F. Keegan, 2004: *Archaeological Reconnaissance at Saint Lucia, West Indies. 4-18-2004 to 5-12-2004 Annual Report*. Online resource,accessed 6 June 2008: http://www.archaeology.leiden.edu/general/img/st.luciareport2004_tcm45-50166.pdf

Hofman, Corinne L., Menno L.P. Hoogland and Annelou L. van Gijn (eds), 2008a: *Crossing the Borders: New Methods and Techniques in the Study of Archaeological Materials from the Caribbean*. Tuscaloosa: The University of Alabama Press.

Hofman, Corinne L., Menno L.P. Hoogland and Annelou L. van Gijn, 2008b: Crossing disciplinary boundaries and national borders. New methods and techniques in the study of archaeological materials from the Caribbean. In *Crossing the Borders: New Methods and Techniques in the Study of Archaeological Materials from the Caribbean*. Corinne L. Hofman, Menno L.P. Hoogland and Annelou L. van Gijn (eds):1-16. Tuscaloosa: The University of Alabama Press.

Hofman, Corinne L., and Loe Jacobs, 2003 (2000/2001): The dynamics of technology, function and style: a study of early Ceramic Age pottery from the Caribbean. *Newsletter Department of Pottery Technology* 18/19:7-43.

Holmes, William H., 1907: Report of the Chief. *25th Annual Report of the Bureau of American Ethnology to the Secretary of the Smithsonian Institution 1903/1904*.Washington: Government Printing Office.

Honychurch, Lennox, 1997a: *Carib to Creole: contact and culture exchange*. D.Phil. Thesis, Oxford University, Oxford.

Honychurch, Lennox, 1997b: Crossroads in the Caribbean: a site of Encounter and Exchange on Dominica. *World Archaeology* 28(3):291-304.

Honychurch, Lennox, 2001: *Ceremonial seat found*. Online article: http://lennoxhonychurch.com/article.cfm?id=362, accessed 17 October 2006.

Honychurch, Lennox, 2006: 'To have a garden is to be a man': Caribs and the transformation of landscape. *Islands, forests and gardens in the Caribbean: conservation and conflict in environmental history*, Robert S. Anderson, Richard Grove and Karis Hiebert (eds):19-41. Warwick University Caribbean Studies. Oxford: Macmillan Caribbean.

Honychurch, Lennox, n.d. *Ancient bowls found*, Online article: http://www.lennoxhonychurch.com/article.cfm?id=391, accessed 17 October 2006.

Hoogland, Menno L.P., 1995: Sainte-Anne: Pointe Helleux. *Bilan Scientifique 1994*:32. Service Régional de l'Archéologie. Basse-Terre: Direction Régionale des Affaires Culturelles de Guadeloupe.

Hoogland, Menno L.P., 1996: *In search of the native population of pre-Columbian Saba. Part 2: Settlements in their natural and social environments*. PhD dissertation, Faculty of Archaeology, Leiden University, Leiden.

Hoogland, Menno L.P., Alistair J. Bright, and Corinne L. Hofman, in prep: *Continuing Rescue Excavations at Argyle, St. Vincent (January 2010)*. Unpublished manuscript, Faculty of Archaeology, Leiden University, Leiden.

Hoogland, Menno L.P., and Hofman, Corinne L., 1993: Kelbey's Ridge 2, a 14th century Taino settlement on Saba, Netherlands Antilles. *Analecta Praehistorica Leidensia* 26:163-181.

Hoopes, John W., and William K. Barnett, 1995: The shape of early pottery studies. In *The emergence of pottery: technology and innovation in ancient societies*. William K. Barnett and John W. Hoopes (eds):1-7. Smithsonian Series in Archaeological Inquiry, Robert McC. Adams and Bruce D. Smith (eds). Washington and London: Smithsonian Institution Press.

Hornborg, Alf, 2004: "Neolithization", ethnogenesis, and material culture: a view from Amazonia. In *Coast to Coast – Arrival: results and reflections. Proceedings of the Final Coast to Coast Conference 1-5 October 2002 in Falköping, Sweden*. Helena Knutsson (ed.):309-344. Uppsala: Societas Archaeologica Upsaliensis.

Huckerby, Thomas, 1914: Petroglyphs of St. Vincent, British West Indies. *American Anthropologist* 16(2):238-244.

Huckerby, Thomas, 1921: Petroglyphs of Grenada and a Recently Discovered Petroglyph in St Vincent. *Indian Notes & Monographs*, Vol 1, No 3. New York: Museum of the American Indian, Heye Foundation.

Hughes, Griffith, 1750: *The Natural History of Barbados in Ten Books*. London.

Hulme, Peter, 1986: *Colonial Encounters: Europe and the Native Caribbean 1492-1797*. London and New York: Routledge.

Hulme, Peter and Neil. L. Whitehead, 1992: *Wild Majesty: encounters with Caribs from Columbus to the present day*. Oxford: Clarendon Press.

Hutchinson, Gem, Sarah George and Christopher James, 2000: *A description of the reef fishery of Laborie, St. Lucia. People and the Sea, a study of coastal livelihoods in Laborie, St. Lucia.* Project document no. 1. Caribbean Natural Resource Institute (CANARI). Online resource: http://www.canari.org/laborie.pdf, accessed 23 September 2007.

Huyghues Belrose, Vincent, 1996: Les sites archéologiques à caractère religieux dans l'histoire de le Martinique. *Bilan Scientifique 1995 DRAC/SRA Martinique*: 31-34. Fort-de-France: Ministère de la Culture.

Im Thurn, Everard F., 1883: Notes on West Indian Stone-Implements, (Illustrated). No.2. *Timehri* 2:252-271.

Irwin, Geoffrey, 1974: The emergence of a Central Place in Coastal Papuan prehistory: a theoretical approach. *Mankind* 9:268-272.

Irwin, Geoffrey, 1992: *The prehistoric exploration and colonisation of the Pacific*. Cambridge: Cambridge University Press.

Isendoorn, A.J. Daan, Corinne L. Hofman and Mathijs Booden, 2008: Back to the source: provenance areas of clays and temper materials of pre-Columbian Caribbean ceramics. *Journal of Caribbean Archaeology* (Special Publication #2):15-24.

Jackson, Ivor, 2004: *Environmental Investigation and Cataloguing, St. Vincent Cross Country Road Project (Final Report)*. Ivor Jackson & Associates, St. John's. Online resource: http://www.gov.vc/Govt/Files/cross_country_final_report.pdf, accessed 17 October 2006.

Jacobson, Katarina, 2002: *Techniques de façonnage et étude de la pâte de la Cedrosan-Saladoïde du site de l'Embouchure de Baillif (Basse-Terre, Guadeloupe)*. Dossier de céramologie. Paris: Université de Paris I.

Jane, C. (ed.), 1988 (1930/1933): *The four voyages of Columbus*, New York: Dover Publications, Inc.

Jesse, Charles, 1953: A note on Bequia: cradle of the Black Carib. *Caribbean Quarterly* 3(1):55-56.

Jesse, Charles, 1963: The Spanish Cedula of December 23, 1511, on the subject of the Caribs. *Caribbean Quarterly* 9(3):22-32.

Jesse, Charles, 1966: An Houre Glasse of Indian News. *Caribbean Quarterly* 12(1):46-67.

Jesse, Charles, 1967: *The Amerindians in St. Lucia (Iouanalao)*. Castries, St. Lucia, St. Lucia Archaeological and Historical Society.

Jesse, Charles, 1973: Petroglyph and rock-cut basins at Dauphin, St Lucia. *Proceedings of the 4th International Congress for the study of pre-Columbian cultures of the Lesser Antilles.* Castries: St. Lucia Archaeological and Historical Society:33-34.

John, C. Lyndon, 2004: *Migrant birds records for Saint Lucia, West Indies.* Online resource: http://www.slubiodiv.org/SLU_Migrant_Birds_Study.pdf, accessed 8th October 2008.

Johnson, Allen W. and Timothy Earle, 1987: *The evolution of human societies: from foraging group to agrarian state.* Stanford: Stanford University Press.

Johnston, Kevin J., 2002: Protrusion, Bioturbation, and Settlement Detection During Surface Survey: The Lowland Maya Case. *Journal of Archaeological Method and Theory* 9(1):1-67.

Jönsson Marquet, Sofia, 2002: *L'art précolombien des Petites Antilles: l'iconographie comparée des pétroglyphes et de la céramique.* Mémoire de DEA. Université Paris I: Panthéon-Sorbonne, Paris.

Jönsson Marquet, Sofia, 2009: Contextual analysis of the Lesser Antillean Windward Islands petroglyphs: methods and results. In *Rock art of the Caribbean.* Michele H. Hayward, Lesley-Gail Atkinson and Michael A. Cinquino (eds):147-160. Tuscaloosa: The University of Alabama Press.

Josselin de Jong, J.P.B. de, 1947: *Archaeological material from Saba and St. Eustatius, Lesser Antilles.* Mededelingen van het Rijksmuseum voor Volkenkunde 1. Leiden: Brill.

Joyce, Thomas A., 1907: Prehistoric antiquities from the Antilles, in the British Museum. *The Journal of the Royal Anthropological Institute of Great Britain and Ireland* XXXVII:402-419.

Joyce, Thomas A., 1916: *Central American and West Indian Archaeology.* London: Phillip Lee Warner.

Kameneff, Léonid, 1995: Sainte-Anne: Savane des Pétrifications. *Bilan Scientifique 1994 DRAC/SRA Martinique*:23-24. Fort-de-France: Ministère de la Culture et de la Communication.

Kantner, John, 2008: The archaeology of regions: from discrete analytical toolkit to ubiquitous spatial perspective. *Journal of Archaeological Research* 16:37-81.

Kappers, Michiel, Scott M. Fitzpatrick and Quetta Kaye, 2007: Automated data collection and 3D modelling of archaeological sites: examining the prehistory and destruction of Grand Bay in Carriacou. *Proceedings of the 21st Congress of the International Association for Caribbean Archaeology.* Basil Reid, L. Antonio Curet and Henri Petitjean Roget (eds):81-90. St. Augustine: University of the West Indies.

Kaye, Quetta, Michiel Kappers and Scott M. Fitzpatrick, 2003: Archaeological survey of Carriacou, West Indies. *Proceedings of the 20th Congress of the International Association for Caribbean Archaeology (1).* Clenis Tavárez María and Manuel A. García Arévalo (eds):391-398. Santo Domingo: Museo del Hombre Dominicano y Fundación García Arévalo.

Kaye, Quetta, Scott Fitzpatrick and Michiel Kappers, 2004: A Preliminary Report on the Excavation at Grand Bay, Carriacou, West Indies, June 28th-July 31st, 2004. *Proceedings of the Institute of Archaeology* 15:84-91.

Kaye, Quetta, Scott Fitzpatrick and Michiel Kappers, 2005: Continued Archaeological Investigations at Grand Bay, Carriacou, West Indies (May 23rd-July 22nd 2005), and the Impact of Hurricanes and Other Erosive Processes. *Proceedings of the Institute of Archaeology* 16:108-114.

Kayser, Olivier, 2001: Saint-Pierre: Centre de Découverte de la Terre. *Bilan Scientifique 2000 DRAC/SRA Martinique*:21-23. Fort-de-France: Ministère de la Culture.

Keegan, William F., 1985: *Dynamic Horticulturalists: Population Expansion in the Prehistoric Bahamas*. Ph.D. dissertation, Department of Anthropology, UCLA. Ann Arbor:UMI.

Keegan, William F., 1991: *Archaeology at Pearls, Grenada: The 1990 field season*. Miscellaneous Project Report Number 47, Florida Museum of Natural History. Online resource, accessed 12 December 2007. http://www.flmnh.ufl.edu/caribarch/grenada.htm.

Keegan, William F., 1992: *The People Who Discovered Columbus: The Prehistory of the Bahamas*. Gainesville: University Press of Florida.

Keegan, William F., 1995a: Modeling dispersal in the prehistoric West Indies. *World Archaeology* 26:400-420.

Keegan, William F., 1995b: Recent sea level fluctuation and population movements in the West Indies. *Proceedings of the 16th Congress of the International Association for Caribbean Archaeology (1)*. Conseil Régional de la Guadeloupe-Mission Archéologique et du Patrimoine (ed.):95-104. Basse Terre: Editions du Ponant.

Keegan, William F., 1996: Columbus was a Cannibal: Myth and the First Encounters. In *The Lesser Antilles in the Age of European Expansion*. Robert L. Paquette and Stanley L. Engerman (eds):17-32. Gainesville: University Press of Florida.

Keegan, William F., 2000: West Indian Archaeology. 3. Ceramic Age. *Journal of Archaeological Research* 8(2):135-167.

Keegan, William F., 2001: Archaeological investigations on Ile à Rat: avoid the –oid. *Proceedings of the 18th Congress of the International Association for Caribbean Archaeology*. L'Association Internationale d'Archéologie de la Caraïbe Région Guadeloupe (ed.):233-239. St. George.

Keegan, William F., 2004: Islands of Chaos. In *Late Ceramic Age Societies in the Eastern Caribbean*. André Delpuech and Corinne L. Hofman (eds):33-44. BAR International Series 1273. Oxford: Archaeopress.

Keegan, William F., 2008: Epilogue: the correct answer requires the right question (and the technology to back it up). *Crossing the Borders: New Methods and Techniques in the Study of Archaeological Materials from the Caribbean*. Corinne L. Hofman, Menno L.P. Hoogland and Annelou L. van Gijn (eds):226-231.Tuscaloosa: The University of Alabama Press.

Keegan, William F., and Jared Diamond, 1987: Colonization of Islands by Humans: A Biogeographical Perspective. In *Advances in Archaeological Method and Theory*, Vol. 10, Michael B. Schiffer (ed.):49-92. San Diego: Academic Press.

Keegan, William F., Scott M. Fitzpatrick, Kathleen Sullivan Sealey, Michelle J. LeFebvre, and Peter T. Sinelli, 2008: The Role of Small Islands in Marine Subsistence Strategies: Case Studies from the Caribbean. *Human Ecology* 36(5):635-654.

Keegan, William F., Corinne L. Hofman and Menno L.P. Hoogland, 2002: *Archaeological Reconnaissance of Saint Lucia, West Indies. 4-28-2002 to 5-19-2002 Report of the FLMNH/ Leiden Expedition.* Online resource: http://www.archaeology.leiden.edu/general/img/st_lucia_2002_tcm45-50167.pdf, accessed 6 June 2008.

Keegan, William F., Corinne L. Hofman and Menno L.P. Hoogland, 2003: *Archaeological Reconnaissance on Saint Lucia, West Indies. 17-04-2003 to 25-05-2003 Annual Report.* Online resource: http://www.archaeology.leiden.edu/general/img/stluciareport2003_tcm45-50200.pdf, accessed 6 June 2008.

Keegan, William F. and Morgan D. Maclachlan, 1989: The Evolution of Avunculocal Chiefdoms: A Reconstruction of Taino Kinship and Politics. *American Anthropologist* 91:613-630.

Keegan, William F. and Reniel Rodríguez Ramos, 2005: Sin Rodeos. *El Caribe Arqueológico* 8:9-13.

Kingsley, Robert G., 1985: *Kin groups and mortuary practices – ethnographic implications for archaeology*. Ph.D. dissertation, Michigan State University, East Lansing.

Kirby, I.A. Earle, 1970: The pre-Columbian stone monuments of St. Vincent. *Proceedings of the 3rd International Congress for the study of pre-Columbian cultures of the Lesser Antilles*, St. George, Grenada:114-128.

Kirby, I.A. Earle, 1974: The Cayo pottery of St. Vincent – a pre-Calivigny series. *Proceedings of the 5th International Congress for the Study of Pre-Columbian Cultures of the Lesser Antilles.* St. John's: The Antigua Archaeological Society:61-64.

Kirby, I.A. Earle, 1978: Some notes of interest to the archaeology of the Antilles. *Proceedings of the 7th International Congress for the study of pre-Columbian cultures of the Lesser Antilles.* Jean Benoist, Francine-M. Mayer and Elisabeth Crosnier (eds):65-68. Montréal: Centre de Recherches Caraïbes of the Université de Montréal.

Kirby, I.A. Earle, 1980: The Carib incursion into the Greater Antilles. *Proceedings of the 8th International Congress for the study of pre-Columbian cultures of the Lesser Antilles.* Suzanne M. Lewenstein (ed.):593-596. Anthropological Research Papers no. 22. Tempe: Arizona State University.

Kirby, I. Earle, and C.I. Martin, 1972: *The rise and fall of the Black Caribs.* Online resource: http://www.svgonline.com/carib_history.pdf. Accessed 10 September 2008.

Kirch, Patrick. V., 1997: *The Lapita Peoples: ancestors of the Oceanic world.* Oxford: Blackwell Publishers.

Kirch, Patrick. V., 2000: *On the Road of the Winds: An Archaeological History of the Pacific Islands before European Contact.* Berkeley: The University of California Press.

Knippenberg, Sebastiaan, 2006: *Stone artefact production and exchange among the northern Lesser Antilles.* Ph.D. dissertation, Faculty of Archaeology. Leiden University, Leiden.

Kocks Consult GmbH, 2008: *Argyle International Airport Project Environmental Impact Assessment, Final Report.* Koblenz: Kocks Consult GmbH. Online manuscript: http://www.svgiadc.com/PDF/FinalReport_05_08.pdf, accessed 23 February 2010.

Kowalewski, Stephen A., 2008: Regional settlement pattern studies. *Journal of Archaeological Research* 16:225-285.

Kozłowski, Janusz K., 1974: *Pre-Ceramic cultures in the Caribbean.* Krakow: Uniwersytetu Jagiellonskiego.

Kremser, Manfred, and Karl R. Wernhart (eds), 1986: *Research in Ethnography and Ethnohistory of St.Lucia: A Preliminary Report.* Horn/Wien: Ferdinand Berger & Söhne.

Labat, Jean-Baptiste, 1979[1722]: *Voyage aux îles de l'Amérique: Antilles, 1693-1705.* Daniel Radford (ed.). Paris: Seghers.

Laffoon, Jason, and Bart de Vos, in press: Diverse origins, similar diets: an integrated isotopic perspective from Anse à la Gourde, Guadeloupe. *Leiden in the Caribbean IV Conference Proceedings.* Corinne L. Hofman and Anne v. Duijvenbode (eds). Leiden: Sidestone Press.

Lange, Frederick W., and Jerome S. Handler, 1980: Archaeology of Mapps Cave: a contribution to the prehistory of Barbados. *Journal Virgin Islands Archaeological Society* 9:3-17.

Lathrap, Donald, 1970: *The Upper Amazon.* Ancient Peoples and Places, Glyn Daniel (ed.). New York and Washington: Praeger Publications.

Laurence, Keith O., 1967: Note of Iere, the Amerindian name for Trinidad. *Caribbean Quarterly* 13(3):45-51.

Le Breton, Adrien, 1998[1722]: *Historic account of Saint Vincent, the Indian Youroumayn, the island of the Karaybes, 1662-1736.* Kingstown: The Mayreau Environmental Development Organization.

L'Etang, Thierry, 2004: Toponymie indigène des Antilles. *Les Civilisations Amérindiennes des Petites Antilles,* Cécile Celma (ed.):32-56. Fort-de-France: Imprimerie Caraïb Ediprinte.

Lemonnier, Pierre, 1986: The study of material culture today: toward an anthropology of technical systems. *Journal of Anthropological Archaeology* 5:147–186.

Lemonnier, Pierre, 1993: Introduction. In *Technological choices: transformation in material cultures since the Neolithic.* P. Lemonnier (ed):1-35. London: Routledge.

Lévi-Strauss, Claude, 1966: *The savage mind.* London: Weidenfeld & Nicholson.

Ligon, Richard, 2003[1657]: *The True and Exact History of the Island of Barbadoes.* J. Edward Hutson (ed.) St. Michael: The Barbados National Trust.

Linné, S., 1929: *Darien in the past: the archaeology of Eastern Panama and North-Western Colombia.* Göteborg: Elanders Boktryckeri Aktiebolag.

Loftfield, Thomas C., 1993: The Bendeshe/Byde Mill Sugar Factory in Barbados: The Ceramic Evidence. *Proceedings of the 14th Congress of the International Association for Caribbean Archaeology.* Alissandra Cummins and Philippa King (eds):408-415. Bridgetown: Barbados Museum and Historical Society.

Longacre, William A. (ed.), 1991: *Ceramic Ethnoarchaeology.* Tucson: University of Arizona Press.

Lorimer, Joyce, (ed.), 2006: *Sir Walter Ralegh's* Discoverie of Guiana. Works issued by the Hakluyt Society, Third Series, No. 15. W.F. Ryan and Michael Brennan (eds). London: Ashgate.

Lovén, Sven, 1935: *Origins of the Tainan culture, West Indies.* Göteborg: Elanders Boktryckeri Aktiebolag.

Lundberg, Emily R., 1980: Old and new problems in the study of Antillean aceramic traditions. *Proceedings of the 8th International Congress for the study of pre-Columbian cultures of the Lesser Antilles*. Suzanne M. Lewenstein (ed.):131-138. Anthropological Research Papers no. 22. Tempe: Arizona State University.

Lundberg, Emily R., 2002: Tutu pottery and ceramic chronology (Chapter 5). In *The Tutu archaeological village site: a multidisciplinary case study in human adaptation*, Elizabeth Righter (ed.):166-198. London: Routledge.

MacArthur, Robert H., and Edmund O. Wilson, 1967: *The Theory of Island Biogeography*. Princeton: Princeton University Press.

Mason, J. Alden, 1941: A large archaeological site at Capá, Utuado, with notes on other Porto Rico sites visited in 1914-1915. *Scientific Survey of Porto Rico and the Virgin Islands* 18(2):209-265.

Mattioni, Mario, 1973: Communication sur les pétroglyphes de la Martinique. *Proceedings of the 4th International Congress for the study of pre-Columbian cultures of the Lesser Antilles*. Castries:25-32.

Mattioni, Mario, 1980: Salvage excavations at the Fond-Brulé site (northeast coast of Martinique). *Proceedings of the 8th International Congress for the study of pre-Columbian cultures of the Lesser Antilles*. Suzanne M. Lewenstein (ed.):553-566. Anthropological Research Papers no. 22. Tempe: Arizona State University.

Mattioni, Mario, 1982: *Salvage excavations at the Fond Brûlé site, Martinique: final report*. University of Manitoba Anthropology Papers 27. Winnipeg: University of Manitoba.

Mattioni, Mario, 1984: *Le site archéologique de Vivé*. Direction des Antiquités de la Martinique. Fort de France:Imprimerie Antillaise Saint-Paul.

Mattioni, Mario, 1990: Objets de Parure Issus de la Fouille de Sondage sur le Site de L'Anse Trabaud (Martinique). *Proceedings of the 11th Congress of the International Association for Caribbean Archaeology*. Agamemnon Gus Pantel Tekakis, Iraida Vargas Arenas and Mario Sanoja Obediente (eds):108-111. La Fundación Arqueológica, Antropológica y Historica De Puerto Rico/La Universidad De Puerto Rico/Recato De Rio Piedras/United States Department Of Agriculture/Forest Service: San Juan.

Mattioni, Mario, and Ripley P. Bullen, 1970: A Chronological Chart for the Lesser Antilles. *Proceedings of the 3rd International Congress for the study of pre-Columbian cultures of the Lesser Antilles*. St. George, Grenada:1-3.

Mattioni, Mario, and Maurice Nicolas, 1972: *Art précolombien de la Martinique*. Musée Départmental de la Martinique, Fort-de-France, Martinique. Paris: Horizons Caraïbes.

McKusick, Marshall B., 1960: *Distribution of ceramic styles in the Lesser Antilles, West Indies*, Ph.D. Yale University, Ann Arbor: University Microfilms Inc.

McKusick, Marshall B., n.d.: *Vieille Case site, Dominica*. Unpublished manuscript.

Mead, Margaret, 1957: Introduction to Polynesia as a laboratory for the development of models in the study of cultural evolution. *Journal of the Polynesian society* 66(2):145.

Meggers, Betsy, and Clifford Evans, 1978: Lowland South America and the Antilles. In *Ancient Native Americans*, Jesse D. Jennings (ed.):543-591. San Francisco: Freeman.

Meltzer, David J., Donald K. Grayson, Gerardo Ardila, Alex W. Barker, Dena F. Dincauze, C. Vance Haynes, Francisco Mena, Lautaro Nunez, and Dennis J. Stanford, 1997: On the Pleistocene Antiquity of Monte Verde, Southern Chile. *American Antiquity* 62(4):659-663.

Mestre, Mickaël, Fabrice Casagrande and Rosemond Martias, 2007: Le Lorrain – Vivé. *Bilan Scientifique 2005*. Fort-de-France: Ministère de la Culture et de la Communication.

Moffitt, John F., and Santiago Sebastián, 1998: *O Brave New People: the European invention of the American Indian*. Albuquerque: University of New Mexico Press.

Moore, Carmella C. and A. Kimball Romney, 1994: Material culture, geographic propinquity, and linguistic affiliation on the north coast of New Guinea: A reanalysis of Welsch, Terrell, and Nadolski (1992). *American Anthropologist* 96:370-392.

Moravetz, Iosif, 2005: *Imaging adornos: classification and iconography of Saladoid adornos from St. Vincent, West Indies*. BAR International Series 1445. Oxford: John and Erica Hedges Ltd/Archaeopress.

Moreau, Jean-Pierre, 1988: *Guide des trésors archéologiques sous-marins des Petites Antilles d'après les archives anglaises, espagnoles et francaises des XVIe, XVIIe, XVIIIe siècles*. Clamart: Editions Jean-Pierre Moreau.

Moreau, Jean-Pierre, 1992: *Les Petites Antilles de Christophe Colomb à Richelieu*. Paris: Éditions Karthala.

Morsink, Joost, 2006: *(Re-)Constructing Constructions: quotidian life and social practice at Anse à la Gourde*. MPhil Thesis, Faculty of Archaeology, Leiden University, Leiden.

Mouer, L.D., and F.H. Smith, 2001: Revisiting Mapps Cave: Amerindian and Probable Slave Occupations of Sinkhole & Cavern, Barbados. *Proceedings of the 18th Congress of the International Association for Caribbean Archaeology*. L'Association Internationale d'Archéologie de la Caraïbe Région Guadeloupe (ed.):301-307. St. George.

Murphy, Reg, and Healy 1995: Paleoecology of the Muddy Bay (Ph-14) site, Antigua: preliminary report. *Proceedings of the 16th Congress of the International Association for Caribbean Archaeology (1)*. Conseil Régional de la Guadeloupe-Mission Archéologique et du Patrimoine (ed.):275-286. Basse Terre: Editions du Ponant.

Murphy, Reg, n.d.: *Image of legged griddle from Antigua*. Online resource: http://www.archaeologyantigua.org/artefacts_leggedgriddle.htm, accessed 8 August 2008.

Myers, Robert A., 1978: Ethnohistorical vs. ecological considerations: the case of Dominica's Amerindians. *Proceedings of the 7th International Congress for the study of pre-Columbian cultures of the Lesser Antilles*. Jean Benoist, Francine-M. Mayer and Elisabeth Crosnier (eds):325-341. Montréal: Centre de Recherches Caraïbes of the Université de Montréal.

Newsom, Lee A., and Elizabeth S. Wing, 2004: *On land and sea: Native American uses of biological resources in the West Indies*. Tuscaloosa & London: The University of Alabama Press.

Nicholl, John, 1607: *An Houre Glasse of Indian Newes, or a true and tragicall discourse, shewing the most lamentable miseries, and distressed Calamities indured by 67 Englishmen, which were sent for a supply to the planting in Guiana in the yeare 1605. Who not finding the saide place, were for want of victuall, left a shore in Saint Lucia, and Island of Caniballs, or Men-*

eaters in the West-Indyes, under the Conduct of Captain Sen-Johns, of all which said number, onely a 11. are supposed to be still living, whereof 4. are lately returnd into England. London. Unpublished manuscript.

Ober, Frederick A., 1899 [1879]: *Camps in the Caribbees*. Boston: Lee and Shepard Publishers.

Oberg, Kalervo, 1955: Types of Social Structure among the Lowland Tribes of South and Central America. *American Anthropologist* 57:472-487.

Oka, Rahul, and Chapurukha M. Kusimba, 2008: The Archaeology of Trading Systems, Part 1: Towards a New Trade Synthesis. *Journal of Archaeological Research* 16:339–395.

Oliver, José R., 1999: The 'La Hueca Problem' in Puerto Rico & the Caribbean: Old problems, new perspectives, possible solutions. *Archaeological Investigations on St. Martin (Lesser Antilles)*. Corinne L. Hofman and Menno L.P. Hoogland (eds):253-297. Archaeological Studies Leiden University 4. Leiden: Faculty of Archaeology.

Oliver, José R., 2008: *Caciques and Cemí Idols: the web spun by Taíno rulers between Hispaniola and Boriquén*. Tuscaloosa: The University of Alabama Press.

Oliver, José R., n.d.: *Taima Taima. A 13,000 years old mastodon kill site in western Venezuela*. Online resource. http://www.bradshawfoundation.com/journey/taima-taima-text.html, accessed 8 August 2008.

Pagán Jiménez, Jaime, Miguel A. Rodríguez López, Luis A. Chanlatte Baik and Yvonne Narganes Storde, 2005: La temprana introducción y uso de algunas plantas domésticas, silvestres y cultivos en Las Antillas precolombinas: Una primera revaloración desde la perspectiva del "arcaico" de Vieques y Puerto Rico. *Diálogo Antropológico* 3(10):7-33.

Palmatary, Helen C., 1950: *The pottery of Marajo Island, Brazil*. Philadelphia: American Philosophical Society.

Parkinson, William A., 2006: Tribal boundaries: Stylistic variability and social boundary maintenance during the transition to the Copper Age on the Great Hungarian Plain. *Journal of Anthropological Archaeology* 25:33-58.

Patton, Mark, 1996: *Islands in Time: Island Sociogeography and Mediterranean Prehistory*. London & New York: Routledge.

Percy, George, 1969 [1608]: Observations gathered out of a Discourse of the Plantation of the Southerne Colonie in Virginia by the English, 1606. Written by that Honorable Gentleman Master George Percy. *The Jamestown Voyages under the First Charter 1606-1609, Vol. 1*. Philip L. Barbour (ed.):129-133. Cambridge: Cambridge University Press.

Peregrine, Peter N., 2004: Cross-cultural approaches in archaeology: comparative ethnology, comparative archaeology, and archaeoethnology. *Journal of Archaeological Research* 12(3):281-309.

Perkin, Francis, 1969 [1608]: Francis Perkin[s] in Jamestown to a Friend in England. *The Jamestown Voyages under the First Charter 1606-1609, Vol. 1*. Philip L. Barbour (ed.):158-161. Cambridge: Cambridge University Press.

Pestle, William J., 2010: *Diet and Society in Prehistoric Puerto Rico: An Isotopic Approach*. Unpublished Ph.D. dissertation, University of Illinois at Chicago, Chicago.

Petersen, James B., 1996: Archaeology of Trants. Part 3: Chronological and Settlement Data. *Annals of Carnegie Museum* 65(4):323-361.

Petersen, James B., 1997: Taino, Island Carib and prehistoric Amerindian economies in the West Indies: tropical forest adaptations to island environments. *The Indigenous People of the Caribbean*. Samuel M. Wilson (ed.):118-130. Gainesville [etc.]: University of Florida Press.

Petersen, James B., Robert N. Bartone and David R. Watters, 1995: Pyroclastic, Storm-Surge and Saladoid Villager Deposits: The Archaeological and Geological Stratigraphy of the Trants site, Montserrat. *Proceedings of the 16th Congress of the International Association for Caribbean Archaeology (2)*. Conseil Régional de la Guadeloupe-Mission Archéologique et du Patrimoine (ed.):40-51. Basse Terre: Editions du Ponant.

Petersen, James B., Michael J. Heckenberger, and Eduardo G. Neves, 2003: A prehistoric ceramic sequence from the Central Amazon and its relationship to the Caribbean. *Proceedings of the 19th International Congress for Caribbean Archaeology (1)*. Luc Alofs and Raymundo A.C.F. Dijkhoff (eds):250-259. Publication of the Museo Arqueologico Aruba Volume 9. Oranjestad: Museo Arqueologico Aruba.

Petersen, James B., Corinne L. Hofman and L. Antonio Curet, 2004: Time and Culture: Chronology and Taxonomy in the Eastern Caribbean and the Guianas. In *Late Ceramic Age Societies in the Eastern Caribbean*. André Delpuech and Corinne L. Hofman (eds):17-32. BAR International Series 1273. Oxford: Archaeopress.

Petitjean Roget, Henry, 1974: La Savane des petrifications (Martinique): un gisement de l'age lithique? *Proceedings of the 5th International Congress for the Study of Pre-Columbian Cultures of the Lesser Antilles*. St. John's: The Antigua Archaeological Society:82-93.

Petitjean Roget, Henry, 1975: *Contributions à l'étude de la préhistoire des Petites Antilles*. Ph.D. dissertation, Ecole Pratique des Hautes Etudes, Paris. Fort-de-France: Société d'Histoire de la Martinique.

Petitjean Roget, Henry, 1978a: *L'art des Arawak et des Caraïbes des Petites Antilles. Analyse de la décoration des céramiques*. Les cahiers du CERAG No. 20. Fort-de-France: Centre d'Etudes Régionales Antilles-Guyane.

Petitjean Roget, Henry, 1978b: Reconnaissance archéologique à l'île de la Dominique (West Indies). *Proceedings of the 7th International Congress for the Study of Pre-Columbian Cultures of the Lesser Antilles*. Jean Benoist, Francine-M. Mayer and Elisabeth Crosnier (eds):81-97. Montréal: Centre de Recherches Caraïbes of the Université de Montréal.

Petitjean Roget, Henry, 1978c: Note sur un vase Arawak trouvé à la Martinique. *Proceedings of the 7th International Congress for the Study of Pre-Columbian Cultures of the Lesser Antilles*. Jean Benoist, Francine-M. Mayer and Elisabeth Crosnier (eds):99-116. Montréal: Centre de Recherches Caraïbes of the Université de Montréal.

Petitjean Roget, Henry, 1978d: Note descriptive de la collection d'objets lithiques de la Librairie Publique de Roseau - Dominique (W.I.). *Proceedings of the 7th International Congress for the Study of Pre-Columbian Cultures of the Lesser Antilles*. Jean Benoist, Francine-M. Mayer and Elisabeth Crosnier (eds):117-135. Montréal: Centre de Recherches Caraïbes of the Université de Montréal.

Petitjean Roget, Henry, 1993: La Vénus impudique de Point des Pies, Saint François, Guadeloupe. Contribution à l'étude de l'art ancien des Antilles. *Proceedings of the 14th Congress of the International Association for Caribbean Archaeology.* Alissandra Cummins and Philippa King (eds): 476-491. Bridgetown: Barbados Museum and Historical Society.

Petitjean Roget, Henry, 1996: *Musée Edgar Clerc. De la découverte de l'île à l'arrivée des Francais – histoire des collections et du musée départemental de préhistoire de la Guadeloupe.* Le Moule: Musée Edgar Clerc/Conseil Général de la Guadeloupe.

Petitjean Roget, Henry, 2002: *De Baloue à Cariacou. Facettes de l'art amérindien des Antilles. Catalogue d'exposition, Écomusée de Martinique 2001-2002.* Fort-de-France: Conseil régional de la Martinique/Écomusée de Martinique.

Petitjean Roget, Henry, 2003: Contribution à l'étude du Troumassoïde et du Suazoïde (600-1200 AD). Une hypothèse sur les causes de la régression du Saladoïde aux Petites Antilles. *Proceedings of the 19th Congress of the International Association for Caribbean Archaeology (1).* Luc Alofs and Raymundo A.C.F. Dijkhoff (eds):227-238. Publications of the Archaeological Museum Aruba 9. Oranjestad: Museo Arqueologico Aruba.

Petitjean Roget, Henry, 2005: Une collection archéologique des Petites Antilles entre au Musée Régional d'Histoire et d'Ethnographie de la Martinique. *La Revue des Musées de France. La Revue du Louvre*:37-46.

Petitjean Roget, Henry, 2007: A propos d'un vase Caliviny de Pearls. Contribution à l'étude de l'usage de la polychromie dans la peinture des ceramiques Amerindiennes des Petites Antilles et sa relation avec les petroglyphes. *Proceedings of the 21st Congress of the International Association for Caribbean Archaeology (1).* Basil Reid, L. Antonio Curet and Henri Petitjean Roget (eds):402-408. St. Augustine: University of the West Indies.

Petitjean Roget, Jacques, 1968a: Méthodes suivies pour la différentiation des niveaux au Diamant: quelques mots sur la typologie. *Proceedings of the 2nd International Congress for the study of pre-Columbian cultures of the Lesser Antilles.* Ripley P. Bullen (ed.):1-8. St. Ann's Garrison: Barbados Museum.

Petitjean Roget, Jacques, 1968b: Etude d'un horizon Arawak et Proto-Arawak à la Martinique à partir du Niveau II du Diamant. *Proceedings of the 2nd International Congress for the study of pre-Columbian cultures of the Lesser Antilles.* Ripley P. Bullen (ed.):64-68. St. Ann's Garrison: Barbados Museum.

Petitjean Roget, Jacques, 1968c: Etude d'un horizon Caraïbe à la Martinique à partir du Niveau III du Diamant. *Proceedings of the 2nd International Congress for the study of pre-Columbian cultures of the Lesser Antilles.* Ripley P. Bullen (ed.):125-133. St. Ann's Garrison: Barbados Museum.

Petitjean Roget, Jacques, 1970: L'archéologie martiniquaise. *Parallèles* 36/37:4-47.

Petitjean Roget, Jacques, and Henry Petitjean Roget, 1973: Etude comparative des tessons gravés ou incisés. *Proceedings of the 4th International Congress for the study of pre-Columbian cultures of the Lesser Antilles.* Castries: St. Lucia Archaeological and Historical Society:157-173.

Pinchon, Robert, 1952: Introduction à l'archéologie Martiniquaise. *Journal de la Société des Américanistes* 41:305-360.

Pinchon, Robert, 1964: L'outillage lithique précolombien de Sainte-Lucie. *Annales des Antilles* 9:11-33.

Plog, Stephen, 1976: Measurement of prehistoric interaction between communities. In *The Mesoamerican Village,* Kent V. Flannery (ed.):255-272. London [etc.]: Academic Press.

Pyne, Nanette M., 1976: The Fire-Serpent and Were-Jaguar in Formative Oaxaca: a contingency table analysis. In *The Mesoamerican Village.* Kent V. Flannery (ed.):272-282. London [etc.]: Academic Press.

Politis, Gustavo G., 2003: The Theoretical Landscape and the Methodological Development of Archaeology in Latin America. *American Antiquity* 68(2):245-272.

Portuondo Zúñiga, Olga, 1995: *La Vírgen de la Calidad del Cobre: Símbolo de Cubanía.* Santiago de Cuba: Editorial del Oriente.

Quinn, David Beers (ed.), 1991: *The Roanoke Voyages 1584-1590: documents to illustrate the English voyages to North America under the patent granted to Walter Raleigh in 1584.* New York: Dover Publications, Inc.

Rafinesque-Schmaltz, Constantine S., 1836: *The American Nations; or, Outlines of a National History; of the Ancient and Modern Nations of North and South America.* Philadelphia.

Rainbird, Paul, 2004: *The Archaeology of Micronesia.* Cambridge: Cambridge University Press.

Rainbird, Paul, 2007: *The Archaeology of Islands.* Cambridge: Cambridge University Press.

Rainey, Froelich G., 1936: A new prehistoric culture in Haiti. *Proceedings of the National Academy of Sciences* 22:4-8.

Rainey, Froelich G., 1941: *Excavations in the Ft. Liberté region, Haiti.* Yale University Publications in Anthropology, No. 23. New Haven: Yale University Press.

Rautman, Alison E., 1998: Hierarchy and Heterarchy in the American Southwest: A Comment on Mcguire and Saitta. *American Antiquity* 63(2):325-333.

Redmond, Elsa M., and Charles S. Spencer, 1994: The Cacicazgo: An Indigenous Design. In *Caciques and Their People: A Volume in Honor of Ronald Spores.* Joyce Marcus and Judith F. Zeitlin (eds):189-225. Anthropological Papers No. 89. Ann Arbor: Museum of Anthropology, University of Michigan.

Redmond, Elsa M., Rafael A. Gasson and Charles S. Spencer, 2008: A Macroregional View of Cycling Chiefdoms in the Western Venezuelan Llanos. *Archeological Papers of the American Anthropological Association* 9(1):109-129.

Reed, Jessica A., and James B. Petersen, 2001. A comparison of Huecan and Cedrosan Saladoid ceramics at the Trants site, Montserrat. *Proceedings of the 18th Congress of the International Association for Caribbean Archaeology.* L'Association Internationale d'Archéologie de la Caraïbe Région Guadeloupe (ed.):253-267. St. George.

Reichlen, Henry, and Paule Barret, 1940: Contribution à l'archéologie de la Martinique: le gisement de l'Anse Belleville. *Journal de la Société des Américanistes* 32:227-274.

Rice, Prudence M., 2005[1987]: *Pottery Analysis.* Chicago and London: The University of Chicago Press.

Richard, Gérard, 2002: Capesterre Belle Eau, arrière plage de Roseau. *Bilan Scientifique 2002.* Service Régional de l'Archéologie. Basse-Terre: Direction Régionale des Affaires Culturelles de Guadeloupe.

Richard, Gérard, 2003: Le site archéologique de la plage de Roseau à Capesterre Belle Eau. Révélateur d'une occupation caraïbe insulaire en Guadeloupe. *Proceedings of the 20th Congress of the International Association for Caribbean Archaeology (1).* Clenis Tavárez María and Manuel A. García Arévalo (eds):15-22. Santo Domingo: Museo del Hombre Dominicano and Fundación García Arévalo.

Righter, Elizabeth (ed.), 2002: *The Tutu archaeological village site: a multidisciplinary case study in human adaptation.* London & New York: Routledge.

Rivière, Peter, 1970: Factions and exclusions in two South American village systems. In *Witchcraft, confessions and accusations.* Mary Douglas (ed.):245-256. London [etc.]: Routledge.

Rivière, Peter, 1984: *Individual and society in Guiana: a comparative study of Amerindian social organization.* Cambridge Studies of Social Anthropology 51. Cambridge: Cambridge University Press.

Roach, C N.C., 1936: Old Barbados, Chapter 1, Arawak and Carib. *The Journal of the Barbados Museum and Historical Society* 3(3):137-148.

Roach, C N.C., 1938a: Old Barbados, Chapter 5, Pottery. *The Journal of the Barbados Museum and Historical Society* 5(2):85-100.

Roach, C N.C., 1938b: Old Barbados, Chapter 5, Pots. *The Journal of the Barbados Museum and Historical Society* 5(3):130-143.

Roach, C N.C., 1938c: Old Barbados, Chapter 5, Rare vessels. *The Journal of the Barbados Museum and Historical Society* 6(1):24-40.

Roach, C N.C., 1939: Old Barbados, Chapter 6, Pottery handles. *The Journal of the Barbados Museum and Historical Society* 6(2):74-86.

Rochefort, Charles C. de., 1658: *Histoire naturelle et morale des Iles Antilles de l'Amérique.* Arnout Leers: Rotterdam.

Rochefort, Charles C. de., 1666: *The History of the Caribby-Islands, viz. Barbados, St. Christophers, St. Vincents, Martinico, Dominico, Barbouthos, Monserrat, Mevis, Antego, &c. in all XXVIII.* Translated by John Davies. London.

Rochefort, Charles C. de., 1992 [1658]: Of what may be accounted polity among the Caribbians. In *Wild Majesty: encounters with Caribs from Columbus to the present day.* Peter Hulme and Neil. L. Whitehead (eds):123-127. Oxford: Clarendon Press.

Rodríguez, Miguel, 1989: The Zoned Incised Crosshatch (ZIC) Ware of Early Precolumbian Ceramic Age Sites in Puerto Rico and Vieques Island. In *Early Ceramic Population Lifeways and Adaptive Strategies in the Caribbean.* Peter E. Siegel (ed.):249-266. Oxford: BAR International Series 506.

Rodríguez Ramos, Reniel, 2007: *Puerto Rican prehistory etched in stone.* Unpublished Ph.D. Dissertation. Department of Anthropology, University of Florida, Gainesville.

Rodríguez Ramos, Reniel, 2010. What is the Caribbean? An Archaeological Perspective. *Journal of Caribbean Archaeology Special Publication 3: Mobility and Exchange from a pan-Caribbean perspective,* Corinne L. Hofman and Alistair J. Bright (eds):19-51.

Roe, Peter G., 1989: A grammatical analysis of Cedrosan Saladoid vessel form categories and surface decoration: aesthetic and technical styles in early Antillean ceramics. In *Early Ceramic population lifeways and adaptive strategies in the Caribbean*. Peter E. Siegel (ed.):267-382. BAR International Series 506. Oxford: Archaeopress.

Romon, Thomas, and Gaëlle Chancerel, 2003: Gosier - Ilet du Gosier. *Bilan Scientifique 2002*:34-36. Service Régional de l'Archéologie. Basse-Terre: Direction Régionale des Affaires Culturelles de Guadeloupe.

Roobol, M. John, and Alan L. Smith, 1980: Archaeological implications of some radiocarbon dating on Saba and St. Kitts. *Proceedings of the 8th International Congress for the study of pre-Columbian cultures of the Lesser Antilles*. Suzanne M. Lewenstein (ed.):168-176. Anthropological Research Papers no. 22. Tempe: Arizona State University.

Roobol, M. John, Henri Petitjean Roget, and Alan L. Smith, 1976: Mt. Pelée and the island population of Martinique. *Proceedings of the 6th International Congress for the Study of Pre-Columbian Cultures of the Lesser Antilles*. Ripley P. Bullen (ed.):46-53. Gainesville: Florida State Museum, University of Florida.

Roosevelt, Anna C., 1991: *Moundbuilders of the Amazon: Geophysical Archaeology on Marajo Island, Brazil*. San Diego: Academic Press.

Roosevelt, Anna C., 1994: Amazonian anthropology: strategy for a new synthesis. *Amazonian Indians from Prehistory to the Present: Anthropological perspectives*. Anna C. Roosevelt (ed.):1-29. Tucson and London: University of Arizona Press.

Roosevelt, Anna C., 1999: The Maritime, Highland, Forest Dynamic and the Origins of Complex Culture (Ch.4). In *The Cambridge History of the Native Peoples of the Americans, vol. 3, South America. Part 1*. Frank Salomon and Stuart B. Schwartz (eds):264-349. Cambridge: Cambridge University Press.

Rostain, Stéphen, and Aad H. Versteeg, 2004: The Arauquinoid tradition in the Guianas. In *Late Ceramic Age Societies in the Eastern Caribbean*. André Delpuech and Corinne L. Hofman (eds):233-250. BAR International Series 1273. Oxford: Archaeopress.

Rouse, Irving, 1939: *Prehistory in Haiti*. Yale University Publications in Anthropology, No. 21. New Haven: Yale University Press.

Rouse, Irving, 1941: *Culture of the Ft. Liberté region, Haiti*. Yale University Publications in Anthropology, No. 24. New Haven: Yale University Press.

Rouse, Irving, 1942: *An archaeology of the Maniabon Hills, Cuba*. Yale University Publications in Anthropology, No. 26. New Haven: Yale University Press.

Rouse, Irving, 1948a: The Arawak. In *Handbook of South American Indians Volume 4: The Circum-Caribbean Tribes*. Julian H. Steward (ed.):507-546. Smithsonian Institution, Bureau of American Ethnology Bulletin 143. Washington: United States Government Printing Office

Rouse, Irving, 1948b: The Carib. In *Handbook of South American Indians Volume 4: The Circum-Caribbean Tribes*. Julian H. Steward (ed.):547-565. Smithsonian Institution, Bureau of American Ethnology Bulletin 143. Washington: United States Government Printing Office.

Rouse, Irving, 1951: Areas and periods of culture in the Greater Antilles. *Southwest Journal of Archaeology* 7(3):248-265.

Rouse, Irving, 1966: Caribbean ceramics: a study in method and theory. In *Ceramics and Man.*

Frederick R. Matson (ed.):88-103. Viking Fund Publications in Anthropology 41. New York: Wenner Gren Foundation for Anthropological Research.

Rouse, Irving, 1976: The Saladoid sequence on Antigua and its aftermath. *Proceedings of the 6th International Congress for the Study of Pre-Columbian Cultures of the Lesser Antilles,* Ripley P. Bullen (ed.):35-41. Gainesville: Florida State Museum, University of Florida.

Rouse, Irving, 1982: Ceramic and religious development in the Greater Antilles. *Journal of New World Archaeology* 5(2):45-56.

Rouse, Irving, 1986: *Migrations in prehistory: inferring population movement from cultural remains.* New York and London: Yale University Press.

Rouse, Irving, 1992: *The Tainos: rise and decline of the people who greeted Columbus.* New Haven and London: Yale University Press.

Rouse, Irving and Ricardo E. Alegría, 1990: *Excavations at Maria de la Cruz Cave and Hacienda*

Grande Village Site, Loiza, Puerto Rico. Yale University Publications in Anthropology, No. 80. New Haven: Department of Anthropology and the Peabody Museum, Yale University.

Rouse, Irving, and Louis Allaire, 1978: Caribbean. In *Chronologies in New World Archaeology.* R.E. Taylor and Clement W. Meighan (eds):431-481. New York: Academic Press.

Rouse, Irving, and José M. Cruxent, 1969[1963]: *Venezuelan archaeology.* New Haven and London: Yale University Press.

Rouse, Irving, and Birgit Faber Morse, 1999: *Excavations at the Indian Creek Site, Antigua, West Indies.* Yale University Publications in Anthropology, No. 82. New Haven: Yale University Press.

Rouse, Irving, Birgit Faber Morse and Desmond Nicholson, 1995: Excavations at Freeman's Bay, Antigua, *Proceedings of the 15th Congress of the International Association for Caribbean Archaeology.* Ricardo A. Alegría and Miguel Rodríguez (eds):445-457. San Juan: Centro de Estudios Avanzados de Puerto Rico y el Caribe/Fundación Puertorriqueña de las Humanidades/Universidad del Turabo.

Rouse, Irving, Louis Allaire and Aad Boomert, 1985: Eastern Venezuela, the Guianas, and the West Indies. Manuscript prepared for an unpublished volume *Chronologies in South American Archaeology,* Clement W. Meighan (ed.). Los Angeles: Department of Anthropology, University of California.

Sackett, James R., 1977: The meaning of style in archaeology: a general model. *American Antiquity* 42(3):369-380.

Sackett, James R., 1982: Approaches to style in lithic archaeology. *Journal of Anthropological Archaeology* 1(1):59-112.

Sahlins, Marshall, 1963: Poor Man, Rich Man, Big Man, Chief: Political Types in Melanesia and Polynesia. *Comparative Studies in Society and History* 5:285-303.

Saitta, Dean J. and Randall H. McGuire, 1998: Dialectics, Heterarchy, and Western Pueblo Social Organization. *American Antiquity* 63(2):334-336.

Sanoja Obediente, Mario, 1979: *Las culturas formativas del oriente de Venezuela: la tradicion Barrancas del bajo Orinoço*. Caracas, Biblioteca de la academia nacional de la historia.

Sanoja Obediente, Mario, and Iraida Vargas Arenas, 1978: The Formative cultures of the Venezuela Oriente. *Advances in Andean Archaeology* 2, David L. Browman (ed.):259-276. The Hague: Mouton.

Sanoja Obediente, Mario, and Iraida Vargas Arenas, 1983: New light on the prehistory of Eastern Venezuela. In *Advances in World Archaeology* 2, Fred Wendorf and Angela E. Close (eds):205-244. New York: Academic Press.

Sapper, Karl, 1903: St. Vincent. *Globus* LXXXIV(24):377-383.

Schultz, Christopher, 1995: The Carriacou hypothesis: bottomless stacked pots, a study in Amerindian fresh water procurement? *Proceedings of the 16th International Congress for Caribbean Archaeology (2).* Conseil Régional de la Guadeloupe-Mission Archéologique et du Patrimoine (ed.):217-228. Basse Terre: Editions du Ponant.

Schwartz, Marion, 1997: *A history of dogs in the early Americas*. New Haven and London: Yale University Press.

Scott, John, 2005: *Social Network Analysis: a handbook*. London [etc.]: Sage Publications.

Serrand, Nathalie, 2001: Occurrence of exogenous freshwater Bivalves (Unionoida) in the Lesser Antilles during the first millennium A.D.: example from the Hope Estate Saladoid site (St Martin, French Lesser Antilles). *Proceedings of the 18th International Congress of the Association for Caribbean Archaeology,* St George, Grenada: Association Internationale d'Archéologie de la Caraïbe, Région Guadeloupe, Mission Archéologique:136-152.

Serrand, Nathalie, 2007: L'exploitation des invertébrés durant l'occupation céramique tardive du sud de la Martinique: Aperçu diachronique au travers des sites de Dizac, Salines, Trabaud et Macabou. *Proceedings of the 21st Congress of the International Association for Caribbean Archaeology (1).* Basil Reid, L. Antonio Curet and Henri Petitjean Roget (eds):421-428. St. Augustine: University of the West Indies.

Service, Elman R., 1971: *Primitive Social Organization* (2nd edition). New York: Random House.

Siegel, Peter E., 1989: Site structure, demography, and social complexity in the early Ceramic Age of the Caribbean. In *Early Ceramic population, lifeways and adaptive strategies in the Caribbean*. Pieter E. Siegel (ed):193-245. BAR International Series 506, Oxford: Archaeopress.

Siegel, Peter E., 1992: *Ideology, Power, and Social Complexity in Prehistoric Puerto Rico*, Ph.D. dissertation, Department of Anthropology, State University of New York at Binghamton, Binghamton. Ann Arbor: UMI.

Siegel, Peter E., 1993: Saladoid survival strategies: evidence from site locations. *Proceedings of the 14th Congress of the International Association for Caribbean Archaeology.* Alissandra Cummins and Philippa King (eds):315-337. Bridgetown: Barbados Museum and Historical Society

Siegel, Peter E., 1996a: An interview with Irving Rouse. *Current Anthropology* 37(4):671-689.

Siegel, Peter E., 1996b: Ideology and Culture Change in Prehistoric Puerto Rico: A view from the Community. *Journal of Field Archaeology* 23(3):313-333.

Siegel, Peter E., 2004: What happened after AD 600 in Puerto Rico? Corporate groups, population restructuring, and post-Saladoid social changes. In *Late Ceramic Age Societies in the Eastern Caribbean.* André Delpuech and Corinne L. Hofman (eds):87-100. Paris Monographs in American Archaeology 14/BAR International Series 1273. Oxford: Archaeopress.

Siegel, Peter. E. (ed.), 2005: *Ancient Borinquen: Archaeology and Ethnohistory of Native Puerto Rico.* Tuscaloosa: The University of Alabama Press.

Siegel, Peter. E., John G. Jones, Deborah M. Pearsall, and Daniel P. Wagner, 2001: Culture and environment in prehistoric Puerto Rico. *Proceedings of the 18th Congress of the International Association for Caribbean Archaeology.* L'Association Internationale d'Archéologie de la Caraïbe Région Guadeloupe (ed.):281-290. St. George.

Sinopoli, Carla M., 1991: *Approaches to archaeological ceramics.* New York and London: Plenum Press.

Sleight, Frederick W., 1965: Certain environmental considerations in West Indian archaeology. *American Antiquity* 31(2):226-231.

Smith, Kelvin, 2006: Placing the Carib Model Village: The Carib Territory and Dominican Tourism. *Indigenous resurgence in the contemporary Caribbean: Amerindian survival and revival.* Maximilian C. Forte (ed.):71-88. New York: Peter Lang.

Soustelle, J., 1934-5: Une pierre-à-trois-pointes de la Dominique. *Bulletin du Museé du Trocadero* 8:12-14.

Spencer, Charles S., and Elsa M. Redmond 1998: Prehispanic causeways and regional politics in The Llanos of Barinas, Venezuela. *Latin American Antiquity* 9(2):95-110.

Spriggs, Matthew, 1989: The Dating of the Island S.E. Asian Neolithic: an Attempt at Chronometric Hygiene and Linguistic Correlation. *Antiquity* 63:587-613.

Spriggs, Matthew, 1997: *The Island Melanesians.* The Peoples of South-East Asia and The Pacific, Peter Bellwood and Ian Glover (eds). Oxford and Cambridge: Blackwell Publishers

Spriggs, Matthew, 2008a: Are islands islands? Some thoughts on the history of chalk and cheese. *Terra Australis* 29:211-226.

Spriggs, Matthew, 2008b: Ethnographic parallels and the denial of history. *World Archaeology* 40(4):538-552.

Stark, J., P. Lajoie and A.J. Green, 1966: *Soil and land-use surveys, no. 20 – St. Lucia.* St. Augustine: The Regional Research Centre of the British Caribbean, The Imperial College of Tropical Agriculture Trinidad, W.I., University of the West Indies.

Stark, Miriam T., Ronald L. Bishop and Elizabeth Miksa, 2000: Ceramic Technology and Social Boundaries: Cultural Practices in Kalinga Clay Selection and Use. *Journal of Archaeological Method and Theory* 7(4):295-331.

Steadman, David W., and Anne V. Stokes, 2005: An Archaeological Survey and Test Excavation at the Saladoid Blanchisseuse Site, Trinidad. *Proceedings of the 20th Congress of the International Association for Caribbean Archaeology (1).* Clenis Tavárez María and Manuel A. García Arévalo (eds):399-406. Santo Domingo: Museo del Hombre Dominicano and Fundación García Arévalo.

Steadman, David W., Paul S. Martin, Ross D. E. MacPhee, A. J. T. Jull, H. Gregory McDonald, Charles A. Woods, Manuel Iturralde-Vinent, and Gregory W. L. Hodgins, 2005: Asynchronous extinction of late Quaternary sloths on continents and islands. *Proceedings of the National Academy of Sciences* 102(33):11763–11768.

Steininger, Fritz F., and Elfriede Mauser, 2002: *Die Molluskenfauna aus den "shell middens" der präkolumbianischen Siedlung von Pointe de Caille, St. Lucia, West Indies. Bedeutung für Ernährungsstrategien und Werkzeugherstellung.* Stuttgart: E. Schweizerbart science publishers.

Steward, Julian H., 1949: South American cultures: an interpretative summary. In *Handbook of South American Indians Volume 5: The comparative ethnology of South American Indians,*

Julian H. Steward (ed.):669-782. Smithsonian Institution, Bureau of American Ethnology Bulletin 143. Washington: United States Government Printing Office.

Steward, Julian H., and Louis C. Faron, 1959: *Native peoples of South America.* New York [etc.]: McGraw-Hill Book Company, Inc.

Stokes, Anne V., David Steadman, Robert J. Austin and Geoffrey Mohlman, 2002: *A reconnaissance cultural resource survey of Grande Anse Estate, St. Lucia.* Unpublished manuscript, Gainesville/Tampa.

Stoneman, J., 1905-07 [1625]: The Voyage of M. Henry Challons intended for the North Plantation of Virginia, 1606. taken by the way, and ill used by the Spaniards: written by John Stoneman Pilot. In *Hakluytus Posthumus or Purchas his Pilgrimes; Contayning a History of the World, in Sea Voyages and Lande Travells, by Englishmen and Others.* Samuel Purchas (ed.), Vol. XIX. Maclehose: Glasgow.

Stuiver, Minze, and Thomas F. Braziunas, 1993: Radiocarbon and *14*C ages of marine samples to 10,000 B.C. *Radiocarbon* 35:137-189.

Stuiver, Minze, Edward S. Deevey Jr. and Irving Rouse, 1963: Yale Natural Radiocarbon Measurements VIII. *Radiocarbon* 5:312-241.

Stuiver, Minze and Paula Reimer, 2010: *Marine reservoir correction database.* Online resource: http://intcal.qub.ac.uk/marine/, accessed 20th December 2009.

Sued-Badillo, Jalil, 1978: *Los Caraibes: realidad o fabula?* Río Piedras: Editorial Antillana.

Sued-Badillo, Jalil, 1995: The Island Caribs: new approaches to the question of ethnicity in the early Colonial Caribbean. In *Wolves from the Sea.* Neil. Whitehead (ed.):61-89. Leiden: KITLV Press.

Sutty, Lesley, 1976a: Archaeological excavations at Miss Pierre, Union Island, the Grenadines. *Proceedings of the 6th International Congress for the study of pre-Columbian cultures of the Lesser Antilles.* Ripley P. Bullen (ed.):66-75. Gainesville: Florida State Museum, University of Florida.

Sutty, Lesley, 1976b: Further excavations at Chatham Midden, Union Island. *Proceedings of the 6th International Congress for the study of pre-Columbian cultures of the Lesser Antilles.* Ripley P. Bullen (ed.):54-65. Gainesville: Florida State Museum, University of Florida.

Sutty, Lesley, 1978: A Study of Shells and Shelled Objects from Six Precolumbian Sites in the Grenadines of St. Vincent and Grenada. *Proceedings of the 7th International Congress for the study of pre-Columbian cultures of the Lesser Antilles.* Jean Benoist, Francine-M. Mayer and Elisabeth Crosnier (eds):195-210. Centre de Recherches Caraïbes of the Université de Montréal, Montréal, Canada.

Sutty, Lesley, 1983: Liaison Arawak-Caliviny-Carib Between Grenada and St. Vincent, Lesser Antilles. *Proceedings of the 9th International Congress for the study of pre-Columbian cultures of the Lesser Antilles.* Louis Allaire and Francine-M. Mayer (eds):145-149. Montréal: Centre de recherches caraïbes, Université de Montréal.

Sutty, Lesley, 1985: An early ceramic effigy bottle from Chatham Pasture, Union Island in the Grenadines. *Proceedings of the 10th International Congress for Caribbean Archaeology.* Louis Allaire and Francine-M. Mayer (eds):401-408. Montréal:Centre de recherches caraïbes, Université de Montréal.

Sutty, Lesley, 1990: A Listing of Amerindian Settlements on the Island of Carriacou in the Southern Grenadines and a Report on the Most Important of These: Grand Bay. *Proceedings of the 11th Congress of the International Association for Caribbean Archaeology.* Agamemnon Gus Pantel, Tekakis, Iraida Vargas Arenas and Mario Sanoja Obediente (eds):242-259. San Juan: La Fundación Arqueológica, Antropológica e Historica de Puerto Rico/La Universidad de Puerto Rico/Recato de Rio Piedras/United States Department of Agriculture/Forest Service.

Sutty, Lesley, 1991a: Paleoecological formations in the Grenadines and the relation to preceramic and ceramic settlements. *Proceedings of the 13th Congress of the International Association for Caribbean Archaeology (1).* Edwin N. Ayubi and Jay B. Haviser (eds):127-147. Reports of the Archaeological-Anthropological Institute of the Netherlands Antilles, No. 9. Willemstad: Archaeological-Anthropological Institute of the Netherlands Antilles.

Sutty, Lesley, 1991b: A preliminary inventory and short essay on ceramic and stone artifacts from recent excavations on Grenada and in the southern Grenadines. *Proceedings of the 12th Congress of the International Association for Caribbean Archaeology.* Linda S. Robinson (ed.):73-86. Fort-de-France: Association Internationale d'Archéologie de la Caraïbe: Martinique.

Sutty, Lesley, 1993: The Use of Genital Sheaths by Insular Prehistoric Cultures: A Unique Case of an Ampullaria Genital Sheath from Carriacou, Southern Grenadines. *Proceedings of the 14th Congress of the International Association for Caribbean Archaeology.* Alissandra Cummins and Philippa King (eds):338-347, Barbados Museum and Historical Society: Bridgetown.

Tartaron, Thomas F., 2008: Aegean prehistory as world archaeology: recent trends in the archaeology of Bronze Age Greece. *Journal of Archaeological Research* 16:83-161.

Taviani, Paulo E., Consuelo Varela, Juan Gil and Marina Conti, 1994: *Christopher Columbus. Accounts and letters of the second, third, and fourth voyages, part 2.* Istituto Poligrafico e Zecca dello Stato. Rome: Libreria Dello Stato.

Taylor, Douglas, 1956: Names on Dominica. *West-Indische Gids* 36:121-124.

Taylor, Douglas, 1958a: Names on Saint Vincent. *West-Indische Gids* 38:106-110.

Taylor, Douglas, 1958b: Carib, Caliban, Cannibal. *International Journal of American Linguistics* 24(2):156-157.

Taylor, Douglas, and Irving Rouse, 1955: Linguistic and Archeological Time Depth in the West Indies. *International Journal of American Linguistics* 21(2):105-115.

Taylor, Ronald V., 1983: Archaeological events in Barbados. *Proceedings of the 9th International Congress for the study of pre-Columbian cultures of the Lesser Antilles.* Louis Allaire and Francine-M. Mayer (eds):571-574. Montréal: Centre de recherches caraïbes, Université de Montréal.

Terrell, John E., 1977: Biology, Biogeography and Man. *World Archaeology* 8(3):237-248.

Terrell, John E., 2008: Islands and the Average Joe. *Journal of Island and Coastal Archaeology* 3:77-82.

Terrell, John E., 2010: Language and material culture on the Sepik coast of Papua New Guinea: using social network analysis to simulate, graph, identify, and analyze social and cultural boundaries between communities. *The Journal of Island and Coastal Archaeology* 5(1):3-32.

Terrell, John E., Terry L. Hunt and Chris Gosden, 1997: The dimensions of social life in the Pacific: Human diversity and the myth of the primitive isolate. *Current Anthropology* 38:155-195.

Terrell, John E., John P. Hart, Sibel Barut, Nicoletta Cellinese, L. Antonio Curet, Tim Denham, Chapurukha M. Kusimba, Kyle Latinis, Rahul Oka, Joel Palka, Mary E. D. Pohl, Kevin O. Pope, Patrick R. Williams, Helen Haines and John E. Staller, 2003: Domesticated Landscapes: The Subsistence Ecology of Plant and Animal Domestication. *Journal of Archaeological Method and Theory* 10(4):323-368.

Thomas, David J., 1972: The indigenous trade system of southeast Estado Bolivar, Venezuela. *Antropológica* 33:3-37.

Tilley, Chris, 1994: *A phenomenology of landscape*. Berg: Oxford.

Torres, Joshua M., 2005: Deconstructing the polity: communities and social landscapes of the Ceramic-Age peoples of South Central Puerto Rico. In *Ancient Borinquen: Archaeology and Ethnohistory of Native Puerto Rico.* Peter E. Siegel (ed.):202-229. Tuscaloosa: The University of Alabama Press.

Torres, Joshua M., and Reniel Rodríguez Ramos, 2008: The Caribbean: a continent divided by water. In *Archaeology and geoinformatics: case studies from the Caribbean.* Basil A. Reid (ed.):13-29. Tuscaloosa: The University of Alabama Press.

Tucek, Charles S., 1971: Radiocarbon, Ltd. natural radiocarbon measurements I. *Radiocarbon* 13: 74-77.

Tucek, Charles S., 1977: Radiocarbon, Ltd. natural radiocarbon measurements II. *Radiocarbon* 19(2):255-256.

Turner, William, 1905-1907[1625]: Part of a Treatise written by Master William Turner, Sonne to Doctor Turner of London a Phisitian, touching the former Voyage. In *Hakluytus Posthumus or Purchas his Pilgrimes; Contayning a History of the World, in Sea Voyages and Lande Travells, by Englishmen and Others*, Vol. IV, Chapter XIII, S. Purchas (ed.):1265-7. Glasgow: Maclehose.

Twinn, Paul, 2006: Land Ownership and the Construction of Carib Identity in St. Vincent. *Indigenous resurgence in the contemporary Caribbean: Amerindian survival and revival*, Maximilian C. Forte (ed.):89-106. New York: Peter Lang.

Ulloa Hung, Jorge and Roberto Valcarcel Rojas, 2002: *Ceramica temprana en el centro del oriente de Cuba.* Santo Domingo: Impresos Viewgraph.

Van den Biggelaar, Don, and Arie Boomert, 2010: *Rescue excavations at the site of the future Arygle International Airport, Southeast St. Vincent (June 2009). With an Appendix by Sebastiaan Knippenberg.* Unpublished manuscript, Faculty of Archaeology, Leiden University, Leiden.

Van Gijn, Annelou, 1993: Flint exploitation on *Long Island, Antigua,* West-Indies. *Analecta Praehistoria Leidensia* 26:156-165.

Van Heekeren, H. R., 1963: *Prehistorical research on the islands of Curaçao, Aruba and Bonaire in 1960.* Studies on the Archaeology of the Netherlands Antilles III. Willemstad: Natuurwetenschappelijke Werkgroep Nederlandse Antillen.

Van Soest, Martijn C., 2000: *Sediment subduction and crustal contamination in the Lesser Antilles island arc: the geochemical and isotopic imprints on recent lavas and geothermal fluids.* Amsterdam: Netherlands Research School of Sedimentary Geology, publication number 20000101.

Vargas Arenas, Iraida, 1979: *La tradicion Saladoide del oriente de Venezuela: la fase Cuartel.* Caracas: Biblioteca de la Academia Nacional de la Historia.

Vargas Arenas, Iraida, 1981: *Investigaciones arqueologicas en Parmana: los sitios de la Gruta y Ronquín, Estado Guárico, Venezuela.* Caracas: Biblioteca de la Academia Nacional de la Historia.

Veloz Maggiolo, Marcio, 1991: *Panorama historico del Caribe precolombino.* Santo Domingo: Banco Central de la Republica Dominicana.

Verdera, Nito, 1994: *Cristóbal Colón, Catalanoparlante.* Ibiza.

Vérin, Pierre, 1961: Les Caraïbes à Sainte Lucie depuis les contacts coloniaux. *Nieuwe West-Indische Gids/New West-Indian Guide* 41(2):66-82.

Verrand, Laurence, 2001: *La vie quotidienne des Indiens Caraïbes aux Petites Antilles (XVIIe siècle).* Paris: Éditions Karthala.

Versteeg, Aad H., 1998: *Caribbean Archaeology, the Archaeology of St. Eustatius.* Online resource: http://home.wxs.nl/~vrstg/eastern/eustatius/eustatius.htm, accessed 16th November 2009.

Versteeg, Aad H., 2003: *Suriname voor Columbus/Suriname before Columbus.* Libri Musei Surinamensis 1. Paramaribo: Stichting Surinaams Museum.

Versteeg, Aad H., and Stéphen Rostain, 2005: *Precolombiana.* Libri Musei Surinamensis 2. Paramaribo: Stichting Surinaams Museum.

Versteeg, Aad H., and Kees Schinkel (eds), 1992: *The archaeology of St. Eustatius: the Golden Rock site*. Publications of the St. Eustatius Historical Foundation 2/Publications of the Foundation for Historical Research in the Caribbean 131. St. Eustatius/Amsterdam: St. Eustatius Historical Foundation/The Foundation for Historical Research in the Caribbean.

Vescelius, Gary, 1980: A cultural taxonomy for West Indian archaeology. *Journal of Virgin Islands Archaeology* 10:36-39.

Vidal, Nathalie, 1992: Le Diamant. *Bilan Scientifique 1991. DRAC/SRA Martinique*:17-19. Fort-de-France: Ministère de la Culture.

Vidal, Nathalie, 1993a: Macouba – Roche à bon dieu. *Bilan Scientifique 1992. DRAC/SRA Martinique*:27. Fort-de-France: Ministère de la Culture.

Vidal, Nathalie, 1993b: Rivière Pilote – Anse Figuier. *Bilan Scientifique 1992. DRAC/SRA Martinique*:38. Fort-de-France: Ministère de la Culture.

Vidal, Nathalie, 1993c: Saint-Luce – Montravail. *Bilan Scientifique 1992. DRAC/SRA Martinique*:28. Fort-de-France: Ministère de la Culture.

Vidal, Nathalie, 1993d: Le Diamant – Dizac plage. *Bilan Scientifique 1992. DRAC/SRA Martinique*:18-19. Fort-de-France: Ministère de la Culture.

Vidal, Nathalie, 1993e: Le Galion – Trinité. *Bilan Scientifique 1992. DRAC/SRA Martinique*:26. Fort-de-France: Ministère de la Culture.

Vidal, Nathalie, 1996: Marigot: La Pointe. *Bilan Scientifique 1995. DRAC/SRA Martinique*:16-18. Ministère de la Culture: Fort-de-France.

Vidal, Nathalie, 2003: La carte archéologique de Martinique. *Proceedings of the 19th Congress of the International Association for Caribbean Archaeology (1)*. Luc Alofs and Raymundo A.C.F. Dijkhoff (eds):14-21. Publications of the Archaeological Museum Aruba 9. Oranjestad: Museo Arqueologico Aruba.

Vidal, Nathalie, and Jean-Baptiste Barret, 1992: Sainte-Luce: Gros Raisin. *Bilan Scientifique 1991. DRAC/SRA Martinique*:35. Fort-de-France: Ministère de la Culture.

Vidal, Nathalie, Benoît Bérard and Olivier Kayser, 2004: En vue de l'etude de l'occupation post-Saladoïde de la Martinique. In *Late Ceramic Age Societies in the Eastern Caribbean*. André Delpuech and Corinne L. Hofman (eds):195-204. Paris Monographs in American Archaeology 14/BAR International Series 1273. Oxford: Archaeopress.

Watlington, Francisco, 2003: The physical environment: biogeographical teleconnections in Caribbean prehistory. *General History of the Caribbean 1 - Autochthonous Societies*. Jalil Sued-Badillo (ed.):30-92. Cambridge: UNESCO Publishing /Macmillan.

Watters, David R., 1994: Archaeology of Trants, Montserrat. Part 1. Field methods and artefact density distributions. *Annals of Carnegie Museum* 63(4):265-295.

Watters, David R., 1997: Maritime trade in the prehistoric eastern Caribbean. *The indigenous people of the Caribbean*. Samuel M. Wilson (ed.):88-99. Gainesville [etc.]: University Press of Florida.

Watters, David R., 2001: Historical archaeology in the British Caribbean. In *Island Lives: Historical Archaeologies of the Caribbean*. Paul Farnsworth (ed.):82-102. Tuscaloosa: The University of Alabama Press.

Watters, David R., and R.B. Miller, 2000: Wood identification in historic sites: inferences for colonial trade and modification of vegetation on Barbuda. *Caribbean Journal of Science* 36(1-2):19-30.

Watters, David R. and James B. Petersen, 1992: *Inter-island settlement pattern variability in post-Saladoid Barbuda and Montserrat, northern Lesser Antilles.* Paper presented at the 57th Annual Meeting of the Society for American Archaeology, Pittsburgh.

Watters, David R. and James B. Petersen, 1993: Preliminary Report on the Archaeology of Rendezvous Bay, Anguilla. *Proceedings of the 14th Congress of the International Association for Caribbean Archaeology.* Alissandra Cummins and Philippa King (eds):348-359. Bridgetown: Barbados Museum and Historical Society.

Watters, David R., and Irving Rouse, 1989: Environmental diversity and maritime adaptations in the Caribbean area. In *Early Ceramic Population Lifeways and Adaptive Strategies in the Caribbean.* Peter E. Siegel (ed.):129-144. BAR International Series 506, Oxford: Archaeopress.

Watters, David R., and Richard Scaglion, 1980: Utility of a transect survey technique in Caribbean prehistoric studies: applications on Barbuda and Montserrat. *Proceedings of the 8th International Congress for the study of pre-Columbian cultures of the Lesser Antilles,* Suzanne M. Lewenstein (ed.):338-347. Anthropological Research Papers no. 22. Tempe: Arizona State University.

Watts, David R., 1994[1987]: *The West Indies: patterns of development, culture and environmental change since 1492.* Cambridge Studies in Historical Geography. Cambridge [etc.]: Cambridge University Press.

Watts, David R., 1999: The Caribbean environment and early settlement. *General History of the Caribbean Volume II: New Societies: the Caribbean in the long sixteenth-century.* Pieter C. Emmer (ed.):29-42. London and Basingstoke: Unesco Publishing/MacMillan Education Limited.

Welsch, Robert L., John E. Terrell and John A. Nadolski, 1992: Language and Culture on the North Coast of New Guinea. *American Anthropologist* 94:568-600.

Whitehead, Neil L., 1984: Carib Cannibalism - The historical evidence. *Journal de la Société des Américanistes* 70(1):69-88.

Whitehead, Neil L. (ed.), 1995: *Wolves from the Sea.* Leiden: KITLV Press.

Wiessner, Polly, 1983: Style and Social Information in Kalahari San Projectile Points. *American Antiquity* 48(2):253-276.

Wiessner, Polly, 1985: Style or Isochrestic Variation? A Reply to Sackett. *American Antiquity* 50(1):160-166.

Willey, Gordon R. (ed.) 1956: *Prehistoric settlement patterns in the New World.* Viking Fund Publications in Anthropology No. 23, New York: Wenner-Gren Foundation For Anthropological Research, Inc.

Willey, Gordon R., and Jeremy A. Sabloff, 1980: *A History of American Archaeology* (second edition). San Francisco: W. H. Freeman and Company.

Wilson, Samuel M., 1989: The Prehistoric Settlement History of Nevis, West Indies. *Journal of Field Archaeology* 16:427-450.

Wilson, Samuel M., 1990: *Hispaniola - Caribbean Chiefdoms in the Age of Columbus*. Tuscaloosa & London: The University of Alabama Press.

Wilson, Samuel M., 1991: The prehistoric settlement survey of Nevis: 1984-1988. *Proceedings of the 13th Congress of the International Association for Caribbean Archaeology (1).* Edwin N. Ayubi and Jay B. Haviser (eds):269-279. Reports of the Archaeological-Anthropological Institute of the Netherlands Antilles, No. 9. Willemstad: Archaeological-Anthropological Institute of the Netherlands Antilles.

Wilson, Samuel M., 2006: *The Prehistory of Nevis, a Small Island in the Lesser Antilles*. Yale University Publications in Anthropology 87. New Haven: Yale University Press.

Wilson, Samuel M., 2007: *The Archaeology of the Caribbean*. Cambridge World Archaeology. Cambridge [etc.]: Cambridge University Press.

Wilson, Samuel M., Harry B. Iceland, and Thomas R. Hester, 1998: Preceramic Connections between Yucatan and the Caribbean. *Latin American Antiquity* 9(4):342-352.

Wing, Elizabeth S., 1993: Animal Exploitation in Prehistoric Barbados. *Proceedings of the 14th Congress of the International Association for Caribbean Archaeology,* Alissandra Cummins and Philippa King (eds):360-367. Bridgetown: Barbados Museum and Historical Society.

Yoffee, Norman, 1993: Too many chiefs? In *Archaeological Theory: who sets the agenda?* Norman Yoffee and Andrew Sherratt (eds):60-78. Cambridge: Cambridge University Press.

Young, William, 1971[1795]: *An account of the Black Charaibs in the Island of St. Vincent's: with the Charaib treaty of 1773, and other original documents compiled from the papers of Sir William Young*. Cass Library of West Indian Studies, no. 18. London: Cass.

Zeidler, James A., 1995: Archaeological survey and site discovery in the forested neotropics. In *Archaeology in the lowland American tropics: current analytical methods and recent applications*. Peter W. Stahl (ed.):7-41. Cambridge: Cambridge University Press.

Appendix 1

WINDWARD ISLANDS SITE CATALOGUE

Appendix 1: Archived under the following persistent identifier:

urn:nbn:nl:ui:13-2of-ohu

Available via: http://persistent-identifier.nl/?identifier=urn:nbn:nl:ui:13-2of-ohu

Appendix 2

RADIOCARBON DATES FOR THE WINDWARD ISLANDS

Appendix 2: Archived under the following persistent identifier:

urn:nbn:nl:ui:13-2of-ohu

Available via: http://persistent-identifier.nl/?identifier=urn:nbn:nl:ui:13-2of-ohu

Acknowledgements

Thanks first and foremost to my initial supervisors and promotors at Leiden University, Prof. Corinne Hofman and Prof. Maarten Jansen, later joined by copromotor Dr. Arie Boomert. I am also grateful to Dr. L. Antonio Curet and Prof. Gert Oostindie for agreeing to be a part of my committee. Thanks to the following colleagues and friends (happily, many fulfilled a double functpion as colleague and friend), who enriched my time spent as a PhD or in one way or another contributed to this dissertation. In no particular order:

Prof. William F. Keegan, drs. Daan Isendoorn, drs. Luc Amkreutz, Dr. Alice Samson, Dennis Bruggink, Dr. Stijn Arnoldussen, Dr. Alexander Verpoorte, Prof. Raymond Corbey, Dr. Bouke van de Meer, Dr. Menno Hoogland, Dr. Gerrit Dusseldorp, Dr. Adriana Churampi, Prof. John Bintliff, Dr. Jago Cooper, Dr. Reniel Rodríguez Ramos, Eduardo Herrera Malatesta MA, drs. Hylke de Jong, drs. Leonardo Pedrosa Negami do Nascimento, Dr. Anna Russell, Jimmy Mans MPhil, Dr. John Hoopes, Dr. Gilda Hernández Sanchez, Dr. Michael Swanton, Dr. Peter Jiménez Betts, Dr. Enrique García, Dr. Humberto Medina González, Dr. Nick Caretta, Dr. Alex Geurds, Joost Morsink MPhil, Angus Mol MPhil, Hayley Mickleburgh MPhil, Franci Taylor MA, lic. Jorge Ulloa Hung and lic. Roberto Valcárcel Rojas. Special thanks to Dr. Sebastiaan Knippenberg for generously sharing his radiocarbon-database with me, and to Dr. Scott Fitzpatrick, Joseph Moravetz, Dr. James Miller, drs. Michiel Kappers, María Antonia Negrete Martínez and Nicola Redway for sharing artefact photographs with me. Many thanks also to Debby Marchena, who kindly donated to me her significant collection of Caribbean and Venezuelan archaeological literature. I owe a great debt of gratitude to all library staff who tirelessly supplied me with endless tomes of archaeological literature and continually extended my loans: Erik and Els (Library Faculty of Archaeology), Syed, Rini, Josephine and Sven (Library Koninklijk Instituut voor Taal-, Land- en Volkenkunde), staff at the University Library and staff at the Rijksmuseum van Oudheden.

Thank you to everybody who extended me kindness and hospitality during my travels in the Windward Islands. Chief among them were Micheline and Anabella Blancaneaux, in the dual role of friends and tireless tour guides for a two-week period in 2004. Furthermore, on Martinique: Dr. Olivier Kayser (S.R.A. Martinique), Dr. Benoît Bérard (S.R.A./Université des Antilles et Guyane), Dr. Sandrine Grouard, Dr. Nathalie Serrand, Mr. Octave Noel and Mme. Cécile Celma (Musée Departemental d'Archéologie precolombienne et de Préhistoire). On Dominica: Dr. Lennox Honychurch and former Carib chief Charles Williams. On Guadeloupe: Philippe Arnoux, Dr. Henry Petitjean Roget and David Laporal (Musée Edgar Clerc). On St. Lucia: Eric Branford and Fortuna Anthony (Saint Lucia Archaeological & Historical Society), staff at the National Archives and John Robert Lee (Folk Research Centre). On Tobago: Eddy Hernandez (Tobago Historical Museum). On Trinidad: Prof. Keith Laurence, Vel Lewis (Trinidad National Museum and Art Gallery), Dr. Basil Reid (University of the West Indies, Trinidad) and Peter O'B. Harris. On Barbados: Kevin Farmer and Dr.

Thomas Loftfield (Barbados Museum and Historical Society). On Grenada: staff at the Grenada National Museum. On St. Vincent: Edgar Adams, Kathy Martin, Roydon Lampkin and the rest of the staff at the National Trust, staff at the IADC and Steve Russell. On Bequia: Nicola Redway.

My travels in the Greater Antilles formed a vital part of my research as well, by confronting me directly with a degree of workmanship and complexity largely unknown to the archaeology of the Lesser Antilles. In the Dominican Republic the following people inspired and helped me: lic. Glenis Tavarez and Gabriel Atiles (Museo del Hombre Dominicano) and Mr. Lenin (Museo Altos de Chavón). On Puerto Rico: Dr. José Oliver (University College London), Juan Rivera Fontán (Instituto de Cultura Puertorriqueña), Luis Chanlatte-Baik and Yvonne Narganes-Storde MA (Universidad de Puerto Rico).

For making my visit to Florida to work on the Bullen collections such an enjoyable experience, I must thank first and foremost Prof. William F. Keegan (Florida Museum of Natural History), for putting me up all week and organizing access to the collections and facilities, and secondly Greg Shaik (Florida Museum of Natural History) for giving permission to work on the collections and for allowing use of his photographic set-up.

On a more personal note, I would like to acknowledge my parents, John and Janet Bright, who gave me a fantastic start in life by always putting my interests before theirs and continually encouraging me to expand my horizons in the face of many personal sacrifices. May this work serve as a testament to their continuing love, support, encouragement and interest. Thanks also to my big sister Kirsty Bright, for looking out for me from an early age and keeping me firmly grounded. Finally, a heartfelt thanks to my partner Iris Briels for accompanying me on my academic journey, for sharing in some of the unforgettable times as well as putting on a brave face when things didn't quite work out, for knowing when to be there and when I was best avoided or ignored, and for reminding me now and again that there is more to life than archaeology.

I owe a big thank you to everyone at Sidestone Press as well (Corné van Woerdekom, Karsten Wentink and Alice Samson) for getting this dissertation printed and published. Finally, a huge word of thanks to the Netherlands Foundation for Scientific Research (NWO) for financing this research and giving me a head start in academia, and to the Faculty of Archaeology, Leiden University, for facilitating my studies and academic career in every way imaginable.